MORE NEW WONDERS OF THE WORLD

JAMES A. ANDERSON

ISBN: 1502486849
ISBN 13: 9781502486844

CONTENTS

FOREWORD

IN NOVEMBER 2007, I came across a web-site on the internet (www.new-7wonders.com) which claimed to have identified the new 7 Wonders of the World from a short-list of 21. I discovered that I had already seen all but two of the seven finalists and all but four of the others on the short-list and decided to visit the rest over the following 3 years. So this is the story of a life-time of travel which took me to these places, rather than a concerted effort to "knock the bastards off" to paraphrase Sir Edmund Hillary about climbing Mount Everest. I wrote about my trips to the seven finalists and the special category Pyramids at Giza in "To the New 7 Wonders of the World" also published by Createspace in 2014. This volume covers my visits to the runners-up in the competition.

If travel is in the blood, I have an excellent pedigree. Born in the Shetland Islands, my DNA traces my ancestors back to the Vikings who arrived in the islands around 800 A.D. Those ancestors got to America in open boats 500 years before Columbus, so they knew a bit about travelling the world.

I didn't make an early start to globe-trotting. Until I was 11 years old, I rarely made it off the 5 miles by 2 (8km x 3) island of Whalsay (population then about 800) on which I was born, just after World War II. Communications were limited then; a small steamer, The Earl of Zetland, called in three times a week on her way from the Shetland capital, Lerwick, to the North Isles. Occasionally in summer, the Earl altered her schedule so that a day trip to Lerwick, known as an "excursion", was possible. Although my mother had a sister living in Lerwick, we only got there about half a dozen times in my first 11 years, usually just on excursion days.

Apart from the limited transport links, we couldn't afford to travel. We did have a pot to piss in - just as well, as the draughty, ramshackle, wooden outdoor toilet was over 50m away, past the byre and its steaming midden and propped up against the ponging hen-house and it was a long way to go for a pee on a cold, dark, winter's night. I used to tell gullible people that we used the same pot in the morning to wash our faces and that our mother then used it to boil up the potato and cabbage soup that was all we had to live on. But that was a lie. We were kept meticulously clean and never went hungry. My father was a crofter/fisherman and there was no money in either agriculture or fishing in those days. Our croft (small farm) had only 7 acres (3 ha) of marginally arable land with a share in the open common grazing in the hills where the sheep were kept. We grew potatoes, turnips, carrots and kale and oats and hay to keep two cows alive during the winter. With some hens to supply eggs and the fish my father brought home, we were largely self-sufficient in basic food. Until I was 8 years old, we had to carry water in buckets uphill from a well as there was no piped water supply: I was at university before an undersea cable brought electricity to the island.

At the age of 11, I went to the grammar school in Lerwick. There was a secondary school in Whalsay but if you wanted to go to university, the only option was exile to the Anderson Institute, living in the hostel where the island children and those from the more remote parts of the Shetland Mainland stayed. It was tough being separated from your family at that age – we only got home for the holidays at Christmas, Easter and summer, with a long weekend in October – but it severed the apron strings and was a first step in preparing me psychologically for future travels.

My horizons broadened again at age 17 when I went to Aberdeen University, a 200 miles (320km), 14 hour, often stormy, boat trip away. During my four years there, I still never got beyond Britain. A week-long Geography field trip based in Stoke-on-Trent in the first year and another in Newcastle in the fourth year defined the limits of my known world. But four years studying Geography kindled my interest in the wider world.

When I graduated in 1967, I had no idea what I wanted to do but fancied something to take me overseas. My chance came when I discovered that the Ministry of Overseas Development was recruiting for their Teachers for East Africa (TEA) scheme. This involved taking a post-graduate Diploma in Education at Makerere University in Kampala and then teaching for two years in Uganda, Kenya or Tanzania. My known world extended to London for an interview and before long I was on my way to Uganda. My world travels had begun.

1

Sydney Opera House, Australia June 1974

By January 1971 my 5 months paid leave after a 3 year teaching contract in East Africa with the British Ministry of Overseas Development was rapidly running out, as were my savings. I had applied to the Ministry for several overseas teaching posts and had an interview in London for one in a Fiji girls' school which I didn't get. I was still waiting word about others in the Bahamas and Malawi when I came across an advert for teachers for New Zealand on 3 year contracts. I was invited to an interview in Glasgow. At the end of the interview, the interviewer sat back and said "Well, that sounds fine. Can you leave on Tuesday?" This was Thursday, so I had a long weekend to get back to Shetland, pack and make it to London for the flight. I was so relieved to be offered the job that I just said "Yeah, no problem". It was, but I made it. This spur of the moment decision was to shape much of my later life.

Research carried out by the Wellington Shetland Society has estimated that there are about 60,000 descendants of Shetland immigrants in New Zealand. Many came out in the 1870s when the New Zealand government promoted and subsidised immigration, with an extensive advertising campaign in Britain, including in the "Shetland Times" newspaper. An early Prime Minister, Sir Robert Stout, was born in Shetland as was Helen Clarke's great grandfather. I had an aunt whose daughter married a New Zealand serviceman posted on Whalsay during World War II. After the war they all three moved to New Zealand where my cousin and her husband both died young in the mid 1950s and my aunt returned to Shetland. The exotic stamps on the letters and the big pink magazines that used to arrive from my aunt and cousin stimulated my interest in the country.

Long distance flights in those days made a lot more stops than the current schedules. We stopped in Frankfurt, then in the middle of the night, with the street lights spread out and twinkling below us, Tehran. Later, we flew over the flooded Ganges/Brahmaputra delta in Bangladesh, known as the Sunderbans, a patchwork of water and greenery stretching for miles. Coming into Bangkok, I saw my first rice paddy fields, a farmer in a conical hat looking up at us as we passed low overhead. In the airport toilet, I was accosted by a shifty-looking character offering to change money at black market rates. We crossed Vietnam, where the war was still raging, via the DMZ (Demilitarised Zone). We landed at the old Kai Tak Airport in Hong Kong, swooping over junks ploughing through the harbour with square, brown, sails and passing so close to a skyscraper that you could practically see coolies slurping noodles in the flats, then down on to the tarmac with the wing flaps screaming as the pilot tried to avoid ending up in the harbour which was rapidly looming up at the end of the short runway.

There was a twelve hour break in the journey in Hong Kong to allow the crew to rest and get some sleep. We were transferred to a hotel in Kowloon. I was tired but couldn't resist the allure of a new destination. I ended up in a joint called the Casino Bar and Night Club in Kimberley Street off Nathan Road, the main street in Kowloon. A girl approached me and said "Hello, Johnny." Although she'd got my name wrong we got along well. The Hong Kong post boxes were modelled on the old red British model, except that for some reason the slot for the letters was vertical instead of horizontal. There was an urban legend that the same principle applied to the anatomy of Chinese girls, only in their case the slot was allegedly horizontal instead of vertical. My scientific investigations to test this theory and get a new slant on things left me barely enough time to get back to the hotel and catch the bus to the airport.

In New Zealand, I had been posted to teach at Kawerau College, down near the Bay of Plenty in the North Island. My first impression of New Zealand was its greenness and the fresh blue sky with fluffy white clouds. The first Maori settlers had called it Aotearoa (Land of the Long White Cloud) and I remember thinking it was a pity that had been changed. Travelling down to Kawerau in the bus we passed through the lush open pasture land of the Waikato dairy farm country with green rolling hills and knolls and into the forested hills around Rotorua. The tree ferns were unlike anything I had seen before, any minute you expected to see a dinosaur's head rear up among them. The volcanic landscape around Rotorua with its hot springs and bubbling lava pools brought home the power of the earth lurking beneath the surface. Mount Tarawera had erupted as recently as 1886, burying several Maori villages under ash and the world famous pink and white silica terraces at Lake Rotomahana under a newly formed lake. A massive earthquake in 1932 had flattened the town of Napier. White clouds billowed from the permanently active White Island volcano in the Bay of Plenty. It was a very unstable country.

Arriving in Kawerau, you could have been forgiven for thinking that you had arrived in hell. The smell of sulphur was overwhelming. The town had been built in the 1950s to house the workforce for the new, giant Tasman Pulp and Paper Mill. The smell from the Mill was truly hellish. The swift flowing Tarawera River ran down the west side of the town supplying water for the mill. The pine-forested hills which were logged for timber for the plant started on the opposite bank, accessed by a bridge. On the other side of the town, the extinct volcanic cone of Mt. Edgecumbe rose above the fertile flat plain which stretched away to the Bay of Plenty. The town had a population of around 7,000 and was laid out in the style of the British New Towns with a central commercial area where all the shops and facilities were located, surrounded by residential districts of weatherboard clad bungalows on generous sized sections. For the first week or two I was billeted in the Kawerau Hotel, the bar of which was the main watering hole for the town – a Wild West atmosphere prevailed at weekends, Dodge City or Deadwood with Maori accents. Draught beer was served in large jugs, even bigger than the most copious German "steins" and drunk from little seven ounce glasses. On my first visit to the bar, I hadn't noticed this latter part of the ritual and started drinking straight from the jug. The barman gave me a pitying look, shoving a seven ounce towards me and said "Here, mate. Most people use one of these." New Zealanders had a strange, schizophrenic, hypocritical attitude to alcohol. Until 1968 the infamous "six-o-clock swill" had been in operation. The pubs had closed at 6.00 pm so men finishing work at 5.00 pm would make a bee-line for the pub and pour down as much drink as their throats could cope with before the bell went. There were horror stories about men lying unconscious in the gutters outside pubs in pools of vomit. I say "men" advisedly as few women went near pubs in those days. Like Prohibition in 1920s America, this was another social-engineering experiment intended to control the demon drink which was obviously less than successful. In 1971 closing time was 10.00 pm as it was in Britain but it was difficult to find a drink anywhere after that so there was still a lot of pressurised drinking as the little hand crept round towards ten.

I was later given a room in the Teachers' Hostel down by the bridge across the Tarawera – I had been promised a new staff house in my contract but apparently it was a long way from completion. A lot of Finns had been brought in to develop the pulp and paper industry and the workforce was predominantly Maori and Polynesians from the Pacific islands. As a result the pupils were an amazing racial mix, some with Maori or Islander features and colouring but blonde hair. They were a fascinating bunch but I quickly learned that the job was more about crowd control or lion-taming than education. One bright spark expressed the opinion that there wasn't much point in going down the academic road when he could walk out of school at sixteen and get a job in the Tasman Mill which would pay twice as much as I could earn as a teacher. At weekends, I used to go down to the Bay of Plenty coast for a swim and sometimes camp overnight on the beach just west of the largely Maori village of Matata. A line of cliffs back from the beach marked an old shoreline, leaving enough room for the road and a railway line and a wide belt of dunes behind the beach. There were some groves of mainly eucalyptus trees in the dunes providing idyllic camping spots. The beach was exposed with crashing surf but I used to dive through the breakers and swim in the calmer waters further out. Coming ashore, I would often be caught by a breaking wave, tumbled head over heels and dumped on the beach, scrabbling for hand and footholds to prevent myself being sucked back out by the undertow. Since I've returned to New Zealand, I've discovered how treacherous this coastline is, with deadly undertows and rips which can carry even the strongest swimmers out to sea. Scores of people are drowned in New Zealand each year in similar circumstances. I realise now that I was mad to swim there alone but I was just twenty-five years old, fit and a reasonably good swimmer and had survived three years in darkest Africa, so the thought that it might be dangerous never entered my head.

One weekend, I was down in the little town of Whakatane on the Bay of Plenty coast to get in some swimming over at Ohope Beach and met an Englishman in a pub who was working as a Town Planner in Auckland. This was a profession that I had thought about taking up when I graduated from Aberdeen University but had been put off by the prospect of several years more studying to qualify. The Englishman told me that there were hardly any qualified Planners in New Zealand and that I shouldn't have any problems getting a job with my Geography degree. Shortly after that I applied for a Planning post with Hamilton City Council up in the Waikato, 128 kilometres (80 miles) South of Auckland and got it. In breaking my 3 year teaching contract, I blew my free return airfare to Britain (and had to pay back the fare out) and was now marooned in New Zealand for an indefinite period.

Hamilton was what was colloquially known as a "cow-cocky" town, a market town serving the surrounding dairy farming region, a sobriquet which also carried connotations of "red-necked" attitudes. However, with a population of 80,000 and growing rapidly, it had really outgrown that role, with an extensive industrial area stretching down Te Rapa Road and a rapidly growing university out at Hillcrest. It had been founded in the late 1860s at the end of the Maori Wars (now generally known as the "Land Wars") in the Waikato. Land confiscated from the Tainui tribe to punish them for their role in the war was distributed to discharged soldiers from the British forces. A survey plan had been drawn up with a framework of streets and mostly quarter acre building sections surrounded by a Town Belt of recreational land. Two separate settlements were laid out originally; Hamilton West and Hamilton East, separated by the wide Waikato River, the longest in the country, flowing down from Lake Taupo. Lake Taupo had been formed by a cataclysmic volcanic explosion around 26,500 years ago which had showered ash across much of the North Island; metres of it underlay Hamilton and it didn't make the best of building foundations. It is thought that this eruption might have contributed to the onset of the glacial maximum (the coldest period) during the last ice age due to its "nuclear winter" effects world-wide. From a professional point of view, Hamilton was an interesting place to work at the time. The Council was preparing an "Area Study" to identify land for city expansion – population projections at the time indicated that it could reach 200,000 by the end of the century; and I was involved in preparing a "Comprehensive Development Plan" to set out the principles of how the growth should take place, which was pioneering stuff for New Zealand at the time. Of course things went pear-shaped for the New Zealand economy after the mid 1970s and this growth never materialised – Robbie Burns had something pertinent to say about "the best laid plans of mice and men" going "aft agley". We turned out to be mice but it was good training for my future career in Planning. We had a "drinking school" after work on Friday nights in one of the town centre pubs, mostly attended by people from the Engineering and Planning Departments. Special occasions, like someone leaving, were known as "five jug nights" – this wasn't five jugs shared among us; it was five jugs each. Afterwards, my favourite drinking hole was the

Hillcrest Tavern, a vast, cavernous place up near the university. These huge suburban taverns were all the rage at the time with live bands at the weekends, sometimes even over-the-hill overseas acts – I remember seeing Millie Small of "My Boy Lollipop" fame at the Hillcrest when she was well past her sell-by date. From Kawerau, I had driven down at the weekends to the white sandy beaches fringing the Bay of Plenty. When I moved to Hamilton, Raglan on the wild, exposed west coast was the nearest beach. My swimming improved no end and towards the end of my time there I even had a go at surfing without ever managing to master it. Looking back, I wish I had started early enough to become competent; I look at surfers now and envy them the adrenalin rush that it brings.

I occasionally went up to Auckland for the weekend. In those days everything closed down for the weekend and the cities tended to empty out. British TV comics could make jokes like "I went to New Zealand but it was closed" and strike a chord. Driving up Queen Street, the main drag, on a Sunday, you could do a U-turn whenever you felt like it without in any way endangering other motorists. But the pubs were lively enough on Friday and Saturday nights. I used to check out the infamous "Snakepit" bar in the South Pacific Hotel on the corner of Queen and Customs Streets to see if there were any stray Shetlanders around. In those days many of my age group and probably a majority from my home island of Whalsay were in the Merchant Navy and New Zealand was a popular destination. The upstairs lounge bar in the Great Northern Hotel on the opposite corner from the South Pacific was another popular haunt. Prince Tui Teko's Maori band used to play there and the Maori comedian Billy T. James sometimes used to appear with them. One night I was making my way to the toilet when I saw a familiar face which suddenly went very white at the sight of me. While I was in the toilet, it dawned on me that it was Harry Poleson from Whalsay who I didn't really know although I had seen him occasionally – he was from the north end of the island and had gone to the other primary school and was in any case three or four years older than me, closer to my brother's age. He had gone to sea shortly after he left school at fifteen. With me being away at boarding school, university and then in Africa for most of the time since then, our paths had rarely, if ever, crossed, when he had been home on leave between voyages. Just a couple of months before we met, my brother had been killed in a car accident in Malawi, in Africa, where he had been working as a vet. When I returned to the bar, I went up to the man and said "Harry?" By this time he had realized who I was and said "Jimmy, my God. I'd heard about Gibbie (my brother Gilbert) and thought I was seeing a ghost." He hadn't seen my brother either for years and had forgotten for a moment that I existed. We had an Irish-style alcohol-fuelled wake for Gibbie.

While in Hamilton, I became fascinated by the history of early European settlement in New Zealand and the wars against the Maori which had led to the founding of the city. At that time, it was difficult to find good information on that period. Racial matters were largely swept under the carpet; it was a taboo subject and there was still an undercurrent of racialism detectable in the mainstream Pakeha (European) population. The revival of the Maori language and their struggle for restitution for land confiscated after the wars and subsequently obtained by unfair means didn't get under way until the mid 1970s after I had left New Zealand. When I came back in 1997, things had moved on. Claims for compensation for Maori land taken illegally were making their way through the Waitangi Tribunal, which had been set up under the Treaty of Waitangi Act, 1975 (several big settlements had already been made, including one with Ngai Tahu, the main South Island iwi (tribe). Te reo Maori (the Maori language) was being taught in schools and there were Maori language tuition programmes on the Maori TV Channel. Glasnost (Russian for openness) had also broken out in the academic world. An excellent documentary series by James Belich, Professor of History at Auckland University, was showing on TV, based on his 1986 book "The New Zealand Wars". In 2003, Dr. Michael King's definitive "History of New Zealand" came out which dealt even-handedly with the colonial struggles and debunked a number of myths about the early settlement of the country. Hone Harawira, a Maori radical, had even made it into Parliament. His brand of reverse-racialism (he was on record as saying he wouldn't let his daughter marry a

Pakeha) acted as a lightning-rod for the hissy-fits and hatreds of the small minority of Pakeha who still harboured racialist feelings towards Maori in general. Bringing the racial issue into the open was probably psychologically healthier than the repression of such feelings which had been the norm in the 1970s.

It is now largely accepted in academic circles, subject to no new evidence emerging, that Maori didn't reach New Zealand until around 1280AD. The earliest traces of fossil pollen from man-induced fires have been found just below a layer of ash produced by the Kaharoa volcanic eruption from Mount Tarawera which has been dated to 1314 AD, plus or minus 12 years. The oldest reliable radio-carbon dating of archaeological artefacts and human remains correspond with this date. Everything points to an origin in the Society Islands, west of Tahiti, probably via the Cook Islands. Obsidian tools, identified as originating from Mayor Island in the Bay of Plenty, have been found on the Kermadec Islands, half way to the Cooks, strongly suggesting that in the early days there were return voyages. Regular European contacts started just over 20 years after Captain Cook had mapped the islands in 1769/70. In 1788, Britain had established a penal colony at Port Jackson (Sydney) across the Tasman Sea in Australia, bringing "Down Under" into regular contact with Britain. The demand for timber, flax, seal oil and skins brought hunters and traders into New Zealand waters and harbours. Whaling ships operating out of Sydney and Hobart (Tasmania) began frequenting the coast in the early 1800s and were soon joined by French and American whalers. The little port of Kororarereka (now Russel) in the Bay of Islands, Northland, grew up to service this industry and soon became known as "the hell-hole of the Pacific" because of its lawless ways. Some Europeans, known as Pakeha Maori, many of them ex-convicts, settled ashore, taking Maori wives. In 1814 the first missionary, Thomas Marsden, arrived in the Bay of Islands. By the 1820s, the timber and flax industries were flourishing, kauri trees from Northland and the Coromandel Peninsula being particularly in demand for ships' masts and spars. Maori had started growing potatoes and escalated their pig rearing to feed visiting ships and were growing flax on a commercial basis. Their favourite payment

for these trade goods was muskets. Maori were a warrior race with fortified "pa" (strongholds) and a history of inter-tribal conflict. The acquisition of muskets led to the Musket Wars, initially within Northland but
then further afield as the Ngapuhi tribe (who were the first to obtain
the new weapons) under their fierce leader Hongi Hika, made raids to
the south. As other tribes obtained these new weapons, Michael King
has written that after 1820 it "developed the momentum of an arms
race", the fighting peaking in the early 1830s. Casualty rates were much
higher than in traditional hand to hand fighting and there were widespread atrocities committed against Maori civilians as well, including
women and children. In 1833, the British Colonial Administration had
sent an "ambassador", James Busby, across from Australia to look after
the interests of British residents and traders. He became concerned
about the effect the Musket Wars were having but also the fact that the
French were sniffing around with colonization intentions and that a
private company, the New Zealand Company, was planning to set up a
colony in what was to become Wellington and possibly set up a government of their own. The outcome was that in late 1839, William Hobson
was sent out from England to establish a colony, resulting in the Treaty
of Waitangi, signed with a number of Maori Chiefs on February 6th,
1840 and subsequently ratified with Chiefs all over the North and
South Islands. Just in time from the British point of view, as a shipload
of French colonists arrived at Akaroa in the Banks Peninsula, south of
what is now Christchurch, in August of the same year.

There were problems with the Treaty and the way Britain started
to administer the country almost from the beginning. Hone Heke, a
Ngapuhi Chief, was unhappy among other things with the capital being
moved to Auckland from Kororareka in 1841, which had reduced his
tribe's "mana" (power/influence) and the hanging of a relative for
murder. He cut down the flagpole at Kororareka in 1844 in protest and
twice more in early 1845 and then later in the year attacked the town
killing 20 Pakeha (Europeans). During the attack a powder magazine
exploded setting fire to much of the town. Further sporadic fighting
against Hone Heke and his ally Kawiti continued in Northland that
year with other Maori groups under Waka Nene fighting on the side of

the colonial administration. (Tribal groups "friendly" to the Europeans came to be known as "kupapa" and featured in most of the later wars as well.) The fighting petered out in a "draw" with neither side able to inflict a decisive blow and no retribution was sought from Hone Heke or his allies. But the British got an early taste of what a formidable foe the Maori could be and how effective a defence their pa provided.

By the 1850s the cracks in the Treaty of Waitangi were already becoming apparent. The Treaty had been written in a hurry and translated into Maori in an even bigger hurry by the missionary Henry Williams. Under it the Maori Chiefs ceded "sovereignty" to Queen Victoria, translated by Williams as the Maori word "kawanatanga" while the Chiefs would retain "full, exclusive and undisturbed possession of their lands and estates, forests, fisheries and other properties" the "chieftainship" aspect of this translated as "te tino rangatiratanga" and "other properties" as "ratou taonga katoa" (all their treasures.) The Maori word closest to "sovereignty" is probably "mana" and it is unlikely that the Chiefs would willingly have given up that. The word Williams used was probably closer to "governorship" in English. Under "rangatiratanga" the Chiefs probably thought they had the right to continue to manage their own affairs without interference from the Crown. The Maori word "taonga" had much wider connotations than "other properties." These cultural and linguistic misunderstandings have dogged the interpretation of the treaty to this day.

But the biggest bone of contention was the amount of Maori land that was being sold to European settlers and the sheer numbers of colonists arriving, which Maori had not foreseen. There were only about 2,000 European residents in the whole country in 1840; by 1858 this had grown to 59,000, while the Maori population had been reduced by the Musket Wars and European diseases to 56,000. The various tribes saw the need to band together to curtail further land sales and in 1856 appointed a Maori King to be based in Ngaruawahia in the Waikato. Previously, there had been no concept of a "Maori nation".

Conflict over a disputed land sale first broke out over the Waitara block north of New Plymouth in 1860 which sparked the first Taranaki War. Imperial forces had to be brought over from Australia to deal with this insurrection and suffered a heavy defeat and 64 casualties unsuccessfully attempting to storm a pa. The settlers were forced to withdraw into New Plymouth which was effectively under siege by Maori for a time and 100 settlers died from diseases brought on by the insanitary, overcrowded conditions. Fighting continued inconclusively into 1861 when a truce was eventually agreed. In that same year, the new governor, Sir George Grey, decided to put down the "King Movement" in order to free up the sale of land. He had a military road built south towards the Waikato from Auckland and a redoubt built at Pokeno. In 1863 he took the opportunity of a fresh outbreak of war in Taranaki to get more troops from the U.K., assembling a force of 20,000 men, which were then used for an invasion of the Waikato in July 1863 under General Cameron. Maori had a maximum of 5,000 warriors to call on, never more than 2,000 in the field at any one time. The first major battle was at Rangiriri Pa in November 1963. After heavy fighting, the Maori withdrew and Cameron was able to enter the Maori King's capital, Ngaruawahia. The King withdrew into the rugged "King Country" to the south in the heart of the North Island. Cameron continued to pursue the Maori fighting force and the final action in the Waikato invasion was at Orakau Pa in 1864, where the Maori defenders were forced to break out through the Imperial army's lines with heavy losses. Their leader, Rewi Maniapoto, is said to have shouted to one of Cameron's officers, "Friend, I shall continue to fight you for ever and ever" before he too retreated into the King Country. Tribes living around Tauranga who were allied to the Waikato Maori continued to resist. They inflicted a heavy defeat on the government forces at Gate Pa but were later caught by surprise at an unfinished pa and defeated and it was all over. Vast tracts of land were confiscated from the tribes which had resisted the invasion and even some who hadn't, laying the basis later for the lucrative Waikato dairy industry and providing residential sites to reward the Imperial troops in places like Hamilton. The Waikato War caused the death of over 1,000 Maori and around 700 Europeans. Maori were never completely defeated: they retreated into the King Country and the government left them alone there. Trouble continued to brew up from time to time. In 1865 a strange religious cult arose in Taranaki called Pai Marire or Hauhau with Christian and traditional elements to it, which developed into an insurrection. General Cameron's successor applied a scorched earth policy, burning Maori villages and crops until it was quelled. The same cult spread to the Eastern Bay of Plenty and East Coast. A German missionary, Carl Volkner, who was suspected of being a government spy, was hung from a tree outside his church in Opotiki and then eaten. This uprising was put down with the help of "kupapa" from the Arawa tribe based around Rotorua. Prisoners were banished to the remote Chatham Islands, 500 kilometres to the east of New Zealand. One of them, Te Kooti, escaped in 1868 by seizing a visiting ship and with a group of followers carried out a guerrilla campaign from the east coast through the Urewera Mountains to Lake Taupo, with raids into the Bay of Plenty and Rotorua, killing a number of Europeans, until he too eventually took refuge in the King Country in 1872. Fighting broke out again in South Taranaki led by a formidable warrior Titokowaru, in protest against land confiscations. He inflicted a heavy defeat on colonial forces led by Thomas McDonnell, killing the Pakeha hero, Von Tempsky. McDonnell's successor Lt. Colonel George Whitmore was also defeated and the Europeans in the district had to retreat to Wanganui. When it looked as if they might have to abandon the area altogether, the Maori threat melted away. It transpired that Titokowara had broken a tapu in a scandal believed to involve another man's wife and his support collapsed. Some non-violent passive resistance to European rule continued in the religious settlement of Parihaka in Taranaki but that was eventually forcibly put down as well. By 1896, the Maori population had fallen to 42,000 from an estimated 110,000 in Captain Cook's time through disease and war and there was concern that it was a dying race. The last spark of resistance came as late as 1917 among the Tuhoe tribe in the remote depths of the Urewera Mountains. Their leader, Rua Kenana, was arrested by a large force of police and imprisoned.

Much more recently, in early 2012, a group of Maori activists known as the "Urewera Four" came before the court essentially charged with operating a training camp for terrorists in Tuhoe country in the Urewera Mountains. Personally, I think what was going on in the depths of the Urewera forests was just a juvenile game of make-believe, political paint-ball games with no likelihood of it ever being translated into reality. For a start, how would they know who to attack? The races are now so mixed that it is often difficult to tell who has Maori blood and who hasn't. How many people could pick out the All Black Dan Carter as being of Maori descent from his facial appearance? One of the accused is a blond haired Pakeha. If he has any Maori blood he looks as if he would easily pass a blood test if having Maori blood was to become a criminal offence with a similar threshold level to the blood alcohol test for drunk driving. I used to see another of the accused, Tame Iti, in the main street in Whakatane from time to time selling Maori souvenirs, when I lived in Ohope. He did not strike me as Osama Bin Laden with a full facial Moko (tattoo). I can see them sitting around a camp fire in the Urewera bush, stoked up with Tui beer and falling helpless with laughter into the embers as they sing a seditious version of the National Anthem:

E i hoa, Atua[1],
Bugger off you Pakeha.
Board your wakas[2], sling your hook,
And take that arsehole Caapeetan Cook.

[1] God of mercy
[2] Canoes

But Maori suicide bombers or urban guerrillas? No way. The jury was unable to reach a decision on the main charge of belonging to a criminal organization and it was dropped but the defendants were given short prison sentences for firearm offences. Tame Iti claimed the guns were for shooting wild pigs in the bush, not the ones who arrested him. Mr. Plod the Policeman has never admitted that he over-reacted or indeed was wrong but the government has since apologised and reached agreement with the Tuhoe tribe settling historical grievances through the Waitangi Tribunal. The compensation in the form of cash, return of confiscated land and devolution to the tribe of the administration of some social services should go some way towards healing old wounds.

Shortly after I joined Hamilton City Council, I was sent on a management training course being held at Lincoln College, on the outskirts of Christchurch in the South Island. Christchurch had been founded by the Church of England Canterbury Association, a private company specifically set up to acquire land and provide the infrastructure for the new settlement. The first ships with colonists had arrived in 1850. The magnificent Cathedral in the city centre would not have looked out of place in any English city. Place names like Manchester Street and New Brighton out by the beach reinforced the Englishness of the place as did the Avon River flowing gently through leafy Hagley Park, punts and all. The substantial stone-built buildings in the centre produced an urban landscape which was more like an English city than the towns I had seen in the North Island, where the verandas overhanging the side-walks and surviving timber buildings evoked visions of Deadwood in Wild West days; in Hamilton weatherboard bungalows encroached on the fringes of the CBD (Central Business District) and the City Planning Department occupied two of those in Milton Street. The landscape around Christchurch was also very different with the broad, flat Canterbury Plain extending away to the snow capped mountains of the Southern Alps. The craggy, volcanic Port Hills separated the city from its port at Lyttleton, but a tunnel underneath the ridge provided alternative access to the winding scenic route over the grassy summit.

Some time later when I had accumulated some leave I took a bus trip down to the South Island, spending a few days in the capital, Wellington, before crossing Cook Strait in the ferry and continuing south as far as Dunedin. Wellington had started life in 1840 as Port Nicholson, founded by the private New Zealand Company. It had become the capital in 1865 because of its central location in the country and the new "Beehive" Parliament Building was an interesting piece of architecture. But the site chosen was unfortunate. It was right on the line of the major fault splitting New Zealand in two, along the edge of two tectonic plates, which would eventually pull the country apart. The fault defined the edge of the Southern Alps in the South Island, ran past the still active volcanoes of Ruapehu and Tarewera in the central North Island and out to sea past the permanently smoking White Island. Everyone had been surprised at the massive earthquakes which had devastated Christchurch in September 2010 and February 2011: nobody had expected that it was in the line of fire. But everyone knew that Wellington was and that something similar happening there was probably just a matter of time.

Dunedin had been founded by Scottish settlers, through a company set up by the Scottish Free Church, the first ships with immigrants arriving in 1848. With a statue of Robbie Burns in the Octagon in the city centre outside the City Council offices, you could tell. Dunedin had benefited from gold strikes in the Otago area, particularly the gold rush following a rich discovery at Gabriel's Gully in 1861. By 1874 Dunedin was the biggest city in New Zealand with a population of 29,000. It had become the main centre for heavy engineering based on iron and steel and the first shipment of frozen mutton to Europe had been sent from a meat works nearby. Speights brewery produced the best beer in New Zealand. The harbour was magnificent: the port had moved out to Port Chalmers on a picturesque peninsula half way out towards the harbour mouth where there was deeper water. The towering Tairoa Head at the harbour entrance housed an albatross colony and the beautiful little sandy coves along the seaward coast of the scenic Otago Peninsula were home to penguin colonies and sea lions. Aramoana, at the harbour entrance, opposite Tairoa Head, had white sand spit beaches backed by pine trees and a seal colony. They actually got some winter down there and when a "southerly burster" of cold air straight from Antarctica rolled in, the temperature could drop by ten degrees centigrade in minutes. But in summer it was beautiful. On my return to New Zealand in 1997, I was to come back to Dunedin as the District Planner.

I only got two or three weeks annual leave at Hamilton City Council which didn't leave much time for travelling. In January 1973 I took a trip up to Fiji. This was my first Pacific island. I flew into Nandi Airport and picked up the hire car which I had pre-booked. On the drive to my hotel, I saw a young man thumbing a lift up ahead and decided to stop for him to get some help to find the Skylodge Hotel where I was booked. When I dropped him off near the hotel he invited me along later to his home in a village just outside Nandi where they were having a bit of a celebration that night. By the time we arrived, the festivities were just getting under way. My new friend, Sitiveni, introduced me to his parents and some of the other guests. Apart from him, nobody seemed to speak much English. They seemed delighted to have an unexpected white man for dinner. I mused that not that long ago I would have been the main course. A meal was served up as we squatted on reed mats outside the thatched huts where the family lived – roast pork and chicken, with taro and yams and taro leaves cooked as a vegetable in coconut milk, all piled on a large taro leaf instead of a plate. Then came the kava, a cloudy white concoction made from a relative of the pepper plant and looking a bit like watery wallpaper paste. It arrived in a huge metal pot, almost missionary size. Sitiveni's father filled a wooden bowl from the pot with a ladle, said a few words, spilled a few drops on the ground, then drained the bowl. Everybody clapped. The process was repeated, only this time the bowl was passed to the next person. When it came to my turn, I wasn't overly impressed with the taste, peppery but bland, a bit like aniseed. It didn't seem particularly potent but it numbed the inside of my mouth. The evening rolled on with some speeches and a few songs and the kava bowls kept coming round and round. It didn't seem to be particularly intoxicating but it was definitely doing something to my head more like an anaesthetic than an alcohol fix. When it was time to leave, Sitiveni escorted me out the path past the banana plantation towards my car. On the way some young girls emerged from the bushes and started chattering to Sitiveni, the discussion punctuated by a lot of giggling and laughter. "They're inviting you to go into the bush with them," he said. Like a good News of the World reporter, I made an excuse and left.

Fiji was hot and sticky after New Zealand. I drove around the south coast of the island from Nandi to Suva, the capital, the mountainous island of Bequ (pronounced Mbengu) lying offshore to the south. I had heard that this island was famous for its fire-walkers. The countryside was lush with tropical rainforest stretching up towards the interior mountains, the coast lined with coconut palms. The road crossed numerous small rivers and streams flowing towards the sea. Large areas were planted in sugar cane. Clusters of thatched roofed houses surrounded by small fields of vegetables, taro, yams and maize and buried among fruit trees and banana plantations, punctuated the landscape. Some beach resort hotels nestled among palm trees along the coastal beaches with tempting names like Reef Lodge and Tropic Sands.

Suva was quite a large town and judging by the number of ships moored at the quays, a busy port. I stayed at the Suva Hotel. Walking round town, I was reminded of East Africa. The shops and businesses were nearly all owned by Asians (Indians), descendants of indentured labourers brought in by the British in the 19th century to work the sugar plantations. Now they almost outnumbered the native Fijians. This was later to create serious political problems and eventually lead to the coup by chauvinist elements in the native population which produced the current military government. Among the shops I spotted a large Burns Philp department store. Branches of this famous trading emporium were found throughout the South Pacific, evoking visions of full-rigged ships and schooners plying between the islands carrying cargoes of copra, sandalwood and Kanakas (native islanders) to be delivered into virtual slavery on plantations in Queensland and elsewhere. In the evening I went into a bar down by the river. The all-male clientele were nearly all already the worse for drink. Pacific Islanders generally didn't handle alcohol well and there were already signs of belligerence so I just had a beer and left. I went on to the Golden Dragon Nightclub above a Chinese restaurant which was packed with sweating revellers in the steamy heat.

I moved back along the south coast to the Coral Coast, the main tourist area of Viti Levu and stayed at the Korolevu Beach Hotel. Tourism was developing on the island by this time but the numbers were nothing like they are now. The view out to Bequ was breathtaking and the water off the white coral sand beaches like a warm bath. It reminded me of the beaches around Mombasa in Kenya and stirred the nostalgia that I still feel from time to time for East Africa.

I started studying for the Royal Australian Planning Institute membership examination while working for Hamilton City Council. This was just a question of getting copies of the syllabus, reading lists and previous exam papers and studying in my own time. I took the annual exams in the office, supervised by Bob Eyeington, the City Planner. It wasn't the easiest way to take what was the equivalent of another university degree but I completed it in 1974. After the final exam, I decided to take a look at Australia and investigate the job opportunities over there. Bill Denbow, an Australian who worked in our office, had contacts in Australia and in particular was a friend of Hans Westerman, who was the Chief Planner in Canberra. Bill fixed me up with a meeting with Westerman and I organized interviews with a couple of Planning Authorities in Sydney and a consultancy firm in Brisbane where one of my former university friends worked.

I flew to Sydney in June 1974. I was impressed with the magnificent setting of the City, the sparkling harbour, dominated by the Harbour Bridge and the newly completed Sydney Opera House (the second of my New Wonders of the World candidates.) Sitting on Bennelong Point at the edge of the harbour and at the tip of the central business district, with the Royal Botanic Gardens alongside and the Bridge nearby, the white sails of the Opera House made a stunning impact. It had been completed in 1973 after an incubation period going back to the late 1940s when Eugene Goosens, the Director of the New South Wales State Conservatorium of Music started lobbying for a venue for theatrical productions. A 1955 design competition was won by Jorn Utzon, a Danish architect and construction began in March 1959. Political interference with the project, which Utzon described as "malice in blunderland", led to his resignation in February 1966 but the project proceeded in his absence.

The design techniques developed by Utzon and the civil engineering firm Ove Arup, including the use of computer aided design, were revolutionary and greatly influenced the development of modern architecture. The design presented enormous technical problems, particularly the roof structure with its sail-like shells of pre-cast concrete. These technical problems, coupled with design changes from the original concept and political interference with the project, resulted in a final cost of $A102 million, an over-run of 1400 percent, and a ten year delay on the original completion date. However, history has delivered some considerable endorsements to the project. In 2003, Jorn Utzon was awarded the Pritzker Prize, architecture's highest honour. The citation said:

> "There is no doubt that the Sydney Opera House is his masterpiece. It is one of the great iconic buildings of the 20th century, an image of great beauty that has become known throughout the world – a symbol for not only a city, but a whole country and continent."

The Opera house was made a UNESCO World Heritage Site in 2007. Clive James, who had abandoned Australia at an early age because it was cramping his immense cultural talents and became a TV personality in the U.K., disparagingly described it as "a portable typewriter full of oyster shells". But he had practically become a Pommie Bastard by living among them so long and picking up bad habits like not washing himself regularly. Anyway, the roof looked more like scallop shells than oyster shells, so Clive obviously didn't know his shellfish. Had he stayed in Australia that could have proved fatal. In "Down Under", the American travel writer Bill Bryson observed that Australia was a country "where seashells will not just sting you but actually sometimes go for you. Pick up an innocuous cone shell from a Queensland beach and you will discover that the little fellow inside is not just astoundingly swift and testy but exceedingly venomous." However, Clive fared better in Britain than his compatriot Rolf Harris. In 2013 Rolf was charged with tying a kangaroo down for immoral purposes, jaking his peg at under-age girls and interfering with two little boys.

Sydney had started life as a penal colony. America had previously served as a dumping ground for Britain's petty thieves but with the American War of Independence, that option disappeared. Captain Cook had spent some time at Botany Bay in 1770 (and later claimed the east coast of Australia for Britain, calling it New South Wales) and it was the aristocratic botanist with him on his ship the "Endeavour", John Banks, who suggested Botany Bay as an alternative. The first fleet of 11 ships, carrying over 700 convicts and their minders arrived in 1778 but finding that Botany Bay was not all that Banks had cracked it up to be – marshy and no permanent water supply for a start – found an ideal site at Sydney Cove in the deep water harbour to the north, Port Jackson. By the time that the transportation of criminals ended in 1868, 160,000 of them had been dumped in Australia, including 25,000 women. Initially, all that the native Aborigines did when they saw the fleet landing was shout "Warra! Warra!" (Go away!) but later put up some resistance. However they were few in numbers, possibly just 4-8,000 in the Sydney region and 300,000 in the whole continent. It is now accepted that their ancestors reached Australia at least 45,000 years ago and possibly as far back as 60,000 BC, somehow crossing at least 100 kilometres (60 miles) of open sea even at the lowest sea levels during the ice age. Their hunting and gathering culture could only support a very low population density and they lived in family groups of 20 to 50 people with no political organization above that. Not having houses, never mind fortified pa like the Maori in New Zealand, they were poorly equipped to resist invasion by Europeans. Since they had no permanent settlements, the British Colonial Administration conveniently solved the land acquisition question by declaring the continent "terra nullius" (empty land), a situation which lasted until the 1970s when it was at last recognised that the Aborigines had some land rights. Aborigines still weren't included in the national census in 1965 and weren't recognised as citizens and given voting rights until 1967. The American travel writer, Bill Bryson, recounts a sorry tale of the atrocities committed against them by the early settlers and government including a particularly horrific incident at Myall Creek in 1838 where 28 Aborigines, including women and children, were massacred by a posse of settlers looking for cattle rustlers. Some of the white perpetrators were eventually hung for that but previous similar actions had gone unpunished. Bryson claims that 20,000 Aborigines were intentionally killed by whites in early colonial times, more than ten times that number dying from diseases introduced by them including an early virulent outbreak of smallpox which left dead bodies lying all around Sydney. This treatment of the native population, coupled with the "White Australia Policy" (immigrants only accepted from European stock, predominantly from Britain) operated by successive governments from the establishment of the Commonwealth in 1901 until discontinued by Gough Whitlam's Labour government in 1972, meant that race relations in Australia in 1974 were a different kettle of fish altogether from in New Zealand, as I was later to discover for myself in Queensland.

In Sydney, I stayed up in Kings Cross, the centre for night-life and still being a committed Philistine, spent my time in the pubs and nightclubs there rather than the Opera House. I had meetings with Planners from both the Sydney City Council and New South Wales Planning Authority. They were involved in developing some interesting concepts for the growth of the city and I got the impression that there were good work opportunities there if I had wanted to apply formally. I visited Circular Quay where the First Fleet had landed and wandered round the Rocks, the earliest settlement area which was starting to undergo refurbishment as a building preservation area. The CBD stretching south from Circular Quay as far as the railway station was a strange mixture of architectural styles from the Victorian period and modern skyscrapers, with Hyde Park providing a welcome green lung. The extensive botanical garden held a fascinating collection of Antipodean plants not found anywhere else in the world. I took a bus out to Bondi Beach, which was a bit run-down at that time and in mid-winter I wasn't tempted to venture into the shark-infested water lapping the golden sand. I took a ferry across the magnificent harbour to the residential North Shore. Port Jackson was what was known in the jargon of my studies of Geography as a "ria", the lower stretch of a river valley, in this case the Parramatta, drowned by sea level rising – like a fiord but without the steep sides. The Harbour Bridge had been completed in 1932 and was a spectacular piece of engineering as well as its contribution to Sydney's iconic harbour scape.

I took a bus to Canberra for my meeting with Hans Westerman. I was not impressed with the Australian landscape after New Zealand. Long stretches of flat, bare, brown grassland, punctuated by stands of the ubiquitous eucalyptus trees, an absence of rural settlements or even signs of human habitation for long stretches, lulled me to sleep, something I rarely do when travelling through new territory. Bill

Bryson in "Down Under" points out that "Australia is the driest, flat-test, hottest, most desiccated, infertile and climatically aggressive of all the inhabited continents" and it showed. And the amazing thing is that the inhabitants call it the "Lucky Country". Now that's optimism for you. Australians were on the whole a cheerful bunch; perhaps not too bright, if their assessment of their continent's attributes and potential was anything to go by, but cheerful with it. The Aborigines had been clever enough not to try to cultivate it. My first impressions of Canberra weren't much better than my gut feelings about the landscape. I'm not a fan of planned "new towns" at the best of times, which may seem strange bearing in mind that I am a professional Town Planner. But Canberra struck me as particularly artificial and lacking in human warmth. The grand design, based on a variety of geometric shapes and axes, looked fine on paper or probably from the air but is obviously not visible from ground level where mortals spend most of their time. I found it soulless and sterile. This impression wasn't helped by the fact that it was pissing with cold rain. The morose Hungarian taxi driver who drove me to my hotel didn't help much either. When I asked him how he liked living in Canberra he said "I don't". Perhaps he was just having a bad day but I could sympathise with him.

Canberra was a purely artificial creation owing its existence to political jealousy between Sydney and Melbourne at the time the Federal Commonwealth was set up in 1901 from the previously independent States. They couldn't decide which city should be the capital so agreed to build a new one somewhere between the two. After seven years of wrangling, the site of Canberra was selected. There is some dispute about what the Aboriginal name means: it apparently could be either "meeting place" or "the hollow between a woman's breasts". Perhaps wisely, they decided to retain the native name rather than call it Crossroads or Cleavage, although "Builder's Crack" or "Buttock Crack" would have been appropriate alternatives. An international competition was launched to produce a design layout for the city, which was won in 1911 by the Chicago architect Walter Burley Griffon and his wife Marion. The plan made use of geometrical shapes such as circles, hexagons and triangles in the layout of roads and the relationships of buildings to each other and featured axes aligned with significant topographical land-marks in the surrounding area. The central feature was to be an artificial, boomerang shaped lake called Lake Burley Griffon, splitting the city in two and providing the setting for the main public buildings. The main roads radiated out from the central Parliament House like the spokes of a wheel. It looked fine on paper. Griffon was appointed Director of Design and Construction and work started in 1913. Progress with build-ing the new capital was slow. Griffon fell out with the Authorities and was sacked in 1920. (Shades of Jorn Utzon and the Sydney Opera House.) The two World Wars and the intervening Great Depression also held things up and it wasn't until Robert Menzies took the bull by the horns and the National Capital Development Commission was set up in 1957 with executive powers to get the job done that real progress was made. The construction of the centrepiece Lake Burley Griffon was completed in 1964.

The meeting with Hans Westerman went well. He said that they had a fairly high turn-over of staff, which didn't surprise me, and if I cared to apply formally, they would let me know about any vacancies that arose. He arranged a drive around the new develop-ment areas with one of his staff. The architecture of many of the individual buildings was impressive as were some of the monuments but it did not alter my initial impression of sterility. Bill Bryson in "Down Under" describes Canberra as "an extremely large park with a city hidden in it" and "a great deal of far-flung greenness, broken at distant intervals by buildings and monuments." He was dead right. It was no place for pedestrians unless they were training for the Sydney Marathon. Bryson also recalled a conversation that he had had with a young girl from Canberra, who was working in Surfer's Paradise in Queensland. It summed up my impression of Canberra perfectly:

Bryson: "So which is better, Canberra or Surfer's Paradise?"
Canberra Girl: "Oh, Surfers by a mile."
Bryson: "It's that good, is it?"
Canberra Girl: "Oh no, Canberra's that bad. I reckon if you were going to rank things by how much pleasure they give, Canberra would

come somewhere below breaking your arm. Well, at least with a broken arm you know it'll get better."

I decided that if I did end up in Australia it would not be in Canberra.

I caught another bus for an epic journey to Brisbane. Distances in Australia are vast; it was 302 kilometres (187 miles) from Canberra to Sydney, then a staggering 1,031 kilometres (639 miles) to Brisbane, taking two full days. For the first leg of the trip to Sydney, I sat beside a girl who told me that her boyfriend had just recently been killed in a car accident. When I told her that the same thing had happened to my brother in Malawi the previous year, she brought out a photo album with pictures from their past together and seemed to be getting some therapeutic benefit from talking about it but it was as depressing as the monotonous landscape passing by the windows. I was beginning to dislike Australia. Eventually, I got to Brisbane, swearing that I'd never get on a bus again. Years later, on my way back to New Zealand from a trip to Papua New Guinea, I spent a couple of nights in Brisbane and really enjoyed the visit. I liked the cosmopolitan atmosphere, the variety of restaurants along the picturesque Brisbane River and top of the range transport system. But in 1974, Brisbane, like Canberra, left me cold. This, of course, was during the time when the Queensland Premier was the notorious, corrupt, right wing/fascist Joh Bjelke Petersen who made Pauline Hansen look like a lily-livered liberal. Bill Bryson recounted that when he was there researching his book "Down Under", the leading political story was a stoush between two politicians called Abbot and Costeloe but Petersen's regime was no laughing matter, particularly his administration's treatment of the Aborigines. Bryson refers to a book by John Pilger which claimed that as recently as the early 1960s Queensland schools were still using a text book which likened Aborigines to "feral jungle creatures". I got talking to some blokes in a pub and inevitably the conversation got around to "Pommie" jokes. There were plenty of them around in New Zealand too but there they were good humoured. In Australia, they were distinctly malicious. Bearing in mind that many Aussies were descended from "Prisoners of Mother England" which the term "Pom" derived from, I found that a bit ironic. I was beginning to dislike Australia even more. I had a meeting at the consultancy firm which I had contacted but my former university friend, Ian Pickles from Rhodesia, whose mug shot I had seen in their promotional literature had left so I didn't get a chance to get any inside information on the firm and life in Brisbane. The projects they were involved in seemed interesting enough and again there seemed to be possibilities for employment but I was already going off the idea of a move to Australia.

In spite of my earlier solemn vow, I took another interminable, even longer, bus trip up the coast of Queensland to Townsville. The impression I got was of a God-forsaken, red-necked, hick town, the terminus for a railway bringing minerals out of the interior to the port. A sign down by the beach warned against swimming due to an outbreak of poisonous fish. I had been warned about their sharks but being bitten to death by fish appealed to me even less. In "Down Under", Bill Bryson points out that Australia "has more things that will kill you than anywhere else." Walking down by the beach, I saw a group of Aborigines, men and girls, sitting under a tree and went across to chat to them. They were drinking beer and already fairly animated. There was a pub just up above the beach so I asked them what it was like. "No idea, mate" was the answer. "They won't let us in there." That was the final straw. As far as I was concerned, the Fat Lady had sung her final aria at the Sydney Opera House. For me, it was all over with Australia.

2

THE ALHAMBRA, GRANADA, SPAIN JUNE 1977

IN JUNE 1976 I finally managed to get a job as a Senior Town Planner with Shropshire County Council, in Shrewsbury, England. It had taken a while since my return from New Zealand towards the end of 1975 because I suspect that potential employers were reluctant to pay travelling expenses from remote Shetland. But when I finally got invited to an interview by Southampton City Council, I wrote to all the Councils that I had current applications with and told them that I would be in England around the date of the interview and ended up with six more interviews scattered all over England. In the end I was offered both the Southampton job and the Shrewsbury one. When I started work, I discovered that the British Royal Town Planning Institute didn't feel that my Australian Planning Institute exam and membership were good enough to meet their high Pommie standards and that I would need to take the final two Parts of their external exam to become fully qualified in Britain and get membership of the RTPI. I studied for this in my spare time and completed the first Part of it in June 1977. Needing a break, I organised a trip to Spain.

There had been an excellent Spanish language teaching series on television and radio which had given me the urge to see Spain when I could afford it and could find the time. I had also invested in a Spanish Linguaphone course so my Spanish had improved no end. I bought a cheap budget airline ticket to Malaga and a booklet of vouchers (through the Thomson Holidays' "Wanderers" package) which could be used in a selection of small hotels (pensiones) in Andalucia, including Granada, where one of the destinations I had in mind was the Alhambra.

In Malaga, I had a voucher for the Hostal Cisneros in Calle (Street) de Cisneros, which turned out to be very central. The street led from the dried-up dribble of the Guadalmedina River to the Plaza de la Constitution, the central square of the city. The main street, Calle Marques de Larios, ran south from the Plaza to the Puerta del Mar where it met the wide, landscaped, east-west boulevard system of the Alameda Principal and Paseo del Parque, lined with palm trees. The old town, with its narrow streets, white-washed houses with wrought iron balconies and red-tiled roofs, lay to the north-east of the Plaza, its little squares lined with bars, cafes and restaurants.

Further to the north-east, on the Plaza de la Merced, was the house where Picasso was born and raised. After the Civil War, General Franco, the Fascist dictator who ruled Spain with an iron hand from 1939 to 1975, banned him from Spain, accusing him of producing "degenerate art". Years later, in the annexe to the Prado Museum in Madrid, I was to see his large, surrealistic painting "Guernica" depicting the horrors of the Civil War following the bombing of the Basque town of Guernica by German and Italian war planes. In 1931 a left wing coalition of socialists, communists and anarchists had won the elections, the King went into exile and a Republic was set up. A right wing reaction set in and the fascist Falange party based on Mussolini's example in Italy attracted a strong following, backed by the army and the church. In 1936, civil war broke out when General Franco mobilised a section of the army against the Republican government. In the bitter fighting over the next three years atrocities were committed by both sides. In Barcelona, the republican stronghold, I was later to see a chapel dedicated to 930 priests and nuns of the diocese who had been killed in the Civil War. In all, 700,000 people were killed in the fighting, 30,000 executed or assassinated and 15,000 civilians killed in air raids. The civil war had been a traumatic experience for Spain, as had the Franco dictatorship which emerged from it. It was still not a subject to raise in polite conversation.

The Cathedral, off Plaza del Obispo on Calle Molina Lario, which ran parallel to and east of the main street, had been converted from a former Moorish mosque, work starting in 1528 and dragging on for 200 years. (A small patio with orange trees, the Patio de los Naranjos, was a survivor from the earlier incarnation as a mosque.) The original plan had been overambitious and funds ran out, leaving one of the bell towers unfinished, giving rise to the Cathedral's nickname, "La Manquita" (The One-armed Lady.) No expense had been spared on the interior. The domed ceiling was 40 metres (130 feet) high, there was an abundance of polished cedar wood and religious paintings and a little museum was crammed with religious artefacts including gold, silver and ivory items. Across the Plaza del Obispo was the red-painted Palacio Episcopal (Bishop's Palace.) The plaza itself had been the scene of burnings at the stake by the Inquisition. (It later formed the set to recreate that horrific scene for the film "The Bridge of San Luis Rey" with Robert de Niro.) The Spanish Inquisition had been set up in 1480 under a papal bull (edict), its main task to root out Moors and Jews who had converted to Christianity (Conversos) but were suspected of secretly still practising their old religions which was punishable by death by hanging or burning alive at the stake. Torture was used to extract confessions. The first Inquisitor-General, Tomas de Torquemada was instrumental in having all Moors and Jews who had not converted to Catholicism banished in 1492. You don't have to dig down very far into Spain's history to find the brutal side of life.

Malaga was a bustling port city, the harbour crowded with craft of all sorts, ferries to Spain's remaining enclaves in North Africa and a large fishing fleet. North-east of the harbour, the wide Malagueta Beach stretched up the coastline with other beaches beyond it. Behind the beach, Malagueta was an up-market residential area.

Rising above the old town to the east was the Alcazaba, the palace and fortress of the Moorish rulers, built between the 8th and 11th centuries AD on the site of a former Roman settlement. The remains of a Roman amphitheatre could be seen just outside the entrance. The Archaeological Museum housed Phoenician, Roman and Moorish artefacts. Above the Alcazaba was the ruins of a 14th century Moorish castle, the Castillo de Gibralfaro, with magnificent views of the old town, harbour and Malagueta Beach spread out below. Immediately below, on the seaward side, was the bullring.

The history of Malaga followed a pattern common to many coastal Spanish cities. It had originally been founded by the Phoenicians, sea-borne traders from the Levant, modern Lebanon. Their North African colony, Carthage, later rose to supplant them with numerous bases along the Spanish coast. The Greeks also set up trading posts. When the Romans defeated both the Carthaginians and the Greeks they incorporated the entire Iberian Peninsula into their Empire for nearly 500 years, Julius Caesar himself being active in the campaigns there. After the fall of the Roman Empire, one group of the barbarians that brought it down, the Vandals, invaded Spain. They were soon followed by the Visigoths who eventually set up a kingdom covering the whole country. During a dispute about the succession to the throne in 711 AD, one faction of the Visigoths invited the Moors from North Africa to help them defeat the rival faction. The Moors were Moslem Arabs who had spread rapidly across North Africa from Arabia following Mohammed's death, incorporating fierce Berber tribesmen from North Africa into their army. Having helped the Visigoth group who invited them across the Straits of Gibraltar to defeat their rivals at the Battle of Guadalete, the Moors stayed and set themselves up as rulers, keen to spread Islam and loot treasure while they were at it. Malaga was the port for one of their main cities, Granada. The Moors were finally expelled by King Ferdinand and Queen Isabella (the "Catholic Monarchs") in 1492, heralding in "modern" Spanish history.

Going even further back to Palaeolithic times, there were extensive traces of the hunting and gathering Neanderthals in Spain, eventually replaced by Neolithic farmers, the Iberians, who had given the Peninsula its name, which meant "Land of Rivers". They had come from hot, dry, North Africa. The Celtic tribes had penetrated into northern Spain. There was an enclave of people in the north, the Basques, whose origins and language were something of a mystery and whose terrorist organization ETA was still actively campaigning for independence. Catalonia, with its own language and history, had shown strong separatist tendencies over the years. Galicia in the north-west also had their own language, closer to Portuguese than Spanish. So it was a hybrid population, much more diverse than my pre-conceived ideas had led me to believe.

Likewise, many of the cultural attributes which I had seen in my mind's eye before coming as typically Spanish had come from outside: grapes and olives had been introduced by the Greeks; the Moors brought oranges, lemons, almonds and palm trees and heavily influenced the architecture; the flamenco now belonged to the Gypsies, a people who had originated in India. But here in Malaga, the second largest city in the province of Andalucia, it all gelled together to create a very Spanish atmosphere, light years away from what I was to see later further down the Costa del Sol. This was the Spain I had come to see.

Considering that it was only two years since General Franco's death, social standards appeared to have relaxed remarkably quickly. If the Generalisimo thought that Picasso's art was degenerate, what would he have made of the pornography on sale in the kiosks in the streets or the shows in the nightclubs such as the Brisamar along the Paseo Maritimo behind Malagueta Beach and near the Bullring? Just south of my hotel in a narrow street off the Municipal Market, street girls were plying their trade quite openly and there were a number of "short stay" hotels. Between the Avenida del Generalisimo Franco (now the Alameda Principal) and the Avenida Heredia, there were about a dozen hostess clubs. These were surprisingly cheap – drinks were not much dearer than in normal bars and even drinks for the girls were not all that expensive. I could even afford the odd bottle of champagne without the prospect of having to face an irate bank manager for a bail out. A typical club was Los Conejitos (The Little Rabbits) on Casas de Campo Street. There was a long narrow bar with stools along it, with incredibly attractive girls spread out along the length of it. If you succumbed to a request for champagne you could retire with a girl to the "Reservados", small, curtained-off alcoves with red upholstered bench seats, coffee tables in front. Here, anything went, again remarkably cheaply. It was a degenerate's paradise and Franco must already have been turning in his grave, perhaps having a sly wank at the thought of what he had missed by being such a buttoned-up, anally-retentive puritan.

Another sign of post-Franco relief was on show in the national parliamentary elections which were taking place, the first since Franco's death. The streets were littered with election posters and leaflets, almost knee deep in places, and heaving with animated crowds of people. There seemed to be a plethora of parties – the Socialist PSOE; Communist PCE; right wing Popular Alliance (AP); Christian Democrats; Social Democrats; Liberals; Maoists; and Marxist-Leninists. Election vehicles, with horns and loudspeakers blaring, edged their way through the crowds. Trumpets blared, drums were being beaten – the noise was deafening. Pent up emotions held in check during 36 years of fascist dictatorship under the baleful eyes of Franco's Guardia Civil were being let loose. It was difficult to conceive anybody in Britain getting so worked up about politics but then we'd had boring democracy for a very long time.

In Malaga I became acquainted with the tapas system of snacking. In the early evening after work people would start crowding into the bars for a drink of beer or wine and to sample some of the snacks on offer. No one ate seriously before 8.00pm at the very earliest, usually nearer 10.00 pm, so tapas tided them over until then. Some of the popular tapas were olives; chorizo (spicy, paprika-red, garlic sausages); Spanish omelette; anchovies; ensaladilla (Russian salad – diced vegetables in mayonnaise); mariscos (seafood) – clams, prawns, mussels, octopus; croquetas (deep-fried balls of chicken or fish mixed with potatoes); albondigas (meat balls); garlic mushrooms; eggplant; green beans; and jamon serrano, wafer thin cured ham from the mountains. Strictly speaking, tapas were just little bite sized platters: a "racion" was a bit larger and a "porcion" almost meal size.

Spanish food appealed to me and I still look out Spanish restaurants wherever I travel. Gazpacho, the cold soup made from fresh tomatoes, cucumber, green peppers, garlic, olive oil, breadcrumbs and seasoning became a favourite. Somewhat heavier on the calories were "cochinillo" – roast suckling pig; and "fabadas asturianas" - a stew including haricot beans, Galician ham, pigs' ears, black sausage and bacon. Another favourite was "pollo al ajillo" – garlic chicken, which came in a number of variations. The roast racks of lamb were also delicious. And you could always find good, cheap wine too.

I took a bus down the coast to Estepona, about 80 kilometers (50 miles) south-west of Malaga, at that time the end of the Costa del Sol strip. On the way in to my hotel from the bus station, I could see the silhouette of Gibraltar on the horizon to the west. In 1994, Paul Theroux passed through Estepona on his trip around the Mediterranean which he wrote about in "The Pillars of Hercules". He referred to it as "awful overgrown Estepona". Fifteen years earlier, that was not the impression it left on me. Although there was a lot of new tourist related development, what remains in my memory is the Casco Antiguo (Old Town): the Plaza de las Flores with its circular fountain and flowers, its three-storey buildings with red-tiled roofs; the Iglesia (Church) de los Remedios, a flight of steps leading up to its whitewashed rococo style façade from the Plaza San Francisco, the statue of a monk in a flowing black habit outside it; the ancient Torre del Reloj (Clock tower) which a leaflet I picked up from the local tourist office said was (sic): "Probably the minaret of a mosk on muslim times." There were also a number of old beacon towers scattered around the town, remnants of an early warning system, some dating back to Roman times, others to the Moors, the latest after the "Reconquista" (recapture of Spain from the Moors) when the coast was plagued by Moslem Barbary Pirates from North Africa and Turkey. There was still a fishing fleet, with auctions down at the harbour in the early morning when the boats returned to port. The palm tree lined esplanade behind the extensive beach was a pleasant place to stroll in the evening when the heat of the day had waned.

The Sierra Bermeja Mountains rose steeply behind the town. The official Estepona Tourist Guide on the internet has this to say about them:

"Sierra Bermeja, always present, always red, always green. Insurmountable barrier as well as link with the inland, invoking the fears to the woods, to the beasts but at the same time welcoming woodcutters, muleteers, resin workers, bandits, maquis and ever hidingplace for fugitives running away from the Romans, from the Visigoths, from the Muslims, from Christians, from the French, from the Liberals or the Absolutists."

They could have added "from Interpol and the CID". The Costa del Sol was to become known as the Costa del Crime, a safe haven for the British criminal fraternity, out of the reach of extradition. The beasts and bandits no longer had to hide in the woods of the Sierra Bermeja, they could live quite openly in the luxury whitewashed villas with swimming pools sprouting up all along the coast which I now retraced back towards Malaga.

The tourist development of the Costa del Sol which Paul Theroux describes as an "utterly blighted landscape" referring to "the meretriciousness, the cheapo appeal, the rankness of this chain of greasespots" was inspired by Franco in the 1960s. He had a vision of revitalising the poverty stricken fishing villages along the coast through the development of a tourist industry financed by funds from America in return for letting them build nuclear bases in Spain. The economic success of the project had had a serious aesthetic and environmental downside. I spent a night in each of Marbella, Fuengirola and Torremolinos. I didn't find these tourist Meccas at that time as offensive as Paul Theroux did fifteen years later: he described this stretch of coast as "a grotesque malignancy, sad and horrible, that was somewhere between tragedy and farce." But I agreed wholeheartedly with his comment that "Spain seemed distant". That was what put me off these places – the adverts for "English breakfasts" and "Fish and

Chips", the fluttering Union Jacks – that wasn't what I had come to Spain to experience. In Torremolinos, I fancied a change from the small pensiones I had been staying in so I booked into a large tourist hotel with a swimming pool. At Reception, I was given the following letter along with my room key:

Dear Clients,

On the last days we have had a lot of problems about some uneducate, insociable and sauvage people staying on the building. (One big umbrella in the pool, all the paper information and book of one travel agency stolen, the door of the elevator on the second floor completely broken etc.,etc.)

We inform with this message to everybody:

1. We have take a very strong measures this is to cut inmediatelly this happenings making a lot of problems and broken the nice holidays of all the good people we have on the house.
2. A special service of the police, dressed with normal clothes, will be done some times during day and night inside and around the building till find the people making troubles to the house and to other clients.
3. We have the all rights and the people making some problem or noise will be tnown out after inform the police.

Please co-operate with us if you know some.

We are very sorry if you are affected of some of this problems out of our control.

The Manager.

Fortunately, I didn't come across any of the "sauvage people" the Manager was after and even managed to avoid getting "tnown out" myself, but this seemed to encapsulate a day in the life of the Costa del Sol.

Back in Malaga, I caught a bus inland, heading for Granada via Antequera. Antequera was a quiet, provincial market town, its red-tiled roofs spread over two hills, surrounded by the peaks and crags of limestone mountains. The centre was dominated by the partially ruined Moorish Alcazaba (palace and fortress) which was approached from the main square, the Plaza de San Sebastian, up the steps of the

Cuesta de San Judas and through the imposing archway of the Arco de los Gigantes, built in 1585. Wherever I looked there were church spires, allegedly 30 of them. The Iglesia (Church) del Carmen was overwhelmingly ornate both inside and out in the Spanish baroque style. The Municipal Museum had a life-size bronze statue of a Roman boy on display and mosaics from Roman villas which had been excavated in the town. About a kilometre from the town centre, in a small wooded park, stood two massive dolmen (burial chambers) dating from around 2500 BC, the time of Stonehenge and the Great Pyramid. They were built from huge slabs of rock and covered with earth, similar to Neolithic and bronze Age tombs found in England, Ireland and as far north as the Orkney Islands. They were believed to have housed the bodies of tribal chiefs. A lot of history was packed into one small town.

In Granada, I stayed in the three star Hotel Los Angeles, at the foot of the hill on which the Alhambra stood. Five storeys high, with an outdoor swimming pool and turquoise trim around doors and windows, this was a step up from the small pensiones I had been using and a giant step up from the lair of the "sauvage people" in Torremolinos. Granada was as Spanish as Torremolinos was not. The gorge of a mountain stream, the Rio Darro, separated the hill on which the Alhambra stood from the Albaicin. The whitewashed buildings of the Albaicin climbed up the other side of the gorge and along the hillside. This was the former Moorish quarter: following the expulsion of the Moors in 1492, many opted to convert to Christianity rather than go into exile and became known as Moriscos. Its narrow streets and squares still had a distinct Arabic feel to it, the little shops in Calderia Vieja and Calderia Nueva off Calle Elvira being straight out of Morocco as indeed were many of their owners, more recent immigrants. White painted "carmines", houses surrounded by gardens shielded from prying infidel eyes by high walls, were strung out along the hillside. The 11th century Arab bath house was one of the oldest Moorish remains. High on the hillside, the Mirador (lookout point) de San Nicholas and even higher, beyond the ruins of the walls of the Moorish city, the Mirador de San

Christobel, afforded fabulous views out across the Alhambra and the city to the snow white peaks of the Sierra Nevada mountains. The white snow caps, shimmering in the bright sunlight, reminded me of the "white villages", clusters of whitewashed houses, which I had seen perched on hilltops on the way up through the mountains to Granada. Some nights, the Alhambra and adjacent Generalife were floodlit, a spectacular sight from these lookout points. From the Cuesta del Chapiz at the eastern end of the Albaicin, the Camino del Sacromonte wound uphill to the Abbey of Sacromonte. This was the Gypsy quarter with some of their old cave houses still occupied including about half a dozen venues where flamenco shows were presented, known as "tablaos". I went to see one in the Cueva de la Rocio. The music and dance of the flamenco had its roots far back in pre-history in North Africa but the Gypsies had adapted it and made it their own since their arrival in Andalucia in the 15th century, originally from Rajasthan in India.

The centre of Granada was around the Plaza Isabel La Catolica where Calle Reyes Catolicos met the main street Gran Via de Colon running northwards beneath the Albaicin. The Plaza Nueva, off Reyes Catolicos, felt hemmed in between the hills of the Alhambra and the Albaicin, its cafes with outdoor tables offering views along the Rio Darro. Around the Cathedral, the maze of narrow streets and alleyways known as the Alcaiceria was the former Moorish silk exchange area. Around its restored horseshoe arches it now housed handicraft shops selling silver jewellery, embroidered silk shawls, ceramics and the full range of tourist souvenirs – flamenco dancer dolls, model bullfighters and bulls, postcards of the Alhambra. The 16th century Casa de los Tiros now accommodated the Tourist Office and History Museum. The Palacio de la Madraza had been the Moorish university and after an interlude as the Town Hall (Ayuntamiento) was again part of the University of Granada. In the Plaza Bib-Rambla there were outdoor cafes, flower sellers, ice cream stalls.

Work on the Cathedral had begun in 1523 and it was a strange mixture of Gothic and renaissance styles. Next door in the Capilla Real (Royal Chapel) down a flight of steps in the crypt, lay the bodies of

King Ferdinand (Fernando in Spanish) and his consort Queen Isabel, the Reyes Catolicos (Catholic Monarchs) whose marriage had united the country and who had finally driven out the Moors in 1492, the same year that they agreed to bankroll Christopher Columbus' trans-Atlantic venture which subsequently paid them big dividends in the form of an overseas empire in the Americas and fabulous amounts of gold and silver. The marriage of Ferdinand and Isabel had brought together the two formerly independent Christian kingdoms of Aragon and Castille. Aragon had earlier been amalgamated through marriage with Catalonia which had previously been part of the Frankish empire that had stretched across the Pyrenees. The area known as Catalonia had been captured by the Moors but won back by the Franks under Charlemagne. However, the Moors continued to attack from time to time in an attempt to regain control. In 878 a local Catalan hero, Wilfrid the Hairy, was seriously injured in a battle against the Moors, aiding the Frankish King Charles the Bald (I'm not making this up.) Thinking hairy Wilfrid was dying, bald Charles granted him his "dying" wish that Catalonia should become independent from the Frankish Kingdom. Since he didn't quite die, Catalonia didn't quite get independence, but Wilfrid was made Count of Catalonia, with a lot of autonomy and full independence came in 988. After that, Catalonia went on to become the most important state in the Mediterranean at the peak of its power in the 14th century with a huge merchant navy and territories in Sicily, Sardinia, Corsica, Naples, parts of Greece including Athens for a while as well as extending on the mainland from Rousillon in France down the Spanish coast to Valencia and the Balearic Islands. This proud history and their own language sowed the seeds of Catalonia's separatist feelings which were to extend into modern times.

1492 was a pivotal year in Spanish and indeed world history. The defeat of the Moors led to the unification of Christian Spain and the discovery of the Americas by Columbus gave it an empire, establishing Spain as the most powerful state in the world for a hundred years and extending Spanish influence across the world beyond the Americas to the Pacific where it annexed the Philippines. The process of European exploration of the world by sea, started slowly and cautiously by the Portuguese half a century previously, accelerated, transforming the world. The expulsion of the Jews in the same year continued their dispersal through Europe which ultimately ended in the Holocaust during the Second World War, the establishment of Israel and whatever results from the current mess in the Middle East which that created.

On Sunday afternoon, I went to see a bullfight. I'd read Ernest Hemingway's "Death in the Afternoon" but otherwise knew very little about the "corrida" or "toreros" as the locals called bullfighting. I'm fond of animals and don't like to see them maltreated. But as a young schoolboy I had often helped my father to slaughter sheep in the autumn when the winter store of mutton was being prepared. My older brother and I would hold the animal down while my father cut its throat with a pocket knife, the blood running into a bucket to be made into black puddings in the entrails. We only had twenty or thirty sheep so I knew all these animals personally – I had seen them grow up from lambs. But I was somehow able to close off the part of my mind that saw them as pets and accept that killing them was just how things were, an annual ritual, economic reality – we needed to eat.

I paid for a seat in "sol y sombra" (sun and shade) bought a programme and hired a cushion to sit on as I had been advised that the seats were just concrete steps. Three matadors (bullfighters) were to fight six bulls in a two and a half hour show. It started with a parade of all the participants with the notable exception of the bulls. Then in the first "tercio" (it was a three act performance for each bull) the bull was teased and played with magenta capes (red rags) by the matador's team (cuadrilla) and the matador himself, to weigh up the bull. (If they'd put him on the scales instead I reckon he would have topped half a ton.) In the second tercio, a picador mounted on a horse protected by heavy padding stalked the bull and repeatedly drove a long lance into its shoulder muscles to weaken it and lower its head for the kill. Then the picadors and the matador himself, all on foot, ran at the bull and plunged pairs of banderillos (long, gaily ribboned, steel-tipped darts) into the bull's already bleeding shoulders. The final tercio was called "la suerte de la muerte" (the act of death). This time the bullfighter was alone with the bull. He invited it to charge him using a small red cape (muleta), nimbly sidestepping it at the last moment. There was little doubt that at this stage of the performance he was risking his life. The bull was bleeding profusely and had been seriously weakened but it still had plenty of life in it and was clearly enraged. One wrong move and the matador would have been dead meat. He had to tire the bull sufficiently to make the final kill which involved leaning in over the horns to stick his sword in between the shoulder blades, a difficult and dangerous move and to make the timing of the coup de grace even more critical a local aficionado sitting next to me later told me that the matador had to chose a moment when the bull's front feet were together. The final despatch was quick and clean. The bull sank to its knees and then slowly keeled over, blood pouring from its mouth, and died. The crowd applauded wildly. The Presidente of the Corrida awarded the Matador both the bull's ears for a job well done. Botas of wine could be seen being raised all round the arena. My neighbours forced theirs on me (I didn't put up much resistance) but drinking from these soft, leather bags which you had to squeeze and direct the thin jet of wine into your mouth was clearly an acquired skill and one that became progressively more difficult the more success you had in hitting the target with the potent red plonk it was loaded with. By the time the sixth bull fell I seem to remember the Matador getting four ears and two tails.

On his trip to research material for his travel book "The Pillars of Hercules", Paul Theroux went to see four bullfights yet he clearly hated them from the beginning to the extent that he wrote: "[T]he only satisfying part of a bullfight to me was seeing a gored matador lying in the sand being trampled flat by the bull's hooves, the bull's horns in the supine torero's gut." Paul's repeated attendance at something that offended him reminded me of the story about the elderly spinster who complained to the police that the man in the neighbouring flat had been regularly exposing himself to her. When the police investigated, they discovered that she would have had to stand on a chair to see into his bedroom. I found that I was able to apply the same detachment to the bullfight that I had as a boy when helping my father to kill sheep, to accept it as a ritual, deeply rooted in Spanish culture. But I never went back to see another one in spite of making five more trips to Spain over the years. The mind is a strange place. Was there something deep down in the recesses of Paul Theroux's psyche compelling him to go back time and again to see a spectacle that he didn't enjoy and didn't approve of? Was there something keeping me from going back to see something which I thought I had enjoyed? Did I subconsciously agree with Paul Theroux? Who knows.

Although the odds were heavily weighted in favour of the matador by the prior weakening of the bull, it wasn't a risk-free profession by any means. Matadors had been killed by bulls and others seriously injured. If the bull's massive shoulder muscles weren't weakened by the lance and darts of the picadors, few matadors would probably survive. It would be suicidal to lean in over the horns to deliver the death thrust without this weakening. If the bull's horns are filed to reduce their sharpness, as is sometimes claimed by opponents of bullfighting, they still looked pretty lethal to me. To quote Corporal Jones in "Dad's Army", I wouldn't like them up me. And if I were a bull, I'd rather go out fighting than in a slaughterhouse, held down helpless while somebody cut my throat.

I deliberately left visiting the Alhambra until the end of my time in Granada. My Guide book and the brochures I picked up from the local tourist office were so fulsome in its praise that it seemed to offer a fitting end to my trip. My hotel was just beneath it and I had seen it from all angles around the city, most spectacularly from the Miradors high on the Albaicin hillside. I had also seen it in different light conditions – early morning, sunset and under floodlights at night. According to the literature, it had originally been whitewashed, the traditional Andalusian wall finish. But its name meant the "Red Fortress" and the red brick now exposed gave it a distinctive appearance, almost a soft glow in certain light conditions. Its silhouette was not particularly striking: it had none of the symmetry of other classic Moslem architecture that I had seen pictures of, such as the Taj

Mahal or the Blue Mosque in Istanbul and the roof lines didn't catch the eye like the Sydney Opera House or some of the cathedrals I had seen in South America with their towering spires. The square, crenellated, tower in the centre of the main palace complex in fact looked quite plain. The reason for this disjointed external appearance became clear as I read up on its history. The original palace had been extended by new palaces added by succeeding Emirs: when the Christians took over, part of the Moorish complex had been demolished to make way for a palace for King Charles V who was also the Holy Roman Emperor and presumably felt he needed something "un-Moorish" to reflect his status.

Granada had been the last stronghold of the Moors as the Christians gradually clawed back the Iberian Peninsula from them. They had arrived in 711 AD, an expeditionary force of 12,000 men, mainly Berber tribesmen under Tariq ibn Ziyal, the Governor of Tangiers, and helped the family of the late Visigoth king to fight off a challenge for the throne from a rival claimant. Their resounding victory at the battle of Guadalete (after which the pretender to the Visigoth throne drowned) suggested to them that the country was there for the taking which they quickly proceeded to do, the Visigoths being disunited and without a king to rally them. For a time, they had the whole of Europe in their sights on behalf of Islam and were only prevented from overrunning what is now France in a desperate battle at Poitiers which the Frankish King Charles "The Hammer" Martel won. It's interesting to reflect, in these days of Al Qaeda and resurgent Moslem fundamentalism, that if this battle had gone the other way, all of us from Western Europe might now be getting down on our knees five times a day to bother the Prophet Mohammed and wiping our backsides with our left hands.

The Moors withdrew to Spain, where only the extreme northwest managed to hold out against them. Gradually, the Christian rulers who had survived there fought back in what became known as the "Reconquista", clawing back the north of the country from the Moors. By the 13th century they had taken the key Moorish cities of Cordoba and Seville and only the Emirate of Granada under the

Nasrid dynasty remained. This was where Moorish culture reached its zenith. At its peak, Granada had a population of 200,000, four times the size of London then. At that time, the Arabs were far ahead of Europe in medicine, mathematics and every other sphere of learning – they translated Greek documents from the vast library in Alexandria, which they had captured and passed the lore of Socrates, Archimedes and all the other Greek philosophers and scientists on to posterity. Their numerical system was adopted in Europe, replacing the cumbersome Roman numerals. They developed the concept of zero and invented algebra, transforming mathematics. In agriculture, they introduced new crops – rice, cotton, sugar cane – and constructed irrigation systems to water "huertas" where these crops and fruit were grown in abundance – oranges, lemons, peaches and pomegranates. And they honed their skills in architecture and the artistic sphere in the Alhambra palace which had been built from the early 14th century.

From the hotel, I walked up to the entrance to the Alhambra through woods of cypress and elm to the Puerta de la Justicia, a gate in the sturdy outer defensive wall which surrounded the hilltop. The wall enclosed an area about 750 metres (half a mile) long. At the north-western end, nearest the Albaicin and towering above the gorge of the Rio Darro, the alcazaba or citadel pre-dated the palace by several centuries. It was now ruined, the outer walls, ramparts and some towers all that was left. On one of the towers, the Torre de la Vela, Ferdinand and Isabela had first raised their flag to celebrate the surrender of the last Moorish Emirate. The north-eastern end of the hill had formerly been taken up with gardens, residences for officials, courtiers and staff for the palace and a mosque. The mosque had been replaced by a church; and a convent, which had been superimposed on the Moorish residential area, had been converted into a Parador – a very expensive luxury boutique hotel. The gardens (the Alameda) remained: they had been planted with roses, oranges, and myrtles by the Moors, irrigated with running water from fountains and cascades supplied through an 8 kilometres (5 miles) long conduit from the Darro River above Granada. They were now a bit overgrown with wild flowers and grass and a dense stand of elms had been introduced by the Duke of Wellington while on campaign there during the Napoleonic Wars.

The four storey Renaissance style early 16th century Palace of Charles V was an impressive looking building in its own right (although rather square and squat looking), but it was entirely out of context with the style of the rest of the palace complex. It housed the Museo de la Alhambra with Moorish artefacts and the Museo de Bellas Artes with paintings and sculptures from the Christian period.

Even close up, the exterior of the Nasrid Palace complex was plain and austere. But once inside, it started to live up to its hype and it soon became apparent why it was later (1984) designated as a World Heritage Site by UNESCO. It was the internal layout and decoration of the various patios and buildings which made it such a magical place. Walls had been coated with stucco, fine plaster which had been carved in relief into elaborate flowing arabesques (decorative patterns based on floral or plant foliage shapes), geometrical designs and Arabic calligraphy in the Moslem tradition; cedar wood ceilings were intricately carved; other ceilings were designed like stalactites or honeycombs and in the great banqueting hall, the Sala de los Reyes, ceiling paintings on leather depicted scenes from hunting and chivalry; coloured azulejos (tiles) had been used as panelling on walls; slender marble columns supported arcades; and perhaps most beguiling of all was the use of fountains with running water and reflecting pools which seemed to induce an atmosphere of peace, calm and coolness. The ambitious objective of the architects had been to create "paradise on earth" and they had come close.

Entrance was through the Mexuar where the Emir heard petitions from subjects and met with ministers. This led into the Patio de los Arrayanes (Court of the Myrtles) where a central rectangular reflecting pond was flanked by myrtle hedges. Viewed from the end of the pond, the square tower of the Salon de Ambajadores (Hall of the Ambassadors) and the horseshoe arches of the marble columns supporting the surrounding arcade were perfectly symmetrical. The hall had been the throne room, its magnificent domed cedar ceiling, 23 metres (75 feet) high, designed to represent the seven Moslem heavens. This was where Ferdinand and Isabel had met Christopher Columbus to confirm their support for his voyage across the Atlantic. Next door was the Patio of the Lions, surrounded by a colonnade of white marble columns, finely perforated filigree work or tracery above the columns: it took its name from the central fountain, an alabaster basin supported by twelve lions sculpted in white marble. The walls were covered part of the way up in blue and yellow tiles. Intricate stucco work on the walls resembled lace. In the Hall of the Two Sisters the vaulted ceiling was the best example of the honeycomb or stalactite patterning. At the end of the complex, a pavilion with a tower and a five-arched portico was all that remained of the oldest palace, the Palacio del Partal.

I walked across to the Generalife, the Emirs' former summer palace, on a hill opposite the Alhambra. The whitewashed building was approached from below through topiary gardens. Here the emphasis was on greenery and water features. The Escalera del Agua was a staircase with water flowing gently down it. The Patio de la Acequia was an enclosed oriental style garden with a long, narrow pool running down the centre of it, jets of water arching above it. In the gardens were tall cypress trees, orange trees, shrubs, hedges and flower beds, a very restful scene.

I fell in love with Spain on this trip and kept returning every few years while I was still living in Britain, five more trips, during which I became reasonably fluent in Spanish. On the Costa Blanca, I discovered Alicante, my favourite Spanish city and Benidorm brought back bad memories of the "sauvage people" of Torremolinos. I was in Alicante in June 1979 for the Hogueras de San Juan (Festival of St. John), ostensibly celebrating John the Baptist but with its origins in a pagan mid-summer sacrifice to the Sun God. A procession of brightly decorated floats wound through the streets bearing weirdly dressed effigies to be burned at midnight in a huge bonfire. Fireworks lit up the sky, bands played, drums throbbed incessantly, trumpets blared and the bars were jumping far into the night. It reminded me of the

Viking fire festival, Up-Helly-Aa, in my native Shetland Islands, only that was in mid-winter and no one would have survived there at midnight in shirt sleeves.

In June 1981, on the Atlantic Costa de la Luz, I visited Cadiz: Christopher Columbus had sailed from there on his second voyage to the Americas and Sir Francis Drake had "singed the King of Spain's beard" in a daring raid in which he burned some warships in the harbour. The defeat of the invading Spanish Armada in the English Channel by Drake in 1588 was the start of the long decline of Spain as the most powerful state in Europe. From Cadiz, I took a side trip inland in searing 40 degrees plus heat to Jerez, the capital of the sherry industry, another icon of Spanish culture. On the way, I saw a rider on a white horse herding a group of bulls in a field beside a vineyard and a little further on a herd of white horses galloping beside the road, images of Spain which stick in the mind. Later, I took a bus down the coast to Algeciras for a ferry trip across to Tangiers in Morocco, where the Moors had originated.

On another trip, I travelled along the rugged Costa Brava from the ancient Roman city of Tarragona as far as Cadaques, close to Salvador Dali's home in Port Lligat. Here, in 1984, the night-life of Barcelona, as catalogued in the "Guia del Ocio" and even on the advert pages of the daily newspapers, was the wildest I have seen anywhere in the world – strip clubs, massage parlours, escort agencies, brothels. By this time poor old repressed Franco must have been spinning in his grave like the sails on one of Don Quixote's windmills in a Levanter gale.

I flew to Seville in the autumn of 1986. Here, the magnificent Cathedral, the largest Christian church in the world, had been built on the site of a Moorish mosque: its minaret had been retained and converted to a bell tower for the Cathedral – the soaring Giralda. Situated at the head of the delta of the Guadalquivir River, Spain's largest, Seville had been the centre of the administration of and trade with the Spanish Empire in the Americas and had grown fabulously wealthy. It had also been the headquarters of the feared Spanish Inquisition.

My last visit, in 1995, was to the capital, Madrid, 650 metres (2,100 feet) above sea level on the Mesita, Spain's parched central Castilian

Plateau, just a small, provincial town with a population of 15,000 when King Philip II made it his capital in 1561 because of its central location in the country. Now it was a bustling, vibrant city of 4 million inhabitants with the royal palace and the Prado filled with art treasures including paintings by Spain's most famous artists, Goya, Velazquez, Zurbaran and with Picasso's "Guernica" in the annexe. In the city centre the Puerta del Sol was the point from which distances were signposted along all the roads radiating out across the nation. I had seen the final destinations of many of them and the magnificent city of Granada where Moorish culture had peaked in the Alhambra and Spain's period of dominating the world had begun in 1492. I had enjoyed my long affair with this diverse and fascinating country.

3

THE EIFFEL TOWER,
PARIS, FRANCE
JUNE 1978

I SAT THE final Part of my Royal Town Planning Institute exam (successfully as it turned out) in June 1978. To celebrate, I decided to treat myself to a trip to Paris. I caught a train down to Dover for the cross Channel ferry to Calais. There were no signs of any blue skies over the White Cliffs of Dover as we left but I did suffer a momentary pang of Vera Lynn induced nostalgia at the sight of them. The English Channel has only been there since sea level rose at the end of the last ice age, which isn't long in the grand scheme of things. It isn't wide but wide enough in the past to protect us from invasion by Phillip of Spain, Napoleon and Hitler. Sure, the Romans got through and the Normans but that was a long time ago. The Romans left when times got tough and the Normans turned into upper class twits with plummier accents than any true Englishman so they eventually succumbed too in a "if you can't beat them join them" way. I'm not particularly jingoistic by nature but there's something about that departure by sea from Good Old Blighty which stirs the nationalistic blood and brings home our separateness from the rest of Europe. I'd left before by air for Africa, New Zealand and Spain but for some reason that did not have the same connotations of leaving the homeland, even if it was just to go next door.

I had booked the three star Hotel Boucherat in Rue de Turenne, near the Place de la Republique. I decided to start my exploration of the city in the area within walking distance of the hotel before getting to grips with the Metro underground train system for places further afield. The Place de la Bastille seemed to be an appropriate place to start, the site of the infamous prison destroyed by the mob at the start of the French Revolution in 1789. That had put an end to the Ancien Regime of kings and nobles and replaced it with a new era of liberty, equality and fraternity, helped along by liberal use of the guillotine, specially invented for the job. There was nothing left to see of the Bastille now, its memory just lingered in the place name   and in the minds of bloody-minded Parisians stirred up by some new real or imagined wrong done to them by the government. I walked west into the Marais district, a swamp until it was developed from the end of the 16th century with magnificent Renaissance style houses for the wealthy such as the Hotel Carnavalet, now the Musee Historique de la Ville de Paris. It had never been a hotel, the word originally just meant "mansion". I stopped to admire the Place des Vosges, the houses built round a square in the early 1600s. At first they almost looked like a modern up-market housing scheme with their uniform, red-gold brick facades but on closer scrutiny there was a wealth of diversity in the shapes, form and decoration of gables, windows and archways. French architecture was distinctive and appealed to me with its mansard roof shapes and blue slate or red ceramic tile coverings. In later travels I was to see it all over the world in places where the French have made their mark from Hanoi to Cape Breton Island. I strolled through the old Jewish quarter around Rue des Rosiers, originally occupied by Sephardim refugees from Spain as early as 1230. Rue Ferdinand Duval had been known as Rue des Juifs (Jews) until 1900. The Rue des Ecouffes was called after a scavenging bird which was a nickname for moneylenders. The French Jews had suffered badly during the Nazi occupation in World War II, some of it with the connivance of the Vichy French collaborators.

A bit further west was the Pompidou Centre, just opened the previous year and named after the former President, whose ugly baby it was. My Berlitz guide compared this architectural crime perpetrated in the name of culture (it housed the National Museum of Modern Art, a library, performance areas and a centre for music and acoustic research) to an oil refinery. Standing in front of it trying to recover from the shock, I decided that that was an insult to Canvey Island. The building was squat, over 40 metres (130 feet) high, on seven levels. It had been designed in the Post-modern/High Tech architectural style by a team including Richard Rogers and the Italian architect Renzo Piano. A report in the New York Times on Richard Rogers winning the Pritzker Prize for architecture in 2007 said that the Pompidou Centre "turned the architecture world upside down". It should have said "inside-out" as its colour-coded entrails hung down the outside, draped over the exposed steel skeleton of the supporting structure. Green pipes carried the plumbing; blue ducts held the heating and cooling systems; electrical wires were encased in yellow; and safety and transportation features like the escalators and fire-fighting equipment were red. In front, in Place Georges Pompidou, jugglers and fire-eaters were performing to a sizeable crowd. It was too much to hope that the fire-eaters would end up burning the monstrosity to the ground.

It may have been the subtle influence of all that exposed plumbing but I began to feel the need to drain the wine lake I had accumulated at lunch time. I asked a passing busker for advice and he pointed towards a square metal box – vaguely resembling Dr Who's time machine – on the other side of the square. There was a screed of instructions on the side of it. It all seemed terribly complicated. As I read, the words started to swim before my eyes. I had a vision of a huge mechanical hand grabbing me, tearing my trousers down, sticking my head in the pan while it was flushing and then hurling me out into the alien landscape of the Planet Wogan in the year 3020 – trousers still around my ankles. I decided to sneak up an alley-way in the time-honoured Parisian fashion, mourning the demise of all things traditional, especially the pissoir.

Nearby, the former market of Les Halles (the equivalent of London's Covent Garden) had been demolished in 1969 and moved to the suburbs. Its replacement, the soul-less Forum shopping centre, was fortunately mostly underground. I walked north up Rue St Denis. As I progressed, I began to notice attractive girls standing in doorways and at the entrance to alley-ways. Their density increased until one lane off to the right was completely lined with them from end to end. I realized that it was going to take me a long time to get back to the hotel.

The following morning, I decided to tackle Montmartre. The Metro proved to be remarkably easy to navigate. I bought a carnet (a strip of tickets) which had to be stamped in a machine at the entrance to the carriages and picked up a map of the network. The lines were distinguished by the end stations, signs saying for example "Direction Porte de Clichy" and there were plenty of interchange points. I climbed up to the Sacre-Coeur (Sacred Heart) Roman Catholic Basilica, on the summit of the Butte Montmartre, the highest point of the city, with a magnificent view out across it from the forecourt – the Eiffel Tower rising in the distance over on the other side of the River Seine. The Basilica had an oriental look about it, more like the Taj Mahal than a traditional church, the domes with mini spires on top like minarets. A portico with three arches was surmounted by bronze equestrian statues of Joan of Arc and King Louis IX who had been declared a saint. Its dazzling white colour, I learned later, was due to the type of limestone it was built from, travertine, which exudes calcite, ensuring that the surface remains white in spite of weathering and pollution. It was relatively new, having been built between 1875 and 1914 and consecrated in 1919 after the end of World War I. Apparently, it had been inspired by a mood of national yearning for spiritual renewal after France's defeat in the Franco-Prussian War of 1870 and the subsequent socialist uprising of the Paris Commune. It symbolised a resurgence of the Catholic Church which had lost much of its power following the French Revolution. The Paris Commune's first insurrection had been in Montmartre: they had executed the Archbishop of Paris. Communards had been blown up by the army when they took refuge in former gypsum mines in the area. The Basilica was a symbol of the restoration of moral order.

There was not much sign of moral order in nearby Pigalle. The display of frilly knickers in the Moulin Rouge was tame compared to what was on offer in the nightclubs along the Boulevard de Clichy leading into Place Pigalle and the streets leading off it. Unlike nightclubs in London's Soho, what was promised was delivered: the live sex shows involved full-on hard-core pornography. In Paris, the tight-arsed, hypocritical approach to sex of the Anglo-Saxon world was absent: none of the sniggering, juvenile tone of the English seaside postcard. The double entendre of the Carry On films was replaced by the single entendre of "what you see is what you get". But getting it was hard on the wallet.

I had lunch in Chez La Mere Catherine in the Place du Tertre. Nobody but a Frenchman or woman could make a plate of raw vegetables (les crudites) so tasty. The French dishes which I sampled during this trip have brought me back to French restaurants all over the world ever since: boeuf bourguinon; confit de canard (duck legs cooked slowly in their own fat, then stored for weeks in earthenware jars); cassoulet (a stew of haricot beans, pork, sausages.) Outside, the square, which used to be the centre of Montmartre where criminals were hanged, was infested with pavement artists, some of whom deserved capital punishment for what they were doing to the faces of gullible tourists. One tapped me on the shoulder and proffered a quick sketch of me that he had made surreptitiously: I glanced at it and pointed to a man across the square. "I think that's him over there." Montmartre had been a Mecca for artists in the late 19th and early 20th centuries. Picasso had developed cubism here. Renoir, Van Gogh, Gaugin had all been residents for a while. I walked over to the Cimitiere de Montmartre where Degas and Stendahl were buried.

In the evening I had dinner in a restaurant in Boulevard Rochechouart not far from Place Pigalle and near the road leading up to the Sacre Ceour. I had steak tartare, raw red meat to beam me for a night in the clubs of Pigalle. There were scores of small hostess clubs where you could get away with all your arms and legs if you just had a drink on your own but once you started buying the girls drinks the meter count started mounting alarmingly. I ended up in a club called the Mayflower in Rue Andre Antoine. The doorman cum bouncer cum minder was a stocky Arab, so muscle-bound he looked as if he had a hunchback. I discovered later that the girls called him Quasimodo behind his hunchback. I got chatting to a girl called Esme who was Dutch. "Esme isn't short for Esmeralda, is it?" I asked her, "like the gypsy girl in "The Hunchback of Notre Dame." "No, it isn't" she said, "but if you buy me a bottle of champagne we can go to a private room and I'll ring your bells." She was remarkably well endowed in the mammary department. I wondered if you could see them from space. Esme, the hunchfront of Rotterdam, I mused. Deep down inside me, where my moral fibre and conscience should have been located, I could hear a hunchback ringing alarm bells.

In the morning, seriously the worse for wear, I headed down to the Ile de la Cite, the little island in the Seine where Paris had had its beginnings. It had started out around 300 BC as a village of Celtic fishermen and boatmen. Then in 52 BC it was occupied by the Romans who expanded onto the left (south) bank, calling their town Lutetia (Marshland). When it was overrun by the barbarian Huns and Franks at the end of the Roman era, it again retracted to the island before spreading again to the left bank in the 6th century AD. But it remained a backwater until 987 when it was made the capital of the Capet dynasty. It then became rich from tolls on shipping and trade passing along the Seine and spread to the right (north) bank. By the 13th century the population was 100,000 and it was the largest city in Western Europe. The island was dominated by the Gothic style Notre Dame Cathedral, built between 1163 and 1345 but largely complete by the 1240s, replacing an earlier Cathedral founded in the 4th century AD. The west façade featured two square towers with double arches. Flying buttresses resembling mammoths' tusks surrounded the nave and apse and a tall spire soared into the sky. An array of leering gargoyles, intended to keep evil away, roosted on a parapet, one of them gnawing at something unrecognisable – perhaps an andouillette, the French version of haggis and equally indigestible. A beautiful rose window encircled a statue of the Madonna and child: there were two more rose windows in the transept. During the French revolution, the Cathedral had been re-dedicated to the Cult of Reason and used as a warehouse to store food.

The bourdon bell called "Emmanuel" in the south tower (the one rung by the hunchback Quasimodo in Victor Hugo's 1831 novel "The Hunchback of Notre Dame") weighed 13 tons and was tolled every hour. According to my Berlitz "Guide to Paris" the famous bourdon bell was "no longer operated by a hunchback but by an electric system installed in 1953." Had the Hunchbacks' Bell-ringing Union really had a closed shop in the Cathedral from Quasimodo's day until 1953? I was standing admiring the "western transept with its majestic towers, spire and breathtaking flying buttresses" as instructed by Mr. Berlitz. I stuck him back in my pocket and stepped off the pavement to take a photograph. Klaxons blared and I was almost engulfed in a breathtaking wave of flying Citroens sweeping across the Seine. Scrambling to regain the pavement, I glimpsed a wild-eyed, fist-waving figure hunched over the wheel of a red Peugeot as it missed me by inches. Quasimodo isn't dead after all, I decided – just made redundant by new technology and taking it out on innocent tourists. But in spite of this latter-day bout of bad temper, I had a soft spot for Quasimodo. I could imagine him looking wistfully back over his shoulder with his wall-eye and plaintively crooning the Hot Chocolate number:

"It started with a cist,

Never thought that it would come to this."

The "Parvis" (Square) outside the Cathedral had been used for public executions during the Middle Ages. At the western end of the island, the imposing early 14th century Gothic palace called the Conciergerie, had been an ante-chamber for the guillotine during the French Revolution. Thousands of prisoners including Marie Antoinette had been held here pending execution. I crossed the Seine to the right bank by the Pont Neuf (New Bridge), the name given (in typically perverse French fashion) to the oldest surviving bridge across the river - built in 1607.

On the other side, I stopped a passer-by and asked him for directions to the Louvre. I knew where it was from my map but I liked to practice my

French from time to time. My informant, who had a Poirot moustache, turned to face downriver and with a flurry of arm waving, issued precise instructions, some of which I even understood. It came to me in a blinding flash, like St. Paul's revelation on the road to Damascus – the answer to the Left Bank/Right Bank conundrum. Frenchmen always point downriver when giving directions; hence, since the Seine flows west, the south side is the Left Bank and the north side the Right Bank – simple when you know the rules of the game.

I was by no means an art connoisseur but I felt obliged to pay the Louvre a visit. It was one of the things one simply had to do in Paris, a way of salving the conscience after all the time spent in the fleshpots of Pigalle and the Rue Saint Denis. It was something you could actually tell people about: it didn't have to be a dirty secret. On the subject of dirty secrets, standing before Leonardo da Vinci's masterpiece, in another flash of possibly divinely inspired enlightenment, I suddenly felt that I'd cracked the enigma of the Mona Lisa's smile – she'd just had it away with the Pope. Moving on, I found the Venus de Milo, a nude statue of the Goddess of Love, Aphrodite, found by a peasant on the island of Milos in Greece in 1820. I'd seen better bodies on some of the strippers in Pigalle but even a cynical philistine like me could hardly fail to be impressed with the craftsmanship. I became increasingly less cynical as I progressed through the galleries: work by Michelangelo; a self portrait of Rembrandt; Rubens' wife and children; a very ugly Austrian Queen by Velazquez – I was amazed she'd paid him for it never mind allowed it to be shown in public. Perhaps for the first time in my life I began to appreciate what art was about.

At the other end of the Tuileries Gardens, in all that was left of the former royal palace burned down by the Paris Commune in 1871, the Jeu de Paume housed the work of the impressionists who had created an uproar in the art world when they burst on the scene in 1874 – Degas, Toulouse-Lautrec, Monet, Manet, Van Gogh, Cezanne, Gaugin, Renoir – names that I knew but whose work I had never bothered to familiarise myself with.

Next door, in the Place de la Concorde, over 1,000 people had been guillotined during the French Revolution, including King Louis

XVI. There still wasn't much concord on show with traffic milling around an island in the middle where the 3,300 years old, 23 metres (75 feet) tall, pink granite obelisk from the Temple of Ramses II in Luxor stood. This had been a gift from Mohammed Ali, the Viceroy of Egypt, in the 1830s but many of the artefacts decorating the public squares and filling the museums of the former colonial powers had simply been looted, including the Elgin Marbles from the Parthenon in Athens which were on display in the British Museum. Napoleon looted a Louvre-full of priceless artefacts while he was in Egypt during one of his world-conquering rampages but had to leave them behind when Admiral Nelson destroyed his fleet at the Battle of the Nile.

I strolled along the "Quais" on the banks of the Seine. So much of the romance of Paris is associated with this area: the stalls of the bouquinistes (book sellers); the bridges, conjuring up the tune and words of the familiar song "Under the Bridges of Paris", making even cynics sentimental. I took a cruise on the river in a Bateau Mouche. This was what Paris was all about.

The following morning I took the Metro over to the Left Bank, the student, Bohemian area of the city, also known as the Latin Quarter as it was where the students had studied Latin. This had been the scene of serious rioting in 1968 when the students had trashed the city. The French seem to be particularly good at rioting as witnessed by the French Revolution and other serious outbreaks of civil unrest in 1830, 1848 and 1871. It was practically the national sport. Disobedience and general bloody-mindedness seemed to come natural to the French. They refused to take "Non!" for an answer although ready enough to give it themselves. The labels arrogant, unfriendly, distant and self-absorbed could all be applied to Parisians as a species although obviously there were individual exceptions. These tendencies were exacerbated by their inability to speak other people's languages and their intolerance of people who couldn't speak theirs. The official campaign against Franglais was a symptom of this. Interestingly, the word "chauvinism" derives from the name of a Frenchman who was famous for it. The people can sometimes put you off a place, as I was later to discover in Russia, Israel and Greece. But in spite of the surly demeanour of all too many of its inhabitants, I liked Paris (and subsequently the other parts of France which I have visited.)

I started off in Place St-Michel, which had been the headquarters of the Paris Commune in the insurrection of 1871. The Boulevard St-Michel ran south from here, at right angles to the Seine: technically the Latin Quarter lay to the east of the Boulevard, St-Germain-des-Pres to the west. In 1968 the students had torn up the cobblestones in the Boulevard to hurl at the police. The area had a rebellious history. The quiet,   narrow streets of the La Huchette and St-Severin districts to the east, with their bookshops and cafes, the little church of St-Julien-le-Pauvre and the Gothic extravaganza of St-Severin with its stained glass windows and bell tower belied this turbulent past. Further up the Boulevard was the Sorbonne where the University had its origins in 1253 as a college for 16 poor students to study theology. I turned east on Rue Soufflot to see the Pantheon. It had been built as a church in the second half of the 18th century, intended to look like the original Pantheon in Rome but had ended up looking more like St Paul's Cathedral. It was now a mausoleum to the great and good of France including Victor Hugo, Voltaire, Emile Zola and Marie Curie. (Dominique Strauss-Khan probably need not apply.) Further east, in the Rue de Mouffetard, a street full of bistros, I had lunch in a Peruvian restaurant where I was able to renew my acquaintance from an earlier visit to South America with pisco sour and ceviche.

In the afternoon, I walked through St-Germain-des-Pres, which had been traditionally the heartland of literature in Paris and the breeding ground for existentialism through its leading-lights Jean-Paul Sartre, Albert Camus and Simone de Beauvoir. I saw the cafes which the literary world had patronised – the Deux Magots, Flore and Brasserie Lipp. I caught the Metro up to Montparnasse, where the centre of gravity of the art world had moved from Montmartre between the two World Wars. This was where "Gay Paris" of the 1920s was at its gayest. "Gay" of course had a different meaning at that time, although Gertrude Stein, one of a group of expatriate writers arriving to join the fun, was as gay as they come in every sense of the word. Ernest Hemingway came, probably to escape prohibition in America,

Henry Millar of "Tropic of Cancer" fame and F. Scott Fitzgerald. I celebrated the cafes they had frequented with a different drink in each of Le Select, Le Dome, La Rotonde and La Coupole. I walked, a bit unsteadily, past the Closerie des Lilas, frequented by Lenin, Trotsky and Hemingway, although fortunately, not at the same time – I don't think their political views were compatible.

I decided it was time to get back to my hotel. It was the rush hour and the Metro was packed: it was sticky hot. For all that, I wasn't complaining – I was jammed up against a nubile blonde and thinking I could quite happily stand there all night. As if in answer to my prayers, the train seemed to lose power and glide to a halt – between stations. Minutes passed, trickles of sweat became rivers, the air was stifling. Further back in the carriage a woman began to scream hysterically, triggering off several children. I managed to get my watch arm up far enough to see the dial without interfering with the blonde too much: I reckoned we had been stuck there for nearly twenty minutes. I could feel panic rising and could sense fear all around me. Then, as suddenly as we had stopped, we moved off again. No explanation. I got off at the next station and walked back to the hotel.

By the following morning, my faith in the Metro had been somewhat restored and I set off to see the really posh parts of Paris and the famous Eiffel Tower. Near the Metro station, I was accosted by a tout handing out business cards on behalf of a certain Monsieur Kalilou, Grand Marabout Africain (Big African Witchdoctor), Member of the Order of Witchdoctors of Africa. From the card I saw that he offered protection against malevolent influences and lack of sexual power, indeed he claimed that he could resolve all problems, even desperate cases. After my experience on the Metro the previous evening and in need of all the "puissance sexuelle" I could muster for another attack on Pigalle, I seriously thought about paying him a visit but better sense prevailed and I made for the Place Charles de Gaulle (popularly known as L'Etoile [The Star] as twelve avenues radiated out from it). Its piece de resistance was the Arc de Triomphe. This imposing decorative archway, 50 metres (164 feet) high and 45 metres (148 feet) wide had been started by Napoleon in 1806 to commemorate his victories in battle but following his defeat at Waterloo and exile to St. Helena , it wasn't completed until 1836. Napoleon did get to use in 1840 when his funeral cortege passed underneath it on its way to his re-burial at Les Invalides, but by that time he had been dead for fifteen years. The names of Napoleon's 128 major battles and the 660 generals who fought in them were carved on the monument. I suppose Napoleon did alright for a boy from Corsica but I can't help thinking that his world-conquering ambitions and megalomania brought about the deaths of an awful lot of Frenchmen who would probably have been prepared to settle for a little less "gloire" in return for a few more years of life.

The magnificent Champs-Elysees stretched all the way down from the Arc de Triomphe to the Place de la Concorde, lined with chest-nut trees and opulent shops, offices, cinemas, restaurants and cafes. This area of the city was known as Les Grands Boulevards. In 1851, Napoleon's nephew seized power and set up the Second Empire as Emperor Napoleon III. He appointed Baron Haussmann to oversee massive redevelopment work that by the fall of the regime in 1870 had transformed Paris into the most magnificent city in Europe. The impressive wide boulevards were central to the plan. The Emperor was alarmed by the popular uprisings of 1830 and 1848: the boulevards were intended to let in light, air and cavalry. Ironically, Haussmann was so dedicated to demolition that he even knocked down his own family home to create the boulevard which now carried his name. Boulevard Haussmann also housed two opulent department stores, an innovation at the time, Au Printemps and Galeries Lafayette. The outrageously decorative Opera House with its gilded winged statues on the roof and colonnaded first floor also dated from this period. The Ritz Hotel on Place Vendome was where Princess Diana had her last meal before her fatal car crash in 1997. The most opulent shopping street of all was the Rue du Faubourg Saint-Honore, where the President lived in the Elysee Palace at number 55. The Palais Royale in the Rue de Rivoli had been built for Cardinal Richelieu in 1639. It passed to the Dukes of Orleans who were prolific spendthrifts and built three-storey arcades around the garden at the rear of the palace to let to small businesses in an attempt to recoup some of their losses. This backfired on them: the shops, restaurants, cafes, and theatres in the arcade spaces became supplemented by gambling houses and brothels and to cap it all on 12th July 1789 a rabble-rouser called Camille Desmoulins jumped up on a table in one of the cafes and made an impassioned speech calling on the people of Paris to rise up against the ruling classes – which they did and the French Revolution had begun.

Across the river, the Eiffel Tower had been built between 1887 and 1889 as the entranceway to the World Fair celebrating the centenary of the French Revolution. The Engineer who gave the tower its name, Gustave Eiffel, had previously done some useful work – built a massive bridge across the Duoro River in Portugal and designed the locks for De Lessep's Suez Canal. But the tower bearing his name had no purpose other than as a lookout tower. It was christened La Dame de Fer (The Iron Lady). A later incumbent of this title, Margaret Thatcher, would not have appreciated being associated with such a useless object, especially a French one. This massive erection could of course be seen as a towering phallic symbol to demonstrate to the world what a big boy France was, something to be venerated and worshipped by generations of serial adulterers like Francois Mitterand and Dominique Strauss-Khan. In his novel "Doctor Criminale" Malcolm Bradbury has a hilarious go at it:

"It seemed to make no sense at all. It was fairly evidently a monument to something but unfortunately there was nothing written on it to say what it was a monument to. It looked like the spire of a great cathedral but the nave was missing and there was no altar to worship at and no particular deity mentioned. It resembled the great new American business skyscrapers going up in the cities of Chicago and New York but because there was no inside to its outside there was not much hope of doing any real business in it. Thirteen years earlier, to celebrate the centennial of another great revolutionary war, the American War of Independence, the French had shipped across the Atlantic another great memorial. This was the Statue of Liberty, sculpture by Bartholdi, interior ironwork by Gustave

Eiffel. But its meaning was absolutely clear, its message, to the huddled masses yearning to breathe free, perfectly plain. This time Eiffel seemed to have omitted something, in fact everything. He had given Paris the ironwork without the statue, the engineering without the sculpture, the torch without the liberty, the bones without the flesh. Today, of course, high on our fine post-modern wisdom, we know exactly what Gustave was all about. Eiffel's Tower was a monument to only one thing: itself. It was a spectacle and there was nothing much to be done with it except look up at its head from its feet or down at its feet from its head or clamber up and down it, staring at the panorama of Paris it opened up and controlled on every side. Leading writers hated it, including Guy de Maupassant, who always dined afterwards in its restaurant, because it was the only place in Paris you couldn't see the tower from."

The tower was indeed unpopular to begin with, much criticised by the public, many calling it an eyesore. The newspapers of the day were full of angry letters. It was originally intended only to stand for 20 years, then be dismantled. I'll leave Malcolm Bradbury to describe its salvation:

"Then, a decade or so later, the French suddenly discovered what the Eiffel Tower was really for. It made the perfect radio transmitter and this meant it was a perfect act of prescience on Gustave's part because radio hadn't even been invented when he put it up."

It was, nevertheless, an impressive piece of engineering. It was 324 metres (1063 feet) tall, similar to an 81 storey building, the tallest structure in the world for 41 years until the Chrysler Building in New York was completed in 1930. Antennae added to the top in 1957 made it taller than the Chrysler Building but there are now several structures which over-top it including ones in Kuala Lumpur, Dubai and Shanghai. It was designed as a lattice tower, made from puddled iron, a very pure form of structural iron. (It needs 50 to 60 tons of paint applied every 7 years to protect it from rust.) A workforce of 300 men joined together 18,308 pieces of iron using 2.5 million rivets.

This workforce was paltry compared to the legions needed to build the Pyramids or Stonehenge. But these were Frenchmen. They had grown up with meccano-sets. They knew a thing or two about screwing.

The Tower was on three levels. I walked up the first two, although I could have taken the elevator. There was a restaurant at the ground level and a bar at level two. A hydraulically operated elevator took me to the top where there was another bar and the view was indeed spectacular.

The Tower had some interesting history attached to it. In 1912 an Austrian tailor had died after jumping 60 metres (195 feet) from the first deck level with a home-made parachute. A.J. Hackett, the New Zealand entrepreneur, had more luck when he bungee-jumped from the top in 1987: he lived and was just arrested. A con man sold it for scrap metal on two separate occasions. Hitler ordered it to be destroyed in August 1944 when the Allies were closing in on Paris but the military governor, General Von Choltitz disobeyed. He ought to have been shot.

Shortly after I got back from Paris, I applied for a job as Deputy Director of Planning with Shetland Islands Council and was offered it. I had come full circle, back to my roots. A couple of weeks before I was due to head north for Shetland, I was driving back to Shrewsbury on the A5 from a football match at Aston Villa in Birmingham when the traffic came to a standstill. I was reaching for the handbrake when there was an almighty crash behind me and my car was rammed into the car in front. A load of frozen chickens had ploughed into my rear end. The car was a write-off. At this time I was broke: the break in Paris had been seriously expensive. I went to see my bank about a loan to buy a car pending the insurance payout and after much shaking of the head and tut-tutting about my conspicuous consumption in Paris they eventually let me have 300 pounds. How times have changed. If I'd gone to them thirty years later before the 2008 financial meltdown they would have been all over me like a rash, thrusting great wads of fivers at me, asking "What were you thinking of buying, a Merc? Would a million do? Someone who can splurge a few grand in Paris nightclubs on bubbly and hunchfronts is just the sort of guy we'd like to loan loadsa money we haven't got to."

With the help of one of my workmates whose father was a big shot at Ford's in Dagenham, I managed to find an old Ford Escort van within my budget. And so I headed north, 300 pounds in debt and all my worldly goods packed into an old Ford Escort. Shetland was booming at this time. Oil had been discovered in the North Sea east of Shetland in the late 1960s and the oil companies had decided to bring it ashore in two huge pipelines from the Brent and Ninian fields to a large oil terminal at Sullom Voe on the islands, costing 1.3 billion pounds to construct. It was due to be opened by the Queen just shortly after my arrival. The population of the islands had burgeoned from 17,000 to 28,000 with the labour force needed to build the terminal and the associated infrastructure. A massive programme of house building was under way to accommodate the workers at the terminal and in the new growth industry servicing the offshore oilfields from the capital, Lerwick, and Sumburgh Airport. More planning applications per head of population were being processed by the local Council than anywhere else in Britain. How things had changed. It was like the Wild West must have been during a gold rush. Accommodation was at a premium. I spent the first few months sleeping on the sofa in my aunt's living room in Lerwick.

4

THE MOAI STATUES,
EASTER ISLAND
JUNE 1998

In 1997, I had returned to New Zealand. Yet another structural review of the management system of the Shetland Islands Council by consultants in 1994 had resulted in a complete shake-up with 5 Executive Managers to replace the 13 Directors based on professional divisions of responsibility. I had become Director of Planning in 1987. Effectively all the Directors' jobs would disappear, making us redundant. We were offered early retirement at age 50 with an immediate pension based on superannuation contributions and pension rights made up to age 60. I was 49 at the time and it was too good an offer to refuse. I was fed up anyway. The job had been a constant struggle trying to persuade successive Councils to control the rampant development which the Islands had experienced in a consistent and legal way. Most months after the Planning Committee meeting, I would feature on the front page of the local newspaper 'The Shetland Times' after a row about something. It was extremely frustrating and stressful. Professional Planners don't actually plan anything: all they do is advise Councillors what they should do and they are under no obligation to

take that advice. All this coincided with a tour I had booked up for to
New Zealand at the beginning of 1995, a group of over 90 people from
Shetland heading out to make contact with the myriad of exiles and
descendants of exiles over there. At the end of the tour, I was left wondering why I had ever left after my first stay there. As soon as I got back,
I applied to immigrate and notified the Council that I would take up
their offer of early retirement if I was successful. The process took 18
months as opposed to 5 days the first time, but in June 1997 I was back
in New Zealand. I very quickly found a job as the District Planner with
the City Council in Dunedin. I liked Dunedin but I soon discovered
that I was back in the same nightmare world of office politics and staff
shortages as I had left behind in Shetland. We were in the process of
holding public hearings on the proposed new District Plan and most
of the work involved was being done by consultants, all of whom were
earning substantially more than me and I was supposed to be the boss.
I decided to give it long enough to master the Resource Management
Act and the new New Zealand planning system and get into the consultancy business myself. In June 1998 I resigned. I had been meaning
to return to Britain that year in any case. I had come out with just two
suitcases in case things didn't work out: now that I was settled there
were a few more belongings to arrange transport for. I had always fancied seeing Easter Island and the giant Moai statues there. I discovered
that I could fly to Papeete (Tahiti) and connect with a Llan Chile flight
there which stopped off in Easter Island on its way to Santiago in Chile,
from where I could continue my trip to Britain via Los Angeles. There
were two Llan Chile flights a week which would give me three nights
on the Island if I stopped off there on one flight and then caught the
next one to Santiago.

As we approached Easter Island at the end of a five and a half hour
flight from Papeete, I could appreciate that this was the most remote
inhabited island in the world – it was another five and a half hours to
Santiago. The island lay 3,510 kilometres (2,180 miles) from the coast
of Chile and 2,075 kilometres (1,289 miles) from Pitcairn Island, it's
nearest inhabited neighbour to the west, where the HMS Bounty mutineers had taken refuge.

The impressive runway stretched almost across the full width of the island where it narrowed towards the south-west tip. Mataveri Airport had been constructed in 1967 but in 1985 the Chilean dictator, General Pinochet, had reached an agreement with America allowing them to upgrade it to take the U.S. space shuttle in an emergency. As we came in to land, I could see the bulk of the island spread out to the east, bare, brown, grassland, with not a tree in sight. It reminded me more of my native, treeless, Shetland Islands than a sub-tropical outpost of Polynesia. The landscape was hilly rather than mountainous, punctuated by the cones of extinct volcanoes. The shape came from three volcanoes which occupied the corners of a triangle: the oldest, Maunga Pukatikei, which occupied the Poike Peninsula in the far distance to the east; Terevaka, the newest and highest at 507 meters (1,678 feet) at the northern apex; and Rano Kau, out of my vision in the south-west corner. It wasn't a large island, just 25 kilometres (15 miles) along the base of the triangle and 12 kilometres (7.6 miles) at its widest, giving an area of 163 square kilometres (63 square miles).

A scaled down replica of a moai statue greeted us enigmatically as we approached the entrance to the modest terminal building. Passengers waiting for the onward flight to Santiago were sitting outside on benches around a neat, colourful garden: the fronds of young palm trees and flowering bushes contrasting with the bare landscape I had seen on the way down, suggesting that the apparent bareness was not natural. I noticed that the slopes of Rano Kau, above the airport, were clothed in eucalyptus and pine trees. I later learned that these had been planted in the 20th century by the Chilean Forestry Commission.

I was picked up at the airport by a driver from the local Kia Koe Tour Company, from whom I had pre-booked tours of the island for the next couple of days. On the way to the hotel, I asked the driver how many people lived on the island. He said that there were somewhere between three and four thousand now and growing. At the time of the 1992 census there had been 2,764 people. The tourist industry was creating new jobs now, he said and descendants of former islanders exiled to Tahiti in the late 19th century were coming back. He added, with a look of distaste, that some of the military people from Chile based on the island were marrying local girls and settling down to stay permanently. I asked him what proportion of the population was native to the island as opposed to Chileans. He replied that in the census 70% claimed to be Rapanui (the local name for the island's inhabitants and its language – they called the island itself Rapa Nui) but that many of those would be of mixed ancestry as the population had fallen to 111 in 1877 and only 36 of them had descendants.

My hotel, the Hanga Roa, was a sprawling, single storey building on the outskirts of the town of the same name, where the island's entire population was concentrated. We had arrived just before midday and I had the rest of the day free, so I walked into town, which was spread out over a fairly large area. The bungalow style houses were mainly built of breeze-blocks with corrugated iron roofs. In "The Happy Isles of Oceania" Paul Theroux described them as "grubby little flat-roofed bungalows with the shape and dimensions of sheds." I found them quite attractive, the gardens a riot of colour – bougainvillea, hibiscus, frangipani, jasmine, orchids, lilies and roses - with plenty of trees, giving a lush appearance in contrast to the rural area seen from the plane. There were replica moai statues and other sculptures in some of the gardens. When Paul had been there in 1991, the streets were unsurfaced and dusty: now the main streets had been paved with oblong red lock-blocks which matched the volcanic soil and the red scoria rocks to be seen in the numerous dry-stone walls. I walked northwards along what appeared to be the main street, Policarpo Toro. I saw several guest houses - residencias - signposted and the Kona Kau Restaurant advertised fresh lobster, a French chef and music and dancing. Wandering around, I came upon an attractive little building: a black Birdman modelled on the frigate bird with a large yellow beak was painted on the façade, a blue fish swimming round it at waist level. There were some souvenir shops – I bought a tiny moai exquisitely carved in shiny black obsidian – a general store and a bakery. Off the main street to the left, down towards the little harbour in Tuumaheke Street, were the government offices, the bank and the tourist office. I turned right into Te Pito O Te Henua (Navel of the World) Street and walked up to the little Roman Catholic Church which stood facing down the street towards the harbour. It was a lovely building with a portico of square white columns decorated with Polynesian motifs. A statue of Christ stood on the roof beneath a simple white cross. The façade was decorated with a spider's web pattern in white, picking out the joints in the rough dry-stone facing of red volcanic rock. People were sitting on the steps and the low dry-stone wall at the edge of the road in front.

I walked back down towards the harbour (caleta) which was sheltered by a breakwater – Hanga Roa means "wide harbour" so by definition it was very exposed to onshore weather. Out on the arm of the breakwater a sad-looking blue-painted figure of Christ stood on a plinth, gazing out to sea, like an adherent of the Birdman cult longing to get away. I could imagine him praying silently "Please, God! Get me out of here." The harbour was crowded with small fishing boats. A couple of moai stood looking across it beside the road running along the waterfront and just past them the thatched roofs of the Bar/Restaurant/Discotheque Pea.

I saw from the map in my guide book that there was a museum and a moai site, Ahu Tahai, less than a mile away along the coast to the north. As I walked along the dusty road, a couple rode past on a pony, the man with his hair in the top-knot style which some of the moai were modelled on, the girl up behind him in a Tahitian style pareu. They shouted "Ia Orana", which I recognised as the Tahitian and presumably Rapanui greeting and they nearly fell off their horse when I replied with the Maori equivalent "Kia Ora". The only birds I saw were hawks, which I later learned were called kara kara and had been introduced by the Chileans to catch rats. There were three separate ahu with moai on them at Ahu Tahai, two with single, large statues, one of which had the red scoria topknot and the third with five Moai of varying sizes, three or four times the height of a man. They all stood facing inland, stylised and therefore similar in appearance but not identical, with long ears, broad noses – just torsos with their arms down by their sides, long fingers clasping their bellies. The altar-like ahu or platforms on which they stood were constructed of dry-stone and must have required a lot of labour to build quite apart from the work that went into making and transporting the moai. They had a vertical face on the seaward side but sloped down at the front where there were the remains of a paved area extending out from the platform.

The museum was a bit of a do-it-yourself job, a hotchpotch apparently knocked together by enthusiastic amateurs but none the less fascinating. There was a section on traditional Rapanui agriculture including the tools used for cultivation; historical photographs and documents; skulls excavated from ahu; basalt fish hooks; obsidian spearheads and other weapons. There were sketches of the traditional oval, boat-shaped houses, the smaller, round, beehive-shaped huts and the ceremonial houses of the Birdman cult still standing out at Orongo. Several oblong shaped stone heads called "potato heads" with eye sockets and rudimentary features, one with round ears, were thought to be the oldest carvings made on the island. Another head had been used to demonstrate the method of making eyes for some of the moai, believed to be a late innovation, as few of them had been found. White coral had been used to create the sclera, red scoria (similar to the top-knot stones) for the irises and black obsidian for the pupils. These gave the statues a very life-like appearance and must have created a sensation on the island when first introduced in a magnificent coup in the one-upmanship game which probably contributed to the eventual collapse of society on the island. Two other artefacts which had fascinated academics researching the island's history were on display: the strange skeleton-like moai kava-kava - wooden carvings of men with cavernous cheeks, beak-like noses, protruding rib cages and back bones; and replicas of rongo-rongo tablets – usually wooden boards covered in hieroglyphic-like symbols resembling a form of writing. Outside the museum stood a 2.5 metre high, reddish coloured moai – clearly not made from the grey tuff of Ranu Raraku quarry where nearly all the statues originated. It had been found near the Hanga Roa cemetery. With a triangular head and large, sunken eyes, it again represented an early style of carving.

In the evening I had a meal at the Kona Koa Restaurant which I had seen earlier. I sampled the raw fish, known as "poisson cru" in Tahiti, the fish marinated in lime juice and paw paw with cucumber, spring onions and chopped red chillies added, topped up with coconut milk. The lobster was reasonably priced, suggesting that the stocks around the island were holding up, unlike in many other parts of the world. There was no sign of the advertised music and dancing but perhaps they went wild at the weekend. Afterwards, I had a walk around a part of town I hadn't visited in the afternoon and came across the Banana Café and Pub, a rusty, tin-roofed shack forming a lean-to on the side of the Kai Nene Supermarket. The moai head on the sign was green, as if he'd had a few too many the night before. There was nobody in the bar and the elderly barmaid was monosyllabic in all the languages I tried so I just had a beer and walked back to the hotel. It was a beautiful clear, calm, starlit night – a Polynesian navigator's dream. Walking down towards my hotel, I could see the bright lights of another large tourist hotel, the Iorana, on the headland below the airport.

In the morning my tour guide Arturo arrived in a mini bus with some loud American voices echoing in the back. An Italian couple and two young Japanese were waiting with me at the Hanga Roa. Easter Island obviously had universal appeal. We drove past the airport to the Vinapu ahu on the south side of the island, Arturo pointing out Maunga Orito on the way, an extinct volcano where obsidian had been mined for tools and weapons. Ahu Vinapu was the site that had got Thor Heyerdahl, the Norwegian ethnographer, excited and inflamed his fixation that the Easter Island statue builders had come from South America. The basalt stonework in the high, vertical back wall of the ahu was as good as anything I had seen in Peru but the individual blocks were not nearly as large, the heaviest weighing 10 tons as opposed to 361 tons in the Sacsahuaman fortress above Cuzco and were trapezoidal in shape rather than the regular, rectangular blocks of the Inca. Arturo told us that they were just a façade, the inside of the platform being filled with rubble. In an attempt to prove his theory, Heyerdahl and five companions had in 1947 launched a balsa wood raft from Lima on the coast of South America and eventually after 101 days made a landfall on Raroia Island in the Tuamotus, which he later documented in his best-selling book "Kon-Tiki." Paul Theroux summed up this feat in "The Happy Isles of Oceania": "In a lifetime of nutty theorising, Heyerdahl's single success was his proof, in Kon-Tiki, that six middle-class Scandinavians could successfully crash-land their raft on a coral atoll in the middle of nowhere." Later, in 1955-56, Heyerdahl led a scientific expedition to Easter Island where he re-erected a fallen moai near Anakena Beach and experimented with techniques of transporting the statues using wooden rollers. The fact that the statue broke suggests that he may even have got that wrong. He wrote up the work of the expedition and developed his theories about the colonising of the island further in his book "Aku-Aku". The gospel according to Heyerdahl was that the first inhabitants, the Long Ears arrived from South America around 380 AD and erected the moai. A few hundred years later, Polynesians arrived who became known as the Short Ears. Initially, the Long Ears enslaved them, using them as a labour force in the moai industry. Eventually, the Short Ears rebelled, wiped out the Long Ears, burning them in a trench on the landward side of the Poike Peninsula where extensive layers of charcoal had been found. This was based on a legend handed down by the islanders about a war between the Long Ears and the Short Ears culminating in a show-down at the same location.

All the moai at Ahu Vinapu had been toppled off the ahu and smashed. Arturo explained that the same had happened at every ahu on the island, all 113 of them with statues on them. (There were nearly another 200 ahu without statues.) All the moai that were now standing had been re-erected in the 20th century. He showed us that large rocks had apparently been placed so that when the moai fell, their necks broke, suggesting a degree of malice towards them. Since Arturo had mentioned Thor Heyerdahl's theory, I couldn't resist a bit of stirring, so I said "Probably served them right if they were South Americans."

"Ah! No!" Arturo said, "There is no evidence that South Americans ever came here before the Chileans annexed the island in 1888. The original inhabitants were Polynesians from the Marquesas Islands who arrived via Mangareva. The Rapanui language is closest to the dialects spoken in those places and the DNA extracted from bones exhumed from the ahu is closely related to Polynesian types and contains geno-types not found in South American natives. Even the rats can be genetically linked back to the Marquesas! The skull types are also Polynesian, many with the rocker-jaw only found among island people. The tools and fishing equipment excavated are also characteristic of Mangarevan styles which came from the Marquesas originally. There are also statues on platforms like ahu in the Marquesas whichresemble the old style ones dug up here - like the one outside the museum. In Tonga, there is a trilithon called Ha'amonga made of three huge 40 ton blocks of stone with one six meters long placed horizontally across two upright ones five meters high, like at Stonehenge and erected around 1200AD - which shows that Polynesian people were able to build large, stone monuments long ago. Heyerdahl argued that the totara reeds found growing in the Rano Kau volcanic crater, which are native to South America, was further evidence of colonization from there but pollen analysis from sediment cores shows that they have been growing there for over 30,000 years and they could very easily have been brought by birds."

I later saw Moai-like statues on a tohua (ahu-like structure called a marae elsewhere in Polynesia) at Hatiheu, in Nuku Hiva, on a 2004 visit to the Marquesas and another at Puamou on the north coast of Hiva Oa, at over seven feet tall, the largest "Tiki" (a stylised figure also common in Maori carvings) in Polynesia outside Easter Island. It had its hands touching its belly like the moai. Paul Theroux reports seeing those same statues on his visit there. On that same trip, I visited Raiatea in the Society islands and saw the huge marae at Taputapuatea where the stone platforms were more impressive than any of the ahu on Easter Island.

I had already read a lot about the origins of the Polynesian people and their ocean voyaging. It was now generally accepted from DNA and linguistic evidence that they had originated in Taiwan, migrating southwards from there between 5,000 and 6,000 years ago. Reaching the Admiralty Islands north of New Guinea they developed the Lapita culture named after a site in New Caledonia where their characteristic pottery was first found. This same pottery can be traced through Fiji to Samoa and Tonga. Archaeological evidence shows that they arrived there around 1,000 BC and developed the distinctive Polynesian culture now seen throughout the Polynesian Triangle with apexes in Hawaii, New Zealand and Easter Island. Very recent re-evaluation of radio-carbon dates using new technology suggests that it may have been another two thousand years before they ventured further east to colonise the Society, Cook and Marquesas Islands, collectively known as Eastern Polynesia. Key to their expansion was the development of canoe technology and navigation techniques. The outrigger provided stability, the lateen sail better

manoeuvrability and tacking ability. The ocean going voyaging canoes with double hulls and sheltered accommodation built across them amidships which were still around in Captain Cook's time impressed him – he wrote that they could outsail his own ship. A medium sized voyaging canoe around 20 metres (65 feet) long could hold about 24 people along with the animals, plants and provisions necessary to establish a colony. In 1999 a replica, the Hokule'a sailed from Mangareva to Easter Island in 19 days. The original colonists could have re-provisioned on the way at Pitcairn Island which would still have been inhabited at that time. (The original Polynesian inhabitants of Pitcairn had died out by the time the Bounty mutineers arrived.)

Polynesian navigation was also relatively sophisticated. Using the sun by day and memorised star maps at night, they were able to plot their courses fairly accurately and get back to where they set off from. Tupaia, a native of Raiatea in the Society Islands, who Captain Cook took with him when he left Tahiti in 1774, could draw a map of the islands as far away as the Marquesas and the Cooks. Making landfall was made easier by observing sea birds which fly out to sea as far as 160 kilometres (100 miles) in the morning, returning at night, giving an island an effective radius of 320 kilometres (200 miles). The movement of migrating birds could have given clues that land lay in the direction of their annual flight patterns: the Pacific Golden Plover migrates from the Arctic to the Society Islands via Hawaii and the Marquesas; the Long-tailed Cuckoo migrates north from New Zealand to the Cook Islands and Tahiti before winter sets in. Islands develop distinctive cloud patterns which can give away their presence. They also interrupt the pattern of sea swells and Polynesian navigators were skilled at interpreting these movements in the sea. I was familiar with this from the Shetland Islands where it was known as the "moder dye": at the height of the "Haaf" fishing for cod and ling in the late 19th century the fishermen would row their open six-oared boats (sixareens) out of sight of land and use the same techniques as the Polynesians to get back ashore again. Floating seaweed, branches and other detritus would have provided further clues.

It is now accepted that the Polynesian settlement of the Pacific was the result of deliberate, planned voyages rather than accidental landfalls – fishing boats blown off course do not carry the women, children and food supplies needed to establish a colony. At first sight it may seem illogical that the Pacific was settled from west to east as the prevailing wind across most of the region is the South-East Trades. However, sailing generally against the wind made it easier to return and there are times when westerlies blow, as much as a third of the time in Samoa and a quarter in Tahiti, longer during El Nino conditions.

There is also archaeological evidence that return voyages were made, even from as far afield as New Zealand. Obsidian from Mayor Island in the Bay of Plenty has been found on the Kermadec Islands half way to the Cook Islands which is believed to be the final departure point for the Maori heading for New Zealand. It would be logical for an initial small group to make the original discovery of a new island, some of them returning to re-provision and bring back more colonists. These long-distance contacts seem to have died out not long after the furthest outposts of the Polynesian Triangle were colonised. In his book "Collapse", Jared Diamond relates how contacts between Mangareva and Pitcairn and Henderson Islands broke down resulting in the populations on these islands dying out. Mangareva also lost contact with the Marquesas where the original settlers had come from. There is some evidence of a colder, stormier climate setting in after about 1400AD which would coincide with the "Little Ice Age" in the Northern Hemisphere, when the Viking colony in Greenland became isolated and died out and Iceland had difficulty maintaining contact with mainland Europe. However, as colonies became established and self-sufficient and friends and relatives in the original homeland died off, the incentive to maintain contact would have reduced over time in any case. Where the reason for the emigration was defeat in war or a family feud as opposed to population pressure on resources or just a pioneering spirit, it would not have been practical or wise to return. In the case of Easter Island there is no evidence that the original settlers ever returned to their Mangareva homeland – no distinctively Rapanui artefacts have been found there or elsewhere in Polynesia. Another indicator that the original voyage was a one-off is that only the chicken and the rat from the standard Polynesian menu survived on the island – no pigs or dogs which were always carried on pioneering voyages. It would seem likely that if these did not survive the first voyage, subsequent trips would have brought them. However, pigs did not make it to New Zealand either in spite of evidence of return voyages.

The Polynesian menu carried with them on their journeys to new islands represented a distinctive part of their culture. In addition to the "livestock" referred to above, there was a characteristic assembly of plants all of which originated in South-East Asia: the coconut palm, the breadfruit tree, bananas, taro, yams, the paper mulberry tree (used to make tapa cloth) and sugar cane. Breadfruit and coconuts do not grow well in Easter Island's cooler, sub-tropical climate: breadfruit tends to blow off the trees in the typical windy conditions before it ripens and never seems to have become established on the island; the coconuts now to be seen at Anakena were a 20th century introduction. One strange anomaly among the traditional Polynesian crops was the kumara (sweet potato) which originated in South America but had spread all over Polynesia, including Easter Island, before the Europeans arrived in the area. This mystery was compounded by the fact that the coconut palm, which is a native of South-East Asia was already in Central and South America when the Spaniards arrived.

So it seems that Thor Heyerdahl had got it all wrong. I'll leave it to Paul Theroux to fire the bullets and deliver the coup de grace in his "The Happy Isles of Oceania":

"Thor Heyerdahl is shrill but mistaken in many of his assumptions. Far from solving the Easter Island mystery, he has succeeded in making the solution more difficult for qualified scientists and made something of a fool of himself in the process. He is an amateur, a populariser, an impresario, with a zoology degree from the University of Oslo. Scientifically, his books have as little value as those of Erich von Danniken, who theorised that the Easter Island moai were carved by people from outer space."

Heyerdahl died in 2002, still convinced that he was right.

We took a detour inland to see the quarry in Puna Pau volcano where the red scoria pukau (topknots) for the moai had been extracted and then headed back to the south coast to Vaipu, another viciously destroyed ahu with broken moai sprawling face down in front of it. A bit further along the coast at Akahanga, more toppled moai and Arturo pointed out other ruins across the bay. The sheer number of these sites was already becoming apparent. Arturo drew our attention to the remains of a large village nearby, the oval, boat shaped foundations of large houses, the floors paved with basalt blocks. He said that there were similar remains all over the island suggesting that there had once been a very large population. He pointed out circular holes in the basalt foundations where wooden poles had been inserted then bent across and tied together to form a framework for the wall covering of woven totara reeds, sugar cane leaves and grasses. They were usually about 3 metres (10 feet) wide and 12 metres (40 feet) long although one near Anakena had been getting on for 25 metres (80 feet) long. There had been three classes in traditional society: the Ariki (chiefs), warriors, navigators and priests; an artisan class including carvers, toolmakers and agricultural specialists ; and the majority who were commoners. The Paramount Chief of the island was believed to be a direct descendent of the legendary leader of the first colonists, Hotu Matu'a. The large, oval houses called "hare paenga" were believed to have belonged to the upper classes.

Jared Diamond's book "Collapse" has a fascinating section on the traditional settlement pattern, agriculture and original flora and fauna of the island. According to his account, the hare paenga of the upper classes were concentrated in groups of six to ten in a 200 metre wide coastal strip, immediately inland from the ahu. The circular, stone-built houses of the commoners, called "hare oka", were further inland, accompanied by oblong, stone-built chicken houses, called "hare moa", 6 to 20 metres (20 to 70 feet) long, 3 metres (10 feet) wide and 2 metres (6 feet) high, surrounded by stone walls for security. There were underground ovens with beach stones (called "umu" elsewhere in Polynesia), gardens surrounded by sheltering circular stone walls and garbage pits (which yielded useful archaeological evidence.) Further inland in the uplands, there appeared to be a type of plantation agriculture with isolated hare paenga but few traces of the commoners' hare oka although roads could be detected running inland from the coast to these areas which Diamond suggests could have been used for access by the workforce. He theorised that the plantations could have been used to feed the labour force engaged in the statue industry. According to Diamond, the island was divided into eleven or twelve wedge shaped tribal territories, each with a stretch of coastline, tapering off inland. This would accord with the pattern typical of other Polynesian islands. Each tribe had several ahu with statues on them, strung out along the coastline, facing inland keeping a stern watch over their former chiefdoms.

Diamond describes various techniques used to increase agricultural productivity: stone-lined pits around 2 to 3 metres (6 to 10 feet) in diameter and over a metre (4 feet) deep, used as composting pits to grow crops; evidence of dams on an intermittent stream flowing off Terevaka mountain, resembling systems used to irrigate taro elsewhere in Polynesia; widespread use of stone walls to shelter crops from the strong winds; and the use of rocks to regulate soil temperature, evaporation and surface water run-off. Crops included the typical Polynesian range: sweet potatoes, taro, yams, bananas, and sugar cane. Early European visitors commented on the fertility of the volcanic soil.

A painstaking archaeological analysis of bones from the garbage pit of a cooking site at Anakena Beach carried out in the 1990s gives an intriguing picture of the early diet of the islanders and how it changed with time. It showed that there had been at least eight species of land birds including herons, rails, parrots and barn owls; and more than 25 sea birds, probably the richest breeding site in Polynesia – albatross, boobies, frigate birds, fulmars, petrels, terns, tropic birds. There were some seal and sea turtle bones but in the lower, older layers, the predominant seafood remains were of the common dolphin, which could only have been caught well offshore using ocean going canoes. Fish bones comprised 23% of the total as opposed to the 90% common elsewhere in Polynesia and there was little shellfish. Easter Island, lying 27 degrees south, is on the cold side for coral formation although some does grow there and the steep drop off into deep water is not conducive to reef formation or fish breeding. The absence of lagoons meant there was no opportunity for fishing or shellfish gathering in shallow, sheltered water. Rat bones outnumbered fish bones, the Polynesian rat (kiore) being an important protein source in the diet. In later layers of the excavation, land birds disappeared completely as did 15 of the sea bird species. This meant the loss not only of the flesh of the birds from the diet but also their eggs. Porpoise bones also disappeared.

Pollen analysis from sediment cores taken from the crater lakes at Rano Kau and Rano Raraku shows that Easter Island originally supported a rich sub-tropical, broad-leaf forest with a relative of the Chilean wine palm predominant, covering 70% of the island. The Chilean palm typically grows to a diameter of a metre (3 feet) and a height of 20 metres (65 feet) taking about 100 years to reach maturity. Casts of the Easter Island variety, found fossilised in lava flows on Terevaka, show diameters of over 2 metres (7 feet) suggesting that it may have been the biggest palm tree in the world. This tree would have provided wine from the sap in the trunk, which, if boiled, could have given sugar; the nuts contained edible, oily kernels; the fronds would have provided material for thatch, baskets, mats and boat sails; the trunks, timber. There was pollen from at least 5 other large trees: two tall species (growing to over 30 metres (100 feet) and 16 metres (50 feet) respectively) and used to make canoes elsewhere in Polynesia – Terevaka means "the place of the canoes"; the hauhau tree, the bark of which provides rope elsewhere; the paper mulberry tree for tapa cloth; another, with a flexible, straight trunk, good for harpoons and outriggers; the Malay Apple had edible fruit; Rosewood and about eight other hardwoods were ideal for wood carving and construction; Toromiro, mesquite and acacia would have been excellent firewood. The sediment cores showed the tree cover gradually being replaced by grasses.

The tour continued on to Rano Raraku, the old volcano where the vast majority of the statues had been carved. The hillside presented a surreal picture as we approached, great heads protruding from the soil where they had presumably been parked awaiting transportation and gradually sunk into the ground. Arturo led us up to see the largest one ever carved, unfinished and still attached to the rock face with a trench in front for the carvers to stand in. It measured 22 metres (70 feet) long and would have weighed about 270 tons when finished. "We'll see the tallest one erected later" Arturo said, "nearly 10 metres (32 feet) high and weighing 82 tons. The heaviest one erected is on the Tongariko Ahu just down below here, 87 tons." He explained that they had been carved using hand-held basalt chisels called "toki" which could still be found lying around in the quarry as if they had just suddenly been discarded. A typical moai would have taken a team of five or six men about a year to complete. A total of 887 statues had been identified, including one stolen for the British Museum, only a quarter ever erected on ahu and nearly a half remaining in the quarry. The rest were scattered along transport routes to their destination. Arturo pointed out traces of old roads – the longest would have extended 9 miles (14 kilometres) to the south-west end of the island. He said that it was fairly clear from island folklore that each represented the deceased head of a tribal lineage. We walked around to see Tukuturi, a reddish coloured, kneeling moai with a beard and features different from the standard conventions, which Arturo said had been almost completely buried.

The comparison with the annual Viking fire festival, Up-Helly-Aa, in my native Shetland Islands struck me. There, a Guizer Jarl is chosen to head a Jarl's squad dressed as Vikings to lead the procession which

tows a replica Viking galley to be burned. Each Jarl chooses a historical figure from the Icelandic sagas or other early Norwegian history to
represent. For a while a few years back this became very competitive,
each squad trying to outdo the previous year's in the elaborateness of
the Viking costumes, armaments and ornaments until it was becoming prohibitively expensive. It occurred to me that much the same
thing had happened on Easter Island. Ingrained human competitiveness would have triggered an escalation in the size of moai carved,
innovations like the red scoria topknots and later the elaborate eye
pieces. This urge to go one better would have been exacerbated by
the fact that the statues played a central role in the island religion
which involved ancestor worship – the earliest European visitor Jacob
Roggeveen witnessed the people prostrating themselves before the
moai. Jared Diamond has pointed out that the size of the statues compared to those found elsewhere in Polynesia can be explained by the
fact that the tuff found in the Rano Raraku quarry, a form of consolidated volcanic ash, is the best and easiest stone for carving to be
found anywhere in the Pacific. He also suggests that there would have
been plenty of surplus labour not needed for agriculture or fishing
as the population built up; the plantations in the uplands could have
provided food for the statue builders, movers and installers. (Members
of the French expedition of 1776 led by La Perouse reported "a soil,
which, with very little labour, furnished excellent provisions and in an
abundance more than sufficient for the consumption of the inhabitants" and that "three days work a year" would be enough to support
the population. This was after the island had been largely deforested.
Roggeveen, visiting over 50 years earlier had reported seeing no trees
taller than 3 metres (ten feet)). The competitive nature of the statue
building is explained by Diamond as a way of channelling natural
human aggression and finding work for "idle hands" when there were
no nearby islands to compete and fight with.

I referred back to the traces of roads Arturo had drawn our attention to earlier and asked him what was known about the transportation of the moai to the ahu. He told us that a number of theories
had been put forward over the years including the local tradition that

they "walked", suggesting some sort of triangular trestle within which the moai would be suspended upright. Thor Heyerdahl had experimented with wooden rollers but the statue had broken.

Years later reading Jared Diamond's "Collapse", I agreed with his conclusion that the most convincing theory had recently been put forward by archaeologists who had experimented with a system known as "canoe ladders" used elsewhere in Polynesia to move huge logs for dugout canoes. These consisted of a parallel set of wooden rails joined by fixed wooden cross pieces. The statue was placed on a wooden sled and dragged along the rails using ropes. The archaeologists calculated that 50 to 70 men, working 5 hours a day could have moved a 12 ton statue nine miles in about a week. Diamond observed that Hawaiians had moved logs heavier than the average moai this way. It is now accepted that all the massive stone monuments erected by stone-age man – Stonehenge, The Pyramids, Mayan temples – were erected by human muscle power, aided by ramps, ropes and levers, provided that there was a large enough labour force available.

We moved down to the Tongariki Ahu set against a dramatic background of the sea cliffs surrounding the Poike Peninsula. Fifteen moai had been re-erected here in 1994 by a group of Japanese archaeologists using a crane, which had struggled with the 87 ton one earlier referred to by Arturo. It was the only one sporting a pukao topknot. The damage inflicted here by the statue toppling episode in the island's history had been exacerbated by a tsunami from the massive 1960 earthquake in Chile which had scattered the fallen moai further inland. The Japanese had done a superb restoration job. Arturo said that the area behind the ahu had been used to cremate the bodies of the deceased. (This was an unusual practice in Polynesia and one that must have needed a lot of firewood, adding to the deforestation problem.)

We drove across the island, past the Poike Trench and then along the north coast to Ahu Te Pito Kura to see Ariki Paro, the tallest moai ever erected and allegedly the last to be toppled in 1840. Further along, we came to Anakena Bay, with a curving beach of golden sand and groves of coconut palms, the only place on the island bearing any resemblance to a Pacific island. Arturo pointed out a single moai standing by itself on Ahu Ature Huke. This was the first one re-erected, by Thor Heyerdahl's expedition in 1955, using the traditional method passed on to him by the local people to whom he had listened for once. The process consisted of building a ramp of stones under the statue's belly by prising it up using wooden levers, steadying it with ropes as it reached the vertical. The plinths on the base of the moai sloped slightly forward to prevent them falling backwards when they finally came upright. Flat stones were then inserted under the front of the plinth to bring them back to the vertical. This was one of the more useful things that Heyerdahl did. Nearby, on Ahu Nau Nau, seven moai had been re-erected, four of them with red topknots and white coral eyes, their black pupils staring atypically out to sea.

There has been some debate over the years about how the 12 ton pukao could have been hoisted onto the heads of the moai. When I was researching this chapter, I came across a simple explanation in Jared Diamond's book: they were erected together with the moai – the pukao would have been lashed onto the moai's head within a wooden framework to create one unit for raising.

Arturo told us that Anakena was where, according to legend, Hotu Matu'a, the founding father of the island's inhabitants, had landed. Being the only beach, this seemed reasonable. The story was that Hotu Matu'a had arrived with his wife and six sons and their families. A second canoe, skippered by Tuu-ko-ihu, contained his extended family. They had named the island Te Pito O Te Henua (The Navel of the World).

Later, in a Wikipedia article on Easter Island, I learned that "pito" could also mean "umbilical cord" and that the name may have reflected the fact that the island was at the "ends of the earth" the outer limits of the living world: the spirit world was apparently believed by the Polynesians to lie in the bowels of the ocean out to the east. The navigators on the voyage to Easter Island would have been familiar with the relatively closely spaced pattern of atolls stretching down from the Marquesas through the Tuamotus to the Gambier Islands where Mangareva lay. The long gap to Pitcairn followed by the even longer span to Easter Island must have brought home to them how much out on a limb or navel cord they were.

The Japanese girl in the group pointed out that the locals called the island Rapa Nui. Arturo smiled, "That is a very strange story," he said. He told us that Peruvian slave raiders had carried off 1500 men (half the island's population) in 1863 to work in the guano mines off the coast of Peru. An international outcry had forced the Peruvians to repatriate them but in the meantime most of them had died. Only a dozen returned, some of whom spread smallpox, which decimated the rest of the population. Men had also been kidnapped from a lot of other islands from the Marquesas south and French bureaucrats from Tahiti were given the job of getting them back to their home islands. There were also men from Rapa, a tiny island away to the west in the Austral Islands group. For some reason confusion arose, in the minds of the French officials, between them and the men from Easter Island, resulting in the latters' home island being labelled Rapa Nui (Big Rapa) to distinguish it from Rapa, to which they added "Iti" (Little) to emphasise the difference and confuse matters even further. Bizarrely, the remaining Easter Islanders, on their return, adopted this name as their own.

This is not as strange as it may sound. The "Navel of the World" name was a legendary label, not in common use. The chiefs and priests who would have been familiar with it had been kidnapped and died. The Easter Island label had been applied by visiting Europeans, originally by the Dutchman Jacob Roggeveen who came across it on Easter Day, 1722 and called it Paasch-Eyland (the 18th century Dutch version.) and the ordinary islanders may not have been familiar with it. Up until the time that the islanders became aware that a wider world existed they would have had no need to call their island anything. The inhabitants of Fair Isle, a remote outpost half way between my native Shetland Islands and our neighbours Orkney, still simply call their home island "The Isle". The Easter Islanders were probably quite happy to adopt a Polynesian name rather than one imposed on them by strangers.

Later, I checked this story on the Internet, where I found a copy of a report for the Smithsonian Institution on an American expedition to the island in 1888/89. The 1891 publication entitled "Te Pito Te Henua" by William J. Thomson, a Paymaster in the U.S. navy, who reported on the expedition, contained the same story. However, it was so garbled that I was none the wiser about the details of the confusion. Paymaster Thomson had nothing in common with his compatriot Ronald Reagan, the Great Communicator, except perhaps when the latter succumbed to Alzheimer's Disease.

One of the Americans in the group asked Arturo when Hotu Matu'a was supposed to have landed. Arturo said that there was some debate about that. Originally it had been thought to be around 300 – 400 AD based on radio carbon dates from charcoal in the Poike Trench and studies of the amount of change in the Rapanui dialect from the original Marquesan language. However, more recent radiocarbon dates from materials excavated from Ahu Tahai and other sites suggested that 800 – 900 AD was more likely. "However," Arturo said, "the genealogy memorised by the islanders and reported to early researchers place Hotu Matu'a in the 12th century."

When I was doing some background reading for this chapter, I came across a 2006 article in the American Scientist by Terry Hunt from the University of Hawaii, who, with his colleague Carl Lipo from California State University had carried out new radiocarbon dating studies on the island and a comprehensive review of the older work in this field. Their conclusion was that there was no reliable evidence of a human presence on Easter Island before about 1200AD. This was in line with similar work done by Atholl Anderson of the Australian State University which dated the first settlement of New Zealand to around 1280 AD, four or five hundred years later than previously believed and intriguingly, as for Easter Island, closer to the genealogical memories of Maori. Similar work elsewhere in Eastern Polynesia by these same scientists suggests that the Society, Cook and Marquesas Islands were only settled between 1025 and 1120 AD, up to a thousand years later than previously believed.

On the drive back to Hanga Roa we passed the site of the former sheep farm at Fundo Vaitea which had dominated the island from the 1870s to the 1950s. The old shearing shed was still there and across the road fruit and vegetables were being grown by Corfo – the Chilean State Development Company. Arturo said that sheep farming had been started in 1870 by a Frenchman from Tahiti called Jean-Baptiste Dutrou-Bornier who bought up land belonging to all those who had died, not just in the smallpox epidemic brought back from Peru but from tuberculosis which had been introduced from whaling ships in the mid 19th century. Dutrou-Bornier came into conflict with the missionaries (who had initially arrived in 1864), burned the houses and crops of their supporters, killing some, until the missionaries left in 1871, taking many of their converts with them to Mangareva. Dutrou-Bornier transported a couple of hundred islanders to Tahiti to work on the plantations of his associates there. By the time he was killed by the islanders in 1877, he owned most of the land outside Hanga Roa and there were only 111 natives left on the island. The sheep farm was then bought by another Tahitian, Alexander Salmon, who bought up all the remaining land except in Hanga Roa where the population was now concentrated. In 1888 he sold out to the Chilean government, which then annexed the island. In the early 20th century, the Chilean government leased out the farm to a Scottish firm, Williamson-Balfour, based in Chile, who effectively ruled the island as the Compania Explotadora de la Isla de Pasqua (CEDIP) until their lease was terminated in 1953. After that, it had been administered by the Chilean navy until 1966, when civilian government was established.

European contacts with the island had been disastrous from the start. Jacob Roggeveen, the Dutch explorer had been the first in 1722. He only made it ashore once as heavy surf had prevented him from landing for a week while he lay offshore. When an armed party of 150 men finally landed, the natives crowded round them as they marched inland: some of the party became alarmed and opened fire, killing 13 islanders. There was then a gap until 1770, when two Spanish ships arrived. Their visit seems to have been peaceful but with more contact with the islanders than Roggeveen it's possible that European diseases were introduced as happened elsewhere in the Pacific and the Americas. Captain Cook followed in 1774 and the French explorer La Perouse in 1776. Following a raid by an American "Blackbirder" (slave-raiding ship) in 1805, the islanders attempted to resist further landings by visiting ships such as whalers but considerable damage had already been done (with an outbreak of smallpox in 1836 and the introduction of tuberculosis around the middle of the century) before the disastrous Peruvian slave raid in 1862/63.

That evening in the hotel bar, I got chatting to an elderly Englishman who was staying in the hotel. I never found out his name or whether he was just a tourist or a visiting academic. The subject got round to the mysterious rongorongo tablets that I had seen at the museum which seemed to suggest that a form of writing had been developed on the island, something which had never happened elsewhere in Polynesia. He said that they appeared to be a very late development. It was thought that the local priests had picked up the idea of writing from the Spanish expedition in 1770 and come up with a system of pictographs to help them remember different religious chants – a sort of aide-memoire or rosary as he put it. There were too many different symbols for it to be based on an alphabet of any sort and there was no correspondence between the symbols used and the petroglyphs found on rocks on the island. The last of the priests had been wiped out in the raid by Peruvian slavers in 1862 so by the time European missionaries arrived in 1864 and asked questions about folklore including the rongorongo tablets there was nobody left who could tell them anything about them. When I got back from Easter Island, I checked this theory and it turned out to be pretty much on the nail with current academic thinking. It's amazing what you learn in pubs.

The tour group re-assembled again the following morning to see the rest of the island. We drove inland to Ahu Akivi, which had been restored in 1960 by William Mulloy and seven moai re-erected. It was unusual in that it was well inland and the moai faced the sea. We continued down a track to visit Ana Te Pahu cave, a garden planted with sweet potatoes, taro and bananas near its entrance. Arturo said that caves like this in lava tubes were to be found all over the island and had clearly been used as houses. "There is one called Ana Kai Tangata (The Cave Where People Are Eaten)" he said, "suggesting that at one time there was cannibalism. Spear heads and other weapons have been found all over the island, so there seems to have been warfare at some time. Even the chicken houses were built like fortresses! And of course there is the legend of the Long Ears fighting the Short Ears at the Poike Trench which Thor Heyerdahl picked up on." We continued down towards the north-west coast to Ahu Tepeu, no moai but an impressive ahu, 3 metres (10 feet) high on the seaward side with large, vertical basalt blocks. Nearby were the remains of more oval shaped and round houses. "This is where Tuu-ko-ihu, the skipper of the second colonizing canoe, is said to be buried" Arturo told us. Gesturing towards the slopes of the Terevaka volcano rising above us, he said "Terevaka means "Place of the Canoes" so at one time there were obviously enough trees to build canoes. Tools for woodworking have been found all over the hillside – stone drills, chisels, scrapers, knives. Yet when Roggeveen arrived, he reported that there were no trees or bushes to be seen over 3 metres (10 feet) tall."

We returned to Hanga Roa and then climbed up the road to the rim of the Rano Kau volcano at over 300 metres (980 feet). The inner crater walls were steep: the lake with its blanket of bright green totara reeds seemed a long way down. We walked along the crater rim to where some circular stone houses were built into the hillside near the edge of the sea cliff overlooking the three little rocky islets (motu) called Motu Kau Kau (which has been described as resembling a broken, rotten dog's tooth), Motu Iti and Motu Nui. "This was the centre of the Birdman cult," Arturo said. "After the moai had fallen out of favour, a new religion took over on the island. The Polynesian creator god, Makemake, was at the centre of it. He was also the god of fertility and responsible for bringing the migrating nesting birds – which was seen as the annual renewal of life. Each year, a Birdman (Tangata Manu) was appointed, following a competition, to be Makemake's representative and ruler of the island for the year.

He went on to describe the annual competition. Each tribal group would nominate a young champion called a "hopu". The hopu had to climb down the cliff, swim a mile out to Motu Iti, wait until a migratory sooty tern had laid an egg, strap it to their foreheads with a red tapa cloth bandanna, swim ashore, climb back up the cliff and present the egg to the chief of their tribe. The winning chief became Birdman: the winning hopu was rewarded with a virgin. Arturo pointed out a deep cleft in the rocks where footholds had been carved on either side around head height from the bottom and petroglyphs of vulvas (komari) etched into the rock face, allegedly showing the difference between a virgin and a non-virgin. In this primitive gynaecological clinic the prospective virgins would stand in the footholds and the priests below them would carry out inspections prior to awarding the winning hopu his prize. Priests will be priests as has become abundantly obvious in the recent scandals involving paedophile priests in the Catholic Church.

While the eggs collected came from the sooty tern, the bird's head on the half-man, half-bird Birdman petroglyphs to be seen all over the rocks in the area, were based on the frigate bird. It no longer came to the island but had been present in the early days as evidenced by the archaeological analysis of bones from a midden at Anakena. The frigate bird held a special place in Polynesian society because of its well-honed homing instincts. It was carried on long sea voyages to help locate landfalls. This makes me think that the Birdman cult may have involved an element of escapism, a desire to get away from the island where things had gone so badly wrong. Identical Birdman petroglyphs have been found in Hawaii, so the concept was not unique to Easter Island (although the competition was) and had presumably been handed down through generations of priests until the time was ripe to re-activate it as the dominant religion and push Makemake to the head of the queue of gods. This juggling of gods seems to have been common in Polynesian society: just before Captain Cook arrived in Tahiti a cult had grown up around the God of War, Oro, which had led to widespread bloodshed throughout the Society Islands.

I could see some advantages that the Birdman cult would have brought to the island, signs of learning from past mistakes. It provided a way of sharing out the leadership of the island among clans without having to resort to warfare; and it provided an outlet for competitiveness in a way much less costly on resources than the moai cult. A by-product was the burgeoning of the petroglyph industry. I've seen estimates of the number of these rock engravings, which are found all around the island, ranging from 4,000 to 6,000. They depicted

Makemake, Birdmen, sea turtles, lizards and fish, not to mention the odd vulva. This would have been a god-send for the redundant moai carvers, a sort of job-creation scheme well ahead of its time. Katherine Routledge had systematically collected the island's traditions in 1919. According to her, the Birdman competitions stared around 1760 and ended in 1878 with the building of the first church by Roman Catholic missionaries who very quickly eradicated the old religions, as they did throughout the Pacific.

Arturo drew our attention to the beehive-shaped cult houses behind us. These were built from flat, over-lapping slabs of basalt quarried from inside the Rano Kau crater. They could only be accessed on hands and knees through low, narrow entrance ways. Arturo said that they had only been used for ceremonial purposes, mainly at the time of the annual egg-finding competition.

With the island circuit complete, Arturo summed up for us what had happened on the island since the original colonists had arrived. "With plenty of food available to begin with from the crops, chickens and rats they had brought with them along with the wild food they found – porpoises, seals, fish and both land and sea birds – the population grew quickly. They cleared forest for agriculture, cut down trees for canoes to hunt porpoises and fish from, for building houses, firewood and to cremate the dead. The large population and fertility of the volcanic soil meant that there was plenty of spare labour to devote to their religion which was based on ancestor worship. The carving of ancestors in the form of moai became an obsession, each tribe trying to outdo the others in the size and decoration of the statues. Moving and erecting the moai needed more wood from the forests and deforestation continued. As the trees disappeared they were no longer able to build canoes to catch porpoises or deep sea fish, soil erosion set in and crops became more exposed to the strong winds without the shelter afforded by trees. The land birds quickly became extinct through hunting and loss of habitat, with the loss not just of their flesh from the food supply but also eggs. Many of the sea birds disappeared too, the remainder retreating to the little offshore islets. With the population continuing to increase while the food supply diminished, famine set in. Eventually, the commoners rebelled against the ariki (chief) and priest class and blaming them and their ancestors in the form of moai for what had happened on the island, they smashed the moai. Warfare went on for a number of years between tribes, led by warriors known as matatoa, with people retreating to fortified caves to live and even the chicken houses were built like fortresses. Human bones split to extract the marrow have been found in garbage heaps near cooking fires in caves, suggesting that cannibalism was practised. The population continued to decline until by the time the first Europeans arrived there were only two or three thousand left. Captain Cook reported that the islanders his crew saw were "poor and distressed, small, lean, timid and miserable."

I later read Jared Diamond's book "Collapse" which contained a detailed description of the downward spiral of events taking place on the island from first settlement, accepting the traditional version as outlined by Arturo and providing some interesting dates and back-up evidence. Pollen samples showed a decline in trees in favour of grasses already by 1300 AD; bones of porpoise, tuna and pelagic fish had disappeared from garbage pits by 1500 AD, suggesting that the wood for ocean going canoes was exhausted by then; no palm nuts with radiocarbon dates later than this same date had been found; wood fuel in cooking fires was replaced by grasses and ferns after 1650; cremation also ended in the 1600s to be replaced with mummification and bone burials; forest clearance reached its peak around 1400 AD and was largely complete by the 1600s. The upland plantations which had been established in the early 1400s came to an end in the 1600s. Chicken houses showed an explosive growth in numbers after about 1650. He also referred to evidence of soil erosion and pointed out that the loss of trees would have exposed the volcanic soil to loss of nutrients and would have reduced the amount of rainfall, exacerbating the loss of productivity. The availability of mulch would also have been greatly reduced. The number of house sites declined after around 1600 AD. No more ahu were constructed or moai erected after about 1620 AD. When he wrote "Collapse", Diamond was assuming the radiocarbon dates placing first settlement around 800-900 AD were correct. If the most recent evidence bringing this forward to 1200 AD is accepted, the speed at which things went downhill is even more startling than Diamond had envisaged.

Diamond's book contained an estimate that the population of the island peaked at around 15,000. I have seen estimates ranging from 3,000 to 30,000. Diamond's figure appears to have been mainly based on estimates made by other researchers based on counting old house site foundations and making assumptions about how many had been occupied at any one time. Michael King in his "History of New Zealand" places the New Zealand population at 110,000 before European contact and observes that a settling group of 100-200 including 50 women could have produced this. The Marquesan population before European contacts reduced it to 2,000 (it's now around 8,000) is believed to have been 80,000 to 100,000.

Later, I came across a challenge to the traditional explanation for the break-down of society on Easter Island as outlined by Arturo and fleshed out in Jared Diamond's book "Collapse". This came in the same 2006 article in the American Scientist by Terry Hunt in which he up-dated the radiocarbon dates for first settlement of the island. Hunt had seized on the idea that rats may have been the primary cause of the island's environmental degradation. He pointed out that the rats which came with the colonists would have found an ideal environment in which to breed: a readily available source of food from palm kernels and bird's eggs; and no predators. Under these circumstances "rats can reproduce so quickly that their population doubles about every six or seven weeks." At that rate their numbers would soon have been into the millions. He pointed out that "almost all of the palm seed shells discovered on the island showed signs of having been gnawed by rats." He also cited examples from Hawaii and elsewhere in the Pacific where rats had apparently played a major role in deforestation.

He then went on to outline an alternative scenario for what happened on the island. The first settlers arrived around 1200 AD. Their numbers grew quickly, perhaps at around 3% annually (he compared this to Pitcairn Island where the growth rate was 3.4% after the Bounty mutineers landed.) At that rate "a colonising population of 50 would have grown to more than a thousand in about a century. The rat population would have exploded even more quickly and the combination of humans cutting down trees and rats eating the seeds would have led to rapid deforestation." He went on to conclude that: "The human population probably reached a maximum of about 3,000, perhaps a bit higher, around 1350 AD and remained fairly stable until the arrival of Europeans. The environmental limitations of Rapa Nui would have kept the population from growing much larger." He went on to conclude that: "There is no reliable evidence that the island's population ever grew as large as 15,000 or more and the actual downfall of the Rapanui resulted not from internal strife but from contact with Europeans."

I came across a further complication in recent research by the German ecologists Andreas Mieth and Hans Rudolf Bork of Kiel University who have studied the process of deforestation on Easter Island. Their study found that: "Over large areas, a single layer of charcoal and ashes several millimetres in thickness can be found deep below the recent surface and on top of the prehistoric garden soils that belong to the period of woodland gardening. The extensive distribution of charcoal layers can only have one explanation: widespread fires in the woodland of Rapa Nui." So they did not buy into Terry Hunt's theory that "the rats done it!"

I don't buy into his theory that the population of the island stopped growing at 3,000 either. The tiny resource poor Pacific island of Tuvalu with an area of 10 square miles (26 square kilometres), less than a sixth of the area of Easter Island, holds nearly 11,000 people. In a recent interview where Paul Theroux was asked about the changes he had seen in Africa over his years of travel he pointed out that when he was a Peace Core teacher in Malawi in the mid 1960s the population had been about a million (actually 4 million in 1966): now it was 13 million. I've been to Malawi to visit my brother's grave and a land flowing with milk and honey it isn't. Lack of resources does not appear to prevent human populations from breeding like rabbits (or indeed rats) unless controlled by disease or war. Short of the Ariki imposing a Chinese style one child policy (which would have been contrary to their own interests as they needed as much manpower as possible for the moai industry) it is difficult to see how the natural growth could have been prevented. Pacific islands are remarkably healthy places without the scourges like malaria, waterborne diseases and yellow fever which plagued tropical Africa and South America. I also doubted that a population of 3.000 could have afforded sufficient surplus labour to produce the array of ahu and moai to be found on the island.

Again, while the European contacts undoubtedly applied the coup de grace to the island through disease and kidnapping, if there was no civil war, as Terry Hunt contended, how do you explain the weapons found, fortified caves being used as dwelling houses, fortified chicken houses, the folklore about fighting between the Long Ears and the Short Ears, cannibalism? Cannibalism was common in Polynesia but it was invariably enemies who were eaten. I've seen the tree outside the church in Opotiki in New Zealand where the German missionary Karl Volkner was hung, prior to being eaten in 1867, accused of spying for the colonial government during the Land Wars with Maori. However, the fact that human bones have been found in Easter Island split to get at the marrow points to a culinary motive rather than a ritual one. If there was no period of starvation on the island, how do you explain the carving of the emaciated wooden moai kavakava? If there was no internal conflict, why were the moai toppled? Warfare was endemic in Polynesia before the arrival of Europeans, nowhere more so than in the Marquesas, where the Rapanui ancestors hailed from and as Herman Melville's stories highlighted. Samoa and Tonga engaged in periodic fighting. In New Zealand, an apparently peaceful colonial era, during which the flightless moa was hunted to extinction, lasted no more than 150 years until, as the population grew and the resources came under pressure, the classical period of history began, dominated by a warrior culture with fortified "pa" all over the islands, massive war canoes and pounamou (greenstone) war clubs. Why should Easter Island have been any different?

Jared Diamond doesn't spell out a specific date for the onset of hostilities on Easter Island but all the indicators point to the late 17th century. This raises an interesting question about the timing of the moai toppling phase. The earliest European visitors, Roggeveen in 1722 and the Spanish expedition in 1770, make no mention of seeing toppled statues. Roggeveen in fact reports that at least some of the islanders were still worshipping them. But he could only have seen a very limited part of the island on his one foray ashore which ended in a one-sided shoot-out. Likewise, I don't know how much of the island the Spanish managed to see. By the time Captain.Cook arrived in 1774, some of the moai had been toppled. When a British ship visited again in 1815, some moai were still standing, including some at Ahu Vinapu. Thor Heyerdahl was told that the tallest one ever erected, Ariki Paro, was the last to be toppled in 1840.

According to Katherine Routledge, the first Birdman cult competition took place in 1760. It occurs to me that the statue toppling may have been the result of the new religion finally taking hold of the whole island rather than during any earlier warfare. New religions tend to take time to become established, witness Christianity. A spot of moai trashing would have made a pleasant day out for a bunch of Birdman bigots, fired up by the new religion, relieved to find something to do with their idle hands and surplus energy now that the fighting was over. The incoming Christian missionaries were certainly ready enough to smash the old Polynesian gods all over the Pacific once they got their pious, bigoted feet in the door.

The charcoal layer above earlier woodland gardens found by the German ecologists was a bit of a puzzle. Two possibilities occur to me: the use of fire as a weapon during the civil wars; or if most of the trees were dead already and there were no signs of re-growth due to the depredations of the rat population on the seeds, it could just have been clearance of literally "dead wood" to provide some fertilizer. In "Collapse", Jared Diamond wonders what they were thinking when they cut down the last tree. Under my second scenario above it could have been: "I'd better cut this bloody thing down before it falls on my house in the next gale; after all, it's been dead for decades." In the second scenario it could have been: "Burn, you Long Eared bastards, burn!"

In 2011, when I was researching material for this chapter, Terry Hunt brought out a book, co-authored with Carl Lipo, called "The Statues That Walked" which elaborated on the theories set out in his 2006 article and drew on more recent fieldwork on the island. This book shed new light on a number of the questions which Hunt's earlier article had raised in my mind. I was particularly impressed with Hunt and Lipo's arguments against a civil war on the island. They pointed out that skeletal remains showed "few signs of lethal trauma." Also that there were no fortifications on the island: the smaller island of Rapa Iti to the west had hill-top fortresses similar to Maori "pa" but there was nothing of that ilk on Rapa Nui. (They suggested that the fortified caves were more likely to have been refuge places used to hide from 19th century "blackbirders".) Perhaps most convincing of all, they argued that the obsidian blades known as mata'a, which had previously been assumed to be weapons, were just multi-purpose cutting and scraping tools – their shape would have made them useless as projectiles in throwing spears and they were too thick and not pointed enough for stabbing. Captain Cook's expedition reported seeing a three feet long carved fighting club and some short wooden clubs like the Maori "patu" but when other early European visitors were attacked by the natives they just had stones thrown at them.

Hunt and Lipo also debunked Jared diamond's theories about the social structure of the island and its settlement pattern. Excavations in the "hare paenga" houses which Diamond had claimed were the houses of the elite "ariki" class had found no traces of domestic artefacts, which corresponded with accounts from early European visitors who had seen nothing in them but gourds. The suggestion was that they were used for ceremonial purposes associated with the "ahu" around which they were grouped. (This function would be consistent with the ceremonial houses at Orongo used by the Birdman cult.) Hunt and Lipo argued that there was no powerful central authority figure forcing the people to erect statues but that the population was widely dispersed over the island in independent tribal groups (presumably like Maori "iwi"). They pointed out that there were no towns or villages which would have been expected in a centralised system. They claimed that the Moai were an

example of what was known in the jargon of sociology as "costly sig-
nalling", a way of bringing the dispersed community together in a centralised, shared activity and establishing a social status pecking order
(or perhaps "pecker" order – "My moai is bigger than yours") as an
alternative to fighting over it. There was an interesting section entitled
"Reasons not to Kill" which argued that, in terms of evolutionary biol-
ogy, avoidance of conflict was the best strategy for long term survival. It
was pointed out that present day Rapanui go out of their way to avoid
conflict. (This would coincide with my own experience growing up on
a small island.)

I was less convinced by the argument that the island's population
never got above about 3,000 people, although obviously if the "hare
paenga" were not dwelling houses, that would seriously throw out the
calculations on housing density on which Jared Diamond had based his
assumptions and Hunt and Lipo pointed out that the structures now
visible had accumulated over centuries and in the absence of more
information on dating it was impossible to tell which had been built
or used at the same time. But I lost the plot when they launched into
a lot of sociological mumbo-jumbo about "bet-hedging" and "cultural
elaboration", suggesting that carving and erecting the moai in some way
helped to keep the population down. I found it difficult to believe that
the Rapanui gave up making babies in favour of making moai ("Not
tonight dear, I've got a moai to move tomorrow.") More persuasive was
their suggestion that female infanticide may have been practised – skeletal remains contained 14% more males than females and all the early
European visitors commented on the fact that there appeared to be far
fewer women than men. Also persuasive was their evidence that producing food on the island had been a struggle from the beginning, as
contrary to what might be expected, the volcanic soils were very infertile
– valuable nutrients had been leached out of them – and the climate
was at the margin for most of the traditional Polynesian crops they had
brought with them. Evidence of this came from the extensive use of
the small, circular, rock enclosures called "matavai" where household
waste and vegetable matter were used to enrich the soil and the extensive areas of "rock-mulch gardening" where broken surface rocks were

used to release nutrients and regulate soil temperature. The authors pointed out that where resources were scarce, the best strategy for long term survival was to limit the number of offspring.

I wasn't convinced at all by Hunt and Lipo's explanation of the end of the moai production line. They wrote that with the arrival of Europeans: "We see…a dramatic shift in the culture of the island away from their focus on statues as signals of prestige and towards the goods of….the Europeans. Some five centuries of tradition of moai construction ended nearly overnight." They argued that a "cargo cult" mentality developed: the islanders built "earth ships" – mounds of earth shaped like European ships where ceremonies were held in an attempt to attract Europeans to come with "cargo". They also argued that the population crash came from diseases introduced by Roggeveen's expedition rather than civil war, writing that: "The population likely soon collapsed to just a few hundred survivors, perhaps in only a few years."

Two things in particular worried me about these theories. According to Jared Diamond, no more moai were carved or erected after about 1620 AD: Roggeveen didn't arrive until 1722 AD and his expedition was only ashore for a day. Bearing in mind that this landing ended in a shoot out, how much direct physical contact was there with the natives? Was it enough to introduce disease? As regards the toppling of the moai, the Authors wrote: "In some cases toppling of statues may have been purposeful but many more likely came down as a result of inattention and lack of maintenance." The evidence that Arturo had shown us of rocks apparently deliberately placed to break the moais' necks had looked pretty convincing.

Hunt and Lipo's explanation of how the moai were transported to the ahu had me convinced. Previously, I had favoured the "canoe ladder" theory which involved the statues being pulled along on sledges lying prone. However, as suggested by the book's title, the authors believed that they "walked", in accordance with the local tradition. A Czech engineer, Pavel Pavel, had come up with this theory, which had been tested in 1986 when Thor Heyerdahl invited him to the island. It involved a group of men pulling an upright statue with ropes to tilt it on edge while at the same moment a second group pulled to twist it into its first step. Careful, rhythmic coordination enabled the statue to be wiggled forward in a walking motion. Using this technique, a small crew could move a moai 600 feet in a day. Two things converted me to this theory: the authors had inspected the moai which had been abandoned along the transport roads and concluded that they had all fallen from upright positions; and they had discovered that the moai were transported to the ahu in an unfinished state where their centre of gravity was ideal for this mode of transport.

The tour ended at lunch time so after a snack at the hotel I wandered down to the other little harbour, Caleta Hanga Piko, just below the hotel. A larger vessel than any I had seen in Caleta Hanga Roa was up on a slipway. I saw some oil storage tanks, sheds and workshops – this appeared to be the industrial area of the town. Two young men were sitting drinking beer outside a shack. They called out "Ia orana" and when I replied "Kia ora" one of them laughed and said in English "You don't look like a Maori." We got chatting and they invited me to join them. I had nothing better planned for the afternoon and thought it might be an opportunity to get an insight into the minds of the locals, albeit already fairly inebriated minds. It turned out that Raoul had spent some time in New Zealand. He had been in Papeete visiting relatives and got a job as a deckhand on a yacht bound for Auckland. Both he and his companion Rene claimed to be native Rapanui although both had Tahitian family connections as well. The subject got round to the relationship between the islanders and the Chilean authorities. By this time quite a lot of beer had gone down. Raoul banged his beer can on the rickety wooden table and said vehemently "We've got the Long Ears back! I'd like to burn the bastards out at the Poike Trench again." I remembered seeing a Chilean policeman on my first day, straddling his stationary motorcycle, black jerkin, dark glasses, crash helmet, face as impassive and merciless as a moai, looking like a cop from Bladerunner. He appeared to be overseeing matters at the local market, perhaps watching that none of the produce was contravening the Chilean equivalent of the Trades Description Act. With the beer fertilising my over-active imagination I pictured a scene where he shouted at one of the market women "Mira, Senora! Ese platano es demasiado curvado para vender."(Look here, Madam! That banana is too bent to sell.) And her replying: "Claro! Porque no metetelo por el culo para arreglarlo." (Obviously! Why don't you stick it up your arse to fix it?) This seemed to sum up the relationship between the two groups perfectly. Years later in 2010 I saw a BBC report that at least 25 people had been injured when Chilean police armed with pellet guns had attempted to evict a group of Rapanui from a building they had occupied for three months, claiming that the land the building stood on had been illegally taken from their ancestors. I wondered if Raoul and Rene had been involved, if they hadn't already succumbed to cirrhosis of the liver.

Flying out towards Santiago, Chile, with the UNESCO World Heritage Site island again spread out below me, I had felt quite satisfied with the answers to all the so-called mysteries of Easter Island worked out over time by a succession of academics: who had carved the statues; when and why; how they had been moved and erected; and what had happened to turn the people against them. But my subsequent reading has raised some serious doubts. Did the population ever rise above about 3,000? Was there ever a civil war? Did the moai just fall down from neglect as claimed by Hunt and Lipo or were they deliberately toppled? If the latter, could it have been the result of religious bigotry after the new Birdman cult replaced the old moai worshipping tradition? Personally, I think the jury is still out on these questions; some mysteries remain. And one very odd thing is still nagging away in the back of my mind that I haven't seen satisfactorily explained anywhere. How did the kumara (sweet potato), a native of South America, come to be a staple item on the Polynesian menu long before Columbus sailed to the Caribbean or Magellan's ship voyaged around the world? Michael King in his definitive "History of New Zealand" assumes that the Polynesians must have made it to the South American continent, left the coconut there and come back with the kumara. Hunt and Lipo also accept this as fact. But there's no evidence of it. I think I can hear Thor Heyerdahl stirring in his grave, "I bloody well told you so. Don't believe everything that Paul Theroux writes."

5

THE STATUE OF LIBERTY, NEW YORK, USA JUNE, 2000

IN JUNE 2000 I took a tour with the American travel company Tauck Tours through the Teton Mountains and Yellowstone National Park, starting in Salt Lake City and ending in Rapid City in South Dakota, travelling across the eastern flank of the Rocky Mountains. I had also arranged to fly on to New York from Rapid City and spend a few days there before continuing on to London. This wasn't my first visit to the USA. In September, 1996, I had taken a two week "Western Discovery" tour with Kuoni, a Swiss company that I had used before for trips to Brazil and the Far East. Since immigrating to New Zealand in 1997, I had also had a couple of stop-overs in Los Angeles and visited Hawaii twice, while travelling backwards and forwards to Britain, so I was already familiar with the American way of life.

I flew into Los Angeles from Auckland. Previous visits had established LA as my least favourite city in the world. It had been the first stop on my 1996 "Western Discovery" tour, my first experience of the United States, and had almost put me off the country before I'd seen any more of it. I'd stayed at the Red Lion Hotel near the Airport and had a day to spare before the tour began. I'd got the impression on the way in to the hotel from the Airport on the shuttle bus that this part of town was an urban desert but it was only when I ventured out on foot the next morning that this impression really came home to me. This was a city for cars, not people, demonstrated by the total absence of pedestrians. I had inquired at the hotel about getting a bus down to Marina del Rey which seemed to be the nearest beach-front area and the receptionist had given me directions to a nearby bus depot and a funny look. When I got there, I began to see why: it appeared that nobody used public transport except down and outs, drunks, ethnic minorities and the mentally handicapped. There wasn't much to see at Marina del Rey, just more concrete sterility. The next morning, the tour started with a trip around the city. We stopped in Venice for a look at Muscle Beach, where a number of beautiful, muscle-bound people, some of indeterminate sex, were working out, roller blading and generally showing off. There were stalls where hippy types in a time warp were offering palm and Tarot card readings. The beach was wide, the sand golden and clean, and the Phoenix palm trees atmospheric but for some reason the water didn't look particularly inviting and I didn't see anybody swimming: since it was an exposed ocean beach, I suspected that there might be dangerous rips; and I knew from my Geography studies that the California Current which flowed down the coast was a cold one. We continued on to Santa Monica pier. On a future stop-over, I stayed at the Pacific Shore Hotel, right down by the beach in Santa Monica and while it was an improvement on the Airport area, I still wasn't overly impressed – for me, it did not live up to its hype. I went to have a beer in a pub one evening and had to queue for a seat – you couldn't just walk in and have a drink at the bar. By this time I was familiar with the American nanny state attitude to alcohol which had led them into Prohibition in the 1920s and 30s when the sale of alcohol had been banned throughout the country, probably the most misguided social engineering experiment ever conducted by mankind, leading to the rise of gangsters like Al Capone and Jack Kennedy's father.

The tour moved on to Hollywood, along Sunset Boulevard to see Sunset Strip with its restaurants and night clubs and through the designer shopping Mecca of Rodeo Drive before driving past some of the fortified homes of the Hollywood stars in Beverly Hills. We stopped at Mann's Chinese Theatre on Hollywood Boulevard to see the Walk of Fame with the names of all the big Hollywood stars encased in stars on the side-walk. The hand-prints in the cement in a patio at the theatre seemed more appropriate to me, bearing in mind the reputation of some of the stars for drink and drugs: getting down on their hands and knees would have been no problem - it could also have saved LA law a lot of bother getting finger prints from them. On another stop-over, I stayed at the Hollywood Roosevelt Hotel, just across the road from Mann's Theatre. This was a livelier area, close to Sunset Strip for the night life but for some reason the glamour of the Hollywood movie scene never rubbed off on me in spite of the big white sign plastered along a hillside above me to the north to remind me where I was. I did see Michael Jackson one afternoon outside Mann's Theatre but soon realized that he was a phoney like most things in Hollywood. There was a big sign advertising Armageddon and I was getting a bit worried that I might have missed something on the TV news until I discovered that it was just a Bruce Willis film. In Hollywood, it was difficult to distinguish fact from fiction. We drove past the Central Business District, a sterile, amorphous mass of skyscrapers with about as much character as a high shelf stacked with cereal packets and then on through some dangerously seedy looking low-rise residential areas and along anonymous six-lane highways back to the sterility of the Airport hotel area. This was urban jungle of the deepest kind.

The following day we had a choice of tours. I opted to visit Universal Studios as I felt that a day of mindless escapism was just what I needed after the depressing impression I had got of the city the day before. This was not something I would have bothered with if I'd been travelling independently as I usually did; but I was pleasantly surprised. Escapism like this is what Americans do best; and God knows they've got a lot to escape from. Disneyland compares very favourably with many aspects of American society. I took the Jurassic Park ride in a raft through white water, being attacked by raptors and T-Rex; and the Back to the Future ride in a space ship – T-Rex again, just missing an ice-age avalanche and a surge of molten lava from an erupting volcano – it was scrotum tightening, adrenalin pumping excitement. I went to the Waterworld show and the Wild Wild West show; it was all good, clean American fun – I even had some apple pie at lunch time. But there's something wrong with a city where the most memorable and enjoyable experience is all make-believe.

The tour moved on down the coast to San Diego. The guide, Geoff, was an ex-US Marine, presumably not long ex as he appeared to be just in his early 30s and he ran the tour like a military operation – every morning there was a wake-up call time; a bags-out time; a breakfast time; and a departure time; and woe betide anybody who was late. Perhaps this was necessary as there was a full bus load, over forty people from a variety of nationalities and with a wide range of IQs. We by-passed San Diego to spend some time in Tijuana. This was Universal Studios' Mexico, the "Down Mexico Way" show, complete with ponchos, Mexican hats, Mariachi bands and the sounds of Tihuana Brass blaring out Latino music everywhere - make believe Mexico. It was one big bazaar, with souvenirs at prices Gringos could only drool at; the same went for the whores hanging out of windows above the shops. Back in San Diego we had a quick tour around the tourist sites; the old town where it all began as a Spanish mission station, the Wells Fargo Office reminiscent of the Wild West days; down the waterfront past some historic ships moored to the quay including the Star of India, past the cruise ship terminal and on to Seaport Village with its shops, pubs and restaurants; and on to the atmospheric Gaslamp Quarter with more restaurants and night-life venues. We spent the night in the Hanalei Hotel, Geoff's very early morning schedule warning of a long day ahead.

I summed up the following day in a postcard to my mother which I found when I was writing this chapter: "We came across the desert yesterday, through Yuma, a long drive, 360 miles with cactus everywhere." But what cacti: east of the Colorado River the weird looking saguaro, like giant candelabra, the stuff of boyhood western films, appeared among the scrub and creosote bushes and we saw tumbling tumble weed. All that was missing was Roadrunner and John Wayne chasing Apaches. The Colorado River formed the boundary between California and Arizona. By the time it reached the sea at the head of the Gulf of California there was very little water left in it. The mighty river which had carved out the Grand Canyon had been pillaged along its course to provide hydro-electricity, irrigate farmland and supply water to the teeming millions in Los Angeles. We saw an example of its use for irrigation in the Imperial Valley where it was used to grow melons, alfalfa and asparagus. There was potentially a serious water problem in the south-western USA. Eventually, Phoenix appeared like a mirage out of the desert, the skyscrapers of the Central Business District floating on the skyline like the backdrop to a science fiction film. It seemed a strange place to build a major city with 3 million people in the metropolitan area; summer temperatures reached away over 100 degrees Fahrenheit. We were staying in the Pointe Hilton Resort on the outskirts of Scottsdale, formerly a separate town where the famous architect Frank Lloyd Wright had been active, but now swallowed up by mushrooming Phoenix which had risen from the red hot ashes of the desert like, well, a Phoenix. I had a twilight stroll in the desert which came right up to the hotel and was surprised at the variety of plants which could survive in this harsh environment.

The following morning we set off for the Grand Canyon. Climbing up the Black Canyon Highway, we visited the ancient Indian cliff dwellings called Montezuma's Castle. It was not a castle, just a prehistoric high-rise apartment complex and had nothing to do with Montezuma who was an Aztec ruler in Mexico City, hundreds of miles to the south, who hadn't been born when the dwellings were abandoned around 1425AD. Apart from those quibbles, it was an interesting example of the pueblo style dwellings found scattered around this part of the arid south-west. They had been built around 700 AD by the Sinagua ("Without Water" in Spanish) people, in a high limestone cliff face above Beaver Creek, a tributary of the Verde River. Five storeys high with some 20 rooms accommodating perhaps 50 people, they were built of stone and mortar. Access had been by ladders for security purposes.

There were traces of an even larger building next door. The people had lived by agriculture, growing beans, corn, squash and cotton on irrigated land below, supplemented by hunting deer and bear. (It fascinates me that homo sapiens developed agriculture independently in different parts of the world using a different suite of crops – rice in the Far East; wheat and barley in the Middle East; and the maize, beans, squash staples in the Americas.) They wore cotton clothes and made pottery and basket ware. Archaeologists believed that the settlement had been abandoned due to droughts or warfare with other tribes migrating into the area.

We carried on to Sedona, in Red Rock Country, where among the startlingly red, sculptured, sandstone hills, the New Age fraternity had detected electromagnetic energy vortexes and had congregated here in droves feeding off the vibes and welfare cheques. Leaving Sedona, we drove through Oak Creek Canyon, the backdrop for many Western movies, rising towards the Colorado Plateau and arriving in Flagstaff set among Ponderosa Pines. Geoff showed us a section of the legendary Route 66 which had once been the main road west from Chicago until superseded by the I-40, part of the Interstate free-way system.. Just a 90 minute drive north from Flagstaff was the Grand Canyon. We arrived in the late afternoon when the light had softened, highlighting the colours in the layered walls of sedimentary rock in the giant ravine. It was a truly magnificent sight, nearly a mile deep, varying from four to eighteen miles across along its 350 kilometres (217 miles) length, the Colorado River flowing through the floor below so distant it looked like a mere trickle. When we left, we were stopped at a police roadblock near the airport, where a lengthy queue of vehicles had already built up. We could see Air force One, the President's plane, parked on the runway and word went round that President Clinton had been in the area that day opening a new section of National Park and was due to leave any minute. Geoff explained that for security reasons some of the Presidential party would leave by plane, others by road and nobody but an inner circle would know whether Bill was up in the clouds or had his feet firmly on the ground. Nothing new for a politician, I thought. Eventually, Air Force One took off with a roar and moments later a cavalcade of cars swept past us. I'm sure I saw Bill in one of them but I hardly had time not to inhale before they had disappeared into the sunset, so I can't be sure. We spent the night in Page on Lake Powell, a huge artificial lake created behind the Glen Canyon Dam, the last of the dams built to harness the power of the Colorado River.

The next morning we drove through the Painted Desert towards Monument Valley. This was Navaho Indian Reservation country, the largest Reservation in the USA, accommodating 250,000 Native Americans. From what we saw, the accommodation was not luxurious. Geoff pointed out a couple of round, half-coconut shaped, mud plastered, Navaho traditional dwellings known as "hogans" but most of the scattered houses were breeze-block shacks with corrugated iron or asbestos sheet roofs often surrounded by derelict cars and other debris. We stopped for lunch and a look at the museum and souvenir shop at Goulding's Lodge. There was a demonstration of traditional Navaho weaving of woollen rugs on hand looms in a hogan; the workmanship was impressive but so were the prices. I recalled that we had seen a few flocks of sheep on the drive in to the Lodge through the Reservation. When Geoff's appointed time to leave arrived, two young Japanese girls were missing. Two minutes passed, Geoff standing at the bus door drumming his fingers on the front seat back. You could have heard a pin drop in the aisle. Another half minute and he swung round, clapped the driver on the shoulder and said "Let's git the hell outa here!" Somebody muttered "It's been a while since Pearl Harbour, Geoff" but not loud enough for him to hear. We moseyed on down to John Ford Point to admire the vista of red sandstone mesas and buttes which had formed the backdrop to so many Western movies from John Wayne's debut in Stagecoach in 1939 onwards – the Three Sisters, Left Mitten, Right Mitten. A renegade Navaho that Geoff had brought along gave us a spiel on the Wild West from an Indian perspective: it sounded as if the characters John Wayne had played all deserved to be hung from the nearest cottonwood tree or at least have had their Levis hauled down and their asses whupped. Still no sign of any pesky Japs. We were given some time to take photographs. A taxi rolled up in a cloud of dust and the Japanese girls tumbled out, looking as if they might at any moment ritually disembowel themselves from shame. Geoff ignored them, looking inscrutable – no peace pipe was going to be lit up here. "Let's hit the trail" he said. Nobody ever missed a deadline again.

The canyon lands of Southern Utah held some of the most beautiful and bizarre scenery that I have seen anywhere. At Bryce Canyon, the Navaho Sandstone had been eroded by water, wind and ice to produce a panorama of multi-coloured rock pinnacles called hoodoos. We drove the 30 kilometres (18 miles) scenic road around the rim of the canyon, which was really an amphitheatre rather than a canyon, the land falling away below us in a series of irregular steps and terraces. Geoff said that there was a natural gradation of vegetation with altitude: Bristlecone Pines up where we were and on exposed rocky slopes unsuitable for other trees; Spruce, Douglas Firs and Aspens lower down the slopes, followed by Ponderosa Pines; and pygmy forest of Pinyons and Junipers in the hotter, even drier bottom lands. It was a wild, desolate but incredibly beautiful landscape – the rock pinnacles were bright orange, pale pink, ochre and red some like Thor's Hammer and The Sentinel standing isolated like gigantic sculptures. The Mormon settler, Ebenezer Bryce, who set up a farm in the area and after whom the canyon was named, summed up the landscape perfectly as "a helluva place to lose a cow." We stayed overnight at Ruby's Inn, just a mile north of the Park entrance, a huge ranch-style leisure complex offering a range of "wild west" activities from horse riding to panning for gold and sapphires. There was a mock up of a one-horse-town street with a jail, mining supplies store and fur-trading post. Or you could walk to the edge of the canyon and drink in the sheer beauty of the expanse of wild, jagged, pink, red and orange pillars spread out before you, bathed in soft light from the descending sun, the silence absolute; and imagine that you were an astronaut just landed on Mars. In the evening, we were taken in a horse-drawn covered wagon driven by a mountain man who claimed this was "Indian country" to a chuck-wagon set up in a clearing in the trees for a cowboy cook-out – a barbecue and a "mess of beans" followed by a hoe-down. More kitsch and make-believe but nevertheless very enjoyable.

The next day we entered Zion National Park through a tunnel from the east which took us into the canyon floor. The canyon had been eroded by the Virgin River which flowed swiftly through it, the walls soaring upwards for 600 to 900 metres (2,000 to 3,000 feet). The Navaho Sandstone shaded pink, orange, red, vermilion and white, eroded into shapes like mushrooms, toadstools, arches and pinnacles. Down by the river, there were meadows with stands of cottonwood, oak and willow trees. Back from the river in the drier areas were prickly-pear cactus with pink flowers and the distinctive Indian paintbrush with its bristly red flowers. The occasional waterfall tumbled down the canyon side.

In Las Vegas we stayed at the Hilton, such an enormous complex that we were given maps of the premises at check-in. The map was of no use in the casino: these places are deliberately designed so that you can't find your way out; there are no clocks or windows so that the clientele can't tell whether it's day or night. I've never been into gambling so I just had a cursory stroll around watching the punters trying to defy the law of averages. It has always been clear to me that the fact that a Mafioso, Bugsy Siegel, started the casino business here in the early 1940s, is a pretty clear sign that the customer is very rarely going to know best in those places. Las Vegas at night was a sight to behold, lit up with neon lights like an oil refinery, the various casinos competing to transport you all over the globe – Paris, Venice, Rome, Luxor, Mandalay, New York, even Camelot – anywhere except the middle of the Mojave desert. It was a make-believe world again but this time good, dirty fun – a place where born-again-Christians could go and be very naughty - secure in the knowledge that since they'd been saved their sins would be forgiven. Unless the wife found the credit card statement.

Next morning we plunged into Death Valley, out of the frying pan of sin and debauchery that was Vegas into the fire of the desert sun at 85 metres (282 feet) below sea level at its lowest point at Badwater, record temperature 57C (134F). It was just punishment for the wicked among us who had spent all night in the casinos or strip clubs. From Zabriskie Point we could see both the highest and lowest points in the area: Mt. Whitney, across the valley in the Sierra Nevada Mountains at 4,460 metres (14,494 feet) capped in snow; and Badwater to the south. Geoff told us that the valley had got its name from a woman in a wagon train that had set out across the desert in 1849 thinking it was a shortcut to the Californian gold fields. They survived as it was so late in the year (December) that the temperature had dropped and they had been able to drink water from melted snow after a snowstorm and later found a spring. As they left, the woman said "Goodbye, Death Valley." We stopped at the visitors' centre at Furnace Creek where springs had created an oasis complete with date palms. There was a display illustrating the environment of the valley, its geology, flora and fauna and its history including the former borax mining industry which had started in the 1880s. Lunch was in Scotty's Castle, a Spanish style hacienda with Moorish touches which had been built in the 1920s by a Chicago insurance executive called Albert Johnson and lived in till his death in 1954 by a desert hobo called Death Valley Scotty who was a friend of Johnson's. We continued north, the peaks of the Sierra Nevada Mountains rising to the west and then turned up into the mountains to spend the night in the Sierra Nevada Inn in Mammoth Lakes, a Swiss-style alpine ski-resort by a lake at the foot of Mammoth Mountain. I'm not sure of the precise temperature range we had experienced that day but it had been the equivalent of from the frying pan to the fire to the fridge, if not the freezer.

We entered Yosemite National Park via Tioga Pass at 3,060 metres (9945 feet) through the crest of the Sierra Nevada. The Tuolumne Meadows lay at 2,650 metres (8,600 feet) on the High Country plateau and the Tioga Road passed through rugged scenery of meadows, lakes and exposed granite rock faces with vistas of eroded granite peaks and domes. We stopped at the visitor centre to orientate ourselves. Driving past the Yosemite Valley entrance we climbed up to Glacier Peak for a birds' eye view of the valley and surrounding peaks. The valley floor lay spread out nearly 1,000 metres (3,200 feet) below; across the valley, the Yosemite Falls plunged nearly 750 metres (2,425 feet) over the edge of the plateau; to the north-east the profile of 2,720 metres (8,842 feet) Half Dome looked like a melon sliced neatly in half. The

Yosemite Valley had begun life as a canyon cut by the Merced River. It had then been widened and carved into a classic U-shape by ice during the Ice Age; then moraine left by the ice had dammed the mouth of the valley creating a lake. Finally, the lake had dried up leaving the flat valley bottom which could now be seen as we drove through it. Harder rocks like the Cathedral Rocks and El Capitan had been more resistant to ice erosion and now towered above the valley sides scoured bare by the glaciers. The minute figures of climbers could be seen high up on the face of El Capitan. We were staying overnight at the Yosemite Lodge near Yosemite Falls and the Village which left time to explore the valley floor. The Merced River had slowed up in its old age and now meandered gently through the valley, flanked by open meadows, wild flowers and flowering shrubs. There were oak woodlands and conifer forests with a mixture of ponderosa pine, incense cedar and Douglas fir. I visited the museum and the Indian Village which brought to life the cultural history of the Miwok and Paiute tribes who had inhabited the valley before the arrival of the white man.

On the way out of the valley in the morning we passed through the Mariposa Grove of Giant Sequoia trees, about 200 of them, the largest tree species in the world. According to Geoff the oldest one dated back 2,700 years. They were so large that in the late 1800s tunnels had been cut through two of them big enough for horse-drawn coaches and later cars. We were headed for San Francisco through the Sacramento Valley with irrigated crops of oranges, almonds and raisins. We passed a very large, very ugly wind farm, the individual turbines clustered close together and seeming to go on for miles. The concept of trying to reduce the environmental impact of industrial complexes appeared to be foreign to the Americans. Crossing the Oakland Bay Bridge, we entered San Francisco. Unlike Los Angeles this was a city where people actually walked in the streets and used public transport, the legendary cable cars – the steepest section on Filbert Street between Hyde and Leavenworth Streets with a 31.5% gradient was a buttock-clenching experience. The city even had a commercial and administrative centre around Union Square. I explored Chinatown and had one of the famous seafood chowders at Fisherman's Wharf. The Haight-Ashbury area was where the Californian hippy culture had developed in the 1960s and later the gay lifestyle had been practised more openly than anywhere else in the world until the Aids epidemic took its toll. American society was a strange mixture of tolerance and intolerance, nanny state and over-permissive-parent state, flower-power and police brutality, Prohibition and drug culture. I walked out onto the Golden Gate Bridge and looked across the Bay towards Alcatraz, the notorious prison island. So much of San Francisco had become familiar to me over the years from films and TV that it was almost as if I had been there before.

We set off through Silicon Valley, headed back towards Los Angeles, the last leg of the journey. In Monterey, there was a statue of John Steinbeck outside Cannery Row, now a strip of shops and restaurants on stilts but in the days when Steinbeck wrote his novel of the same name, the centre of the sardine canning industry until its collapse from overfishing in 1945. We took the scenic seventeen mile coastal drive from Monterey down to Carmel, stopping on the way for an obligatory photograph of the Lone Pine (actually a Cypress, Geoff said, always keen to be precise) perched on a rock outcrop with a backdrop of Pacific Ocean. There was also a colony of seals and some very entertaining prairie dogs which appeared to be auditioning for a Disney movie. Carmel was Clint Eastwood's town: he had been mayor and woe betide any citizen or visitor who besmirched its pristine townscape. This was an enclave for the filthy rich and it would make Clint's day to run bad guys out of town. The 160 kilometres (100 miles) drive down the Big Sur was one of the great drives of the world. The road hugged the rocky coast, sometimes cut into the cliff face, sometimes carried on bridges, always with spectacular views along the desolate, rocky shoreline with surf crashing and a mist of sea spray hanging in the air. In this wilderness area, forests of Monterey cypress trees, giant redwood, and stands of oak had survived American environmental rapaciousness. At San Simeon we glimpsed Hearst Castle high on a hill above the road, the former lair of the reclusive newspaper tycoon Randolph Hearst. Just outside San Luis Obispo, we stopped at the Madonna Inn to visit what must be the most eccentric gent's toilet in the world, a rocky grotto with gilt mirrors and water cascading down the stone face of the urinal. You wouldn't have been surprised if Fred Flintstone had shambled into the stall beside you. They advertised a Caveman Room (137) where the stone shower was supplied from a waterfall and the king-size bed could accommodate "two primates". The whole place from its fancy sign with a stage coach to the over-the-top honeymoon suites and brothel-style pink furnishings and décor, flowers everywhere, was American kitsch at its very best. We stopped for the night in Santa Barbara which had been destroyed in an earthquake in 1925 and rebuilt in "Mediterranean" style, all red tile roofs and whitewashed walls, the tone set by the old Spanish mission station around which the town had developed. The following day it was back to Los Angeles and the end of the tour.

My tour of the Tetons and Yellowstone in June 2000 started in Salt Lake City. The group was billeted in the Hilton, right in the city centre, 42 of us, all but five American. I had never been a great fan of group tours and had mixed feelings about my previous "Great West" tour de force with Geoff the ex-Marine but public transport in the areas we were headed for was virtually non-existent and the problem with a self-drive car through spectacular scenery is that it's difficult to watch both the scenery and the road. A tour also afforded a unique anthropological opportunity to observe Homo Americanus in their own habitat: I hadn't been overly impressed with most of the members of the species that I'd encountered abroad and on my last tour. On the afternoon of the first day we got under way with a trip out to the Great Salt Lake just west of the city. Large as it was, it was just a remnant of the former Lake Bonneville which had formed from melt water at the end of the ice age. Centuries of evaporation had concentrated the salt level until now you could have pickled herring in it, although amazingly some species of microscopic shrimp was able to survive. The salt flats around it had been used by boy racers like Donald Campbell to set land speed records and occasionally kill themselves. Just to the west of here at Promontory Point, a ceremony had been held in 1869 joining the railways which had been converging on each other from the west and east coasts, uniting the country and heralding in the main era of the "Wild West" as immigrants flooded west to take advantage of land offers under the Homestead Act of 1862.

In the evening, I went out to see if I could find somewhere to get a drink. I was aware that Utah, with its Mormon majority (70% of the population), was still effectively in the Prohibition era – at one time you could have as many wives as you wanted but couldn't buy a double whisky for love or money. I stumbled on a promising looking dive called the Dead Goat Saloon where the clientele looked too degenerate to be drinking orange juice and country music was wailing from an old-style jukebox. I walked up to the bar and ordered a beer from a barman who had a goatee beard and a face to match. "Are you a member, Sir?" he enquired. I explained that I was an overseas tourist and had just arrived in town that day. "No problem," he said, "I'll make you out a temporary honorary membership." And so I became an Honorary Member of the Dead Goat Saloon on the spot, entitled to get as pissed as a newt, prohibition or no prohibition. The previous ill-fated attempt at social engineering in the 1920s, when liquor had been banned throughout the States, had made fortunes for bootleggers like President Kennedy's father Joseph and numerous Mafia bosses. Utah obviously hadn't learned any lessons from that; they were still flogging a dead horse, or in this case, goat.

In the morning we had a tour of the city, starting with Temple Square where the magnificent Salt Lake Temple stood, its six spires soaring up towards heaven. Work had started on it in 1853 and it had taken 40 years to complete. Beside it, the Mormon Tabernacle, built to house meetings of the cult, had a roof shaped like an elongated dome, supported by 44 sandstone pillars so that it looked like a cross between a giant turtle and a deformed centipede. Next to the Tabernacle, the Salt Lake Assembly Hall had been built in Victorian Gothic style, looking like a miniature medieval cathedral. The northern side of the square was occupied by a bulky white office block resembling a wedding-cake. The whole area was beautifully landscaped with trees, shrubs, flowers and a fountain in the middle of the square. The Mormon religion (the Church of Jesus Christ of Latter Day Saints) had been founded by Joseph Smith, a farm labourer from New York State, who in 1820 claimed to have seen visions of the Angel Moroni (So why aren't they called the Morons?) who showed him a golden tablet, which he translated into the Book of Mormon setting out the principles of the new religion, including the belief that polygamy was good. Amazingly, this claptrap caught on and the cult grew in size. However, their beliefs attracted hostility and the sect moved to Illinois where the same thing happened again and in 1839 Smith was killed by an angry mob. Their new leader, Brigham Young, eventually decided that the only way to escape persecution was for them to "go west, Young Mormon" and in 1847 their covered wagons fetched up in Salt Lake City. At that time, Utah was still part of Mexico so they were outside of American jurisdiction. The following year, the war with Mexico brought the western part of the continent into the USA and the Mormons were once again in trouble with authority, particularly over their practice of polygamy. At one point in 1857 war even broke out with the federal government. Utah wasn't recognized as a State until 1896 after the Mormons had agreed to forego their Moroni-given right to polygamy.

We visited the Brigham Young Historic Park with a statue of the famous polygamist and the Pioneer Memorial Museum with memorabilia of the early settlers, Brigham Young's life story, and an eclectic assembly of dolls, clocks and guns. An underground passage led to the former Carriage House with a pioneer wagon, sleighs, handcarts and a blacksmith's shop. The Beehive House, Brigham Young's former two storey home had a large beehive on the roof, representing industry, the guide said. Outside, straddling Main Street, a Japanese style gateway was surmounted by a giant metal eagle with a 6 metres (20 feet) wingspan, hovering above the middle of the street. The archway framed the domed Utah State Capitol on the hill above, closely modelled on its namesake in Washington. Outside the Capitol, amongst a colourful display of red flowering cactus and marigolds, there was a statue of Massasoit, the Wampanoag Indian Chief who in 1621 had ceded 12,000 acres (4,725 hectares) of land to the Pilgrim Fathers for their Plymouth Plantation and started the chain of events which ended with the Indians losing all their land. The deal had been brokered by another Wampanoag, Squanto, who had been kidnapped and carried to Europe by earlier explorers and learned to speak English before being repatriated. He had shown the Pilgrim Fathers how to grow maize which saved their lives when their imported crops failed. It was sad to think how the kindness of those two men had been rewarded by future generations of settlers. From outside the Capitol the attractive City Hall building stood against a backdrop of the snow-capped Wasatch Mountains to the east, where we were headed next, Twin Peaks rising to 3,454 metres (11,330 feet). Park City lay at 2,120 metres (6,900 feet) in the Wasatch Mountains, about an hour's drive from Salt Lake City. It had started life as a silver mining town in the 1860s and a strip of well-preserved historic buildings remained in Main Street, converted to galleries, shops, restaurants, bars and hotels. The town was now a ski resort and nearby an array of impressive facilities were being prepared for the 2002 Winter Olympics. There had been the usual accusations of bribery and corruption in the process of bidding for the games but that now appeared to have become so commonplace that it was virtually an Olympic event in its own right. Park City was also home to the Sundance Film Festival founded by Robert Redford in 1981.

The following morning we drove north past the Great Salt Lake again and into Idaho for lunch, before crossing into Wyoming and heading for Jackson. This was a Wild West holiday town with the Sundance Inn, regular gunfights in the town square and an archway made entirely from deer antlers. Just north of Jackson was the entrance to the Grand Teton National Park and Jackson Hole, a valley which extended north for 50 miles between the Teton (Tit) Range to the west and the Gros Ventre Mountains (Big Stomach in French) to the east. Some French mountain-man must have been feeling lonely when he named these landmarks. The valley was drained by the Snake River, flowing south from Jackson Lake. We were staying the night in Jackson Lake Lodge, on a bluff overlooking Jackson Lake with a magnificent view across to the 40 miles long Teton mountain range, with twelve jagged peaks rising over 12,000 feet (3,700 metres), the highest point, Grand Teton, soaring to 13,770 feet (4,237 metres). These were the newest mountains in the Rockies, their straight frontage defined by a fault line, the sharp granite edges of their peaks chewed by glaciers, snow caps glinting in the setting sun. When I wandered out onto the veranda to enjoy the view, I spotted a moose beneath me, motionless, staring at the same scene as me. It obviously never got tired of it.

In the morning we took a raft trip on the Snake River. The river flowed through meadows and stands of cottonwood trees. We saw moose, a couple of buffalo, Canada geese, ducks and a beaver dam and a bald eagle sitting on a tree stump. Back from the river, terraces had been carved into the glacial moraine. The mountain slopes were clad with conifers, Lodgepole pine grading upwards into Douglas fir and spruce. The guide said that there were still plenty of black bears and grizzlies up there. Away from the river, in the drier parts of the valley, he said, the vegetation was mainly just sage brush supporting a lot of sage grouse. In the afternoon I took the hotel shuttle bus over to Colter Bay Marina on the lake with a good close-up view of Mount Moran and had a look around the visitor centre. The John Colter Chuckwagon restaurant looked appetising but we were being fed at the Lodge that night so I didn't sample their chuck.

The following morning we set off for Yellowstone National Park, the oldest one in the world, having been designated in 1872 – a remarkable first for Uncle Sam, not generally known for his Greenie tendencies. We followed the Snake River for a while, then its tributary the Lewis, past Lewis Lake, skirting Yellowstone Lake and then swinging west across the continental divide to the Old Faithful Inn, where we were to stay the night. The Park was centred on a volcanic plateau at an average height of over 2,400 metres (8,000 feet) with over 10,000 geysers and hot springs, more than half those in the world. It was what is known as a shield or super volcano with a huge dome of magma (molten lava) lying below the surface. The last time it blew its top around 640,000 years ago it created a caldera measuring 28 by 47 miles across (45 by 75 kilometres). When a similar volcano in

Sumatra blew up around 76,000 BC to create Lake Toba it is believed to have almost reduced homo sapiens to extinction through its effects on weather patterns – creating the equivalent of a "nuclear winter". An earlier explosion at Yellowstone had been dated to 1.3 million years ago. Assuming that the magma accumulated at a constant rate, you didn't need to be a mathematical genius to work out that we were due another one any day now. After lunch, I wandered out for a look at the Old Faithful geyser erupting. It went off every 80 or 90 minutes, lasting between 2 and 5 minutes and shooting 35 to 55 metres (120 to 180 feet) into the air. It was surrounded by yellow, orange and brown deposits caused by cyanobacteria and there was a hellish smell of sulphur – perhaps it should have been called Old Nick. The Old Faithful Inn was an impressive building, built in 1904 from local Lodgepole pine logs and stone, it was one of the largest log structures in the world. In the lobby there was an immense stone fireplace and a hand-crafted clock of copper, wood and wrought iron. The dining room featured etched glass panels and an impressive timber ceiling.

Next day we went for a tour of the Park. Lodgepole pine covered 60% of the Park, comprising 80% of all the forested area. There had been a recent fire which had burned off an extensive part of the forest. Previously, these fires had been fought, but the guide explained that they were now largely left to run their course as it was a natural process and helped to regenerate new growth. We saw a herd of buffalo (American bison). The guide said that the buffalo had practically become extinct in the wild in the 1880s but some ranchers had protected herds on their land and some of these had been re-introduced into the wild in the Park and now numbered about 3,000. This wasn't popular with ranchers surrounding the Park as they tended to stray out and carried brucellosis, a disease which could be transmitted to cattle. Likewise, he said, the Gray Wolf had been hunted to extinction in the area but had been re-introduced to the Park from Canada in 1995 and were now breeding, much to the annoyance of neighbouring farmers who were allowed to shoot any they found preying on their stock. At Mammoth Hot Springs, marble-like travertine had precipitated out from the boiling water to produce curtain-like terraces of rock. We stopped at Canyon Village to see the Grand Canyon of the Yellowstone, a 20 miles (32 kilometres) long gash carved in yellow and orange rhyolite rock by the Yellowstone River which fell 152 metres (500 feet) over two sets of waterfalls. We saw more buffalo in the open meadows of Hayden Valley before arriving at our overnight stop at the Lake Yellowstone Hotel right down on the Lake, looking across it to the snowy peaks of the Absaroka Mountains. I took a walk along the lake towards where the Yellowstone River flowed into it. A buffalo was grazing near a large shed so I crept up on it behind the shed to get a close-up photograph. There were dire warnings everywhere about not getting too close to these powerful, unpredictable beasts. A little further on another sign read: "Due to bear danger, the area beyond this sign is closed to all travel." This time, I didn't push my luck.

Next day we left the Park via the North-East Entrance and briefly crossed into Montana, "Big Sky Country". We stopped in Cooke City, a small one-horse town nestled at the foot of a rugged, forested mountain. There was some tourist accommodation, restaurants, cafes and bars relying on Park visitors. One establishment had a life-size model of a Grizzly Bear mounted on the roof ridge: it was so life-like that I jumped when I first spotted it; I thought it was about to leap down onto me and tear me limb from limb. There should have been a sign warning people with weak hearts about it. We followed the Chief Joseph Scenic Highway to Cody where we were to spend the night in the Holiday Inn. Cody was Buffalo Bill's town: he had helped found it in 1895. Buffalo Bill, alias William F. Cody, had been a Pony Express rider as a teenager before serving as a US Army scout during the Civil War. When the war finished, he supplied buffalo meat to the workers on the transcontinental railway, earning his nickname. With the completion of the railway in 1869, he continued hunting buffalo, but now with more sinister connotations. The 1870s was the decade when the showdown between the Plains Indians and the influx of settlers moving west reached its climax. The Plains Indians relied on the buffalo for their livelihood, not just its meat for food but its skin for shelter and clothing: it was the centre piece of their culture.

The US Government hit on a strategy to bring the Indians to heel. The Army paid hunters like Buffalo Bill a bounty for every buffalo killed. If the buffalo were exterminated, the Indians would starve, forcing them to come into the Reservations, an early manifestation of the Concentration Camp, which were being set up to accommodate them. This policy is neatly summed up in "Bury My Heart at Wounded Knee" by Dee Brown:

"When a group of concerned Texans asked General Sheridan if something should not be done to stop the white hunters' wholesale slaughter [of the buffalo] he replied: "Let them kill, skin and sell until the buffalo is exterminated, as it is the only way to bring lasting peace and allow civilization to advance."

From the beginning of 1872 to the end of 1874, 3.7 million buffalo were killed, only about 150,000 of those by Indians.

Dee Brown gives a lurid account of what happened next. In 1874, the Comanche Indians led a raid to drive the white hunters from the buffalo grazing land which had been reserved by treaty for the exclusive use of Indians. 700 warriors attacked the white hunters' base at Adobe Walls near the Canadian River but they were driven off and later congregated in the Palo Duro Canyon in Texas with hunters from other tribes – including Cheyenne, Kiowa, and Arapaho. The canyon was a last refuge for large buffalo herds as it had springs, streams and green buffalo grass when the plains above were parched. The Government ordered General Sheridan to force the Indians to return to their Reservations. Five separate columns of soldiers were dispatched from five surrounding forts, thousands of "bluecoats" armed with repeating rifles and artillery. One of the columns caught the Indians by surprise, burned their tepees, destroyed their winter supplies of buffalo meat and slaughtered a thousand of their ponies used for hunting. The Indians scattered but the soldiers methodically hunted them down, the survivors returning to their Reservations. By the 1880s the buffalo were practically extinct. This was one of the dirtiest tricks ever played anywhere in the world in the ethnic cleansing game.

With the buffalo gone, Cody started a Wild West Circus with real, live cowboys and Indians, including for a while the Sioux Chief Sitting Bull and toured the world with it from 1883 until World War I. In Cody in 1902, he built the Irma Hotel, where I had lunch and an advert said: "Cody Gunslingers Appearing Nightly at the Silver Saddle Saloon". I couldn't make it as I went to the "Nite Rodeo" instead at a stadium just outside the town. This was as authentic an exhibition of calf rop-ing and bare-back riding of bucking-broncos and bulls as you'll ever see. Back at the Irma, the gunslingers would have been firing blanks but these cowboys were genuinely risking life and limb. There was a life-like equestrian statue of Buffalo Bill brandishing a rifle outside the Buffalo Bill Historical Centre, which reputedly had "the most compre-hensive assemblage of material on the wild west in the world." As well as a section on Buffalo Bill's life and the history of the West, there was the Gallery of Western Art, a Firearms Museum and a Research Library. Unfortunately the section I was most interested in, the Plains Indian Museum, was closed for refurbishment. In the exhibition I discovered that Butch Cassidy and the Sundance Kid had holed up in Cody for a while: it always came as a shock to me that characters like these from school-days western comics and films were real people.

From Cody, we drove through canyons and high passes in the Bighorn Mountains into the Powder River country of open, high alti-tude grassland. This area had been the last refuge of the Sioux people outside Reservations and a few miles to the north was the site of the Battle of the Little Bighorn where Crazy Horse had wiped out General Custer's 7th Cavalry. We were due to stay the night at The Ranch at Ucross, a working ranch but also operated as a tourist attraction. As we approached, the sky grew darker, huge black clouds piled up and all of a sudden all hell broke loose, crashing thunder, blinding lightning and pouring rain – it was as if the bus was driving under a waterfall. We had had beautiful weather up until now but this was a reminder that in mountainous regions the weather can be unpredictable and danger-ous. We made it to the Ranch at very slow speed but any programme of ranching activities was a washout, literally.

Next day we headed into South Dakota and the Black Hills. The Black Hills of Dakota were an offshoot from the Rockies, detached from the main range. Rising over 2,150 metres (7,000 feet) the bare granite peaks were in places eroded into weird shapes such as the Cathedral Spires in the area known as the Needles of the Black Hills. They got their name from their dark green blanket of Blue Spruce and Norway Pine which looked black from a distance. Dissected by swift flowing streams and gorges, the Hills had been sacred to the Sioux tribe. An 1868 treaty between the tribe and the US Government stipulated that:

"No white person or persons shall be permitted to settle or occupy any portion of the territory [The Black Hills] or, without the consent of the Indians, to pass through the same."

In spite of this, some gold prospectors sneaked in, convinced that there was "gold in them thar hills". In 1874 the Government ordered General Custer to make a reconnaissance into the Hills with over 1,000 men, including geologists and miners, to ascertain the extent of any gold reserves. They cut a trail in for their supply wagons which later became known as the "Thieves' Road". Custer reported that there was an abundance of gold and prospectors started to flood in, the army doing little to stop them. The Government tried to buy the land from the Indians, who refused to sell; then they tried for mineral rights, which were again refused and negotiations broke down.

By this time the Government was becoming concerned that Indians remaining free outside the Reservation system were a threat to that system and a danger to settlers due to unrest over the Black Hills issue. It issued an ultimatum to groups of Sioux under Sitting Bull and Crazy Horse to come in to the Reservations or be hunted down. The ultimatum expired and army columns set out to bring them in. The free Indians congregated in a large village in the valley of the Little Bighorn River, around 10,000 people, perhaps 4,000 warriors. General Custer found the village and ordered Major Reno to attack it from the south but he was driven off and Custer's' 7th Cavalry, approaching from the north, ambushed and slaughtered. The Indians dispersed but were hunted down mercilessly. Sitting Bull retreated to Canada; Crazy Horse eventually gave himself up but was later bayoneted to death while allegedly "resisting arrest" at Fort Robinson. The Government confiscated the Black Hills and the remaining Sioux hunting grounds in the Powder River country. The free ranging Indians were disarmed, their ponies confiscated and they were confined to the Reservation – they were finished as a threat to the white man.

Subsequently, the Sioux Reservation was reduced in size. Then, in 1882, the Government proposed to break it up to provide land for settlers now streaming in from the east, involving the loss of another 50% of the remaining reservation. A Commission was set up to negotiate this and Sitting Bull appeared before it – he had returned from Canada and been arrested but released from prison in 1883. At his first appearance he gave the Commission a piece of his mind and walked out. On his return, Senator John Logan summarised the Government's attitude to the Indians:

"You are on an Indian Reservation merely at the sufferance of the Government. You are fed by the Government, clothed by the Government, your children are educated by the Government and all you have and are today is because of the Government. If it were not for the Government you would be freezing and starving today in the mountains. I merely say these things to you to notify you that you cannot insult the people of the United States of America or its Committees. The Government feeds and clothes and educates your children now and desires to teach you to become farmers and to civilize you and make you as white men."

In 1889 the Sioux Reservation was broken into small islands which became surrounded by white settlement.

After a lunch of buffalo kebabs at the K-Bar-S Restaurant in Keystone (the waitress assured me that they were from ranched stock and not rustled from Yellowstone Park) the tour moved on to Mount Rushmore National Memorial. Over 300 metres (1,000 feet) above us on the granite face of 1,760 metres (5,725 feet) Mount Rushmore, the stony faces of former Presidents Washington, Jefferson, Lincoln and Theodore Roosevelt looked down on us from on high. Washington's head was 18 metres (60 feet) high, his nose 6 metres (20 feet) long, his mouth over 5 metres (18 feet) wide – swollen headed, nosey and big mouthed enough for any politician. The Monument had been completed in 1941, just months before the Japanese attack on Pearl Harbour and had taken 14 years to complete under the guidance of the sculptor Gutzon Borglum.

A bit to the west was the work in progress of a giant statue of Crazy Horse. This was a project started by the sculptor Korczak Ziolkowski in 1948 and since his death in 1982 carried on by his family, financed by a foundation relying on private donations – not surprisingly the Federal Government had refused to fund a memorial to the man who had killed the national hero General Custer. When complete, the statue would be the largest in the world, measuring 173 metres (563 feet) high by 197 metres (641 feet) long depicting the Chief seated on a horse with his arm outstretched pointing ahead. So far, his head and the horse's head had been sculpted and there was a hole through the rock promontory where his armpit would be but there was a long way to go. There was a model of the intended final product in the nearby Crazy Horse Orientation and Communications Centre, where Sioux Indian culture was promoted. We watched a fashion show with Sioux girls in traditional dresses, using a tepee as a changing room.

To the south, a solitary stone monument in the Pine Ridge Indian Reservation commemorated where on December 29th, 1890, at least 150 mostly unarmed Lakota Sioux men, women and children had been massacred by the US Army's 7th Cavalry - the Wounded Knee Massacre Site. The tragedy had begun earlier in the year when a member of the tribe, Kicking Bear, had returned from a trip to Pyramid Lake, Nevada, where he had met Wovoka, a Paiute Indian prophet who had founded the Ghost Dance religion. Wovoka preached that Indians who performed the Ghost Dance would be carried up into the air while the earth was covered with a wave of new soil which would bury the white men. The suspended Indians would then be returned to earth along with their dead ancestors and great herds of buffalo and wild horses. Kicking Bear introduced the dance to the Sioux Reservations and it caught on like wildfire – the people danced from dawn far into the night. Women were particularly attracted to the new religion as it promised the return of warriors killed in the Indian wars. The Government became alarmed although the cult advocated non-violence. They thought that Sitting Bull was behind it and ordered his arrest, during which he was killed. They then set out to arrest Big Foot, another Chief suspected of fomenting disorder, and disarm his followers. At their Reservation on Wounded Knee Creek, one Indian, who was deaf, was slow to surrender his rifle and in a scuffle with soldiers it went off. The soldiers panicked and opened fire on the Indians who retaliated with knives, clubs and the few guns they had left. The Army then opened up with the four big Hotchkiss machine guns they had mounted above the camp, killing Indian men, women and children indiscriminately and some of their own men. Fleeing Indians were pursued and cut down by out of control troopers. In all, at least 150 Indians were killed (some estimates put the figure as high as 300) and 50 wounded. This took ethnic cleansing of the native people to new heights.

We spent the last night of the tour in the Hotel Alex Johnson in Rapid City. The hotel had been built in 1928 and according to their promotional literature Johnson had envisaged it as "a cultural show-piece that paid tribute to the people of the Great Sioux Nation"; a bit late perhaps. It was decorated with Lakota Sioux art and artefacts, 100 years old Navaho rugs, buffalo hides and old photographs. A farewell dinner had been laid on, which gave me an opportunity for some anthropological reflections on my fellow tour members. It was amusing to see how the group sub-divided itself among the different tables. I had got the impression throughout the tour that there had been a lot of subtle goings-on to determine the net-worth in dollar terms of fellow group members. When it was discovered that I was a mere public servant, a town planner of all things, with its connotations of socialism and state regulation, my social status plummeted: I would certainly not be at the top table. Looking round, you could have put a place card on most of the tables with a wealth range which would have covered all the occupants. I had identified two couples as filthy rich, older men with young "Trophy Wives" who were always impeccably dressed and tended to keep themselves apart from the hoi-polloi. I had placed a Californian lady travelling with her 30 something son, who was in computers in Silicon Valley, also in that category. Sure enough, they made up the "top table". As far as I could see there were two exceptions to this wallet-size based pecking order. Three very merry widows from Georgia, who called themselves the "Southern Belles", had put together a "Confederacy Table". They had been very friendly towards me but clearly I wasn't "Gone with the Wind" material. I was no Rhett Butler. I could never deliver a line like: "Frankly, my dear, I don't GIVE a damn!" or flog a slave like him. The Confederacy table was no place for people like me. The other exception was the "Latino Table", with the three Spanish American couples, although they all seemed to be equally well-heeled too. There were no African Americans in the group. There were also very few single people: I ended up at the table with an elderly Jewish lady from New York who was on her own and the two "overseas" couples – one from England and the other from Germany, neither of whom had appeared to mix much with the rest of the group. This segregation was perhaps not all that surprising: the old adage that the British and Americans are "one people divided by a common language" is not far off the mark. It was difficult to find common ground: for the most part their knowledge of the wider world was vague; and the most popular American sports like American football, baseball and basketball are black boxes to Europeans. While individual members of the group had been friendly enough towards me, the economic snobbery got up my nose as much as the class system in Britain. On the whole, I felt that old King George III had not been as mad as he was cracked up to be when he let them go after that storm in a teacup known as the American War of independence.

I had booked an extra night in Rapid City after the end of the tour in order to take a trip up to Deadwood, just a 45 minute drive north on the edge of the Black Hills. I remembered seeing the 1953 film "Calamity Jane" starring Doris Day and the words of the song from it "The Deadwood Stage" (Whip-Crack-Away!) came back to me on the drive up:

"Oh, the Deadwood stage is a-rollin' on over the plains
With the curtains flappin' and the driver slappin' the reins."

Calamity Jane had been a real, live character and so had Wild Bill Hickock, another denizen of Deadwood, who had been shot in the back while playing poker in a saloon there, holding the "dead man's hand" – aces of spades and clubs, eights of spades and clubs and possibly the nine of diamonds. Deadwood was a gambler's paradise again. It had been falling into serious decay until, in a desperate attempt to regenerate the economy, gambling had been legalised in 1989. By 1990, 83 gambling licences had been granted and the main street became "Gambler's Alley". I had a look around the Silverado and the Gold Dust Casinos. Kevin Costner, the star and director of the film "Dances with Wolves" which had been filmed in South Dakota and Wyoming, with much of the dialogue in the Lakota Sioux language, had bought a shop and converted it to a casino. Taxes from the gambling joints had been used by the City Council to restore the town's historic buildings and it was looking good again.

That night, back in Rapid City, I went into a pub for a beer after dinner. It was a bit dark and dingy and there were just half a dozen customers, all drinking alone. Looking round, I realized that they were all Indians, looking morose and already drunk. I wondered what Massasoit and Squanto, who had welcomed the Pilgrim Fathers, would make of this now. What George III's former subjects had done to the Native Americans was a crime against humanity and I was seeing one result of it now. Later, I saw a Wikipedia article on the internet on the 19th century American doctrine of "manifest destiny" which held that the USA was inevitably destined and had a God-given right to spread across the continent and was used to justify the war in 1848 which seized the western half of the country from Mexico and the Indian wars. The article included a reproduction of an 1872 painting called "American Progress", an allegorical representation of the settlement of the West. It showed a giant Columbia, a personification of the US, leading settlers west, stringing telegraph wire as she went, Native Americans and animals fleeing in terror.

I flew on to New York City, where I had booked a room in the Edison Hotel on West 47th Street between 8th Avenue and Broadway. It had obviously once been a very smart place but was now showing its age badly, although the Rum House Bar was good. However, the location was excellent, near Times Square and the Theatre District and not far from Central Park. The Manhattan system of street names was not very imaginative but it certainly made navigation easy. New York had been founded by the Dutch in 1626 when it was known as New Amsterdam. Legend has it that they paid the Algonquin Indians the equivalent of US$24 for the whole of Manhattan in goodies which would now be sourced from The 2$ Shop. The New York real estate market was born. In the early days, it was a den of pirates and prostitutes (nothing much changes through history as the 2008 collapse of the financial markets due to piracy by the inhabitants of Wall Street showed) until Peter Stuyvesant arrived to clean up the town, like a latter day Wyatt Earp in Tombstone, Arizona. (Of "The Gunfight at the O.K. Corral" fame.) Wall Street took its name from a wall built by the Dutch across the peninsula to keep out the Indians and the British: it crashed for the first time in 1664 when it was over-run by the British during one of the 17th century wars between Britain and Holland. The Dutch recaptured New Amsterdam ten years later but it was returned to Britain by treaty and remained in their hands as New York.

I walked down to Times Square, plastered with advertising billboards dedicated to the capitalist religion which had not yet fallen into disrepute. I had discovered that Gray Line operated a "Hop-on, Hop-off" tour of Manhattan which went round all the tourist sights in a red, open-topped, London-style, double-decker bus. A ticket was valid for two days and included a ferry ticket and entrance to the Statue of Liberty and Ellis Island. With the limited time I had available in the City, this seemed an ideal way to cram in as much sight-seeing as possible. I decided to spend the first day doing the full circuit and leave the visit to the Statue and Ellis Island out in the harbour for the second day as the tour leaflet recommended allowing three or four hours for that. Like San Francisco, the landmarks of New York had become so familiar to me through photographs and films as to produce a sense of deja-vu. I had also become acquainted with some of the iconic buildings through my Town Planning studies so it was almost like seeing old friends again. We passed Macy's, the famous Department store and I hopped off at the Empire State Building. When it was completed in 1931, this was the tallest structure in the world at 443 metres (1,454 feet) with 102 storeys. It had since been surpassed but remained the highest building in New York. In the lobby there were posters and other memorabilia of King Kong, a reminder that this was where the 15 meters (50 feet) tall ape had met his fate in spite of all Fay Wray's attempts to save him in the 1933 movie. I walked down 5th Avenue, New York's up-market shopping equivalent of London's Bond Street, past the Flatiron Building, which is considered to be New York's oldest skyscraper, completed in 1902, its odd triangular shape sometimes described as resembling an ocean liner as well as the clothes iron which gave it its nickname. Washington Square was the heart of Greenwich Village, the home of the beat generation in the 1950s and 60s but now rapidly moving up-market. I walked down MacDougal Street for a look at the Café Wha where Allen Ginsberg, Bob Dylan and Jimi Hendrix had hung out.

I hopped back on the bus at Union Square and we continued in a loop through Greenwich Village, past Soho, Little Italy and Chinatown, then swinging round the tip of the peninsula past the World Trade Centre and Battery Point, where the ferries left for the Statue of Liberty, and into Wall Street, home of the New York Stock Exchange and as events were to prove in 2008, the biggest collection of crooks on earth. We continued along East River, with the Brooklyn Bridge to our right and then north along 1st Avenue through East Village to the United Nations Building where I got off. The imposing building, completed in 1952, had been designed by Le Corbusier and its blue glass reflected the surrounding monuments and sculptures including a large globe. The 18 acres (7 hectares) site was not part of the USA: the UN had its own police force, post office and other public services – in this respect it was like the Vatican City in Rome. An air of reverence and gravity for the high-minded but not very effective organization was afforded by the stained glass windows by Chagall. I walked along 42nd Street past the Chrysler Building, another New York icon with its soaring spire. When it was completed in 1930, it was the first building to rise above 1,000 feet (305 metres) and the tallest in the world until trumped by the Empire State Building the following year. Just beyond, the concourse of the 1913 vintage Grand Central (Railway) Terminal was something to behold, the ceiling of the vast space decorated with back to front constellations of the zodiac and with a four-faced clock, each face made of opal, valued at between 10 and 20 million dollars.

I rejoined the bus for its circuit around Central Park. We drove through the Upper West Side past the Lincoln Centre, the Natural History Museum, the Cathedral of St. John the Divine, the largest Gothic style cathedral in the world and then swung east into 125th Street and Harlem, the centre of African American culture. We passed the Apollo Theatre, where black singers from Billie Holiday, Dinah Washington and Ella Fitzgerald to Stevie Wonder and Marvin Gaye had made their names and James Brown was later to lie in state. We passed the Harlem Market and Mosque, a reminder that there was a substantial Moslem community in the area. Parts of the district were run-down and dangerous looking but there were signs of gentrification with some fine restored old brownstone buildings: it looked as if Harlem was on the up. I got off for a walk through Central Park. This massive green space (it was over 5 kilometres [3 miles] long from north to south by 1500 metres [a mile] wide) had been laid out in 1858 and was a complete contrast to the teeming city surrounding it. I walked down to the picturesque Bethesda Fountain by The Lake: it was amazingly peaceful after a hectic day.

The following morning, I took the bus again down to the World Trade Centre and went up to the "Top of the World", the glass observatory on the top floor, from which there was a magnificent view of the city and out to the Statue of Liberty and Ellis Island in the harbour. It was an eerie experience, just over a year later on 9/11, to watch planes fly into the building. I carried on down to Battery Point and caught a ferry out to Ellis Island. The Island had served as the centre for processing new immigrants from 1892 to 1954. The imposing red-brick main building with its twin oriental-looking towers had been beautifully restored as a museum, the tiling and vaulted ceiling of the Great Hall inside a work of art. In the early 1900s, more than 2,000 immigrants had arrived at the centre every day, over 22 million during the course of the centre's operation. The museum contained an archive of those who had passed through, compiled from passenger manifests of ships docking at the island.

I caught the ferry again on to Liberty Island, where the Statue of Liberty stood, bearing aloft her torch of freedom. Strangely enough, the initiative for the statue had come from France. In 1865, a French politician with a very long name, Eduard-Rene Lefevre de Laboulaye had first suggested a monument to celebrate American independence and France's role in bringing it about (the French had supported the colonists against their British rulers) and had inspired the young sculptor Auguste Bartholdi to pursue the idea of a gift from the people of France to the United States to symbolise the spirit of successful revolutions in both their countries. France was to pay for the monument, America to provide the site and the money for the plinth. By 1874 the French had raised the money for the statue but it took a concerted campaign in his newspaper by the press baron Joseph Pulitzer to raise the money for the plinth. The statue was made in France and transported in sections for assembly on the site. The architect of the Eiffel Tower, Gustave Eiffel, designed the internal iron-mongery to support the copper cladding. The statue, called "Liberty Enlightening the World" was formally dedicated by President Grover Cleveland in October 1886.

It was an impressive sight on the small 12 acres (5 hectares) Liberty Island, the robed, female figure, representing Libertas, the Roman Goddess of Freedom, standing on a tall plinth, 93 metres (305 feet) from ground to torch flame. Her right arm held the torch of freedom aloft and in her left hand was a tablet with the date of the American Declaration of Independence, July 4, 1776, inscribed on it, intended to symbolise the rule of law. The seven rays of her halo symbolised the seven seas and the seven continents as well as helping her torch to enlighten the world. The statue had originally been a brown copper hue. However, it had fairly quickly taken on a green patina of verdigris as the copper oxidised, which gave her a softer, more venerable appearance. In the former museum in the base (its contents had been moved to the Ellis Island Museum) there was a plaque with a poem written in honour of the statue by Emma Lazarus, entitled "The New Colossus":

"Give me your tired, your poor,

Your huddled masses yearning to breathe free,

The wretched refuse of your teeming shore.

Send these, the homeless, tempest-tost to me.

I lift my lamp beside the golden door."

Not everybody was happy with the sentiments expressed by the monument when it was erected, suggesting that it was all just a tad hypocritical. According to Wikipedia, shortly after the dedication, the Cleveland Gazette, an African American newspaper, suggested that the statue's torch should not be lit until the United States became a free nation "in reality". Its Editor wrote:

"Liberty enlightening the world, indeed! The expression makes me sick. This government is a howling farce. It can not or rather does not protect its citizens within its own borders. Shove the Bartholdi statue, torch and all, into the ocean until the "liberty" of this country is such as to make it possible for an inoffensive and industrious coloured man to earn a respectable living for himself and family, without being ku-kluxed, perhaps murdered, his daughter and wife outraged and his property destroyed. The idea of the "liberty" of this country "enlightening the world" or even Patagonia, is ridiculous in the extreme."

He could probably have put in a word along the same lines for the Native Americans as well. Four years after the Statue of Liberty was inaugurated, The US 7th Cavalry massacred a village of Sioux Indian men, women and children at Wounded Knee in South Dakota.

6

THE KREMLIN, MOSCOW, RUSSIA JUNE 2005

DURING 2004, I decided to take a trip back to the Shetland Islands from New Zealand the following year by rail. I'd read a few travel writers' accounts of trips on the Trans-Siberian Railway, including Eric Newby, Dervla Murphy and Paul Theroux, and it sounded interesting – in the sense of the old Chinese curse: "May you live in interesting times." I decided not to do the full seven days, 9,289 kilometres (5,806 miles) marathon from Vladivostok to Moscow but to take the Trans-Mongolian from Beijing which joined the Trans-Siberian line near Ulan Ude, east of Lake Baikal. This would still involve five full 24 hour days on trains. I planned stops in Ulaan Baatar, Irkutsk and Ekaterinburg to break the journey and get a taste of Mongolia and Siberia, and then spend a few days in Moscow to see, among other things, the Kremlin. From Moscow, my plan was to carry on by train all the way to Amsterdam, from where I could get a flight to Edinburgh. I discovered that buses were more practical for the section of my planned route between Riga in Latvia and Warsaw, via Vilnius, the capital of Lithuania. I borrowed a Russian language self-tuition package from the library and started to give myself a crash course in Russian.

In June 2005, I flew to Hong Kong and then on to Beijing to catch the Trans-Mongolian train to Ulaan Baatar, the capital of Mongolia. This first leg was scheduled as a 30 hour, 1,551 kilometres (969 miles) sojourn, part of which was through the Gobi Desert. The taxi driver dropped me a good two hundred metres from the station entrance: I wasn't able to figure out why. I found the platform without much difficulty as signs and the Arrivals and Departures board were in English as well as Mandarin. Even more helpful, the positions where the coaches would stop were identified by their numbers on the platform. I was booked on train No.23 which arrived at the platform well before the scheduled departure time. I found my 1st class sleeper compartment, two narrow bunks with a table between them, small but clean and comfortable looking. The coach attendant showed me the wash room and toilet down at the end of the narrow corridor, basic but clean. Nobody turned up to occupy the other berth so it looked as if I had the compartment to myself as we left right on time at 7.40 am. I'd prepared myself for the long journey with a lot of hours of reading material: Leo Tolstoy's "Anna Karenina" (I'd already read his punishingly long "War and Peace " which would have been more than enough to fill in the idle moments of a trip to Mars); Boris Pasternak's "Doctor Zhivago" (David Lean's 1965 film of the book was one of my all-time favourite films – I'd seen it three times in Kampala, Uganda with my African girlfriend, Marita); and some Russian language aids – a phrase book, dictionary, Cyrillic alphabet and vocabulary cards. To begin with, I didn't need these distractions, as the Chinese landscape slipped past. We stopped at Nankou to have a rear engine attached to help push us over the mountains ahead. At Badaling, we emerged from a long tunnel to see a stretch of the Great Wall appearing on ridge lines above us. I had visited it in 2002 on a tour through China and the sight of it again brought back forgotten memories. We continued through a series of tunnels, each time emerging to a view of a new section of Great Wall. At Kanzuang, the rear engine was detached. Shortly afterwards we crossed the San

Gan River, where there were farms and orchards and a backdrop of mountains. I was surprised how quickly the time passed just watching the scenery with the occasional foray out into the corridor to see the other side of the tracks and observe my fellow travellers – there were some other Europeans but the majority were locals. At lunch time, I went along to the dining car and had some beef noodles and a Tsingtao beer. The menu had a reasonable selection of Chinese dishes and the noodles were delicious. I thought British Rail's catering corps could have learned some lessons from them. The Chinese décor incorporated the obligatory red and green dragons here and there. I was glad that I'd opted for a bit of variety on the trip: this was a Chinese train; I assumed the next leg from Ulaan Baatar would be on a Mongolian one; and then from Irkutsk I would be at the mercy of the "babushkas" (carriage attendants/grandmothers) of Mother Russia.

As we approached the industrial city of Datong, we passed through the coal mining area of Hebei Province. After Datong, we entered Shanxi Province, still seeing sections of the Great Wall from time to time. Beyond Jining, the green hills and valleys petered out and we were into the fringes of the Gobi Desert in the semi-autonomous Province of Inner Mongolia. Around 9.00 p.m. we drew into the border town of Erlian where we were gone over by Chinese Customs and Immigration and had the wheels changed in a huge shed. Mongolia, following Russia's lead, used a wider track gauge than the rest of the world. Each carriage had to be lifted of its underlying bogie and swung across to the wider version, a process taking about an hour. When we crossed into Mongolia, darkness had fallen and we spent another couple of hours in the border post at Zamyn-Udd while Mongolian Customs and Immigration officials slowly made their way through the carriages. I got a few hours sleep and woke up when we reached Sainshand after 5.00 am. We were in deepest Gobi by now and I watched the flat, arid landscape slip past. Amazingly, even in this bleak, desolate wilderness an occasional group of gers appeared (round tents made from canvas with layers of sheep's wool felt, sometimes called yurts) with herds of sheep, goats, horses and camels. How they could survive on the few sparse clumps of grass and shrubs visible was beyond me. I went back to sleep. We stopped in Choir around 9.00 am: there was a group of multi-storey apartment buildings standing in the middle of nowhere. A friendly local out in the corridor said it was a former Soviet military airbase but was now empty. Mongolia had cut its self free from the USSR's apron strings in 1991 after the collapse of the communist system. As we continued north, the desert gave way to steppe grassland and approaching Ulaan Baatar through the rolling hills of the Bogdkhan Uul Mountains, trees appeared and gers became more numerous with bigger herds of horses, sheep and goats. We arrived in Ulaan Baatar bang on time at 1.10 pm.

I was staying at the Chinggis Khaan Hotel in the centre of the city. Old Chinggis was everywhere; the local beer even bore his name. He was credited with having unified the local tribes into a nation in 1206 AD. They then went on to conquer a huge swathe of the known world reaching as far west as Hungary and Poland and were at the gates of Vienna when political unrest back home led them to withdraw. They had ruled China as the Yuan Dynasty and subdued Mesopotamia and Persia. One group, known as the Golden Horde or Tatars kept the Russian rulers under control and extracted tributes from them until Ivan the Terrible finally managed to throw off the yoke in 1552. Their descendants ruled India as the Mogul Emperors: all this from a population of no more than a million at the time. But they had a horseback mounted army of 100,000 men armed with a lethal bow and arrow which they fired from the saddle and that was the weapon of mass destruction of its day. When on campaign, they could live off mare's milk and blood from their ponies and so were highly mobile. They also employed terror tactics to encourage cities to surrender to them. Any city that resisted and had to be taken by force of arms had their entire population massacred as a lesson to others.

Walking around Ulaan Baatar now, it was difficult to envisage this glorious past. But they had always been a nomadic race. Their capitals had always been just temporary ger encampments. The present site had been permanently occupied since 1778 but again had just been essentially a ger camp until the 1920s. The Manchus who had founded the last Chinese dynasty, the Ching, were related to and closely allied with the Mongols and Mongolia was part of the Chinese Empire when the last Emperor was deposed in 1912. They had broken away from China at that time but at the end of World War I in 1918 China invaded to bring them back into the fold. Then in 1921, Russia invaded and aided by a local communist insurgency pushed the Chinese out. In 1924, a communist republic was set up, essentially just a puppet of the new USSR. The city was renamed Ulaan Baatar (Red Hero) to commemorate this event. An equestrian statue of the local hero who had led the communist insurgency, Damdin Sukhbaatar, stood in the central square, Sukhbaatar Square, and behind him the modern Parliament building with its classical columns. Coming into the city on the train, I had seen it sprawling for miles along the north side of the valley of the insubstantial Dund Gol (River). In the taxi to the hotel from the station I had passed streets of characterless soviet-style multi-storey apartment blocks and strangely impermanent looking low-rise housing often with gers in the yards as if even the permanent structures had been designed with moving away in mind. Now in the city centre and along the main street, Peace Avenue, which led into it, the public and commercial buildings had the austere look associated in my mind with soviet architecture. So the city was really just the product of what had amounted to a Soviet occupation from 1924 until the collapse of communism in 1991 when Mongolia had had its own velvet revolution and broken free. I had walked past a statue of Lenin on my way into the centre from my hotel and all the signs were in the Russian (Cyrillic) alphabet. It was now a bustling metropolis of around a million people, a third of the country's total, and there were harbingers of a blossoming economy in the form of some Chinese style glass tower blocks. I had read that Mongolia had promising reserves of copper, coal, gold and other minerals and that the multi-national vultures were hovering around. There were also a surprising number of international restaurants and western style bars. In the evening I had one of the best French meals I've ever eaten in Le Bistro Francais, just north of the Parliament building – the duck magret was exceptional and they even had French wine at reasonable prices. I normally sample the local cuisine when I'm travelling but what I had read about Mongolian food didn't tempt my taste buds. In 'Riding the Iron Rooster' Paul Theroux wrote that: "The Mongolians had a way of making food inedible or disgusting and they could transform even the most inoffensive meal into garbage, by serving it cold, or sprinkling it with black carrots, or garnishing it with a goat's ear." While young yak's udder braised in fermented mare's milk (and garnished with a goat's ear) may well have been to die for (probably painfully), I decided to put off exploring the Mongolian haute cuisine trail for another day. I went along to the Budweiser Bar, just off the main square, for a drink after the meal and was invited to join a very jolly group of four revellers from the Government Policy and Planning Department who were obviously having a night on the town and decided that it was government policy that foreigners like me shouldn't be drinking alone. The two men would have been in their mid thirties, the girls younger. They all spoke good English. One of them, Batsuren, presented me with his business card which identified him in English as a Senior Officer. They were excellent company and Batsuren had travelled a lot outside Mongolia and was well informed about world affairs. However, as the drinks flowed, the conversation got less serious and when I told them that I was having a tour of the city the following morning which included a performance of traditional music and dance, Batsuren threatened to give me a preview of traditional throat singing, the girls shrieking "No! No!" They had obviously heard him before. I decided to leave before the conversation got round to another Mongolian obsession, wrestling, and I was invited to participate in a demonstration.

I was picked up for the city tour in the morning, just myself in a mini-bus with a driver and guide. We crossed the valley to the Winter Palace of the Bogd Khan, their last king and the former head of the Buddhist faith in Mongolia, believed to have been a living Buddha like the Dalai Lama. It had been built between 1893 and 1903 but converted to a museum when the communists took over and cracked down on religion. It was full of stuffed animals – he had had a zoo – and a ger was lined with the skins of snow leopards, 150 of them according to the guide – I was too sickened to count them. There was an excellent view of the city from the palace, spread out along the valley side opposite, and there were some pleasant stands of trees. As we drove around the city, I was amazed at the number of gers tucked in among the permanent buildings. According to Paul Theroux when he passed through in 1987 on his Riding the Iron Rooster trip, 35% of the population lived in gers. We visited the National History Museum just off the main square where there was an excellent display on the Golden Horde which had set out to conquer the world in the 13th century and an interesting Stone Age section with some exquisite gold artefacts found in graves. There was a section on the various ethnic groups with examples of their costumes, hats and jewellery, some incorporating an amazing amount of silver ware – presumably not worn to milk the yak. A furnished ger was the centrepiece of a section on traditional culture with farming implements, domestic utensils and musical instruments. We finished in the section on the 1990 Democratic Revolution, the outcome of which history will no doubt eventually reveal: the jury was still out. Nearby was the Museum of Natural History where the highlight was undoubtedly the dinosaurs, especially the pair fighting, which according to the guide had been buried alive in mid scrap 80 million years ago – possibly by a sand dune collapsing on top of them. I wondered if they might have been having sex: "Darling, did the earth move for you?" We moved on to the Gandan Monastery, out on the west side of town. Buddhism had had a spectacular revival since the fall of the communist regime. In 1937 the communists had suppressed religion and carried out purges against the priesthood. Around 900 monasteries were destroyed and Gandan, which had housed 5,000 monks, was partially destroyed, the rest used to house Russian officials and as stables for their horses. Throughout the country, Buddhist monks were killed, jailed, or conscripted into the army, the survivors joining the laity. In 1944, part of Gandan had been re-opened as a government show piece to demonstrate to foreign visitors that Buddhism hadn't been completely eradicated. Now there were again 900 monks, with temples, colleges and a university within the complex. Monasteries and temples were being rebuilt all over the country. The main temple was full of Bhudda statues including one 26 metres (78 feet) tall made of bronze covered in gold. This was a recent replacement: the original, which had been stolen by the Russians, had been commissioned by the Bogd Khan (Chief Priest) in 1911 in the (vain) hope that it might restore his eyesight which he had lost through syphilis. I didn't inquire how come a celibate monk, nay, a living Buddha, caught syphilis in the first place but I suppose monks will not be monks from time to time like the rest of us. Some medieval Italian popes had had the same problem. Perhaps it was just another miracle – if you could have an immaculate conception, why not an immaculate dose of the clap?

After the tour, I went to a supermarket to stock up on food and drink for the next leg of my journey to Irkutsk the following day. My trip notes pointed out that there was no restaurant car on my train, which was probably just as well if Paul Theroux had got his culinary information correct. He had visited food shops and listed what he saw there including basins of yellow goats' ears, chunks of rancid mutton and chicken feet. The menu had obviously improved since he'd been in town: I managed to find some salami, bread, biscuits, cheese, butter and fruit, fruit juice, tea bags and a bottle of vodka – another dubious gift from Mother Russia to her Mongolian vassals: there were an awful lot of drunks around town.

Train No.5 to Irkutsk left right on time at 1.50 p.m. This leg was a bit shorter, 1,120 kilometres (700 miles) and just over 24 hours duration. The layout was the same as the Chinese train with two bunks in the first class compartments but everything seemed to be a bit shabbier, worn-out looking. This time, I had a cabin mate, a man in his forties wearing a dark suit who introduced himself in English as Valentin. He looked Mongolian but said he was from Ulan-Ude in Russia. I later discovered that he was a Buryat, one of the native Siberian tribes that the Russians had absorbed as they conquered their "Wild East". They were closely related to the Mongols and it emerged later that Valentin could understand and speak Mongolian as well as a bit of English. He said he was a Civil Engineer. The scenery north of Ulaan Baatar was rolling grassy hills with patches of wild flowers and grazing animals around the ubiquitous gers. In a siding at Zuunkahara, there was a long line of wagons loaded with logs. Valentin said that there was a big trade in timber to China from Siberia now. He added with a rueful grin that an awful lot of copper wire and even pipelines went in the same direction, pirated by the Russian Mafia from moribund factories which hadn't been able to compete in post-communist times and even from still operational infrastructure projects. South of Darkhan, the grass-land became less lush and green and birch and pine trees appeared on the hills in the distance. I thought I saw a yak, which Valentin con-firmed. I said it was a bit odd, considering that Mongolia and yaks tend to be inseparable in the Western mind, that this was the first one I'd seen. He said that they were more common in the remote mountain areas. We stopped in Darkhan, a large industrial town of Soviet-style apartment blocks. I had brought out the vodka bottle just before we arrived and poured us each a shot. Valentin spotted a little stall on the platform where a Mongolian equivalent of a babushka was selling mut-ton dumplings – "buuz" he called them. He said since I was providing the vodka, he would provide the antidote – he claimed that they were good for soaking up the effects of the alcohol. I still hadn't sampled the local cuisine so this seemed like a good opportunity. The buuz turned out to be excellent. Valentin said that you could get similar ones in Russia which were colloquially known as "pissing dumplings" because of the way the juice squirted out of them when you stuck a fork in. We arrived at the border at Sukhbaatar before 9 p.m. and by the time we had cleared Customs and Immigration and crossed over to the Russian side at Naushki for an even more thorough going over it was dark. The Russian border officials were stony faced and brusque to the point of rudeness. They searched diligently, even lifting floorboards in the cor-ridor, on the lookout for contraband and back-handers. The regime might have changed but no-one had given these people a course on customer care yet. They fitted my preconceived idea of the profile of a Soviet apparatchik perfectly. The border crossing must have taken over five hours but we managed to make it relatively painless: the vodka bot-tle ebbed steadily and Valentin proved to be a very entertaining com-panion. He said he was badly out of practice in English but with the aid of my Russian phrase book and dictionary and my own rudimentary Russian it was amazing how wide ranging a conversation we managed to have. I pumped him for information about what things had been like in Russia following the collapse of communism and it sounded as if anarchy had ruled under Boris Yeltsin in the 1990s. He said that the Mafia had more or less taken over Irkutsk and they still had a strong hold there, particularly in the drug trade which had precipitated an HIV and Aids epidemic through needle sharing and prostitution to support drug habits. Unemployment had soared in Siberia with factories closing down when they had to compete in a capitalist system. The environmental and health problems generated from some of the formerly secret nuclear installations east of the Urals and from leaking oil pipelines were only now coming to light. He said that a lot of people were turning to drink or religion to provide solace. Buddhism was making a strong comeback among his tribe, the Buryats, and even the old religion, Shamanism, was undergoing a revival, people worshipping the sun, moon and the natural world. I told him that that made more sense to me than all the cock and bull preached by the major world religions. Sometimes you can discuss politics and religion with complete strangers over a drink without ending up killing each other. We eventually made it out of Naushky headed for Ulan-Ude through the valley of the Selenga River which I had glimpses of through the darkness before we turned in. Valentin said that we were in his native land now, Buryatiya.

We arrived in Ulan-Ude around 7.15 a.m. Valentin was leaving the train here. He looked like I felt, severely hung-over, as we shook hands. We had joined the Trans-Siberian Railway proper at Zaudinsky, 13 kilometres (8 miles) east of Ulan-Ude so from here it was steadily westwards all the way to Moscow. The wild scenery on the way to Irkutsk was some of the best on the whole trip. We started off following the Selenga River as it wound between forested hills, the spruce, fir, pine, larch combination of the "taiga" which I was to become all too familiar with as I progressed through Siberia but which had a novelty factor after the desert and steppe lands of Mongolia. Not far out of Ulan-Ude, we swung across the river on a bridge, giving spectacular views along the valley. Just past Selenga station, we left the river to make its way into Lake Baikal and then a bit further on we emerged from the forested hills and a vista of the vast blue lake opened up in front of us, the cliffs on the other side visible in the distance. The line now followed the shore of Lake Baikal for 200 kilometres (125 miles) passing in and out of tunnels blasted through the cliffs lining the lake. Inland, to the south, there were glimpses of the snow capped Khrebet Khamar Daban mountain range which rose to nearly 5,000 metres (16,000 feet) along the Mongolian border. We stopped at Mysovaya (Babushkin) where there had been a gap in the Trans-Siberian railway between 1900 and 1904 which had been plugged by an ice-breaker ship carrying trains across from Port Baikal on the other side of the lake at the mouth of the Angara River. It had initially been thought that building a line around the south end of the lake would be prohibitively expensive but the ferry service was not a success due to weather interruptions and an experiment with a temporary line laid across the ice in winter ended disastrously when a train plunged through and sank. So the lake shore route was built after all. At Baikalsk, a huge pulp and paper mill spilled its effluent into the erstwhile pristine lake and you could smell the sulphur in the air even with the train windows shut. I had lived in Kawerau in New Zealand for a while next to the massive Tasman plant of the same type and knew that they were not good neighbours. From Sluydyanka near the end of the lake, the line now cut across country through forested hills directly towards Irkutsk. In the 1950s a giant hydroelectric dam had been built across the Angara River at Irkutsk, flooding the section of railway from Irkutsk to Port Baikal. The old line between Port Baikal and Sluydyanka was still open, a little-used branch line, but now being promoted as a scenic route for tourists and railway buffs. We arrived at Irkutsk station at 2.15 p.m., exactly on schedule again. I was impressed.

I was booked into the Rus Hotel in Ulitsa (Street) Sverdlova, right in the city centre. The 2003 edition of the Lonely Planet guide said it was "comfortable, great value and usually booked solid." They didn't mention that it was staffed by the most unfriendly, unhelpful, hard-faced women I have ever encountered. Perhaps they were former tractor drivers or shot-putters re-trained for the hotel industry but their training obviously hadn't got the concept of customer service across to them. The bedroom was reasonably clean but the plumbing and electrics left much to be desired – the hot and cold taps were the wrong way round, the sink plug was missing (this seemed to be standard in Russia including on the Trans-Siberian), the shower temperature adjuster knob kept falling off, only half the lights worked and there were bare wire ends hanging down where a lamp had been removed. Paul Theroux had described a similar scenario in a hotel on Lake Baikal in "Riding the Iron Rooster". He had added the comment: "How had these people sent rockets to Mars?" The breakfast the following morning was the worst I have ever had thrown at me: there was no choice, take it or leave it – cold, lumpy porridge, black bread so stale and hard that if I'd dropped it on the floor it would have bounced back onto the table and some sort of spam-like cold meat so greasy and gristle-infested that it was inedible. It brought to mind Paul Theroux's description of Mongolian food – all that was missing was a pig's ear garnish.

After I'd checked into the hotel and half-scalded myself when the shower knob fell off, I decided to take a walk around the city centre. I asked at Reception if they had a map of the city but got what I came to know and love as the standard stony-faced answer to all my inquiries or requests: "Nyet" (No.) But there was a map in my guide book, so I retrieved it and set off down Ulitsa Sverdlova to the river. The large, ugly, Soviet-era pile of the Intourist Hotel stood near the river bank. A sort of riverside park had been laid out along Gagarina Boulevard which paralleled the river. Here and there small groups of morose drunks were sitting on the embankment wall or grassy slope below it, swilling beer. At the foot of the main street, Karl Marx Street, there was an obelisk commemorating the building of the Trans-Siberian Railway line. Nearby was an impressive statue of Tsar Alexander III who had initiated the Railway project in 1891 and a bust of Yuri Gagarin, the first man into space, no doubt much to Paul Theroux's surprise. Presumably someone had checked Sputnik for loose wires before he launched off. On the inland side of the riverside promenade, facing each other across Karl Marx Street, stood the 1804 White House, the former residence of the Governors General of Eastern Siberia, now the university library and the brick-built Regional Museum, dating to the 1870s and formerly housing the Siberian Geographical Society. Further up Karl Marx Street, the Drama Theatre was an attractive, classical style building and behind it there was an impressive stadium. A bit further on a statue of Lenin stood defiantly, as if he was still in charge – his spirit was certainly still alive in the sour-faced apparatchiks at the Hotel Rus. I turned off Karl Marx Street towards the central market building. I noticed that there were a lot of shaven-headed, bull-necked types sitting outside some of the shops. I thought they must be security guards and then I remembered what Valentin had said about the Mafia's hold on the city; the sort of protection they were providing probably had a sinister side to it. I also noticed that there didn't seem to be much in the way of window displays of merchandise. It was as if the old Soviet days of rationing and queuing for staple goods were still with us, when there was nothing to display. There was certainly no shortage of goods any more in the market building but it was all very old fashioned looking. There was a dairy products section where individual vendors were ranged behind an array of large metal urns with milk, buttermilk, sour milk, curds. There seemed to be little effort made to make the displays of goods attractive: the predominating business ethos seemed to be "take it or leave it"; an appropriate logo would have been a fist with the middle finger sticking up. It was as if now that capitalism had arrived, they didn't have a clue how to operate it. The people looked miserable as if smiling had been banned by some latter day Stalin. The men had a beaten, hang-dog look about them and looked scruffy, unkempt. The women, on the other hand, were well dressed, albeit in the style of "Tart Magazine" rather than "Vogue", high heels, shiny tights, miniskirts, pink or fake leopard-skin tops and heavily made up – it occurred to me that they might not be able to smile through the layers of powder and paint even if they'd wanted to. I made my way across past the Circus and the Central Telegraph Building to the administrative centre on Ploshchad (Square) Kirova, dominated by the turgid, Stalinist slab of the Regional Administrative Building. I later learned that a magnificent Cathedral had been demolished on Stalin's orders to provide the site for this lump of concrete. Miraculously, three churches had survived out behind it and to the side: the Gothic style Polish Church which had been built by Polish exiles who were Catholic; the white-washed Church of Christ the Saviour, which dated back to 1706; and right down by the riverbank, the exotic Bogoyavlensky Cathedral with its green onion-shaped domes and salmon-pink trim around its white towers. A bride and groom in full wedding regalia were posing for photographs in front of it.

In the evening I went for a meal in the Lancelot Restaurant in Ulitsa Kievskaya, off Karl Marx Street. It was a mock-medieval style place in a basement with a wrought-iron portcullis above the entrance and deco-rated with swords, shields, halberds and banners. They specialized in grilled meats served on wooden plates. I had a shashlik accompanied by aubergines and garnished with half an orange – no pigs' ears here. Afterwards I went along the Hotel Angara on Kirov Square for a drink. It looked much more up-market than the Rus and there was a lively bar in the attractive lobby with mini-skirted bar maids who had discovered how to smile. I thought I had made a bad choice of hotel but when I got back to my Gulag (Concentration Camp) the Rus, I looked up what Lonely Planet had to say about the Angara which was: "Don't be fooled by the fancy foyer"; that the cheapest rooms were 'disgracefully shabby"; and that the higher standard rooms were "passable by old Soviet-era standards but very overpriced": so much for Russian tourist accommodation.

I had booked a tour of the city for the following morning and my guide, Viktor, arrived at the hotel to collect me. He was young, just out of University where he had studied "tourism" he said and he spoke excellent English. I was encouraged that perhaps the Authorities were making an effort after all to wean the population away from Soviet ways. We started off at the obelisk to the Trans-Siberian Railway down by the river. Viktor said that the line from Moscow had reached Irkutsk in 1898, following the old post road from Chelyabinsk at the south-ern end of the Ural Mountains, which had formerly been the east-ern terminus of railway lines. The line from Vladivostok had arrived at the other side of Lake Baikal in 1900. The railway had been seen as a means of tying the vast country together as the trans-continental railroads had done in America in the 1870s. It had also been seen as a way to promote re-settlement of some of European Russia's over-crowded rural population to Siberia: the serfs had been freed in 1861 and internal travel restrictions lifted but social unrest had continued and Tsar Alexander II had been assassinated in 1881. The railway was also intended to stimulate economic development in Siberia and exploit the forest and mineral resources. Its potential military value had been demonstrated in the Russo-Japanese War of 1904-05 when the early system had proved inadequate to support the war front and the Russian fleet sent round to the Far East by sea had been destroyed by the Japanese.

We moved on to the History Museum. Russia had started expanding into Siberia after Ivan the Terrible had defeated the Tatars at Kazan in 1552 and Astrakhan in 1556. He then authorised the Stroganov merchant family to open fur-trading posts east of the Ural Mountains aided by Cossack mercenaries under Yermak Timoffeevich. Forts were built ever further east, reaching the Ob River by the 1580s, the Yenisey by the end of the 16th century and the Pacific coast by 1639. Traders even crossed into Alaska which belonged to Russia until 1867 when it was sold to the USA for around 2 U.S. cents an acre to raise funds after an economic collapse in Russia following the Crimean War. There was fighting with Valentin's people, the Buryats, and other native Siberian tribes, who were the equivalent of American "Red Indians", the Cossacks being the "cowboys" with Tsarist troops sometimes filling the role of the U.S. cavalry manning the forts. The forts became the nucleus of towns, Irkutsk being founded in 1651 and becoming the main base for expansion further east. It also became the focus of the trade route into China carrying furs and ivory south and tea and silk north which was later followed by the Trans-Mongolian line. In 1879, a fire had burned down three-quarters of the wooden city but the gold rush to the Lena River basin in the 1880s brought new prosperity and it was rebuilt with many impressive brick mansions. The construction of the railway brought in floods of migrants to Siberia from European Russia, 5 million between 1891 and 1914. Then, after Stalin's first 5

Year Plan in 1929, Irkutsk had been designated as an industrial and scientific centre and grew rapidly while the establishment of the Gulag system of slave-labour camps brought thousands of unwilling immigrants to Siberia to develop the mining industry, forestry and to build infrastructure. In World War II, Stalin had moved as much industry as possible further east into Siberia away from the invading Germans, especially production for the military effort. The discovery of oil and gas in the 1950s and '60s brought development of industries along the Trans-Siberian including a petro-chemical plant to Irkutsk. The giant Angara dam completed in 1956 had provided massive amounts of hydro-electric power.

We had a look at the churches around the Administration Building that I had seen the previous day and then drove out to the Znamensky Monastery, standing among trees and built in 1762. Outside it, a statue had been controversially erected the previous year of the White Russian leader Admiral Kolchak, near where he had been executed by the Bolsheviks in 1920, at the end of the Civil War which had erupted after the Bolsheviks seized power in October 1917. This had been the background to the Doctor Zhivago novel. We moved on to visit the Volkonsky House Museum where one of the leading legendary "Decembrists", Count Sergei Volkonsky, had lived. The "Decembrists" had been a group of aristocratic army officers who had attempted to stage a coup against the Tsar in December 1825 but failed. Those who hadn't been massacred in the central square in St. Petersburg when the coup was quelled by forces remaining loyal to the Tsar or subsequently executed were exiled to Siberia to do forced labour, mainly in the silver mines near Chita and Nerchinsk, east of Ulan-Ude. Many of their wives had followed them and set up home in Irkutsk, where they were joined by the exiles when they finished their sentences or were ultimately granted an amnesty by the next Tsar. The wives had promoted a lively cultural and social scene in Irkutsk. The mansion was near a little pink church and built round a courtyard with stables and servant's quarters. Part of it had been restored in period style and there was a photographic exhibition including family portraits. Nearby, we had a look at some very attractive old wooden houses with carved, decorative, wooden fretwork around the windows, doors and eaves which resembled lace work.

The following morning, I had a tour booked down to Lake Baikal, about 70 kilometres (45 miles) away. We stopped to look at the massive 2 kilometres long Angara dam and the ice-breaker "Angara" which had transported rail passengers across the lake in the early days of the Trans-Siberian. Viktor said she had been built in kit form in Newcastle-upon-Tyne and assembled at the lake. The Angara River was the only outlet from Lake Baikal: but there were over 300 rivers and streams flowing into it. The statistics relating to Lake Baikal were astonishing: it was over 600 kilometres (nearly 400 miles) long by 60 kilometres (38 miles) wide; over a mile deep on the western side; and it held the biggest volume of fresh water of any lake in the world, 20% of the world's supply that wasn't tied up in ice caps – more than all the North American Great Lakes combined. And it was getting bigger: it was on the edge of two tectonic plates which were pulling apart and would eventually detach Eastern Siberia from the rest of Russia. We stopped in the little village of Listvyanka down by the lake shore, a picturesque settlement of wooden cottages with brightly painted shutters and a bubbling, swift running stream flowing through it. A beautiful little wooden church with a spire, St. Nicholas, stood by the stream. It had been raining on the drive down to the lake but now there was just an intermittent drizzle, overcast and cold with a nippy wind blowing off the lake. The previous day in Irkutsk had been bright sunshine with the temperature in the high twenties centigrade. It was obviously a very variable climate. There was an outdoor market down at the little harbour with stalls of wooden carvings and utensils, jewellery made from local semi-precious stones, some paintings and other souvenirs. I bought a plate made from beautiful soft, light, cedar wood with local wild animals carved into it. A number of stalls were selling smoked fish which were being prepared over wood fires in tin boxes, the smell of wood smoke and cooking fish filling the air and the smoke swirling around like fog. The fish were called "omul", a member of the salmon-trout family. I bought one to sample and it was delicious so I bought some more to take with me on the next leg of the train journey the following day – I had read what Paul Theroux had to say about the food on the Russian trains and was not expecting much from the restaurant car. Some fishing boats and craft for cruises on the lake were moored to a jetty nearby but it wasn't much of a day for pleasure cruising as the rain set in again. We called in at the Baikal Limnological Museum with displays on the natural history of the lake, maps, models, stuffed animals and a small aquarium with a couple of "nerpa" – cute-looking, black-eyed freshwater seals (the only freshwater ones in the world and a bit of a mystery as to how they got into the lake in the first place), some giant sturgeon and some nice, fat omul which made me feel hungry again. On the way back to Irkutsk, we stopped at the Taltsy Museum of Wooden Architecture, a collection of traditional Siberian wooden buildings salvaged from sites where they had been threatened with demolition. They were spread out picturesquely in clearings among the trees along the riverbank. When we got out of the car, Viktor sprayed me liberally with insect repellent from a plastic drum: he said the gnats, midges, ticks and mosquitos were savage, sometimes so bad they couldn't take visitors around the site but today should be O.K. It was a fascinating and photogenic display now that the sun had finally come out. There were farmsteads, a watermill, a church, chapels and perhaps most impressive of all an old wooden "ostrog" (fort). There were some ancient babushkas in traditional costume sitting outside some of the buildings with facial expressions and body language that said "if you take my photograph, I'll kill you." When I tried to sneak shots of them from outside their field of vision they appeared to have eyes in the backs of their heads, perhaps a skill honed during years of surveillance by the KGB.

The next day I was back at the station to catch train number 9 for the longest leg of my trip, the full length of Western Siberia to Yekaterinburg, at the south end of the Ural Mountains, 3,371 kilometres (2,107 miles) and scheduled to take 48 hours. The first sight of the provodnitsa (carriage attendant) came as a shock. This was no wrinkly old babushka; she was young, good looking, beautifully dressed. She showed me my compartment, the communal wash room/toilet at the end of the carriage (no sink plug, I noted) and the samovar (hot water urn for making tea) out in the corridor, but it was like being shown round by a robot, no glimmer of human warmth and as for a smile, forget it. She later showed herself to be arrogant, bossy, treating her customers as if we were prisoners on the way to the Gulag. The railway had remained a state-managed monopoly, so I suppose old habits died particularly hard in that context. I had just finished stowing my luggage and organizing reading material when a man in his fifties and a girl around twenty came into the compartment. She introduced herself as Natasha and her father as Nikolai, speaking fluent English and to my surprise smiling, friendly. She said she was a student at the university in Irkutsk and her father had been visiting her and was now heading home to Yekaterinburg. "He doesn't speak any English" she added. I replied in Russian that I only spoke very basic Russian but held up the phrase book. "Ah!" she laughed. "That should help." She stayed on board to chat until it was almost time to leave. I was beginning to suspect that there were two sides to the Russian personality: a social and private side; and an official and public one. In her private life, the provodnitsa might well be the life and soul of the party. We left right on schedule at 4.20 p.m. We were soon into the never-ending "taiga" (forest) following the Angara River as it made its way to join the Yenisey. We stopped briefly in Angarsk which my guide book described as "oil-rich" but there was nothing visible from the train to confirm that. Likewise at Usole-Sibirskoe which Lonely Planet said supplied much of Russia's salt and many of its matches. It occurred to me that it was ironic that I was going to leave Siberia without seeing a salt mine – like leaving Mongolia without seeing a yak. For a while Nikolai and I tried to make conversation using the phrase book but it was hard work. I established that he'd been a footballer and was still involved in the game either as a manager or a coach. When he learned that I was from Scotland, he beamed and said "Kenny Dalgliesh kharasho! Good!" the only English word he ever spoke. After a while he went out, indicating with a grin, an elbow movement and the word "piva" (beer) that he was going to look for a drink. We stopped for half an hour or so in Zima at getting on for nine o'clock in the evening, allegedly a "former exile town" the name of which meant "winter". I got out to stretch my legs and get some fresh air. I had got up that morning with a cold after getting soaked a few times at Lake Baikal and not being dressed for the chilly wind off the lake. It had gradually been getting worse all day and by now my nose and eyes were running steadily and my head had developed that stuffed-up feeling as if it was metamorphosing into a turnip. I decided to go to bed early and try to sleep it off. I went to the toilet and discovered that there was no paper left. Just to test the system (I had been forewarned about this and had my own roll with me) I knocked on the providnitsa's door and feeling like Oliver Twist, asked for some more. Predictably, like Mr. Bumble the Beadle, her reply was "nyet" with a "you must be joking" smirk on her face. I woke up around midnight with Nikolai stumbling around trying to get into his bed. His mission in search of alcohol had clearly been successful.

The next morning, my cold was no better: I had started sneezing and a dry cough was developing. Just before the industrial city of Krasnoyarsk with a population of around a million (I couldn't decide whether "kiss my arse" or "scratch my arse" was the best mnemonic to remember it by) there were some prominent forested hills, a welcome break from the endless flatland of Siberia and then we were on a kilometre long bridge across the massive Yenisey River and into the station. We stopped long enough to have a wander around the station. Babushkas were selling snacks on the platform but I didn't see anything that appealed to me. After Krasnoyarsk, the scenery was not inspiring, long stretches of dark, gloomy, forest with the occasional clearing where it had been logged-out and the very occasional village of single-storey wooden houses with steeply sloping roofs designed to shed snow and surrounded by wooden fences. Brief stops were few and far between. I made good progress with Doctor Zhivago. I was finding Anna Karenina hard work and hadn't got much past the opening line: "Happy families are all alike; every unhappy family is unhappy in its own way." This tale of marital infidelity among upper class twits in 19th century Tsarist society wasn't really to my taste but it was better than the scenery if the worst came to the worst. At lunch time I went along to the dining car to check if it was as bad as Paul Theroux had described. It was. I ordered something described as chicken and peas. It was very accurately described, a shrivelled, over-fried chicken leg on a small side-plate with a dollop of cold, mushy, tinned peas. I asked for "khleb" (bread) and a single slab of rubbery black rye bread was brought back with a grudging look. The chicken had been fried in some sort of rancid oil or fat and it was jaw-numbingly tough. The beer was good, however, so I decided to restrict my use of the dining car to drinking. The day was fading when we got to Novosibirsk, with a population of 1.5 million, the largest city in Siberia. It was here that Akademgorodok had been built, a centre for academic and scientific research, where some of the best minds in the USSR had been brought together and presumably taps and electrical wiring were properly connected. I had read that it had suffered badly from brain-drain after the collapse of communism. After the station, we crossed the mighty Ob River (at over 5,300 kilometres (3,300 miles) it was the fifth longest river in the world) on another kilometre long bridge. By the time I surfaced the following morning, we were well past Omsk on the Irtysh River and on the long run in to Yekaterinburg, where we arrived on schedule again at 4.00 pm. Two days on the train on the stretch had been enough. Any longer would have run a serious risk of madness. When Paul Theroux had reached Moscow at the end of his trip all the way from Vladivostok in "The Great Railway Bazaar" he had been muttering "Monkey!" at everyone as he left the train.

I was booked into the Magister Hotel on 8th March Street which the Lonely Planet guide described as "small and friendly". This time they were spot on. The English speaking receptionist even gave me a street map before I'd asked for it and showed me on it where to catch the No.15 tram which ran up the street the hotel was on and then along the main street, Prospekt Lenina. I couldn't fault the room either. I went for dinner to the riverside Kamenny Most restaurant, just a couple of blocks north and then east over the Iset River on Ulitsa Malysheva. I had a bowl of borscht (beetroot soup) which didn't do much for me but the beef Stroganoff in its sour cream and mushroom sauce with blinis (pancakes) was good. I walked back across the river and then west three blocks to the Old Dublin Pub: yes, the Irish theme pub had reached Siberia. It was quite lively and obviously popular with expatriates from the languages I heard being spoken. I got chatting to a Scotsman at the bar whose firm was involved in some joint venture to open up a new minerals deposit in the Urals. He'd already had a bit to drink and was scathingly cynical about what he was involved in – the lack of environmental controls over mining and the amount of corruption at government level. I was worried for his sake in case some of Vladimir Putin's old mates from his KGB days might be within earshot. He got on to the subject of Chelyabinsk, a city just south of Yekaterinburg, where Beria, Stalin's Chief of the Cheka (Secret Police) had overseen the building of a nuclear complex using 70,000 forced labourers from the Gulag in the late 1940s. The radioactive waste had just been dumped in lakes and rivers. In 1957 there had been an explosion in a reactor which had spread radioactive material over a wide area (worse than Chernobyl, he claimed, only it had been hushed up). Then in a drought in 1967, a bog where waste had been dumped had dried out and radioactive dust had blown around again. Now, he said, the number of deformed foetuses and babies being aborted and born dead in the area was horrific. (I recently read Kim Traill's 2009 book "Red Square Blues" which confirms this same story.)

Breakfast next morning at the Magister was quite good and there was even some red and black caviar. I had obviously made a good hotel choice this time. I had booked a half-day tour of the city and Olga, my guide, arrived to collect me after breakfast. She was tall, young and beautiful and dressed like a fashion model but strangely agitated and a chain smoker – I wondered if she was on drugs. We started off at the Istorichesky Skver (Historical Square) where the city had been founded by Tsar Peter the Great in 1723 as part of his push to exploit the minerals in the Ural Mountains. There was a statue of the two men whom he had commissioned to found the city. A dam had been built across the Iset River to create the City Pond which had been used to power water mills to drive an iron forge and a mint. The dam and pond now just served an ornamental purpose but an old water tower had been preserved and old mining and metal processing equipment was on display in the adjacent Museum of Architecture and Technology. The City Hall with a statue of Lenin out in front of it was just to the west along Prospekt Lenina on the Square of 1905. We moved on to visit the Urals Mineralogical Museum, an eclectic collection of minerals not just from the Urals but some from all over the world, which had been a private collection. We walked up past the attractive Opera and Ballet Theatre to have a look at the statue of Yakov Sverdlov – the city had been re-named Sverdlovsk after him in 1924 and only reverted back to the old name in 1991. He had been Lenin's right hand man in the October 1917 Bolshevik coup but had died in the flu epidemic of 1919. He was believed to have been behind the murder of the Tsar and his family in 1918. Now he stood there covered in birds' shit as if the pigeons had delivered the verdict of history on him. Over behind the main post office, the Icon Museum was housed in an attractive Byzantine style building. It had been starting to drizzle when we came out of the Mineralogical Museum and was raining by the time the mini-bus picked us up again. Stupidly, since my cold was as bad as ever, I hadn't taken a waterproof. We drove up to see the site of the mansion, Ipatyev House, where the Tsar Nicholas II, his wife and five children had been massacred. It was now just marked by a marble cross as the building had been demolished in 1977 during Boris Yeltsin's time as Communist Party boss in the city in case it became a shrine for monarchist sympathisers and subversives. But history has a way of biting back. Just alongside was the magnificent Byzantine Church of the Blood, recently completed to commemorate the royal family. The Russian Orthodox Church had taken the cult of the Romanovs to a ridiculous level by conferring sainthood on them. There was a display dedicated to them in the basement. Stories which had come out since the fall of communism and documented by Greg King and Penny Wilson in their book "The Fall of the Romanovs", suggested that the massacre had been a horrific, amateur and botched affair. The man entrusted to carry out the deed had been a highly placed officer in the Cheka, Yakov Yurovsky. It had been done in the middle of the night, the family roused and brought down to a basement room on the pretext that they were going to be moved somewhere safe as there was danger of a White Army attack. The eleven executioners had used hand guns and some of them were drunk. Several of the children had survived the first salvos as they had jewellery and gems sown into their clothes which deflected the bullets and they had to be finished off individually. It was so messy that some of the hardened assassins had vomited. The Romanovs had ruled Russia since 1613 and despots they had undoubtedly been but nobody deserved to die the way they had. It had been a horrible end to a dynasty.

In the afternoon, after the tour, I had a chance to look around the rest of the city using the apparently efficient tram system. Yekaterinburg now had a population of over a million and a half and was Russia's third largest city. It had got a boost in World War II when Stalin moved industries east away from the Nazis and it had been out of bounds to foreigners until 1990 due to the amount of production related to the military. I had read that it had been infested by the Russian Mafia in the 1990s but was now cleaning itself up. Certainly I saw no signs of the skinhead types I had seen in Irkutsk and the people didn't have the look of despair on their faces so prevalent in Irkutsk. The shopping streets were livelier too. I bought myself a "matryoshka", the traditional Russian wooden dolls which fit inside one another. There was one that featured Stalin, Khrushchev and Brezhnev but I settled for Putin, looking as arrogant and constipated as ever, Yeltsin, with a drunken leer on his face and Gorbachev, with his trademark birthmark on his forehead. I recalled that Winston Churchill had described Russia as "a riddle wrapped in a mystery inside an enigma." I had just bought a blotch-head, wrapped in a piss-head inside a big-head badly in need of an enema. Some old wooden houses had survived with the same intricate carving around the windows, door lintels and eaves that I had seen in Irkutsk and there were some attractive onion-domed Orthodox churches. The industry was located outside the city centre which was clean, tidy and relatively unpolluted.

Train number 15 left Yekaterinburg at 9.15 am for the 1,814 kilometres (1,134 miles) 24 hours run to Moscow. During the night, I had been running a temperature, sweating and with the beginnings of a sore head. I realized that my cold had become a flu following the soaking I had got during the city tour. I was joined in my compartment by a woman in her forties dressed in a business costume and carrying a briefcase. When she heard my Russian accent she switched to English. She was one of these confident, self-possessed women that Russia seems to mass-produce, equally at home in the business world or in a previous era driving a tractor or welding the fuselage of a Mig fighter plane. There was no segregation of the sexes in allocating berths on the Trans-Siberian. I apologised to her for my flu after an uncontrollable bout of sneezing and said I hoped I wouldn't bring her down with it. She said she would go and see if she could find a spare berth in a compartment with a female occupant in any case and came back shortly saying "Success." Out in the corridor, I got chatting to a woman with a New Zealand accent who said she was part of a group that had travelled all the way from Vladivostok. When she heard that I lived in New Zealand she invited me to meet some of the rest of the group but I declined politely warning her about my state of health. She said that several members of the group had the same problem and a couple had food poisoning. It sounded as if she hadn't enjoyed the experience.

The Ural Mountains were a serious disappointment. Every map I'd seen showed the rail line between Yekaterinburg and Perm running across them but I saw nothing resembling a mountain. I had a similar experience later with the Jordan River in Israel which I had imagined as a roaring torrent but it turned out to be a dribble. We were also supposed to pass a marker showing the boundary between Europe and Asia on the watershed of the Urals but I must have blinked and missed it. We stopped in Perm. This was the setting for part of "Doctor Zhivago". The doctor and his family had fled to their estate at Varykino near the city during the civil war between the Bolsheviks and the White Russians and his lover, Lara, played by Julie Christie in the film, had moved to Yuriatin which was based on Perm. A notorious Gulag, Perm 36, believed to have been the worst of them all, was also nearby and had only been closed in 1992. Paul Theroux described visiting it in "Ghost Train to the Eastern Star." The Gulag or Concentration Camp system had started as early as 1918 when Lenin had decreed the "red terror" against opposition to the

Bolshevik regime after civil war had broken out with the White Russian faction. He had said that: "Anyone who dares to spread the slightest rumour against the Soviet regime will be arrested immediately and sent to a concentration camp." Prisoner of War camps were originally used after the prisoners had been repatriated at the end of hostilities in 1917 and since there had been 2 million POWs there were plenty of vacancies. The system was later escalated by Stalin in the 1930s to implement his 5 Year Plans. Nobody in their right mind would have gone voluntarily to work in the mines in places like Kolyma and Magadan in remote north eastern Siberia so they were staffed by forced-labour exiled to the Gulags on trumped-up charges designed to produce a slave labour force. Getting on for nightfall we reached the Volga at Nizhny Novgorod with another long bridge across the huge river. It was a beautiful, hot, sunny evening even this late and people in summer clothes were sitting on the grass on the railway embankments watching the train pass and others were stretched out along the river banks. I had another fevered night's sleep, waking up now and then sweating. We arrived at Moscow's Yaroslavl Station on schedule at 9.15 am.

I was booked into the Rossiya Hotel for four nights. It was a mammoth, 3,200 rooms, Soviet monstrosity, but in an ideal location just off Red Square. I had booked tours for the next two days but I had the rest of the day free so I set off to explore the city. St. Basil's Cathedral was just minutes away, the building that I had always associated with Moscow. It reminded me of a giant cruet set, with onion-domed towers of salt, pepper, mustard and a taller, slimmer, vinegar jar. Or it could have been a tray of ice cream cones, the ribbed, scalloped, sworls of the domes looking like scoops of exotic ice creams. The colours were startling – green, orange, gold, yellow with some red and blue. The combination of shapes and colours was so intricate and psychedelic it looked as if it had been moulded from plastic. It had been built by Ivan the Terrible between 1555 and 1561 to celebrate his victories over the Tatars, each of the nine chapels dedicated to a separate victory. I walked north through the cobbled Red Square with the high wall surrounding the Kremlin on my left, past the Saviour's Gate leading into the Kremlin complex, surmounted by a red 70 metres (230 feet) high tower with a clock, past Lenin's Mausoleum and into the GUM department store on the east side of the square. Inside, under the arched glass roof, there were no signs of the fabled shortages of Soviet days: arcades of smart shops ran down either side and through the centre of the building – Benneton, Christian Dior, Estee Lauder, interspersed with cafes and restaurants. At the far end of the 500 metres (1600 feet) long Red Square stood the Historical Museum, its red brick façade and twin spires completed in 1883 in what my guide book called the Russian-Revival style. Alongside it, the attractive little tangerine-coloured Kazan Cathedral had been re-built in the early 1990s, Stalin having had the original one demolished in 1936. There was a painting of the Kazan Virgin above the main entrance: presumably virgins were a scarce commodity in Kazan. I carried on past the equestrian statue of Marshal Zhukov, World War II hero of the Battle of Kursk and the defence of Stalingrad. The Resurrection Gate had been rebuilt in 1995: the original had been demolished by Stalin in 1931. Its twin arched gateways and twin red towers with their slender green spires known as tent spires were a perfect lesson in symmetry. The pleasant green lung of the Alexander Gardens stretched south below the west wall of the Kremlin with monuments to the "Hero Cities" which had borne the brunt of the fighting in World War II and the Tomb of the Unknown Soldier at its north end. Just to the north, Maneznaya Square was beautifully landscaped - ponds with fountains spouting like geysers among trees, prancing horse sculptures and an obelisk. The huge, underground, Okhotny Ryad shopping mall extended along beneath the Square to Tverskaya Street, the city's main street, which stretched away to the north. Just across Tverskaya, the Duma (Parliament) had been relocated from the White House, which had been trashed by Boris Yeltsin during an abortive coup against his drunken presidency. I walked up Tverskaya as far as Pushkin Square with its statue of the famous poet. From what I had seen there was no doubt that capitalism was alive and well in Moscow. Prada, Hermes, Louis Vuitton, Macdonalds were all there with billboards advertising Marlboro cigarettes, vodka, beer, chocolate. There were bars, restaurants, nightclubs, casinos. On the streets, Mercedes cars were two a kopek (100 kopeks = 1 rouble).

I took the Metro down to the Arbatskaya district. When I exited, I saw that the station had been designed with the shape and colour of the Soviet red star. The pedestrianised Old Arbat Street was a bit touristy with an art market, portrait painters, buskers, jugglers and souvenir shops. However, the pastel painted shops in old merchant houses created a more relaxed atmosphere than the bustling, ultra-modern Tverskaya area. I bought a copy of the English language "Moscow Times" and went into a café for lunch. The newspaper was full of adverts for pubs, nightclubs and Escort Agencies – there appeared to be a plethora of Irish theme pubs. At the end of the street the towering skyscraper of the Foreign Ministry was one of the seven "wedding cakes" built after World War II in paranoid "Stalinist-Gothic" style to demonstrate how well the USSR had recovered from the war. I took the Metro back to Kitai-Gorod station and walked back to the hotel through what had been the original settlement that had grown into the current metropolis of ten million people. I was exhausted, my flu still persisting and I slept until dinner time. I managed to drag myself out for an evening meal but any thoughts of sampling the night-life offered in the Moscow Times were out of the question.

In the morning my tour guide, Irina Pavlova, arrived to take me for a city tour. She was in her late twenties, small, good-looking and confident, dressed casually in jeans, which was unusual in my experience so far for working Russian women but it suited her free spirit. We started off in Red Square. Irina said that it had originally been a wide moat along the Kremlin wall which in the 15th century had been filled in. It had originally been used as a market square but the wooden stalls had frequently burned down. It had also been used for public addresses by the Tsars and for public executions and then for huge military parades in Soviet times. The first Kremlin fortress had been built in the 12th century and a walled merchant's town profiting from trade along the adjacent Moscow River had developed alongside it in the Kitai-Gorod area. Both had been sacked by the Mongols in the 13th century but rebuilt and Moscow had eventually succeeded Kiev as the capital of the incipient Russian state, the headquarters of the Orthodox Church also moving there. The Kremlin, including the existing walls had been rebuilt in stone at the end of the 15th century by Tsar Ivan the Great using Italian architects. The old wooden city of Kitai-Gorod and most of the rest of Moscow had been burned to the ground in 1812 to deprive Napoleon of the prize of capturing it and rebuilt in 19th century style. Irina pointed out where Stalin and Brezhnev had been buried along the Kremlin wall alongside Lenin's Mausoleum. We drove over to see the Lubyanka, the former headquarters of the KGB and still housing their successors the FSB. The huge, square, orange-coloured eight-storey slab dominated the square in front. We moved on to see the Bolshoi Theatre, a beautiful neoclassical building with a column lined façade surmounted by a pediment with sculptured angels, above which a statue of Apollo, the Greek god of light and music, drove his chariot loaded with the sun across the sky. The current building had been completed in 1856 after earlier ones had been burned down. Across the street in Revolution Square, a statue of Karl Marx was leaning on a broken lump of rock with the inscription: "Workers of the world unite." It occurred to me that the crumbling rock was a fitting epitaph to his dream of a socialist paradise as he surveyed, no doubt pissed-off, the flowering of capitalism around him. We drove on and stopped at the resurrected, gold-domed Cathedral of Christ the Redeemer, rebuilt between 1994 and 1997 at Mayor Yuriy Luzhkov's behest to replace the one destroyed by Stalin in 1931. Lenin had said that religion was the opium of the people: Stalin had tried to wean them off it by wholesale destruction of churches and murdering around 95,000 priests. Irina said that Stalin had planned a grandiose Palace of the Soviets for the site, 315 metres (1,034 feet) high, surmounted by an 100 metres (328 feet) high statue of Lenin but the project had later been dropped. Just opposite, over on the end of an island in the Moscow River, a sailing ship bearing a huge statue of Tsar Peter the Great had apparently run aground. This was no great surprise as Peter was a notorious piss-head, prone, during bouts of drunkenness, to trash the houses where he stayed in Europe when he went there to pick up some tips about modernising Russia, including ship-building. He had obviously been drunk at the helm yet again. As we drove south, Irina pointed out Gorky Park on the other side of the river. I said I'd read the book by Martin Cruz Smith and seen the film. She said that it had been filmed in Finland. We stopped to visit the Novodevichy Convent which had been founded in 1524. The Smolensk Cathedral was in the centre of the complex, its creamy white walls topped with green onion-shaped domes and a gold one. A six-tiered, red-walled, baroque-style bell tower stood nearby, rising to 72 metres (236 feet). Attractive buildings, some with gold onion domes, were scattered all around the site. Krushchev was buried in the adjacent cemetery. We ended the tour at Sparrow Hills, where a summit vantage point provided an excellent overview of the city. The area was dominated by Moscow State University, another of Stalin's seven skyscraper "wedding cakes."

Irina had struck me as highly intelligent so I decided to pick her brain on the demise of communism. She said she had been too young to understand what had been going on under Gorbachev but from what she had read since, he had been naïve to hope his "perestroika" (economic reform with some relaxation of state monopolies and limited free enterprise) and "glasnost" (openness, more freedom of speech) policies would work. She said most people agreed that the whole communist system had become so rotten in its last years that once rigid control was relaxed it was bound to collapse like a pyramid of playing cards. Under Boris Yeltsin, anarchy had broken out both in economic and social terms. The Russian Mafia had flourished. With the new personal freedom, old moral standards had broken down and wild nightclubs, strip clubs and prostitution had mushroomed. Yeltsin's cronies, mostly high officials in the former Communist Party, had bought up state assets at knock down prices to privatise them and become obscenely rich "oligarchs" while ordinary people were starving without the social security safety net that communism had provided. A huge gap had developed between the "haves" and the "have nots" and people brought up under communism resented that. When the economy had collapsed in the late 1990s most people had lost their savings. Now, under Vladimir Putin, things were settling down. She thought that most people in Russia valued security above personal freedom and actually wanted strong leaders like him. She grinned and said that she wasn't personally convinced that democracy had all the answers either if it produced leaders like George W. Bush. "Touche" I said.

I had asked Irina for advice on where to cash travellers' cheques and she volunteered to come and give me a hand at the end of the tour. I soon discovered why. At the bank, we waited ages to be attended to and then there was a wad of complicated forms to fill in, all with multiple duplicates. We had to wait again to be let into a room (which had to be opened with a key) where we handed over the cheques and the forms. We then had to queue again at a window to get the cash. It took well over an hour. Like Paul Theroux on the subject of space travel, I wondered: "How do these people manage to run an economy?" Back at the hotel, I was exhausted and fell asleep. I was still so tired in the evening that I just got something to eat in the hotel and went straight to bed.

In the morning, Irina appeared again for a tour of the Metro system and the Kremlin. I was feeling seriously ill but decided to persevere. The Metro system was amazing. It had been the centrepiece of Stalin's first 5 Year Plan, started in the early 1930s and designed to impress. In the Teatralnaya Station, ceramic panels depicted the different cultures of the republics in the former USSR, their national costumes shown in ceiling panels above gleaming chandeliers. The main hall at Revolution Square had life-size bronze statues of "red heroes" standing in marble-lined arches – Red Guards, workers, farmers, sailors, sportsmen and sportswomen. Komsomolskaya Station was named for the Communist Youth League which had played a major role in building the system. It had two stations: one on the original, appropriately named, red line; the other on the circle line. The first was lined with rose-coloured marble pillars with panels showing heroic Metro workers; the second a much more elaborate affair with stucco mouldings and glittering chandeliers. There were gold mosaics of military parades and historical figures.

We moved on to visit the Kremlin, entering through the Trinity Gate in the western wall, approached over a ramp above the Alexander Gardens. On our left was the Arsenal, originally built by Peter the Great in 1701. There were some canons standing outside but presumably some more modern weapons inside as it was out of bounds. Even more out of bounds were the Presidential Palace and offices just beyond it. The Kremlin was an impressive complex of palaces and religious buildings. It covered 27 hectares (68 acres) with 2,230 metres (7,316 feet) of walls which were up to 20 metres (65 feet) high and 6 metres (20 feet) wide. There were 4 gates and 20 towers spread out around the walls. We walked past the State Kremlin Palace, an ugly modern structure built in 1961 to house Communist Party congresses but now used for opera, ballet and concert performances. We came to the Tsar Canon, cast in 1686 and weighing 40 tonnes. It had never been fired. A bit further on was the Tsar Bell, the largest in the world, weighing over 200 tonnes. It had never been rung. I was beginning to think there was a dirty joke there somewhere featuring a Kazan Virgin and to wonder how many more White Elephants we would come across. A large piece which had broken off the bell was propped up against the plinth. Between the useless bell and canon Ivan the Great's Bell Tower was the tallest building in the complex at 81 metres (265 feet) with a golden onion dome. It had been built in 1505-08. It had later been extended by the Assumption Belfry, with 21 bells and another golden dome and later still by an annexe with a green tent-spire roof. We walked through into Cathedral Square. The 15th century rebuild of the Kremlin had featured three magnificent Cathedrals which were grouped around the Square: the Uspensky (Assumption) for coronations; the Blagoveshchensky (Annunciation) for baptisms and weddings; and the Archangelsky for state funerals and royal tombs. With their towers and golden onion domes they were breathtakingly beautiful and the interiors were filled with lavish icons, paintings, frescos, murals and mosaics. The largest building in the complex with 700 rooms and a 125 metres (410 feet) long white and yellow façade was the green-roofed Great Kremlin Palace, the present building completed in 1849 for the Moscow residence of the Royal family when visiting from the then capital St. Petersburg. It was now used for receptions for foreign dignitaries. Our last stop was the State Armoury where the treasures accumulated by the Tsars over the centuries were displayed. It had been completed in 1851 as a museum in the same style as the Palace. There were thrones, crowns and ornate hats (including Ivan the Terrible's "Cap of Kazan"), coronation dresses (including Catherine the Great's one) and carriages. I was particularly fascinated by the Faberge Eggs collection. One, which was also a musical box, was set in a model of the Kremlin; but my favourite incorporated a model of a Trans-Siberian train. A separate exhibition, the State Diamond Fund, featured diamonds, jewellery, crowns and other state regalia including the Orlov Diamond, set in Catherine the Great's sceptre and the largest sapphire in the world.

By this time, I was out on my feet. Every bone and muscle ached, the sweat was running off me, every step was an effort and breathing set off a noise in my chest like a kettle boiling. I said to Irina that I would have to go back to the hotel and see if I could find a doctor. She said the hotel should have a doctor on call and she would come with me and sort it out. When we arrived she sent me up to the room and said she would bring the doctor up. I collapsed on the bed. Just ten minutes later she appeared with an elderly woman in a white coat whom she introduced as Doctor Malysheva. "She doesn't speak any English," Irina said. "So I'll stay with you to translate and she'll need a thousand roubles." (About twenty pounds sterling.) I recalled a quotation from Anton Chekhov, the Russian playwright: "Doctors are the same as lawyers; the only difference is that lawyers merely rob you, whereas doctors rob you and kill you too." The doctor asked a few questions about my symptoms and past medical history and then took my temperature. I heard Irina asking her what the reading was and understood the answer "sorak" (40C). I knew I was in trouble. The two of them entered into a long conversation and I could see that Irina was arguing with the doctor about something, quite forcefully. Eventually, Irina turned to me and said: "She says you have pneumonia and ought to go into hospital, but I said no, not into our hospitals. It's better if you stay here and I'll keep an eye on you." So that was settled. The doctor drove an injection into my buttock with a heavy duty syringe which looked as if it had been designed for use on woolly mammoths and left. Irina went away to pick up a course of antibiotics and some other tablets. When she returned she also had cartons of milk and buttermilk which she said would be good to build my strength up and a supply of food. When I was paying her for the supplies, I gave her an extra 1,000 roubles but she handed it back with an offended look. "What's this for? I don't need paying for helping someone who's in trouble." She said that the doctor had directed that I was to stay in bed and then left, saying she would come back in the morning. I set my alarm clock to wake me when I needed to take pills but apart from that slept right through until Irina knocked on the door next morning. She'd brought more food and another carton of buttermilk and stayed to chat for a while. She showed me photos of her family, a ten year old son and chubby little four years old Mariana. I remarked that her son looked Mongolian and she said her husband was a Tatar from the Volga region. He had a catering business in the university. I was feeling a lot better and being in bed with Anna Karenina was a lot more interesting than I'd thought it was going to be. In the afternoon I felt strong enough to get up and wander along to a café in the hotel for a coffee. The following morning, Irina appeared again with the doctor who took my temperature. It had come back down to normal. I was due to catch a train that evening to Riga in Latvia. Irina said she had organised it for me to keep the room until a driver from her tour company picked me up at 4.30 pm to take me to the station and that the doctor had said it should be O.K. for me to travel but that I was to take it easy. After the doctor left, I pressed her again to take some money for all her trouble but she was adamant that she didn't want anything. I said what she had done for me was above and beyond the call of duty and added in Russian "Bal'shoe spasiba." (Thank you very much.) "Och'im priyatna" she said. (It was a pleasure.) She kissed me on both cheeks and left with a wave. She was living proof that you shouldn't judge a book by its cover or a people like the Russians by the hard exterior shell they show to the world

I made it to the station for my overnight train connection to Riga. In Riga, I managed the tours I had pre-booked but my system was just ticking over and I tired quickly. On the way down to Vilnius in Lithuania, an over-taking car clipped the bus and we had to stop and wait for the police to turn up. It was hot and we all got out to sit on the grass verge. I fell asleep and the driver had to shake me awake five hours later when we were ready to continue. In Warsaw, I was amazed how well the old town had been rebuilt from the rubble of World War II: if I hadn't known everything had been destroyed, I would have been convinced the buildings were the originals. I had been to Berlin before, just after the wall had come down and it was interesting to see how the integration of the two halves of the city was proceeding. I had a tour out to Potsdam Palace. Amsterdam was my favourite European city and I had been there a number of times. I had a steak in my favourite restaurant, the Argentijns on Warmoestraat but it would have taken more than a lump of red meat to build up stamina for a visit to the adjacent red light district. Back in Shetland, after plenty of rest, I thought I had recovered. In August, I flew to Dublin and hired a car for a week to drive round the west coast of Ireland through Cork, Kerry, Killarney and up as far as Galway. It pissed with rain most of the time and I could hardly see the road never mind the scenery. I caught another cold. When I got back to New Zealand, I was still coughing and after a couple of weeks I went to the doctor. I was diagnosed with bronchitis: more antibiotics. Travel Agents should be made to print a warning on all itineraries in the same way as tobacco companies on cigarette packs: "Travel can seriously damage your health – especially in Russia."

7

STONEHENGE, ENGLAND
AUGUST 2006

I HAD LIVED in England for over two years between 1976 and 1978, working as a town planner for Shropshire County Council and living in Shrewsbury. During that time, I had never bothered to see the tourist sites of Merry England such as Stonehenge. My priorities were pubs, clubs and football. There were allegedly 99 pubs in central Shrewsbury, within the ox-bow loop of the River Severn which enclosed it. I can't personally vouch for this. When we went on a pub crawl, I used to lose count after eight or nine. My local was the Old Bell, just down the road from the Shirehall, where I worked and the statue of Roland Hill, the man credited with starting the British postal service, on his tall column. I occasionally used to turn out for their football team. Serious weekend drinking was done in the Yorkshire Rose in the town centre and then either Mr. Pews, a members only club near Shrewsbury Town's football ground, where I occasionally used to meet team members drowning their sorrows or the less salubrious Cascade Club at the bottom of the Wyle Cop where you could smell the urinals out in the street.

I rarely missed a Shrewsbury Town home game at the Gay Meadow – how the visiting teams must have loved taking the piss out of the Shrewsbury players about that name in those homophobic days when you could still joke about it. A group of us even went to away games occasionally, to exotic places like Wrexham and Chester. When Shrewsbury was playing away, I would sometimes go into Birmingham to watch Birmingham City or Aston Villa and occasionally even venture as far as London to see Arsenal or Spurs. When I was in London, it never occurred to me to visit the historic and cultural treasures of the capital like Westminster Abbey, the Tower of London, St. Paul's Cathedral, the British Museum or the National Gallery. I walked or drove past the Houses of Parliament and Buckingham Palace, but that was about it. I wouldn't go as far as to say that I was a yob or that I had a drink problem – most of my mates led a similar life style and I rarely touched alcohol during the working week. Besides, I managed to pass the Royal Town Planning Institute's entrance examination during that time by private study in my own time so I obviously wasn't a complete waster. But I certainly wasn't heavily into cultural pursuits or exploring England's heritage.

And so, older and wiser, on my way back to New Zealand in August 2006, I took a train to Salisbury and hired a car to do a tour of the tourist attractions of Ye Olde England which I had completely ignored when I had lived there. I had by this time managed to see all the London sights on stopovers over the years but I had yet to visit archaeological sites like Stonehenge, Avebury and Roman Bath, cultural centres like Shakespeare's home town of Stratford-Upon-Avon, the "Dreaming Spires" of Oxford and scenic landscape areas along the Channel coast and the Cotswolds. All of these were easily accessible from Salisbury.

In Salisbury I stayed in the venerable old Kings Arms Hotel, a black and white Tudor style pub with rooms to let and an excellent restaurant. It was in St. John Street just opposite the St. Ann Street Gate through the medieval wall surrounding Salisbury Cathedral Close. The Cathedral was a magnificent Gothic style structure, built between 1220 and 1258, its pointed arches and flying buttresses supporting a soaring 123m (400 feet) spire, the tallest in Britain. Inside, the 70m (228 feet) long nave was lined with columns of Purbeck stone from the south coast, separated by graceful archways and supporting the arched roof. In the north aisle was one of the oldest working clocks in the world dating from 1386 AD. The Chapter House held one of the four remaining copies of the Magna Carta, the agreement drawn up between King John and his barons in 1215 AD, restricting the absolute power of the monarchy and in particular providing legal protection against arbitrary arrest and imprisonment. Also in the Cathedral was a fascinating scale model of Old Sarum, an ancient town the remains of which I later visited just on the outskirts of Salisbury. Old Sarum had pre-dated Salisbury as the main town in the area, one of the most important in the west of England at the time. William the Conqueror had convened one of his earliest Councils there. It had started life as an Iron Age fort with impressive ramparts. However the site was exposed on a wind swept hill and there were problems with the water supply. In 1219 AD the bishop was given permission to build a new cathedral on the site of the present day Salisbury Cathedral beside the River Avon and Salisbury grew at Old Sarum's expense. By the 14th century the old cathedral had been demolished for building material and Old Sarum practically abandoned. Judging by the model, it must have been a fascinating place in its day.

From the St. Ann Street Gate, within Cathedral Close, a number of beautiful old houses lined North Walk, Choristers Green and West Walk. Some of these were contemporary with the Cathedral but many had been renovated in the 18th century in the attractive Queen Anne style and there were later Georgian   examples. Arundells, the home of the former Prime Minister, Edward Heath, was in West Walk. In the evening, I had a meal in the Haunch of Venison, a pub opposite the Market Square in a building dating from 1320 AD, when it was built as a church house for the adjacent St. Thomas's Church. The church had been named after St. Thomas Becket, Archbishop of Canterbury, who was murdered at the behest of King Henry II. In the first floor dining room of the pub, I sampled their signature dish, the haunch of venison, with creamed potatoes, parsnips and juniper jus. Later, having a drink downstairs, the barman drew my attention to a mummified hand and a pack of 18th century playing cards displayed in a small side window. He said they'd been discovered in 1903 during some renovation work. Presumably someone had been caught dealing off the bottom of the pack. In the morning I had a look at the 1495 "Doom" painting in the church, depicting Jesus sitting on a rainbow at the Day of Judgement with visions of heaven and hell on either side of him. Hell was of course the most interesting with a number of naked figures including a miser with his money bags and a woman who actually had her clothes on – an attendant told me she was supposed to be a female alehouse keeper. Surprisingly, in view of the display next door, there were no card-sharps.

Stonehenge was just a dozen or so miles north of Salisbury, set in the open country of the Salisbury Plain. I had read a lot and seen TV programmes about the monument and the various theories about what its purpose was, none of which seemed to be conclusive. I knew that it had been dated to the Neolithic period and early Bronze Age between 3,100 and 1600 BC during which it had been constructed in stages and so was contemporary with the Pyramids in Egypt. I had been interested in archaeology since childhood – there were remains of a Neolithic house and burial just outside the boundary fence of our croft on the island I was born on and the bases of stone walls dating from the same period could be traced from there through the neighbouring hills. Shetland had numerous archaeological sites dating from this period as did the neighbouring Orkney Islands with the stone circle called the Ring of Brodgar, Scara Brae village and the impressive Maes Howe burial chamber. The people who built Stonehenge or close relatives, had thus been able to reach the remotest islands of Britain. I had also studied pre-history as part of my Geography degree at Aberdeen University and had kept up with new developments in archaeological research over the years so I had a good general knowledge of the subject and the context in which Stonehenge stood. From the work of the Ancient Human Occupation of Britain project (AHOB) as documented in Chris Stringer's book "Homo Britannic: The Incredible Story of Human Life in Britain", I knew that the first evidence of humans in Britain, stone tools found in East Anglia, dated back as far as 700,000 years ago, when hippos, rhinos, elephants and lions had been living there, during a particularly warm interglacial period.

These people hadn't been our species, homo sapiens, but descendants of "homo erectus", the ancestor of the Neanderthals. The evidence was that people were forced out of Britain during periods of glaciation (possibly seven phases since the earliest traces of man) returning during interglacials. The earliest signs of homo sapiens, the Paleolithic Cro-magnon people, dated to around 40,000 years ago but they were in turn forced out as the glaciers of the last Ice Age advanced south, reaching their greatest extent around 20,000 BC by which time Britain wouldn't have been habitable. As the ice receded again, about 11,500 years ago, hunter-gatherers of the Mesolithic period were able to move back into Britain and traces of their culture had been found in the Stonehenge area. Around 4,000 BC new people moved into Britain, farmers, growing crops and raising livestock. Agriculture had developed in the Middle East as early as 9,000 BC and gradually spread west, either through the movement of people seeking new land as populations grew or through diffusion of the idea to neighbouring tribes. It was these Neolithic agricultural people who had built Stonehenge.

Most of the theories relating to the purpose of Stonehenge involve religion, burial and measurement of the seasons. It has been established that the stones are aligned to catch the rays of the sun at the mid-summer and mid-winter solstices along the line of the approach road, The Avenue. Knowledge of the seasons and time would have been vital to agricultural people to guide the planting and harvesting seasons. Other civilisations, such as the Maya in Central America were obsessed by it. The ancient Egyptians worshipped the sun god Ra and sun worship was common in other cultures. It therefore seems likely that Stonehenge served both as an astronomical clock and a religious centre. Burials in all cultures are integral to religion so it is to be expected that there would be burials associated with the site.

There has been debate over the years about how Stonehenge was built, how it was possible for primitive people to manhandle such huge blocks of stone without the aid of machinery. The same question has been posed about the Pyramids, the Mayan temples and the Moai Statues on Easter Island. The standing stones at Stonehenge are indeed huge. The sarsen (sandstone) stones in the outer circle, of which there were originally 30, weighed about 25 tons and originated in the Marlborough Downs 20 miles (32 Kilometres)   away, as did the 50 ton blocks in the outer horseshoe, some of which were hoisted up to form trilithons with one block resting across two uprights standing over 7 metres (24 feet) tall . The dolerite bluestones which formed an inner horseshoe in the monument weighed about 4 tons each and originated in the Preseli Mountains 250 miles away in Wales, while the altar stone placed within the horseshoe was thought to come from Carmarthenshire or the Brecon Beacon Mountains, also in Wales. It has now been accepted that the construction materials for the Pyramids, the Mayan temples and the Easter Island Moai were moved purely by manpower using ropes, sledges, wooden rollers and earthen ramps for raising stones, where possible also using waterways to float stones on rafts or barges. The agricultural society at Stonehenge would have been able to support surplus labour not needed for immediate food production and the labour demands of farming is in any case sea-sonal. It has been estimated that it would have taken about 600 men to drag a 50 ton block from the Marlborough Downs to the site. Wooden rollers would have been readily available as the landscape would still have been largely wooded at that time.

The Neolithic stone circle at Avebury lay 20 miles (32 kilome-tres) further north, part of the same UNESCO Heritage Site listing as Stonehenge, along with a number of other archaeological sites in the area: West Kennet Avenue, the 1.5 miles (2.5 kilometres) long proces-sional way leading into Avebury from the south, lined with 100 pairs of standing stones; Silbury Hill, 40m (130 feet) high, the largest man-built mound in Europe, purpose unknown; West Kennet Long Barrow, England's finest burial mound, its entrance flanked by huge sarcen stones, the roof made from massive overlapping capstones and where fifty skeletons had been found. Avebury itself was the largest stone cir-cle in Europe, measuring about 330m (1,072 feet) in diameter. There were originally 98 sarcen standing stones, some weighing over 40 tons and ranging in height from 3.6 to 4.2 metres (11.7 to 13.6 feet). Within the outer stone circle had been two inner rings, the northern one measuring 98 m (318 feet) in diameter with originally 27 stones, the southern one 108m (351 feet) across with 29 stones. Beyond the outer ring, a 5.5m (18 feet) high earth bank with a ditch 6 to 11m (20 to 36 feet) deep inside it had formed the perimeter of the site.

This complex of stone circles, processional ways and burial mounds could only have been the product of a sophisticated, well organised society with a complex culture involving elaborate rituals. Fred Flintstone look-alikes they were not. They had pottery for storing food and drink, razor sharp tools and weapons made from flint, with bronze implements appearing later, pick-axes made from red deer antlers capable of digging deep ditches. They were able to transport massive stones over long distances and construct impressive monuments from them. They were also in contact with mainland Europe: human remains found at Stonehenge have been attributed to people from as far away as the Mediterranean, the German Alps and Brittany in France, suggesting that overseas trade was well developed.

It was difficult to see the overall picture of Avebury as the village encroached into the circle and it was dissected into quarters by roads running across it from north to south and east to west. Most of the stones were now missing and you had to figure out the layout as you went around – I had picked up a useful map and brochure from the little tourist office in the village. However, this mixture of old and relatively new made it more interesting than Stonehenge, which stood in stark isolation in an open landscape like a museum exhibit. The Avebury complex was part of the village scene. Wandering around, it was fascinating to ponder on what the stone circle had been used for – the archaeologists have never figured this out, other than it must have served some ceremonial, ritual or religious purpose. Funerary rites, ancestor worship, ceremonies to appease malevolent spirits have all been suggested. Some archaeologists think that the taller, narrower stones may have been male symbols, the shorter, more squat shaped ones representing females. One of the stones, the Barber stone, had a fascinating story attached to it. In the 1930s, archaeologists had re-erected many of the stones which had been buried during a frenzy of religious destruction directed at these symbols of Devil worship. Under the Barber Stone, they had found the skeleton of a man with coins in his pocket dated to around 1320 AD, a pair of scissors and a lancet, the implements of a barber-surgeon. Evidence suggested that the stone had fallen on the man and crushed him while it was being buried. He may just have been passing through the village and stopped to see the fun. This may have curbed the enthusiasm of the circle wreckers who could have interpreted it as the Devil getting his own back. In any case, much of the monument was spared as later records show. In 1349 the Black Death struck the village and during and for a while after that the people would have had better things to do than worry about a few old stones. Another outbreak of religious fervour took place in the 17th and early 18th centuries with the rise of Puritanism. During this phase, fires were lit around some of the stones and then water poured on to weaken them so that they could be smashed with sledge hammers and used as building material. Again this frenzy passed, following criticism from local antiquarians but the majority of the stones had gone. The Northwest sector of the site had the best remaining array of stones, including the massive 65 ton Swindon Stone, one of the few never to have been disturbed. Partial restoration of the site, including re-erection of many of the buried stones, had been carried out in the 1930s by the archaeologist Alexander Keiller: a museum named after him, with artefacts from the site, was housed in the former stables of Avebury Manor. The village itself was picturesque with some white-washed thatched cottages, St. James Church and graveyard, the Great Barn and the 16th century Avebury Manor. I had lunch in the black and white, half-timbered, Tudor style Red Lion pub, near the centre of the circle, its neat thatched roof flopping over the ridge-lines like a wig.

I drove down through Dorset and stopped in Tolpuddle in the valley of the River Piddle which eventually piddled into the sea at Poole Harbour. Tolpuddle was the home of the Tolpuddle Martyrs, 19th century heroes of the trade union movement. I went into the museum dedicated to their story, located at the end of a strip of workers cottages built in 1934 to commemorate the centenary of the events which immortalised them. By 1830, farm workers in the remoter parts of southern England were suffering hard times; wages had fallen to seven shillings a week and were due to be reduced further to six shil-lings. Mechanization and other innovations arising from the agricul-tural and industrial revolutions were creating a surplus of labour in rural areas. In remote areas, landowners did not have to compete with the higher wages which workers could earn in London and the northern industrial towns and could get away with screwing down wages. In 1832 six Tolpuddle men got together to form the Friendly Society of Agricultural Labourers to campaign for a minimum wage of 10 shillings a week. Trade Unions had been legal since 1825 when the Combination Acts had been repealed but bizarrely an obscure law from 1797 prohibited people from "swearing secret oaths to each other", which the Tolpuddle six were alleged to have done in setting up their Society. Following a complaint from a local landowner to the Prime Minister, the men were arrested, found guilty and sentenced to transportation to Australia for 7 years. I had been to Australia and my heart bled for these men. But, fortunately, the story had a happy ending. There was a public outcry, a petition was raised for their release which collected 800,000 signatures and thousands of people marched in protest in London. All but one of the Martyrs (he had a previous conviction) were released after two years and returned to Britain to a heroes' welcome. The Trades Union Congress host an annual Tolpuddle Martyrs Festival in the village to promote the ideals for which the men suffered. Nearby Puddletown, with some attractive white-washed, thatched cottages, was the model for Weatherbury in Thomas Hardy's novel "Far From the Madding Crowd". I saw the cot-tage where he was born on my way into Dorchester, the setting for his novel "The Mayor of Casterbridge". On a hill above the southern approaches to Dorchester stood Maiden Castle, the largest Iron Age hill fort in Britain, enclosed by huge, steep-sided chalk ramparts. The Romans had captured it in 43 AD and the skeleton of an ancient Briton had been disinterred with a Roman crossbow bolt in his back. In the Dorset County Museum, where artefacts from the site were on display, I remarked to an attendant, "Surely not an Englishman run-ning away?" and got a very dirty look – he obviously knew a Scottish accent when he heard one.

I drove a few miles north from Dorchester on the A352 to the village of Cerne Abbas to see the Giant, a massive nude figure carved into the chalk on a hillside above the village. Wielding a huge knobbly club and a massive erection he measured 55m (180 feet) tall and 51m (167 feet) wide, his club 37m (120 feet). There was no information on the interpretive signboard about the size of his erection. The figure had been formed by digging trenches about 30cm (12 inches) wide and deep through the grass and soil to expose the underlying snow white chalk. Speculation had been rife over the years as to when he had been carved and why. Theories ranged from him being a pre-Roman Celtic representation of the Greek hero Hercules to a Saxon deity. Sadly, modern research suggests something less romantic; that he's actually just a piece of graffiti – a cartoon of Oliver Cromwell, carved by servants working for the Royalist Lord of the Manor during the English Civil War. Cromwell was apparently sarcastically called "England's Hercules" by his enemies. I later discovered that an archaeological investigation in 2008 using special equipment had discovered that the original carving included an animal skin hanging from the outstretched left arm. Hercules was often depicted like that with a lion skin, lending credence to the Cromwell spoof theory. The study also suggested that the size of his erection had resulted from a re-cut of the trenches in Victorian times which had merged a circle representing his navel with an originally smaller penis, rendering him the first recipient of penis enlargement treatment, long before the days of computer spam offers. There is no evidence that Oliver Cromwell ever underwent penis enlargement – he was a big enough prick already.

I spent the night in Weymouth, in a small hotel on the Esplanade behind the wide sandy beach. Weymouth was an archetypal example of an English seaside resort, popularised when allegedly mad King George III took a dip there in 1789. Considering the temperature of the water in the English Channel he undoubtedly was mad. His statue adorned the end of the Esplanade with some pygmy palm trees planted nearby, presumably intended to give the impression that the water was warm. A little further on was an attractive red and blue

Georgian style clock-tower. A candy-striped beach hut advertised cockles and prawns and the beach was covered in deck-chairs – it was a beautiful sunny day. I didn't see any old men with white handkerchiefs knotted over their heads Michael Palin style but there may still have been some of them left. Away to the east, white cliffs glinted in the sun all the way to the Isle of Purbeck, which, like the nearby Isle of Portland, wasn't an island; but both were famous sources of building stone, used for example in Salisbury Cathedral, St. Paul's Cathedral in London and the United Nations building in New York. I had lunch al fresco at the Galley bistro, down by the old harbour, full of fishing boats and yachts and lined with pastel coloured Georgian houses, pubs and restaurants.

I set off to explore a section of the "Jurassic Coast", starting at the alleged Isle of Portland and heading west as far as Lyme Regis. The stretch of coastline from the Isle of Purbeck westwards to Exemouth had been designated a World Heritage Site for its geological interest. Earth movements had tilted the rocks and erosion exposed them so that older rocks appeared in the west getting younger as you went east – 185 million years of geology in the 153 km (95 miles) of coastline. The cliffs were packed with fossils, including the spiralling ammonites, one of the earliest marine life forms – from which amazingly we've all descended. The Isle of Portland ceased to be an island around 6,000 years ago when it started to be attached to the mainland by Chesil Beach, a 25 km (17 miles) long ridge of pebbles and shingle, 15m (49 feet) high, trapping a lagoon inside it which is narrowing by 5m (16 feet) a year as the beach migrates landward. Portland's central plateau rose to 154m (500 feet) scarred by centuries of quarrying the white limestone. The red and white striped lighthouse on Portland Bill at the seaward tip looked like a giant stick of rock. I stopped at Abbotsbury Swannery on the shore side of the lagoon protected by Chesil Beach. It had been started by monks from the adjacent monastery about 600 years ago and every year in May some 600 wild swans appeared to nest. In Lyme Regis, I walked out along the Cobb, the breakwater sheltering the little harbour which had been made famous by the film of John Fowles' novel "The French Lieutenant's Woman" but there was no sign of Meryl Streep. This was also where the Duke of Monmouth had landed in 1689 in an abortive rebellion to restore the Stewart Kings to the throne.

I turned north and drove on to Bath, a spa town in Roman times and again in the 18th century when washing once more became popular in England – although Australians dispute this. I checked into the Abbey Hotel after a nightmare passage through one way streets, with no entry signs and pedestrian precincts every time I wanted to turn in a certain direction. It was not a city for driving so I set off on foot to explore. Turning left on North Parade, I crossed the Avon River, which snaked around the central city and walked up to the old centre, the little square called the Abbey Churchyard in front of the Abbey and the Roman Baths. The Roman town had grown up here around the baths built to take advantage of three hot springs. The healing powers of the springs had been known to the ancient Britons and a shrine dedicated to their Goddess of Healing, Sulis, had preceded the Romans, who named their town Aquae Sulis – the Waters of Sulis. After the Romans abandoned Britain in the 5th century AD, their town fell into disuse and decayed during the Dark Ages. A Saxon abbey and convent were built on the site of the present day abbey in the 8th century and the settlement revived. The present abbey dated from a re-build in 1499.

I had a look around the abbey and then went to see the Roman Baths which had been beautifully restored, the terrace above the green-tinged waters of the main pool lined with statues. A museum held the artefacts excavated from the site including a gilded bronze head of the Roman Goddess of Healing, Minerva.

Bath had been given a new lease of life early in the 18th century. A wealthy businessman, Ralph Allen (who would now be called a "Developer" or possibly a "Speculator") aided by an upper class dandy, Beau Nash, who became the town's Master of Ceremonies, responsible for organising the social whirl, combined to popularise the town as a spa for the wealthy upper classes. A property boom resulted in some of the most attractive Georgian style housing developments in Britain including the Circus and the Royal Crescent, designed by the talented architect John Wood and later his son of the same name. The city centre was peppered with elegant buildings from this period – the Theatre Royal, Queen Square. I walked back across the Avon over Pulteney Bridge, designed by Robert Adam in the style of Ponte Vecchio in Florence, with little shops on either side. The whole city has been designated a UNESCO World Heritage Site.

I set out from Bath to explore the Cotswolds. Although called the Cotswold Hills, the landscape was not actually hilly, the rolling appearance resulting from the valleys eroded by the rivers flowing east. The underlying rock was oolitic limestone, much finer grained than the carboniferous limestone which forms craggier, rougher country like the Pennines. The edge of the oolitic limestone formed an escarpment facing west above the valley of the River Severn and the land fell away eastwards in a dip slope from there, dissected by rivers such as the Windrush. The stunning landscape which resulted had been designated as an Area of Outstanding Natural Beauty (AONB) by English Heritage. The oolitic limestone made an excellent building stone, soft and easy to cut when quarried but hardening on exposure to the air. Ranging in colour from pale grey in the south to cream, through golden honey to brown in the north, it provided the character of the built environment in the walls of cottages, villages and churches. It had even been used as roofing material, splitting easily to form tiles, which being heavy, influenced the building style, through needing heavy wooden beams to support them.

I drove east to the village of Lacock, its curving streets flanked by cottages and houses, some half-timbered and whitewashed others in warm grey Cotswold stone, all 18th century or older, many medieval. The upper storeys of some houses overhung the ground levels; others stood gable on to the street. The outside of the 18th century Red Lion pub was decorated with hanging baskets of flowers. The former Lacock Abbey had been converted to a stately home in the mid 16th century. In the Lady Chapel of the 11th century Church of St. Cyriac, the ornate tomb of Sir William Sharington had a recess with moss covered stones, lilies and three little wooden crosses. One of the houses featured in the Harry Potter films as the home of the boy wizard.

I carried on north to Castle Combe, once voted the prettiest village in England. It had a 13th century market cross with a pyramid shaped tiled roof and the medieval Church of St Andrew. Old weavers' cottages huddled around the medieval packhorse bridge which crossed a swiftly flowing stream heading for the nearby Avon River. The stream had once been lined with more than 20 woollen mills. Sheep had made the Cotswolds. Roman landowners had kept sheep on their estates near Cirencester and the tradition had endured into Anglo-Saxon and Norman times. The native breed known as Cotswold Lions could produce fleeces weighing 28 pounds. Initially the wool was exported to the Low Countries where towns like Ghent and Bruges grew rich making cloth from English wool. In the 14th century King Edward III arranged for Flemish weavers to be brought over to England to develop a woollen industry which soon came to dominate the English economy, the Cotswolds accounting for more than half the production, with over 500,000 sheep. There was plentiful fuller's earth in the area to clean the wool and the swift flowing streams provided sites for spinning and weaving mills. The area prospered and fine houses and churches – which came to be known as Wool Churches – were built.

I drove on north through the Cotswold landscape, fields bordered by drystone walls, remnants of the original mixed woodland along watercourses and on hillsides – oak, elm, beech and yew trees. In the north Cotswolds, I stopped briefly in Bourton-on-the-Water with 18th century bridges spanning the Windrush River. It was touristified with an abundance of gift shops. Nearby were the picture postcard villages of Lower and Upper Slaughter, lying along the River Eye amid gentle, wooded hills. The name derived from the old English word "slaughtre" meaning "muddy spot" – it didn't look like a place prone to massacres. Here the houses were of honey coloured Cotswold stone, mostly dating from the 16th and 17th centuries. In Lower Slaughter, the River Eye flowed gently between low banks which had been faced up with stonework. I wandered across a little footbridge with ducks swimming around below. The splendid 17th century Manor House was now a hotel. The 19th century corn mill was now a museum with a teashop, one of the few brick buildings in the village. Upper Slaughter was characterised by large two-storey houses with dormer windows, most with Cotswold stone roof tiles. The Norman era Church of St. Peter had an impressive tower with battlements. Sir Edwin Lutyens, the designer of New Delhi, had worked here between 1906 and 1910, renovating some existing houses and designing new ones. On my way north, I saw a set of medieval stocks on the enormous market green in Stow-in-the-Wold, an attractive little town with a plethora of antique shops. As I left the Cotswolds, I pondered on the irony of the fact that economic disaster had produced the landscape which was now such a tourist attraction. From around 1750, the woollen industry had started to collapse in face of competition from northern towns like Leeds and Bradford where cloth could then be made much more cheaply using the new-fangled steam power and factory systems brought in by the industrial revolution. By 1850 it was more or less all over for the Cotswolds, poverty was rife and there was even starvation. Too many eggs had been put in the wool basket. By the end of the 1914-18 War only a few flocks of the Cotswold Lion sheep remained and it had become a rare breed. There's nothing like poverty to promote conservation. Little money was available to spend on property renewal and the fine buildings created during the wool boom remained as if set in 18th century aspic.

In Stratford-upon-Avon, I stayed in the Shakespeare Hotel, fittingly enough in the home town of England's greatest playwright. The hotel was a black and white Tudor building, the interior full of low beams and period furniture. Some of the rooms were named after Shakespeare's plays but I saw no signs of a 'Much Ado About Nothing' room. I walked down to the Shakespeare Centre in Henley Street which was built in 1964 to commemorate the 400th anniversary of the great man's birth. It incorporated the restored timber-framed building where his father, for a time the Mayor of Stratford, had lived. Rooms had been furnished in Elizabethan style and an adjacent exhibition told the story of Shakespeare's life. Next door to the Shakespeare Hotel in Chapel Street was the next stop on the Shakespeare heritage trail, Nash's House, where his granddaughter Elizabeth had lived. It was furnished in period style and housed a museum of local history. Adjacent to Nash's House was all that was left of New House where Shakespeare had lived after he retired and returned from London and where he died. Nothing remained but some foundations and two wells, the site now accommodating a colourful Tudor style garden and two mulberry trees, one allegedly grown from a cutting from a tree planted by Shakespeare. The story behind the fate of New House was fascinating. In the mid 18th century, the house belonged to the Reverend Francis Gastrell. Shakespeare was by this time already famous and the places associated with him already on the tourist trail, much to the Reverend's annoyance. So many people came to sit beneath the mulberry tree where the Bard had reputedly sat that, in a fit of rage, the Reverend cut it down. This brought the wrath of the local community down on him and in 1759 he retaliated by demolishing the house, after which he was run out of town. Considering the hordes of tourists who now swamp Stratford, many locals probably have some sympathy for the irascible clergyman. A block away was Hall's Croft, where Shakespeare's daughter Susanna had lived with her husband, a doctor called John Hall. It was a beautiful, half-timbered building, furnished in period style with an exhibition on medieval and Elizabethan medicine, including some gruesome instruments. The Doctor was renowned for his scurvy cure and apparently specialised in some other treatments involving dead pigeons and peacock's droppings which may have been less successful.

I drove out to Anne Hathaway's Cottage on the western edge of the town, where Shakespeare's wife had been born on a farm. To call the building a cottage was a bit of a misnomer; it was a substantial 12 roomed farmhouse in the traditional timber frame/wattle and daub infill style with a thatched roof. It was furnished in period style with some original furniture including a wooden "courting settle" (nowadays it would be called a sofa) on which it was speculated William and Anne may have indulged in some "Chesterfield rugby" – she was already pregnant when they got married. There was an Elizabethan style garden outside and just beyond, the Shakespeare Tree Garden, with specimens of all the trees mentioned in his plays. I looked around for Burnham Wood but perhaps I couldn't see the wood for the trees. Mary Arden's House, the family home of Shakespeare's mother, was in Wilmcote, about 5 km (3 miles) north-west of the town. There is apparently some doubt about which of the buildings there she actually lived in; until recently it was believed to be the main farmhouse, a fine early 16th century building with a half-timbered frontage and gabled dormer windows but there were now suspicions that it may have been a less salubrious building nearby. The farmhouse had been in continuous occupation and so was perfectly preserved when bought by the Shakespeare Birthplace Trust in 1930 and converted into a museum. They had later acquired the adjacent Glebe Farm and the whole complex was now the Shakespeare Countryside Museum, with a dovecote, farm equipment, a cider press, rare-breed farm animals and a falconry. An exhibition illustrated the work of country craftsmen such as blacksmiths, coopers and wheelwrights. I had a pint in the nearby pub, predictably called The Mary Arden, with a painting of the good lady on the sign outside. I asked the young barmaid if Shakespeare's mother used to drink there and she told me with a straight face that she had until she was banned for singing dirty songs. I reminded her that that was how rumours started. That evening, I had Kerala chicken cooked in coconut milk in the Coconut Lagoon in Sheep Street, the best Indian restaurant I had come across anywhere in the world.

The following morning was warm and sunny and I took a stroll along the bank of the Avon. I started in Bancroft Gardens where in the Gower Memorial a bronze Shakespeare sat being entertained by Lady Macbeth, Prince Hall, Falstaff and Hamlet. Further along was the Royal Shakespeare Theatre and the Elizabethan style Swan Theatre. I finally came to the Holy Trinity Church where the Bard lay buried beneath a simple stone in the chancel.

In Oxford, I climbed the Carfax Tower, all that's left of the 14th century St. Martin's Church, to get an overview of the central city. A sea of university colleges lay spread out below me, 38 according to the leaflet I'd picked up in the tourist office, the earliest dating back to the 13th century, now with 20,000 students. In the early days there had been serious friction between the students and the townspeople, culminating in the St. Scholastica's Day Massacre in 1355 when 63 students and 30 townspeople were killed in armed rioting. Students never are very popular with the locals in university towns but this was ridiculous. I walked down St. Aldate's to Christ Church College, Tom Tower soaring above the main entrance with its 7 ton bell 'Great Tom'. The tower had been designed by Sir Christopher Wren when he was Professor of Astronomy at the University. He must have thought about giving up the day job after that. The Dining Hall was on the south side of the vast expanse of grass in Tom Quad. The walls were lined with portraits of former students including some of the 13 Prime Ministers who had attended the College. Albert Einstein had been there as well but I didn't see him in the rogue's gallery. Henry VIII and his daughter Elizabeth 1st were both there. Henry had been heavily involved in founding the college after he fell out with Cardinal Wolsey, who had started it – they had quarrelled over women and religion of course, what else? In the Cathedral, a notice beside a side door contained dire warnings about not opening it. In spite of this, a tour guide was white-rabbiting on to a party of tourists about Alice in Wonderland, the door wide open. I thought he must be mad as a hatter. I infiltrated them and had a look out. Sure enough there, across a lawn, was the green door set in a high wall that Alice had gone through into Wonderland. The author of the Alice books, Lewis Carroll (alias Charles Dodgson) had been a Mathematics tutor at the College and many of the characters and scenes in the books were based on people and places in the college – he wrote the first book just to amuse the Dean's daughter, Alice.

I walked back up to the High Street and had a wander through the covered market with stalls selling food of all kinds – butchers, delicatessens, coffee, but also T- shirts and souvenirs, clothes and footwear; a modern, medieval fair. I continued along High Street, past Brasenose College, where there were allegedly carvings of monks picking their noses and vomiting and Michael Palin had studied. Next door was the 14th century Church of St. Mary the Virgin with its soaring spire. Just across the street was University College where Bill Clinton didn't inhale, long before he met Monica Lewinsky, who may or may not have swallowed. I turned up Catte Street, the twin mock-Gothic spires of All

Souls College on my right and three of the most iconic buildings in the city in quick succession on my left – the round Radcliffe Camera with its massive dome; the Bodleian Library; and the magnificent Sheldonian Theatre, the first major work of Sir Christopher Wren, who was still Professor of Astronomy when he designed it. Someone must surely at that point have said "Christopher, for God's sake give up the day job." He went on to design St. Paul's Cathedral in London. Architecture probably paid better than teaching in those days too. Further along Broad Street, a brick cross in the road surface marked where Bishops Latimer and Ridley had been burned at the stake in 1555; a year later, Archbishop Thomas Cranmer was dragged from his trial in the Church of St. Mary the Virgin to suffer the same fate. Scorch marks from the fire could still be seen on the gate of Balliol College. Henry VIII's eldest daughter Mary had succeeded to the throne and as a staunch Catholic had set out to snuff out the Protestant Reformation brought about by her father. The bishops refused to recant their Protestant faith and suffered the ultimate penalty. I retraced my steps and passed into New College Lane under the Bridge of Sighs, modelled on the original in Venice. New College had been founded in 1379 – age was relative in Oxford. Turning left into High Street again, I arrived back at my hotel, the Eastgate Townhouse, opposite Magdalen College.

In the evening I went on a pub crawl. The Eagle and Child was in St. Giles Street, opposite St. John's College, where Tony Blair had studied spinning and how to invade Iraq. It had been the local of J R Tolkien, author of 'Lord of the Rings' and 'The Hobbit' and C S Lewis, who wrote 'The Chronicles of Narnia'. Both were professors in the English Faculty of the university. Apparently they would get quite loud discussing ideas for fantastical novels. Your average drunk can get carried away with tall tales getting on for closing time but with the sort of imaginations these guys had the sky would not have been the limit. I had dinner in the Brasserie Gerard in George Street; garlic prawns, coq au vin, tarte au citron and quite a lot to drink – Monte Verde Sauvignon Blanc, Muscat de Beaunes and a Grand Marnier with the coffee: I was on a pub crawl after all. I called in to the White Horse in Broad Street, opposite the Sheldonian Theatre. This had been one of Inspector Morse's favourite pubs in the TV series. Mulling over a pint, it occurred to me that compared to some of the mayhem that had gone on in Oxford in the past – massacring students, burning bishops – the sorts of crimes Morse had to solve were kid's stuff. I tried to remember the embarrassing first name that Morse always refused to use. Was It Alice? No, she was in Wonderland. Bilbo? No, he was a Hobbit. My brain wasn't functioning well. I blamed the drink. It would come back to me.

In the morning I wandered across the road to Magdalen College, dominated by the 48m (144 feet) high Great Tower, completed in 1509. It had been used as a vantage point during the Civil War when Oxford became the Royalist headquarters after the Battle of Edgehill in 1642. The chapel had a beautiful stained glass window and a 15th century copy of Leonardo da Vinci's painting 'The Last Supper'. The cloisters surrounding the central quadrangle were populated with grotesque stone statues, gargoyles, some representing the seven deadly sins, some biblical figures. They were supposed to have provided inspiration for C S Lewis's fertile imagination. There was a bust of Oscar Wilde, a former student, in the Hall, now the refectory. I strolled along Addisons Walk, a path along a branch of the Cherwell River, some deer from the adjacent Deer Park grazing in the water meadows. Across the road from Magdalen, the botanic gardens had started life as a herb garden to study plants for medicinal purposes; much more exotic tropical species now lurked in the greenhouses down by the river. I set out across Christ Church Meadow, following the River Cherwell. Punts glided past, poled by pairs of would-be gondoliers, shades of Brideshead Revisited. Black and white cows grazed in the meadow. It was an idyllic scene, vintage England. Suddenly, it came back to me – Inspector Morse's first name – Endeavour! Fancy calling someone after Captain Cook's ship. No wonder he was such a sad bastard. I had a pint in the Head of the River pub down on the Thames, here called the Isis. A couple of rowing eights flashed past, perhaps dreaming of glory in the annual boat race with the old enemy, Cambridge.

The following morning, I caught a bus out to see Blenheim Palace, the ancestral home of the Dukes of Marlborough and the birthplace of Sir Winston Churchill. It stood just outside the attractive village of Woodstock, 8 miles (13 kilometres) north of Oxford on the A44. The land and money to build the palace on it had been gifted to John Churchill, the 1st Duke of Marlborough, by Queen Anne, in recognition of his victory over the French at the Battle of Blenheim in 1704, during the War of the Spanish Succession. It was a magnificent, sprawling, baroque style building, set in 2,000 acres (813 hectares) of parkland. It had been designed by the architects Sir John Vanbrugh and Nicolas Hawksmoor, the park laid out by the famous landscape architect Lancelot 'Capability' Brown. It had been designated a UNESCO World Heritage Site in 1987.

The Great Hall was aptly named, with its 20m (65 feet) high ceiling decorated with a painting showing scenes from the 1st Duke in battle, lighted by windows high up in the walls. Sculptures stood in alcoves and framed portraits hung behind a high balcony. There were two tours on offer, one of the state rooms and the Churchill Exhibition, the other upstairs to the virtual reality show "Blenhiem Palace: The Untold Story". The state rooms were magnificent, full of oil paintings in gilt frames, portraits of the various Dukes, porcelain, tapestries and chandeliers hanging from the ceilings. The Long Library was 55m (179 feet) long; the Red Drawing Room more intimate with gilt framed paintings of family members, an open fireplace and ornate candle holders. We saw the room where Sir Winston Churchill was born in 1874. The story of his life was told in the Churchill Exhibition. The high tech virtual reality show upstairs was more fun. It was conducted by the ghostly image of Grace Ridley, lady's maid to the 1st Duchess, who told us stories about the family and servants spanning the 300 years since the palace was built, aided by talking portraits and animated figures who emerged, literally, from the woodwork. It was the best production of this type I had seen. After the tours I went to see the separate exhibition "Churchills' Destiny" in the former stables, which covered the lives of both John Churchill, the 1st Duke and Sir Winston, drawing parallels between them. It covered the history of the War of the Spanish Succession which brought the 1st Duke his fame and fortune.

Out in the Park, I took the miniature railway to see the Pleasure Gardens with a maze and butterfly house and then took the Gardens Lakeside Walk to see Blenheim Dam and Cascade. Finally, I strolled across the Grand Bridge, spanning the artificial Great Lake and made famous in a Turner painting and made my way up to the tall Column of Victory with the 1st Duke perched on top. I exited via the Woodstock Gate to the village and had a late lunch in the Bear Hotel, an ivy-covered 13th century coaching inn, with open fireplaces, bare stone walls and low exposed beams – quintessential Olde England.

On my way back to Salisbury to deliver the rental car, I stopped in Uffington to see the famous White Horse. Carved in chalk on a hillside, this was an authentic prehistoric creation, dating to the Bronze Age - unlike the Cerne Abbas Giant. Archaeological investigations involving optically stimulated luminescence in 1994 had produced dates ranging between 1400 and 600 BC and you can't argue with technology like that. However, all that optical stimulation had still not produced an explanation of why the 110m (357 feet) long beast had been carved. A similar image had been found on Iron Age coins. However, I came across an article in Wikipaedia which may offer a clue. Apparently, in Ireland in the Dark Ages (still on-going there), the initiation ceremony for a new king required him to mate with a white mare. A graphic eye-witness account records that: " Held by several men, her hind quarters adequately spread, she was presented to the future king to couple with." This wasn't just some Irish jiggy-jiggy and horsing around; according to the article, similar rituals went away back in Celtic and Indo-European traditions. So perhaps the Uffington white horse was just a piece of Bronze Age pornographic graffiti. If the Cerne Abbas Giant had been around in the Bronze Age, this theory could even have explained his erection. But the mystery remains. Sometimes, as in the case of Stonehenge, a bit of mystery does no harm – it helps to stimulate the imagination. It was too late to call in Inspector Morse on either of these cold cases; the poor bugger had died without ever solving the mystery of why his parents had saddled him with a first name like Endeavour.

8

ANGKOR WAT, CAMBODIA
AUGUST 2006

FRESH FROM MY trip through Merry England to the mysterious
Stonehenge, I landed in Cambodia which, during Pol Pot's regime in
the late 1970s, had probably been the least merry country on earth,
ever – more akin to hell – and where the temples at Angkor represented a tectonic shift since the time of Stonehenge in man's ability
to create magnificent monuments to the Gods. I had booked a tour
with Travel Indochina, an Australian firm based in Ho Chi Minh City
(Saigon). I had travelled with them before in Vietnam and China: I
liked their informal style and the small groups they specialised in. I
was staying in the Hotel Cambodiana, in the capital, Phnom Penh,
down by the confluence of the three rivers which provided the setting
for the city: the mighty Mekong, flowing down from Tibet; the Tonle
Sap, which drained the massive lake of the same name to the west;
and the Tonle Bassac, which re-joined the Mekong at the head of its
delta on the Vietnam border. It was a strategic location, the reason
why the rulers of Angkor adopted it as their capital when they abandoned the area around Angkor Wat in the 1430s. Before I left for the
tour, I had read two very interesting books: 'Pol Pot: The History of a
Nightmare' by Philip Short; and 'Collapse: How Societies Choose to

Fail or Survive' by Jared Diamond. The latter didn't specifically cover the end of the civilization in the Angkor Wat area but it provided useful pointers to the factors which may have been involved. Coupled with the travel guides I had read, I therefore had a reasonable amount of background information about what I was about to see.

The tour group met with the guide in the hotel in the afternoon of the day I arrived. There were only two other group members, Ann and Malcolm from Australia, both around my age. I didn't catch the guide's name but it sounded like Dook (spelled 'Deuch' in Philip Short's book but pronounced 'Dook') , the name of the notorious head of the Tol Sleng Prison which we were to visit later. I hoped he didn't share any of the character traits of his namesake or we were in for a terrifying trip. He was a local Khmer (the name given to the inhabitants of Cambodia and their language) – Travel Indochina didn't provide Aussie guides for groups of less than 7 people.

We started with the National Museum, next door to the Royal Palace and not far from the hotel. The exhibits were displayed in courtyards around a lush tropical garden: an eight-armed statue of the Hindu god Vishnu dating from the 6th or 7th centuries; a slightly later representation of Shiva; and an 11th century sculpture of Jayavarman VII, the greatest of the Angkorian god-kings. Many of the sculptures and carvings from Angkor Wat and the surrounding temples had been brought here for safe keeping during the years of civil war. There was also a display of pottery and bronze artefacts from pre-Angkorian periods. The Funan kingdom in what is now the southern Vietnam coastal area had flourished from around the 1st to the 6th centuries AD, trading with China, India and Indonesia; later the Chenla kingdom around the Phnom Penh area and to the east of Tonle Sap had blossomed with the development of wet-rice cultivation. The country had had a long and distinguished history.

In the early evening, when some of the heat had gone out of the sun, we took a cyclo tour of the city and saw some of the landmarks from French colonial times – the railway station, the Post Office and some fine old hotels. The French had taken out a protectorate over Cambodia in 1864, ostensibly to protect it from the unwanted attentions of Thailand and Vietnam, with which it had been in conflict on and off for centuries. Independence had come in 1953 when the French finally gave up the struggle against insurgencies opposing their rule. But their legacy remained in the architecture and the food.

In the morning we went to visit the Royal Palace complex, entering through the Chan Chaya Pavilion, where classical Cambodian dance performances used to be held. The Palace itself was still occupied by the royal family and out of bounds but we had a look at the throne room where coronations took place. The Khmer Rouge had destroyed many of the contents when they took over the city in 1975, before Prince Sihanouk returned from exile. They had had a similar attitude to historic treasures as the Red Guards in China. The piece de resistance was the Silver Pagoda with its floor of over 5,000 silver tiles, each weighing a kilogram. It had originally been built of wood by King Norodom in 1892 but rebuilt in more substantial materials in 1932, including Italian marble steps leading up to the entrance. The steeply raked roof was covered in green and gold tiles, with elaborately carved gilded beams and antler-shaped finials. Inside was an Emerald Buddha on a gilt pedestal. The Pagoda had been inspired by Bangkok's Wat Phra Keo (Temple of the Emerald Buddha). A 90 kilogram Golden Buddha was encrusted with literally thousands of diamonds and other precious stones. There were also silver, bronze and marble Buddhas. Bejewelled masks were on display - which had been used in dances and ceremonies - and gifts from visiting heads of state. Outside in the compound stood an equestrian statue of King Norodom, a bell tower and shrines to some ex-kings and one of Prince Sihanouk's daughters. The covered gallery around the perimeter of the compound was lined with a 600 metres (1,950 feet) long mural of the Hindu epic, the Ramayana, the illustrations more gory than the Indian version, according to Dook. Bizarrely, the Pagoda had served as the HQ of the Khmer Rouge leadership for a time after they captured Phnom Penh. They had even slept there. This may have been a blessing in disguise as much of the contents had been spared the vandalism which the rest of the Palace complex was subjected to.

I was fascinated by the life story of Prince Sihanouk which was inexorably bound up in the history of Cambodia since World War II. He had come to the throne in 1941 aged 19 and played a major role in winning independence from France in 1953. In 1955 he abdicated in favour of his father to take part in the elections to establish a government for the new country. Under the constitution, real power lay with the government rather than the monarchy. His party won the election with a landslide majority and remained in power for twenty years. However, in 1970, Sihanouk was ousted in a coup and went into exile in China. A right wing clique, closely allied with the Americans and led by Lon Nol, took over and intensified the struggle against the communist insurgency which had escalated during the 1960s. Bizarrely, Sihanouk now allied himself and his supporters with the Khmer Rouge which in 1975 captured Phnom Penh and took over the government. However, he was sidelined by the Khmer Rouge leadership - who jettisoned their moderate supporters to pursue all out communism - and was under virtual house arrest in the Palace during Pol Pot's time in power. When Vietnam invaded in 1979, ousted the Khmer Rouge and set up a puppet government, Sihanouk escaped and again went into exile in China, returning in 1990 after the Vietnamese had left. After an unsuccessful attempt to regain political power in the elections to form a new government, he resumed the throne again in 1993. However, he had a stormy relationship with the new government and fearing that they were plotting to abolish the monarchy, in 2004 he abdicated for the second time, this time in favour of his son. It had been an eventful life.

We drove on to Tuol Sleng Prison which was located in the southern part of the city. It was housed in a former secondary school and had been called S-21 (Security Office 21) by the Khmer Rouge. Ironically, Deuch, the man in charge of the establishment, had been a schoolteacher. To the inmates, he must have been the headmaster from hell. It was set up in May 1976 for the interrogation and extermination of people accused of opposing Angkar, the name the Khmer Rouge gave to their organization. Many of the victims were members of the Khmer Rouge itself, including many senior figures. On a board outside was posted the school rules, in its new incarnation as a detention centre, ten commandments giving a chilling insight into the mentality of the people who ran it:-

1. You must answer accordingly to my questions. Do not turn them away.
2. Do not try to hide the facts by making pretexts of this and that. You are strictly prohibited to contest me.
3. Do not be a fool for you are a chap who thwarts the revolution.
4. You must immediately answer my questions without wasting time to reflect.
5. Do not tell me either about your immoralities or the revolution.
6. While getting lashes or electrification you must not cry at all.
7. Do nothing. Sit still and wait for my orders. If there is no order, keep quiet. When I ask you to do something, you must do it right away without protesting.
8. Do not make pretexts about Kampuchea Krom* in order to hide your jaw of traitor.
9. If you do not follow all the above rules, you shall get many lashes of electric wire.
10. If you disobey any point of my regulations you shall get either ten lashes or five shocks of electric discharge.
    * Southern Vietnam
    *

Inside, the faces of the victims stared out at us from the walls, men, women and children. If one member of a family was suspected of sub-version, all members were arrested. Meticulous records were kept, like under the Nazi regime in Germany. Each prisoner was photographed on admission and then again after torture and in some cases even after death. The downstairs classrooms had been subdivided into one-man cells measuring 0.8 by 2 metres. The windows were covered by iron bars and tangles of barbed wire. The shackles used to fasten the prisoners to the floor or walls were still in place. The prisoners slept on the floor without mats, mosquito nets or blankets. They had to ask permission from the guards to relieve themselves or even to change position while trying to get to sleep; otherwise, if they were caught, they were whipped. They were tortured to extract confessions: the instruments used were on display. Children from ten to fifteen years of age were trained as guards. They became exceptionally cruel, like the child soldiers in some countries in Africa. During the period of its operation, more than 17,000 victims were taken to the extermination area at Choeung Ek, known as the Killing Fields, our next destination.

The Killing Fields, a former longan orchard, were 15 kilometres (10 miles) outside the city and had a peaceful, rural feel on the initial approach with a scattering of attractive trees. But we were soon brought back to reality at the sight of some of the 8,000 skulls of the victims behind the glass panels of the pagoda-shaped memorial. Many of them had been bludgeoned to death to save bullets, the back of some of the skulls crushed like eggshells. The bodies had been disinterred, blindfolded and bound, from some of the 129 communal graves on the site. Some young children were playing among the pits and mounds representing excavated and untouched mass graves. Bits of bone and cloth were visible in the pits. They smiled angelically and waved at us as we walked around, oblivious to the horrors that had been perpetrated in their playground.

The man ultimately responsible for those horrors, Pol Pot, was something of an enigma. He was not an ignorant, uneducated savage like Idi Amin. His real name was Saloth Sar – Pol Pot was one of many aliases he used when operating clandestinely against a succession of governments. His father was relatively wealthy owning 50 acres (20 hectares) of rice paddies (ten times the average in his village): he used to employ the poorer villagers to help with the planting and harvesting. The family was well placed socially: his aunt got a post in the royal household and later her daughter became one of Crown Prince Monivong's concubines. There was no social stigma attached to this; quite the contrary - it was a considerable status symbol. When Monivong became king, Sar's sister became his favourite concubine. Sar used to visit them at the Palace when he went to Phnom Penh, aged 9, to study – first as a novice in a Buddhist monastery for a year then at a catholic private school where the lessons were in French. He had a privileged up-bringing – only a handful of locals could afford a Western-style education in those days. He later went to college in Phnom Penh and then won a scholarship to study in France in 1950. It was there that he got involved with a left wing student group, the Cercle Marxiste – many of the subsequent Khmer rouge leadership belonged to this group. He later joined the French Communist Party. However, Philip Short, writing in his book "Pol Pot", was of the view that he was more influenced in his later actions by the French Revolution than the writings of Marx, Stalin and Mao.

In January 1953 Sar returned from France to investigate which of the various revolutionary groups the Cercle Marxiste should support. At that time the Cambodian communists, the Khmer Viet Minh, were relatively weak, just a group within their Vietnamese counterparts fighting against French rule. However, the Cercle decided to throw in their lot with the Viet Minh but aim to gradually break away from Vietnamese control. Sar joined them in the jungle just months before independence. After the ceasefire in Vietnam in August 1954, following the defeat of the French at Dien Bien Phu, Sar returned to Phnom Penh. Part of his group's objective had been met with the ending of French rule but they still wanted rid of the monarchy and its associated feudal structures. Initially Sar was involved in the legitimate political process to establish a government for the newly independent country, campaigning with the Democratic Party, left wing but not overtly communist. However, the incipient Khmer Rouge also had an underground wing operating in secrecy which he was also a part of. He led a double life with a beautiful upper class girlfriend, reputedly liked to have a good time, enjoying music and dancing and drove a flash car belonging to his sister who had been the old king's concubine. He was described as amiable, always smiling. However, the elections turned out to be a disaster. Sihanouk's party swept the board and to rub salt into the wound, Sar's upper class girlfriend ditched him in favour of one of the wealthy successful candidates. On the rebound, he married a fellow communist, five years older than him and no beauty, who subsequently had a miscarriage which left her unable to have children and later developed chronic schizophrenia. It's difficult to tell whether personal circumstances like these had any influence on the sort of man he was to become but it seems likely to have embittered him. After the elections, the Vietnamese communist party, which still controlled the Cambodian branch, ruled that the Cambodians should not pursue an armed struggle against Sihanouk's government as he was believed to have left wing sympathies but continue both overt and underground political activities. Sar devoted himself to the underground branch with a cover as a teacher of history and French literature in a private school. He was reputedly very popular with his pupils. In the early 1960s, Sihanouk launched a campaign of repression against the communists, banning all left wing newspapers, assassinating their overt leader and condemning to death the next two most senior operatives, leaving Sar as the new leader. A list of known left wing subversives including Sar was published and he fled to the jungle near the Vietnamese border where the Viet Minh were operating in Cambodian territory along the Ho Chi Minh Trail. It was now that he adopted the code name of Pol Pot and armed insurgency against Sihanouk and then Lon Nol began in earnest. Ironically, it was the blanket B-52 bombing by Lon Nol's American allies along the Ho Chi Minh Trail in eastern Cambodia, starting in 1970, that swelled the ranks of the Khmer Rouge and enabled them to take over the country in 1975.

The first action of the Khmer Rouge was to empty out the cities including Phnom Penh, expelling the inhabitants to the rural areas where they were to be organised into agricultural cooperatives. In 1975 there were over two million people living in Phnom Penh but most of these were refugees from the American bombing and civil war elsewhere in the country. However, there were about half a million who had no recent ties with the countryside. Thousands died in the evacuation and Lon Nol supporters and his military were systematically executed. It was while domiciled at the Silver Pagoda that Pol Pot and the senior leadership of the Khmer Rouge decided on their strategy for ruling the country. Since 1975 they had been allied with Prince Sihanouk and his wealthy, aristocratic supporters. Many intellectuals and professional people had also supported the Khmer Rouge cause, preferring them to the corrupt regime of Lon Nol. They were believed to be a relatively moderate socialist group led by the left wing intellectual Khieu Samphan and Ieng Sary. Amazingly, it was a year after the take-over until it was made publicly known that Angkar was a communist organization and that Pol Pot was the leader. This self-effacing side to Pol Pot's character, hardly typical of other 20th century tyrants like Hitler, Mussolini, Stalin, Saddam Hussein and Idi Amin was another of the enigmas surrounding him, although the regime as a whole was obsessed with secrecy. What the leadership decided at the Silver Pagoda was to discard their moderate allies and go for full, unadulterated communism; to transform the country into a giant, Maoist, peasant-dominated, agricultural cooperative. Their philosophy was spelled out by Khieu Samphan in a seminar for party members returning from abroad. The aim, he explained was to destroy private property on both the material and mental planes. Evacuating the towns to root out the bourgeoisie was the first step on the material plane. "The moment you allow private property," he said, "one person will have a little more, another a little less and then they are no longer equal. But if you have nothing – zero for him and zero for you – that is true equality." On the mental plane, he said "Everything you think of as yours – family, parents, wife must be sacrificed for the good of Angkar – men, women and children separated and segregated." Angkar would become the family. "The knowledge you have in your heads, your ideas, are mental private property too – you must wash your minds clean." At the end of the seminar, the delegates were told to keep these ideas to themselves as "if the masses knew what we have been discussing, they might become discouraged."

The practical implementation of this philosophy included the abolition of money and markets, even barter was discouraged; law courts, newspapers, postal services, overseas telecommunications and air services, other than a couple of flights a week to China, were discontinued. The population was set to work in gangs clearing new land for rice cultivation and digging irrigation channels in echoes of ancient Angkor. No wages were paid. Food, a few bowls of watery rice a day, and clothing, black shirt and trousers, car-tyre sandals and a chequered scarf, known as a krama, were provided by the state. It became a slave state. Foraging, hunting and even picking up windfall fruit were prohibited as this could create inequalities. The working day was 12 to 15 hours followed by nightly seminars with self-criticism and lectures by the village leaders on the need to "work hard, produce more, love Angkar, build and defend the nation, reject selfish, individualistic Western-style capitalism." The same mantra was relayed by state radio. There was no free time. People had to stop saying "I" and use "We" instead. Weddings were collective for a minimum of 10 couples; families were broken up, children over seven years old separated from their parents to live communally with Khmer Rouge instructors. The Buddhist temples were closed and the monks put to work in the fields. The numbers taken out of the agricultural workforce to dig ditches and clear land, coupled with the inadequate food from the communal kitchens, sickness and lack of incentive to work, resulted in poor harvests and famine. Thousands died of starvation. With the break-down of health services and lack of hygiene, malaria and dysentery took a further toll. No value was put on human life. The representatives of Angkar had a mantra which they used to repeat when executing people:-

"To keep you is no profit; to destroy you is no loss."

The mental pressure of indoctrination re-enforced by hunger, lack of sleep and long hours of physical labour reduced the population to virtual automatons.

The leadership saw that the system wasn't working. Rather than accepting that the system was wrong, they blamed subversive elements within their own ranks. Prisons like Tuol Sleng were set up to root out the traitors to Angkar: S-21 was not a one-off; there were others like it all over the country. Ironically, it was the purge of alleged dissidents in the Eastern Zone, starting in 1977, which lead to the downfall of the regime. So many of the senior political and military leaders in that area were purged in places like Tuol Sleng that it was relatively easy for the Vietnamese, enraged by incursions into their territory by the Khmer Rouge, to invade and overthrow them. During their time in office, some 1.7 million people died in Cambodia out of a population of around 8 million. One disturbing thing among many is that this was perpetrated by a very small leadership group and a party organization which never numbered more than about 10,000.

This wasn't the end of Pol Pot and the Khmer Rouge. They fled to the Thai border and aided by the bizarre politics of the cold war in the 1980s continued to be a thorn in the flesh of the Vietnamese backed government and its successor once the Vietnamese left. Vietnam was backed by the Russians and on very bad terms with the Chinese. A Disneyland scenario developed whereby the Khmer Rouge, although ousted from power, retained Cambodia's United Nations seat, supported by America, Thailand and China. Things changed after the Vietnamese left in 1979. The Khmer Rouge refused to participate in the elections eventually arranged for 1993 and continued the armed struggle. However, without their former outside backers, following the end of the cold war in 1990, they were gradually worn down. Pol Pot set up a hit on one of his fellow leaders Son Sen, suspecting him of subversion, in which his whole family was massacred. The party had had enough. In 1997 the senior military commander, the one-legged General Ta Mok arrested Pol Pot and he was sentenced to house arrest for life. He died the following year. The remaining top leaders, Khieu Samphang and Nuon Chea gave themselves up in 1999. General Mok was finally arrested and imprisoned. It was all over for the Khmer Rouge at last.

Philip Short has attempted to explain Pol Pot and the Khmer Rouge in terms of the influences on them. He suggests that they applied the ideals of the French Revolution, the practices of Maoist China, the methods of Stalinism and some home grown concepts stemming from their Buddhist up-bringing. The French Revolution provided the lesson that there was no middle way, no compromise allowed, never to do things by halves. In shades of Robespierre, 1975 became Year Zero. The guillotine became the gun and the bludgeon. Mao taught them that they could have a communist revolution from an agrarian, peasant base without worrying about an intermediate stage of proletarianism a la Marx. Stalin instilled the need for constant vigilance against internal dissent and purges to cleanse the party. Finally, Buddha preached mind control and the evils of private property. In his year in a Buddhist monastery Pol Pot had been taught the spirit of detachment, not to covet material things, the abandonment of personal ties, the suppression of individuality in both thought and behaviour. The Khmer Rouge believed that their ultimate aim should be for the population to have no personality at all, to destroy the individual. That sounds suspiciously like Nirvana.

On the way back from the Killing Fields, we called in at the Psar Themei Market, an Art-Deco style building with a distinctive yellow dome. Apart from fresh food there were plenty of fake designer watches and clothing on display and some gold and silver jewellery of dubious authenticity, a veritable bootlegger's paradise. We took a cruise on the Mekong River. During the monsoon season, which ran from May to October, the river level was so high that the flow of the Tonle Sap River reversed and it flowed back into the lake. The lake level rose by some 6 metres (20 feet), providing water and silt for the wet-rice crop and replenishing fish stocks. We were forcibly reminded that this was the monsoon season when the skies opened and the land disappeared from sight.

In the evening, I was heading out to have dinner at the Riverhouse Restaurant and Lounge when I met Ann and Malcolm who were going to a Khmer restaurant which Dook had recommended. They invited me to join them. When I mentioned the place that I had been meaning to go to, Ann said "It's not one of those brothels, is it?" She had obviously got me sized up already. The Khmer restaurant was in Sisowath Quay, the street bordering the Tonle Sap River. Our table on the first floor looked down on the busy street scene below. The food was excellent. I was familiar with Thai and Vietnamese food from previous visits to these countries and Khmer food seemed to be a hybrid between the two. We were due to have a cooking demonstration in Siem Reap and I was looking forward to learning a bit more about the local cuisine. We shared a selection of dishes including amoc – baked fish with coconut curry, chilis and lemongrass served on a banana leaf – and a delicious stir-fried eggplant with beef. Afterwards, I took a taxi along to the Riverhouse, a bit further along the same street. I had a look at the menu in the downstairs restaurant, a mixture of French style and local dishes, more up-market than where we had eaten but with more up-market prices too. The lounge upstairs was fairly quiet. There were a few older European men with young local girls, par for the course in that part of the world, but none of the brothel-type activity Ann had suspected. Cambodia had developed an unfortunate reputation as a paedophile's paradise and I had seen plenty of dodgy looking massage parlours on our tours of the city so there was no doubt a seedy side to it. But we were leaving early to head for Siem Reap and Angkor Wat so I didn't investigate the night-life further.

On the way to Siem Reap, a five or six hour drive according to Dook, we stopped in the little town of Skuon to sample the local delicacy – sautéed spiders. I had eaten deep-fried locusts under lamp posts in Kampala in my youth – the locals used to wait until they turned dizzy flying around the lights and fell to the ground before popping them into woks of boiling oil on charcoal braziers. They were very tasty, although that opinion should be viewed in the light of the amount of beer which we had consumed before sampling those snacks. When I returned to Shetland after my stint in East Africa, one of my party pieces, fuelled by alcohol, had been to pluck daddy-long-legs out of the air and eat them live. However, the fried spiders weren't to my taste and the Australians weren't impressed either. I said I was surprised to hear that since presumably like all Australians they had been brought up on a diet of witchetty grubs and other bush tucker. It was a small revenge for the brothel comment. We passed through the town of Kampong Thom near which Pol Pot had been born and a little further on stopped at a ruined Hindu temple dating back to the days of the Angkor Empire, a gaggle of children outside seeking alms. Dook told us that the road we were following had only recently been resurfaced making road transport easy now, even in the monsoon season. He said that it followed the line of an old road between Phnom Penh and Angkor which was confirmed when we crossed a thousand year old bridge at Kampong Kdei, the balustrades in the form of the mythical Naga serpents, a common feature of Angkorian architecture.

We arrived in Siem Reap and checked into the Day Inn Resort. Siem Reap was an untidy, sprawling city of 700,000 people with dusty streets, strung out along the Siem Reap River, the source of the irrigation system around which the Angkor civilization had been built. We were up before dawn to see the sun rise over Angkor Wat. The Angkor civilization could be dated back to 802 AD when Jayavarman II proclaimed himself to be a god-king and declared independence from his Javanese overlords. This took place at Phnom (Mount) Kulen, now a sacred mountain to the Khmers, 50 kilometres (20 miles) east of Angkor Wat - which had been built by Suryavarman II early in the 12th century AD.

We arrived at Angkor Wat in the half light of early dawn, the sun not yet above the horizon. I was immediately impressed by the sheer size of the complex – it was believed to be the largest religious structure in the world. It lay within a rectangular surrounding moat 190 metres wide and measuring 1.5 by 1.3 kilometres, the temple complex within it measuring 1,025 by 800 meters, the central beehive tower soaring 65 metres (216 feet) above ground level. We crossed the moat, a sandstone causeway leading towards the temple. In a tower in the entrance gopura (pavilion) set in the high laterite perimeter wall, was an eight-armed, 3.25 metre high statue of the Hindu god Vishnu, to whom the temple had been dedicated. A Buddhist nun was selling incense sticks outside the tower: the temple had later been converted to a Buddhist shrine and had remained in use as such after the Khmer rulers left, leaving it in a good state of preservation over the years while the other temples in the area had been reclaimed by the jungle.

Once through the entrance gate, the full extent of the temple came into view. The design was based on the Hindu temple mountain concept, the central tower intended to represent the sacred Mount Meru, home of the gods in Hindu mythology, the four lower towers at the corners of the second of the three levels being the lower mountains surrounding the central peak. An avenue lined with naga balustrades passed between two libraries and two pools to the front of the temple. We stopped by one of the pools to wait for the sun to rise behind the temple. Coupled with the early morning mist it wasn't ideal conditions for photography. There was some debate about the reason for the orientation of the temple facing west which was unusual for a Hindu temple, although Vishnu was associated with the west. The theory was that it had been intended to serve as a tomb for Suryavarman II as well as a temple – west was associated with death in Hindu mythology, the sun setting on life. God-kings tended to like impressive tombs, the pyramids for the Egyptian Pharaohs being the prime example.

Just inside the entrance was the Gallery of a Thousand Buddhas where devotees had left statues of Buddha. Just remnants were left, many having been destroyed over the years, others moved to the National Museum in Phnom Penh for safe-keeping. There were carvings everywhere, over 3,000 voluptuous, bare-breasted apsaras, dancing girls for the gods. Around the base of the temple stretched a series of magnificent bas-relief carvings showing battle scenes from the Hindu epics the Mahabharata and the Ramayana; a triumphant battle march by Suryavarman II's army; horrific scenes from the Buddhist concepts of heaven and hell; and the bizarre legend of the "Churning of the Ocean of Milk". Dook explained this latter good versus evil story to us. A team of gods (devas) had lined up against a bunch of devils (asuras) to churn the sea to obtain the elixir of immortality, using a serpent wound around a mountain, which was supported by Vishnu in an incarnation as a turtle. The gods held the serpent's tail, the demons its head. Initially, they produced a poison, which Shiva drank to save mankind, but before he could swallow it, his consort Parvati grabbed his throat to save him from sacrificing himself, which explains why he is sometimes depicted blue in the face. The elixir was eventually produced and fortunately tails won- the gods got their hands on it. But when the divine garuda was flying across India with it in a jar, it spilled four drops on the cities where the Khumb Mela festival is now held. There was some more about the demons later getting hold of some of the elixir which resulted in the eclipses of the sun and moon but by this time I had lost the plot. I marvelled at the ingenuity of the ancient Hindu priests who had dreamt all this up and the fact that such beliefs had endured into modern times. Tolkien and C S Lewis couldn't have done better over a few beers in the Eagle and Child pub in Oxford. Unless of course they'd come up with something along the lines of a virgin giving birth and her son rising from the dead to float up to heaven. Now that would really be ridiculous. The murals had to be read anticlockwise, the reverse of the normal in temples, another clue that the temple had also been a tomb – in Hindu funeral services, rituals take place in reverse order. I climbed up the excruciatingly steep steps to the third and highest level of the temple, nearest to God and holiest and so deliberately difficult to reach. Here in the central tower there had originally been a gold statue of Vishnu riding a garuda (winged man-bird) who was also supposed to have represented the god-king. It had been removed when a later king made Buddhism the official religion.

Building a temple this size had been a massive undertaking; digging the surrounding moat in itself a prodigious feat. The surrounding walls had been built from laterite - local clay - but the temple itself was constructed from sandstone blocks. These had been transported from Mount Kulen, 50 kilometres away. It was estimated that over 5 million tons of stone was used, equal to the amount used in the Great Pyramid in Egypt. An estimated 40,000 elephants had been involved along with rafts and barges on the Siem Reap River. The construction had taken 40 years, virtually the whole of Suryavarman II's reign. Building the Great Pyramid had taken 20 years and involved around 100,000 workers: even allowing for the longer construction period for Ahgkor Wat and the use of elephants, it still must have needed a colossal workforce.

We took a trip up in the hot air balloon moored near the temple, rising to 200 metres on the end of a cable. From up there you could see the remnants of the vast irrigation system which had supported the Angkor civilization. Part of the huge Western Baray (reservoir) still remained, just north of the airport. It had been constructed in the 9th century and measured 8 by 2 kilometres, the size of 4,000 football fields, the largest reservoir on earth until the industrial revolution. It had been made using mounds to contain the water rather than dug out but the manpower needed must still have been huge. A similar project during Pol Pot's regime to create a reservoir measuring 800 by 40 metres had taken 20,000 workers 5 months to complete. The Eastern Baray, on a similar scale to the Western one, had silted up, but with Dook's guidance, you could make out the shape of it. Likewise, traces of the network of drainage canals and ditches criss-crossing the area could be seen. Over 1,000 square miles had been served by the system, twice the area of Los Angeles.

We moved on to Angkor Thom, just north of Angkor Wat. In 1177, less than 30 years after the completion of Angkor Wat, the Chams, a Hindu empire based in central Vietnam, attacked and destroyed the city built around the temple, occupying the area for four years. In 1181, a new king, Jayavarman VII defeated them and started building a new city, Angkor Thom, which at its height accommodated over a million people, including those in the surrounding irrigated area, at a time when London had 50,000 inhabitants. The city had been square in shape, each side 12 kilometres long, enclosed by an 8 metre high wall, surrounded by a moat 100 metres wide. We approached the gate to the city along a causeway , lined with large statues of gods on the left and demons on the right, all set to churn the ocean of milk again. The gate was 20 metres high, decorated with elephant's trunks and with an enigmatic face on each of the four elevations of the towers above the wall level. The centrepiece of the city had been the Bayon Temple. Like Angkor Wat it was designed in three tiers. The lower two were square, again lined with bas-reliefs depicting ferocious battle scenes with the Chams; linga (stone penis) worship; a circus; and scenes from everyday life. Again there were numerous apsaras. The third tier was circular and here the enigmatic face was everywhere. Supposed to represent the Buddha but allegedly bearing a strong resemblance to the god-king Jayavarman VII, it smiled out from all four elevations of 54 towers, 216 images in all. The haunting faces gave no clues as to what they were thinking. I was reminded of a comment I had seen in Philip

Short's book 'Pol Pot', made by Ieng Sary, one of the Khmer Rouge leadership group. Referring to his former leader, Pol Pot, he said "You could not tell from his face what he was feeling. Many people would misunderstand that. He would smile his unruffled smile and then they would be taken away and executed." I wondered if history had repeated itself during the Pol Pot regime.

Just north of the Bayon Temple was the Terrace of Elephants, a 350 metres long viewing platform for the aristocracy to watch public ceremonies taking place in the main square in front. Its retaining walls were decorated with garudas, lions and a parade of elephants, mahouts on their backs. At the end of it was the Terrace of the Leper King, a 7 metre high platform with a nude statue on top. The front of the retaining wall was covered in carvings of apsaras and court scenes. Dook told us that carvings elsewhere suggested that Jayavarman VII had suffered from leprosy. He said that the theory was that the terrace had served as a royal crematorium.

In the afternoon we took a cruise on the Tonle Sap on a little boat with a roofed, open-sided deck shelter supported by a gallery of posts. Down towards the lake, the houses were built on stilts to cope with the 6 metres (20 feet) rise in the level of the lake during the monsoon season. They were fairly flimsy, built of bamboo slats around a framework of poles. We passed a cart pulled by two bullocks loaded with bananas and corn cobs. Out on the lake we passed floating villages, pretty much self-contained. We visited a shop. A little food stall beside it was offering fried water snakes fresh from the lake. A pet monkey was chained up nearby. People were fishing from canoes. Dook said that many of the fishermen were of Vietnamese origin. Plants were growing on bamboo rafts filled with soil – chilli peppers, lemon grass, mint, banana plants. I even saw a family of pigs on a raft. We stopped to visit a floating crocodile farm, a new industry in the area, producing skins for the fashion industry. A little boy was paddling around the farm in a large basin, completely at home on the water. A girl of seven or eight was paddling around in a tiny canoe accompanied by a toddler. I held up a fifty riel note (about 10 pence sterling) and pointed at my camera. Her face broke into a huge smile and she paddled furiously in to the side of the raft, grabbed the note and backing off again, held up her hand in a Churchillian V-sign. No enigmatic, Pol Pot smile here, she was clearly delighted.

The following morning we set out by tuk tuk (motorised three-wheeled taxi) to visit two more temples; Ta Prohm, just to the east of Angkor Thom, and Preah Khan, just to the north. Ta Prohm was where some of the scenes in the 2001 film 'Lara Croft: Tomb Raider' had been shot. I immediately spotted the tree where Angelina Jolie had fallen through a hole. Little had been done in the way of restoration here. The crumbling towers and walls were strangled by huge fig trees with flying buttress roots like giant squid. It was much as it had looked when first re-discovered by French explorers in the 19th century. Preah Khan was much larger than Ta Prohm, surrounded by a moat and wall, the temple itself enclosed by a wall measuring 700 by 800 metres. Four processional walk-ways to the gates were again lined with statues all set to churn the ocean of milk. Dook explained that the temple had been a centre for major festivals. It was much better preserved than Ta Prohm and more restoration work had been done. The pattern of a central tower sanctuary surrounded by vaulted galleries was similar to the other temples we had seen as were the carvings of apsaras.

In the afternoon we went along to the Baray Petit Garden Restaurant , housed in a traditional wooden Khmer house, set in a beautiful garden, for a cookery demonstration. I was familiar with most of the ingredients from Thai and Vietnamese cooking – lemon grass, galangal, turmeric, kaffir lime, garlic, basil, mint – but the secret ingredient in the main dish, kreung beef on skewers, was so secret that I never figured out what it was. The mysterious kreung also featured in the stir-fried "long beans kreung and chicken". The "lemon grass with chicken" soup was very similar to a Thai soup but the salads –"white cabbage with chicken and cucumber" and "vermicelli with chicken" were not fiery like the typical Thai salads. At the end of the demonstration we were given a little leaflet with the recipes for a souvenir.

In the evening I took a tuk tuk round to the Carnets d'Asie for dinner. It was an unusual place combining a handicrafts boutique, art gallery and bookshop with the restaurant. The menu was a mixture of French style and local dishes. I had scallops from Sihanoukville down on the coast and duck in orange sauce as a main. It was relatively expensive by Cambodian standards, the duck costing 9 US dollars. A Ricard, an imported French pastis, was 3 US dollars.

On the final day we headed out to visit two of the outlying temples, Banteay Srei and Boeng Mealea. Banteay Srei was 32 kilometres north-east of Siem Reap, about a 45 minutes drive. It was a Hindu temple dedicated to Shiva and had some association with women. It was small and built from pinkish stone. What distinguished it was its carvings, considered to be some of the best anywhere in the world, delicate, intricate depictions of women holding lotus flowers, scenes from the Ramayana – it was breathtakingly beautiful. Boeng Mealea, further to the east, was a complete contrast, overgrown with jungle and vines, nature rampant. It had been built in the 12th century by Suryavarman II to the same floor plan as Angkor Wat and was enclosed by another massive rectangular moat, the sides measuring 1.2 kilometres by 900 metres, now mostly dried up. Inside we had to clamber over piles of fallen masonry. A wooden walkway led to the central tower, which had collapsed. Boeng Mealea was quite close to Mount Kulen, the sacred mountain where the Angkor civilization had begun and where the sandstone for Angkor Wat had been quarried. Dook pointed it out to us. He also told us about Kbal Spean, the River of a Thousand Lingas, which was just nearby. There, lingas (stone penises) had been carved into the bed of the Siem Reap River, the source of the irrigation water for the Angkor area, as a fertility symbol to ensure a plentiful rice harvest. He also reminded us that the area was still littered with land-mines after the civil war. I suspected that he was trying to discourage us from asking to visit Kbal Spean. "It's just as well you told us that," I said "or Ann would have been clamouring to go and see the lingas." Another small revenge for her "brothel" comment in Phnom Penh.

At its peak, the Angkor Empire was massive, stretching from Burma in the west to Vietnam and Malaysia. Scientific research, including the analysis of soil samples from the reservoirs and drainage canals suggests that the problems leading to its collapse started as early as

1300AD with the hydraulic system starting to silt up. The forest cover had been stripped from a wide area to accommodate and feed the large population and this would have resulted in soil erosion, clogging up the drainage system. The massive self-aggrandizing temple building programmes by the god-kings would have absorbed manpower which could otherwise have been used to maintain the hydraulics. Problems with the irrigation system would have created food shortages and mal-nutrition. Apart from that, trouble was brewing from Thailand which had been under Angkor control. Powerful kingdoms developed there in Sukhothai and subsequently Ayudhaya which challenged Angkor's rule and in 1431 the Thais attacked and conquered Angkor Thom. What was left of the Angkor rulers fled to Phnom Penh and set up shop again on a much more modest scale. It seems likely that they were already weakened by food shortages and a haemorrhaging of people towards the Phnom Penh area long before the Thais attacked. Human remains from the period show signs of malnutrition. A bridge dating from late in the Angkor period is roughly built from temple blocks, a sign of decline and decay. But the greatest achievement of the Empire had endured – Angkor Wat. When the French explorer Henri Mouhot came across it in the mid 19th century he wrote that it was "a rival for the temple of Solomon and erected by some ancient Michelangelo" and that "it might take an honourable place beside our most beautiful buildings. It is grander than anything left to us by Greece or Rome and presents a sad contrast to the state of barbarism in which the nation is now plunged." On that latter note, I wonder what he would have made of the Khmer Rouge. In 1992, Angkor Wat had been designated a UNESCO World Heritage Site.

After my return from Cambodia, I kept in touch with events there. Deuch was eventually arrested and tried by the tribunal set up to bring the remaining Khmer Rouge leaders to justice. He admitted to being responsible for the deaths of 16,000 people and was sentenced to nineteen years in prison. It hardly seemed adequate. Nuon Chea, Brother No.2, had also been arrested and was next in line to be tried. People I talked to who had also visited Cambodia would invariably say "Weren't the people so friendly, always smiling?" I would have to agree

but in the back of my mind would be the comment made by Ieng Sary about Pol Pot's smile which had come back to me when contemplating the enigmatic faces at the Bayon Temple. Philip Short points out that every atrocity the Khmer Rouge committed can be found depicted on the stone friezes at Angkor or in paintings of Buddhist hells. There is a photograph in his book of government soldiers carrying severed heads of Khmer Rouge victims. They say that there's no use crying over spilt milk, churned or otherwise. Over the centuries plenty has been spilt in Cambodia and plenty of blood too. So why not smile? The alternative would be crying and Deuch had prohibited that on the rule board outside Tuol Sleng Prison.

9

The Parthenon, Athens, Greece June, 2007

I'D SEEN THE Parthenon from the air in 1970 on the descent to the old Athens Airport on a scheduled stop between Cairo and London on my way back to Britain after three years living in East Africa. In 2007 I decided to renew my acquaintance with it and see a bit of the rest of the country, so I organized a stopover in Greece on my way from New Zealand to spend the Northern Hemisphere summer with what was left of my family in the Shetland Islands. My mother had died at the age of 103 at the beginning of the year, followed by my older brother a week later from cancer and I had inherited the old family home.

A brand new airport had been built for the 2004 Athens Olympics out at Spata, 27 kilometres (17 miles) south-east of the city. It was linked to the metro train system which took me in to the city centre at Syntagma in 30 minutes. I was booked into the 3 Star Philippos Hotel in Mitseon Street, just south of the Acropolis where the Parthenon stood. This was my introduction to the cavalier way in which the Greeks treat tourists. My room was designed around the lower section of a staircase which presumably had served some purpose in an earlier incarnation of the hotel but now just started near the ceiling and ended a bit past the middle of the floor, the bed fitted in on one side of it and a desk with the TV on the other side. I had never seen anything like it and I'd stayed in some flea-pits in my time, but this hotel was in all the tour company brochures. Besides, the TV wasn't working so I went to Reception to see if I could move to a room a bit closer to what I'd paid for. No chance, the hotel was fully booked and as far as the TV went, the handyman had gone home. The two guys on Reception looked highly amused: Tourist Baiting was obviously a popular subject in all the Greek hotel management courses.

I'd booked a morning bus tour of the city to get my bearings. The first stop was the Temple of Olympian Zeus, the largest in Greece at 96 metres (315 feet) long by 40 metres (130 feet) wide, which perhaps explained why work on it had started in 515 BC but hadn't been completed until the Roman Emperor Hadrian finished off the job in 132 AD. Apparently it had been started by one of the Tyrants who had ruled Athens in the early days before they embraced democracy and subsequent rulers had been reluctant to finish a monument which was the brain child of a Saddam Hussein look-alike and of course in a democratic system, local government finance for an expensive project like that no doubt came under close scrutiny. Only 16 of the original 104 Corinthian columns remained, each 17 meters (56 feet) high. It had been constructed of Pentelic marble, the same stone as the Parthenon, which we could see silhouetted on top of the Acropolis above us. The temple had contained a statue of Zeus inlaid with ivory and gold (the ivory for his skin and gold for his clothes) and a huge statue of Hadrian but both had long gone. Just outside the temple site, Hadrian's Arch, erected in 131 AD, marked the boundary between the original Greek city and the Roman extension. The Romans had defeated the Macedonians (who at that time controlled most of Greece except Sparta) in 196 BC and then again decisively in 168 BC at Pydna, after which they absorbed Macedonia into the Roman Empire, the rest of Greece becoming a Protectorate. After political dissent in the Protectorate, the Romans sacked Corinth in 146 BC and the whole of

Greece became a province of Rome. Further unrest in 86 BC led to the Roman Commander Sulla having to subdue Athens which effectively ended Greek resistance to Roman control. The period of Greek dominance in world affairs was over.

The bus tour continued past the Panathenaikos Stadium where the first of the modern Olympic Games had been held in 1896. The impressive Zappeion Exhibition and Conference Hall and the Presidential Palace, with the beautifully landscaped National Gardens, were across the street. As we turned west into Eleftheriou Venizelou Street, the tour guide pointed out the Benaki Museum on the opposite corner and told us that there were several other excellent museums just to the east in the up-market Kolonaki residential area, including the Museum of Cycladic Art and the Byzantine Museum. He said that Kolonaki was also the place for expensive restaurants and designer shopping so I made a mental note to avoid it. Rising above Kolonaki was Lykavittos Hill, which with the Acropolis dominated Athens' skyline. The white-washed old Agios Georgios Church perched on its craggy summit. The Parliament Building had the Tomb of the Unknown Warrior on the wall in front, guarded by a couple of Evzones, the Greek equivalent of the Grenadier Guards at Buckingham Palace. If you were trying to take the piss out of a soldier, you couldn't do much better than make him dress up in the uniform the Evzones wore – white tights under a frilly white wide-sleeved dress with a pleated skirt, red shoes with black pom poms and what looked like a horses tail hanging down from their silly red berets. Syntagma Square out in front of the Parliament building was the centre of modern Athens with the main streets leading off it and the metro station there the hub of the public transport system. The neo-classical Parliament building had originally been completed in 1843 as the Royal Palace for the first king of Greece, a German called Otto, following independence from the Turkish Empire in 1832 and had remained in that use until 1924 when Greece finally threw out King Constantine and became a Republic. The north side of the square was dominated by the opulent Hotel Grande Bretagne. We continued up Panepistimiou Street, past Schliemann's House, now the Numismatic Museum. Schliemann was the German amateur archaeologist who had identified and excavated the site of Troy in present day Turkey and the alleged tomb of Agamemnon in the Bronze Age city of Mycenae in the Peloponnesian Peninsula. Further up the street on the right hand side was the Roman Catholic Cathedral and then a group of fine 19th century neo-classical style buildings – the Athens Academy, the University and the National Library. At the seedy-looking Omonia Square, we turned south down Athinas, past the Central Market to Monastiraki Square where we swung east, skirting the Plaka, the old city, to the Greek Orthodox Church Cathedral, known as the Mitropoli. It had been dedicated in 1862 after 20 years in the building, using marble from churches demolished during the Turkish occupation. Standing dwarfed next to it was the tiny Byzantine era church Panagia Gorgoepikoos dating back to the 12th century AD. Its modest size, 7.5 metres (25 feet) by 12 metres (40 feet) reflected the fact that by the 12th century, Athens had shrunk to the size of a village. The picturesque little building was constructed from Pantelic marble, weathered to a golden yellow colour, its roof and dome clad in red tiles. We arrived back at Syntagma Square and then turned south, still skirting the Plaka, past the Russian Orthodox Church of St. Nicodemus and the Anglican Church of St. Paul's, before arriving back at Hadrian's Arch and swinging west towards our last stop – the Acropolis and the Parthenon. On the way in towards the entrance to the Acropolis, the guide pointed out the two amphitheatres built into the south face of the hill – the theatres of Dionyssos and Herod Atticus. The former had very ancient origins (although it had been re-built in the 4th century BC and enlarged by the Romans to seat 17,000) and was considered to be the birthplace of Greek tragedy, with plays by Euripides and Sophocles performed there in the 5th century BC. The smaller theatre nearer the entrance to the Acropolis and seating 5,000 had been built by a Roman consul between 161 and 174 AD and was again being used for performances.

The flat-topped, steep-sided limestone rock of the Acropolis with a surface area of about 3 hectares (7.5 acres) rose 150 metres (490 feet) above sea level and was a natural fortress. There was evidence of Neolithic settlement there and a defensive wall had been built round it by the Mycenaeans around 1500 BC during the late Bronze Age. When Athens emerged from the dark ages (which followed the end of the Mycenaean civilization, when Greece was over-run by the Dorian barbarians from the north) the Acropolis became a religious centre with a temple dedicated to the Goddess Athena, built there in the 6th century BC. But all the buildings now standing on the summit dated from the Golden Age of Athens between 460 and 430 BC. Athens had been destroyed by the Persians in 480 BC following the defeat at Thermopylae when everything standing on the Acropolis had been razed to the ground. However, following the Athenian annihilation of the Persian fleet at the naval battle of Salamis later in the year and the expulsion of the remaining Persian ground forces from northern Greece the following year, Athens entered a period when, as leader of the Delian League (called after the island of Delos which had formerly dominated most of the Greek islands), it controlled an empire covering the Islands, parts of Asia Minor and the Black Sea coast and colonies in the Western Mediterranean as far away as Spain. With wealth generated from trade within this sphere and silver from the mines at Lavrio near Cape Sounion, Athens, under the leadership of the statesman Pericles aided by the architect Ictinus, master of works Callicrates and the sculptor Phidias, was able to embark on a programme of construction which produced some of the finest buildings the world has seen, including the Parthenon, the jewel in the crown of the Acropolis building group.

We climbed up to the impressive entrance to the Acropolis, the Propylaea, which as well as guarding the entrance had served as a public meeting place and art gallery. Like the other buildings on the summit, it had been built from marble from Mount Pentelicus, about 16 kilometres (10 miles) away. With its Doric and Ionic columns, it was a fine piece of architecture in its own right. Just on the right of the Propylaea complex, stood the small Temple of Athena Nike (the Victor) just four Ionic columns wide, each 4 metres (13 feet) high, built to celebrate the victories over the Persians. When we emerged from the Propylaea it immediately became clear that the summit was again a building site as it had been in Pericles' day. The Parthenon was shrouded in scaffolding and tarpaulin and its perimeter littered with builders' rubble and equipment: it was one of the untidiest building sites I'd ever seen – Callicrates, the original clerk of works, would probably have had a fit. Restoration work on the building had been going on for years and had a while to run yet. It was disappointing – photography was pointless – but no doubt when the work was finished it would be worthwhile, the ancient building preserved for posterity. And it had been a magnificent building: 70 metres (230 feet) long by 30 metres (100 feet) wide with all the main dimensions on a 9:4 ratio to make it perfectly symmetrical. Visual trickery had been used to counteract the laws of perspective – the columns bulged slightly in the middle to make them look straight and leaned inwards to make them seem vertical; and the stepped base curved upwards slightly at the centre to make it seem level from a distance. A single row of Doric columns 10 metres (34 feet) high surrounded the building, supporting the roof, which had been covered with large, overlapping marble tiles laid on wooden beams, now of course gone. Inside the pillars, a marble wall had enclosed the cella, the two interior rooms, one of which had contained the huge 12 metres (40 feet) high gold and ivory covered statue of the Goddess Athena to whom the temple was dedicated, the other serving as the treasury for the Delian League. Each gable had a triangular pediment beneath the sloping roof surfaces, which had been filled with stone sculptures – the western gable portraying the struggle between Athena and the Sea God Poseidon for the right to be the patron of Athens; the eastern one the birth of Athena, the Goddess of Wisdom and Intelligence. Along the wall-head, above the architraves (marble lintel beams lying across the columns), had run a sculpted frieze, most of which remained. The original had been painted in blue, red and gold and must have been a magnificent spectacle. Another frieze had run around the top of the inner wall around the cella probably depicting the procession climaxing the Great Panathenaea, the four yearly festival in honour of Athena. This was from where Lord Elgin, while British Ambassador in Constantinople, had misappropriated most of the "Elgin Marbles", which were now in the British Museum. In 1801 he had had permission from the Turkish authorities to study and copy the artwork on the Acropolis buildings but it was doubtful if that included the right to take any of it away – the original document (firman) signed by the Sultan had been lost. This was now a bone of contention between the British and Greek governments. Just across from the Parthenon on the north side of the hill was the Erechtheion, a temple named after an early mythical king of Athens and believed to have been dedicated to a number of gods including Athena, Poseidon and Hephaistos, the God of Fire and Blacksmiths. The portico on the south side was known as the Porch of the Caryatids (Maidens) as its roof was supported by columns sculpted in the form of young girls. The ones now to be seen were copies, five of the originals being in the Acropolis Museum and the sixth in the British Museum, having been stolen by Lord Elgin.

The damage to the buildings on the Acropolis reflected the history of Athens and Greece. The glory days of Athens which had made their construction possible effectively came to an end with Athens' final defeat in 404 BC by Sparta in the Peloponnesian Wars which had dragged on for nearly 30 years. However, it remained an important city during the subsequent periods of Spartan and then Macedonian dominance of Greece and was an important cultural centre in Roman times. Apart from a couple of the sackings by barbarians (the Herulians in 267 AD and the Goths under Alaric in 395 AD) which the Roman Empire was prone to, the downward spiral of Athens began when the Roman Empire was split between East and West parts and Constantinople was built as the capital of the Eastern Roman Empire, with Athens' cultural functions moving to the new capital. The adoption of Christianity as the official religion of the Empire meant that the temples on the Acropolis no longer had their original function – the Parthenon was converted to a church in the 5th century AD. In 1204 the Crusaders sacked Constantinople and the Eastern (Byzantine) Roman Empire started to break up. Greece and other parts of it were fought over by the French, Catalans, Florentines and Venetians and Athens declined to little more than a large village. In 1456 it was occupied by the Ottoman Turks, the Parthenon converted to a mosque with a minaret added and the Erechtheion used as a harem. In 1687 the Acropolis was again serving as a fortress for the Turks in an attack by the Venetians. A Venetian cannonball came through the roof of the Parthenon and exploded the powder magazine which the Turks had installed in the building. Severe damage was done and to make things worse the victorious Venetians looted sculpture from it, Lord Elgin taking a leaf from their book just over a century later. In 1827, during the Greek War of Independence against the Turks, a Turkish shell scored a direct hit on the Erechtheion, almost destroying it. So it was hardly surprising that some scaffolding and tarpaulin was now in place in an attempt to restore some of the damage dealt out over the centuries.

The tour ended at the Acropolis so I walked down to the smooth rocky outcrop of Areopagus Hill, which the tour guide had told us was an excellent vantage point from which to photograph the Acropolis towering above and to look out across the remains of the Ancient Agora (Market Place) and Roman Forum. The Areopagus Hill had been the site of the law courts in classical Greek times. Just across from it on the lower slopes of Filopappos Hill, the Pnyx had been the place where the Ekklesia (Citizen's Assembly) met to discuss and vote on matters of state. Athens gets the credit for being the birthplace of democracy with all citizens getting a say in political decisions but the definition of a citizen was tightly subscribed. Women, slaves, debtors and immigrants were barred from voting. At its peak, the population of Athens was around 300,000 of which a third were slaves. With women making up half the remainder and a lot of foreigners due to Athens' far-flung trading links, perhaps only about 10% of the population were involved in the democratic process.

The sites of the Ancient Agora and later Roman Forum had been built over during the Ottoman era but in 1931 permission had been granted to demolish the houses in order to carry out archaeological excavations. The site had become a treasure trove of ancient remains. I walked down to the Roman Forum where the octagonal Tower of the Winds had survived over the centuries, standing 12 metres (40 feet) high and 8 metres (26 feet) in diameter. It had been a combined water-driven clock and weather vane and had a frieze below the conical roof with figures personifying the eight wind directions. The foundations of various

Forum buildings had been excavated including the bases of columns. The central markets had been moved here during the time of Caesar and Augustus and it had been the commercial centre of Roman Athens. Nearby were the remains of Hadrian's library. The best preserved building in the Ancient Agora was the Temple of Hephaestus, which had survived the wear and tear of the centuries better than the Parthenon, which it resembled in style, down to the frieze around the roof-line and the triangular pediment space which looked as if it had contained sculptures too. In the early 1950s the Stoa of Attalos had been fully restored on the original foundations using traditional materials. This two storey, colonnaded, roofed arcade of shops, had dominated the east side of the Agora until it was destroyed in a raid by the barbarian Heruli tribe in 267 AD. It was now a museum to house the finds from the surrounding archaeological site where work was continuing.

In the evening, I walked up to the Plaka, which with Monastiraki and Psirri to the north had been pretty much all that there was to Athens before it was made the capital of independent Greece in 1834 with a population of just 6,000. The narrow streets and alleyways still had an Ottoman feel to them and this was tourist territory with the shops and restaurants heavily orientated to that trade. I walked up Vyronos Street, called after the English poet Lord Byron, who had lived for a time in the main square of Plaka, Plateia Lysikratous, where the street ended. Byron was a hero in Greece as he had died of fever in Mesolongi in 1824 while involved on the Greek side in their War of Independence. The main street of Plaka, Adrianou, was lined with tavernas and souvenir shops. Nestling on the slopes of the Acropolis was the Anafiotika district, with narrow, stepped lanes and whitewashed houses and an occasional island style blue-domed roof. It had been built by people from the Cycladic island of Anafi, who had come to Athens to build the Royal Palace for King Otto in the 1830s. With its displays of bougainvillea, roses and jasmine in gardens, window boxes and hanging baskets, this was the most attractive area of Athens that I found. There were a number of restaurants up the narrow lanes and I decided to have dinner at one where a bouzouki player was pretending to be Zorba the Greek and there were outdoor tables. I had a selection of mezedhes for a starter, including dolmadhes (vine leaves stuffed with rice) and tzatziki (yoghurt, cucumber and garlic) and then souvlaki (pork grilled on skewers) with a side dish of fried aubergines and courgettes, washed down with a carafe of red wine. When the handwritten bill arrived, I did a double take: there were things there that I hadn't eaten and the total was well in excess of the figure my mental arithmetic came up with. I took it down to what looked like the manager manning the till. He summoned the waitress who had served me and eventually we managed to sort out the confusion. They were both smarmy and apologetic but I could recognise an attempted rip-off when I saw one. I wandered over to the rather grungy Psirri district where I had seen some promising looking bars earlier and had a few ouzos in a taverna with a live band playing Greek music. The night-life seemed to be lively, but the area was distinctly seedy and I caught a taxi rather than walk back to the hotel. As we drove off, I noticed that the meter wasn't running, so I tapped it and said in my rudimentary Greek "Put meter." He said something in Greek that I didn't understand and then added in English "Not working." When we got to the hotel he asked for a ridiculous fare. Fortunately, I'd checked the going rate in my tourist guide book before going out, so I just swore at him and threw him a note for what I thought would be about the right amount, less than half what he had asked for. He didn't go ballistic, which suggested that I had still probably paid over the odds. I was becoming seriously fed up with the Greek version of hospitality to tourists.

The following afternoon, I took a bus tour out to see the Temple of Poseidon at Cape Sounion. The 70 kilometres (43 miles), hour-long drive southwards down the west coast of the Attica Peninsula took us through some fishing ports and beach resorts, now effectively suburbs of Athens, with views out across the islands in the Saronic Gulf to the Peloponnesian Peninsula. The gleaming white marble columns of the temple to the God of the Sea was an imposing sight, standing starkly exposed on a rocky headland, 60 metres (200 feet) above the sea. There was a strong on-shore sea breeze and surprisingly powerful waves were crashing at the base of the cliff, creating a cauldron of white foam. The Aegean Sea stretching out to the south was flecked with the white-caps of breaking waves. It was easy to understand why a sea-faring people would want to keep on good terms with the sea and any god that might dwell in it. Sixteen of the original 40 or so columns of the temple remained standing on a stepped platform, with the architrave lintels surviving across most of them. There had been a shrine to Poseidon here since the 7th century BC and a later temple had been destroyed by the Persians after their victory over the Greeks at Thermopylae in 480 BC. The present temple dated to 440 BC, contemporary with the Parthenon. The tour guide told us that Lord Byron had carved his name on one of the columns – an early graffiti artist and carrying on the tradition of vandals like his fellow countryman and upper-class twit Lord Elgin.

I had booked a four day tour of the main tourist sights on mainland Greece: the Peloponnese with Mycenae and Olympia; the oracle at Delphi; and the Byzantine monasteries at Meteora. We stopped at the Corinth Canal, which had been cut in 1893 across the Isthmus of Corinth so that ships travelling east-west could avoid the long detour around the Peloponnesian Peninsula. The idea of connecting the Gulf of Corinth to the Aegean Sea across the 6 kilometres (4 miles) wide isthmus had first been mooted in ancient times and Nero had made a start during the Roman occupation but cutting the 90 metres (290 feet) deep, 24 metres (79 feet) wide trench through solid rock had had to wait the advent of modern explosives and heavy machinery. It was already too narrow for large, modern ships but still useful for small cargo boats, cruise ships and leisure traffic. The tour guide told us that there was little left to see of the ancient city state of Corinth as it had been razed to the ground by the Romans but there were still substantial remains of the Roman city built to replace it and the hill-top fortress of Acrocorinth. We drove south along the Saronic Gulf to visit the amphitheatre at Epidauros. This remarkably preserved theatre had been built in the late 4th century BC and was again being used for performances, renowned for its near-perfect acoustics. The original structure had had 34 semi-circular rows of limestone benches around the central stage, the Romans adding a further 21 to give a seating capacity of 14,000 accessed by 36 staircases. The circular stage was

20 metres (66 feet) in diameter and the banked seating spanned 114 metres (374 feet) across. Constructing it, even with today's technology, would be a major project. In ancient times, Epidauros had been an important religious, therapeutic and medical sanctuary, dedicated to the God of Healing, Asklepios and there were remains of this function nearby, including a snake pit thought to have housed sacred serpents. I was glad that medicine had advanced a bit since then. We crossed over the peninsula to Nafplio on the Argolic Gulf, the capital of newly independent Greece from 1929 until Athens took over five years later. It was an attractive little town, huddled beneath two impressive fortresses behind and with the smaller, Venetian Bourtzi fort on an island off in the harbour. The waterfront was lined with hotels, restaurants, cafes, bars and boutique shops housed in neoclassical style buildings with flowers on balconies and in public gardens – it brought home how drab most of Athens had been.

What remained of Mycenae wasn't far away. The Mycenaean civilization had existed in the late Bronze Age from around 1700 BC until it collapsed around 1100 AD. As well as the fortified citadel here at Mycenae, traces of the civilization had been found elsewhere in the Peloponnese and at Athens and Thebes. The site of Mycenae had been discovered and excavated by the German, Heinrich Schliemann, in 1874. He had studied Homer's "Iliad" and "Odyssey" and believing them to be based on fact, had used clues from them to locate first Troy and then Mycenae. We entered the site through the massive Lion Gate, taking its name from the lions carved above the lintel. Just inside, below the path, was what the archaeologists had romantically named "Grave Circle A". This was where Schliemann had found the gold death mask which led him to claim that he had "gazed upon the face of Agamemnon." Agamemnon had been the king who had organized the siege of Troy which was reckoned to have taken place around 1250 BC: the mask had been dated to 300 years earlier than that so whoever's face it was, it wasn't Agamemnon's. The settlement had been surrounded by a massive wall, 13 metres (42 feet) high and 7 metres (23 feet) thick, made of stone blocks weighing up to 6 tons. They had obviously been expecting trouble. A path led up to the hilltop where the site of the former royal palace had been identified. In common with all the archaeological sites that I saw in Greece there was nothing in the way of signage or interpretive displays to bring the site alive for visitors. If we hadn't had a tour guide to explain what was what we might as well have been strolling around a scree slope or an abandoned quarry. I had seen the same apparently blasé, off-hand attitude to the historical heritage in Rome years before. Prior to my arrival in Greece, I had felt strongly that Britain should return the Elgin Marbles to Athens where they belonged; already, I wasn't so sure.

We continued on towards Olympia, with a short stop in Tripoli, the capital of Arkadia, which had given its name to idyllic rural landscapes worldwide. With grassy meadows, cultivated fields, orchards and olive groves and a backdrop of pine forested hills, it was indeed attractive countryside. The tour guide pointed out a road leading south which went to Sparta, the war-like city state that had ended Athens' period of greatness and whose warriors had defended the pass at Thermopylae against the Persians and died to a man. We carried on through the rump of Megalopoli which had been an important city in ancient times but now just boasted a huge, polluting, coal-fired power station. When we hit the coast, we turned north, skirting the Ionian Sea on our left until we arrived at our hotel in the modern village of Olympia for the night.

There wasn't a great deal left of the original site of the Olympic Games. The first recorded games had taken place in 776 BC and were held every four years until the Eastern Roman Emperor Theodosius I banned them in 394 AD as part of a purge of pagan festivals: Theodosius II ordered the destruction of the temples in 426 AD. Earthquakes had completed the job. Again there was no signage to identify the individual buildings or to interpret what had gone on. The site contained one of the original Seven Wonders of the World, the Temple of Zeus, in whose honour the games were held. Now all that was left was the base of a few of the original columns and some shattered columns which had tumbled down. If it hadn't been for our guide, we wouldn't have known what it was. Part of the colonnaded courtyard of the athletes' training centre, the Palaestra, had been re-erected and the 7th century BC Temple of Hera had survived a bit better than Zeus' one which was a couple of hundred years younger. The entrance to the stadium had been through a walled passageway with a stone vaulted roof: a small section of the roof remained. You could still see the start and finish lines of the 120 metre sprint track and the judges' seats. The stadium had been able to seat 45,000 people and it was now difficult on this desolate spot to envisage the five day spectacle with running, long jump, javelin, discus, wrestling, boxing and chariot and horse racing. It was a men only affair; women and slaves were even banned from watching.

We left for Delphi, crossing the impressive new suspension bridge over and high above the Gulf of Corinth and then following the north coast of the Gulf past extensive olive groves and on to the mountain village of Arahova, perched on a rocky spur on the flanks of Mt. Parnassos at 960 metres (3120 feet) above sea level. It was now a ski resort and it felt like it even in June – for the first time since I'd arrived in Greece I felt cold. The village's rural origins were apparent in the goods for sale in the shops lining the main street and in the narrow alleyways off it – cheese, honey, hand-woven woollen carpets, rugs and quilts and embroidery. I sampled the local red or rather purple wine in a bar with a stupendous view out over the Gulf of Corinth and it helped to warm the cockles of my heart. We retraced our route the 12 kilometres (7.5 miles) back to Delphi village and checked into our hotel for the night.

The setting of Delphi on the rocky, pine forested flanks of Mt. Parnassos above a valley of cypress and olive trees was spectacular. It was renowned in ancient times as the dwelling place of Apollo, the God of Prophesy, among other things, and an oracle, in the form of a priestess, had been present there from at least as early as the 8th century BC. After Delphi became an important city state in the 6th century BC, the sanctuary entered its golden age with people coming from all over the ancient world to consult Apollo, for a fee, on what course of action they should take both in public and private life. By no means all the questions put were of earth shattering importance: tablets had been found which queried the faithfulness of partners, whether friends could be trusted and if new jobs should be taken. The priestesses had sat above a fissure in the rock and it is believed that subterranean gasses may have had a hallucinogenic effect. They are also believed to have chewed laurel leaves and poppies which would have had a similar effect. The stoned ravings of the Priestess were supposed to pass on Apollo's advice to a priest who would interpret it and deliver it in verse. It sounded as if there was a lot of room for messages to get lost in translation here. The advice given was generally ambiguous, allowing the priests to hedge their bets – if things went pear-shaped they could always say "Ah! But what I actually meant was...." Legend has it that Alexander the Great went to consult the oracle before setting off on his expedition to conquer the world. When the priestess told him to come back the next day (she would have fitted nicely into the modern Greek tourist industry) he dragged her out by the hair and she said: "Let me go. You're unbeatable." Alexander is supposed to have replied: "I have my answer" and went on to conquer the world. What she probably deliberately forgot to mention was that he would die at the age of 33 in the process. The oracle had been shut down in 393 AD by Theodosius after the Roman Empire became Christian and pagan practices were purged.

The steep Sacred Way snaked up the site from the entrance past the site of the Agora, where religious objects had been sold, to a series of Treasuries, where each city state had housed offerings of artwork and money to Apollo. The Athenian one had been fully restored. Just past it was the Rock of the Sybil where the oracle had originally sat before relocating to a chamber beneath the floor of the Temple of Apollo dominating the site above, some of its columns having been re-erected. Above the Temple, the well-preserved theatre had seated an audience of 5,000. A further steep walk took us up to the Stadium where the Pythian Games had been held every four years, the second biggest sporting event in ancient Greece after the Olympic Games. A music festival had also been held there to celebrate Apollo's mythical slaughter of the serpent Python, which sounded as if it should have been a Monty Python's Flying Circus sketch. The 200 metres (655 feet) long stadium had been partly hewn out of the rock face and could seat 7,000 spectators, some of the banked stone seats remaining. The museum housed sculptures and architectural remains excavated from the site including works of art from the Treasuries. There was a scale model of the sanctuary coloured in white, blue, marble, gold and terracotta. A life-size bull was made of beaten silver sheets with gold trimmings. There was a model of the Sphinx and perhaps most impressive of all, a life-size bronze statue of a charioteer. The guide pointed out the Omphalos, a sculpted cone representing the centre of the world. Greek legend held that Zeus had released an eagle from each end of the world and they had met at Delphi.

We left the centre of the world and headed north for Kalambaka, where the Byzantine monasteries of Meteora were located. This was backwoods Greece, a long way from the centre of the world. Kalambaka, with a population of around 8,000, was very much a one donkey town. It had been almost wiped off the map by the Nazis in World War II and the buildings were all post-war. We were staying in the Hotel Orfeus on Pindou Street at the east end of town. I had a walk up the main street, Trikalon, in the evening. There were quite a few cafes and bars but the clientele was almost exclusively male, giving the place a Middle Eastern feel. Emancipation for women had obviously not yet arrived here – it had taken a lot longer to throw off the Turkish yoke mentally than physically. But the setting of the town was spectacular, nestling below the towering rock pinnacles which gave the Meteora area its name which meant "suspended in the air". The pillars were the heavily eroded remains of a deep layer of sedimentary rock uplifted from the sea having been compressed by tectonic forces to produce faulting, erosion exploiting the resulting cracks to wear away the softer sandstone, leaving harder rocks in the conglomerate standing as tall, smooth, isolated crags above the Plains of Thessaly. In the morning, we drove through the village of Kastraki, surrounded by red pinnacles, to the Monastery of the Great Meteoron, the first to be founded, in the 14th century AD. By that time, the Byzantine Empire was on the wane and Turkish incursions into Greece had begun – the monks needed a safe haven. Hermits had been living in caves in the rocks since the 10th century AD but now they became a refuge for much greater numbers: by the 17th century there were 24 monasteries. Now only 6 active ones remained. The pinnacle on which the Great Meteoron stood was over 600 metres (2,000 feet) high and the logistics of building on these isolated peaks was staggering – road access and paths cut in the rock had only been provided in the 1920s. When the monasteries had been built, access had been by rope ladders, the building material hauled up in nets or baskets suspended from ropes raised by winches. We saw an example of one of those at the nearby Monastery of Verlaam. The interior of the Great Meteoron was beautiful and peaceful with its katholi-con (church) and frescoes showing the persecution of Christians by the Romans. We carried on to visit St. Stephen's Monastery which appeared to be a much more commercial operation with nuns busy selling religious souvenirs and DVDs of Meteora. On the drive back to Athens we passed through Thermopylae where the Spartan defenders had eventually been wiped out by the Persians in 480 BC. An imposing statue of their leader, Leonidas, stood beside the road.

I flew out to Crete and took a taxi in to the Lato Hotel in Heraklio, where I was to be staying. This proved to be an excellent boutique hotel and their top floor restaurant with an outdoor terrace overlook-ing the harbour and the massive floodlit Venetian fortress of Koules served the best meals I found anywhere in Greece. Heraklio had undergone a period of growth under Venetian rule from 1217 (when they took over Crete following the sacking of Constantinople by the Crusaders in 1204, which led to the decline of the Byzantine Empire) until 1669 when they finally succumbed to the Ottoman Turks. The massive fortified city walls built by the Venetians were still in exis-tence, perhaps not surprisingly, as they had been strong enough to fend off the Turks for 21 years after the rest of Crete had fallen to them. Heraklio had been badly damaged by German bombing in World War II but some of the Venetian heritage had survived includ-ing the vaulted arcades of the Arsenal where ships had been built and repaired down by the old harbour; the ornate 1628 Morosini Fountain, with four stone lions spouting water (sporadically), in the main square, Plateia Venizelou; and the restored Loggia, just off the square, which had been a gentleman's club in Venetian times but now housed a lesser breed, the City Council. There were a number of cafes, restaurants and bars around Plateia Venizelou and the attractive church, Agios Markos Basilica; just to the north, El Greco Park was beautifully landscaped with trees and flowers. El Greco, the famous Renaissance painter, had been born either in Heraklio or the village of Fodele but moved to Venice to study under Titian and then to Toledo in Spain where he made his name and died in 1614. The city Market was located just south of the square in a street named for the year 1866 (there seemed to be a fetish for naming streets after historical years and dates) with colourful displays of fruit, vegetables, cheese, honey and other produce and foodstuff. Over on the east side of town, just north of Plateia (Square) Eleftherios, the Archaeological Museum held a wealth of artefacts excavated from the various sites of the Minoan civilization on the island. The statue of another hero of Crete, Eleftherios Venizelos, who had been Prime Minister of Greece for a long period early in the 20th century, dominated the Square. Another famous son of Heraklio, Nikos Kazantzakis, the author of "Zorba the Greek" was buried in the Martinengo Bastion of the city wall at the south end of the old city – you could walk along the top of the wall from there to the waterfront in about an hour.

I took a tour out to see the Minoan capital at Knossos, just 5 kilometres (3 miles) south of Heraklion. Until the Englishman, Sir Arthur Evans, excavated the site between 1900 and the early 1930s, the Minoan civilization was believed to be mythological, associated with the Greek legend of King Minos and the Minotaur, half man, half bull, resulting from a liaison between the King's wife and a prize bull and kept locked up in a labyrinth under a palace at Knossos. It came as a surprise to the archaeological world when Evans' excavations uncovered a civilization going back to the time of the Great Pyramids in Egypt (2500 BC). It is now believed that the people who developed the Minoan civilization were early Bronze Age migrants into Crete from what is now Turkey, arriving around 3,000 BC. There had been Neolithic farmers on the island since about 7000 BC. The first so called palace at Knossos and others elsewhere on the island had been dated to around 1900 BC but there appeared to have been a massive earthquake around 1700 BC so the remains now visible dated to after that. Substantial damage had been incurred again around 1500 BC and then total destruction by fire a hundred years or so later, when the Minoan civilization effectively ended. The jury is still out on what caused the collapse of the Minoans but they would have been seriously weakened by a massive tsunami from the volcanic eruption on the island of Santorini to the north just before 1600 BC. Archaeological evidence suggests that the tsunami may have produced a wave 23 metres (75 feet) high which would have destroyed coastal settlements and shipping – the Minoans were seafarers trading with the Levant, Egypt and North Africa as well as other parts of Greece. Knossos was far enough inland to have escaped direct physical damage from the tsunami but the economic impact must have been enormous – its port on the coast would have been wiped out. The Mycenaeans from mainland Greece occupied Crete after the fall of the Minoans but it is not known if they had a hand in their downfall.

Covering nearly 2 hectares (4 acres) and with around 1300 rooms, the building complex at Knossos was clearly more than just a palace as there was evidence of storage areas for agricultural produce and metallurgical workshops. It is generally accepted that Evans let his imagination run away with him a bit when identifying what was on the site and his reconstructions of some areas in modern materials (for example concrete pillars for wooden ones) has come in for criticism but I preferred it to the absence of efforts at interpretation on the archaeological sites I had visited on mainland Greece. The engineering was impressive with evidence of channelled water supply, sewerage and surface water drainage systems and paved roads. Evans had even reconstructed a bath and an en-suite flushing toilet in what was believed to be the queen's quarters. There was a throne room with a gypsum throne flanked by benches and with frescoes of the mythical griffon. The brightly coloured, replica frescoes (the originals were in the Archaeological Museum in Heraklio) helped to bring the site alive – one near the north entrance depicted the capture of a wild bull; another in the queen's apartments featured dolphins, fish and sea urchins. An assembly of huge earthenware jars (pithi), some 2 metres (over 6 feet) tall had been used to store olive oil, wine and grain. There were remains of a theatre. The site was fascinating but the lack of signage would have made it difficult to navigate and understand without the help of a guide.

The tour continued on to the Lasithi Plateau about 840 metres (2750 feet) above sea level, a fertile agricultural area with fields of grain and potatoes, apple and pear orchards and almond trees. At one time there had been 20,000 windmills with white canvas sails, erected in Venetian times to raise water for irrigation but few were now left and even fewer operational, having been replaced by mechanical pumps. We stopped at Tzermiado, one of the small farming villages, for lunch. In the afternoon we paid a visit to the Dikteon Cave, where Zeus was alleged to have been born. Ancient Greek theology was bizarre in the extreme – it made virgin births and dead blokes floating up to heaven almost credible in comparison. The tour guide's story was that in the beginning there was a great void called Chaos out of which came the Elder Gods (Titans), led by Cronos. Zeus was the sixth of Cronos' children. Cronos had eaten all the earlier ones as he had heard a rumour that one of them was going to kill him. (Child abuse and dysfunctional families were obviously not just modern social phenomena.) Zeus' mother tricked Cronos by feeding him a stone instead of Zeus (he probably thought it was just one of her rock cakes that she'd left in the oven a bit too long) and spirited the boy away to another cave. When he grew up, he gave Cronos a powerful emetic (or possibly laxative) which made him bring up the other children who ganged up with Zeus to give battle to the Old Gods and defeat them, taking over the universe as the pantheon of Olympic Gods which the ancient Greeks worshipped – Apollo, Poseidon, Athena and God knows how many more. "Ho, hum," I muttered. It never ceased to amaze me how gullible the human race was when it came to god bothering. The path up to the cave was long and steep and it was very hot. I was beginning to wonder if it was worth it, a thought reinforced by the sight of a griffon vulture hovering above us, no doubt planning to feast on the carrion of any tourist who collapsed. A bit further on, an old man dressed in the traditional Cretan garb of high boots, baggy jodhpurs and shirt with a crocheted head-scarf, all in black, was preying on us as well, loitering there with a donkey, ready to give a lift to the weak-minded. It worked: an overweight American woman, who had been complaining loudly to the guide, climbed aboard and without a trace of shame rode off into the sunset – Calamity Jane re-incarnated. When we got to the cave, there was a long flight of steps leading down into it. No sign of Zeus but there were plenty of stalactites and stalagmites in the limestone grotto and the exercise had probably done us all good, apart from Calamity Jane.

Another day, I took a bus tour to western Crete. Crete was a long (170 kilometres [106 miles]), narrow island with a backbone of mountains running more or less the full length, rising to 2,456 metres (7,982 feet) in Mt. Ida. We could see the craggy peaks over on our left as we drove along. We passed through Fodele, the village which claimed El Greco as its own, set in a fertile valley with a river running through it and orange and lemon groves. Driving through olive tree country, with Mt. Ida towering above us, still with some snow on it in June, we arrived at the 16th century Arkadi Monastery. This was the scene of an atrocity during a revolt in 1866 against the Turkish occupation of the island. Hundreds of local people (perhaps as many as a thousand) from the surrounding area, including women and children, had taken refuge in the monastery. Two thousand Turkish soldiers arrived to deal with the insurrection but the locals refused to surrender and the abbot set alight a store of gunpowder in the building, killing everyone (including the Turks) apart from one little girl who was blown into a tree but survived. The incident was commemorated in a little museum beside the monastery. Crete had had more than its fair share of tragedies in warfare over the years. In 1941, during the Second World War, the Nazis had massacred the entire male population of the village of Anoghia to the east of here.

We continued west to the town of Hania, the former capital of Crete until Heraklio took over in 1971, the snow-capped Lefka Ori (White Mountains) rising above it to the south. Here the Venetian and Turkish heritage was much better preserved than in Heraklio. In the old town, inside the remnants of the old walls, Venetian town houses had been attractively restored and some old wooden Turkish houses had survived. The old Venetian harbour was enclosed by a breakwater with a lighthouse at the end of it. A mosque had even survived the liberation from the Turks, standing down by the waterfront. The harbour esplanade, Akti Koundouriotou, was lined with cafes, restaurants, tavernas and boutique hotels. At the seaward end of it, the massive bastion of the Firkas Fortress, which had been built to defend the harbour entrance, was now the Naval Museum. I had lunch in a restaurant on the waterfront. I couldn't decide between the gyros (cones of pita bread filled with meat, potatoes and yoghurt) or spanakopita (spinach and cheese pies) so I had some of both and some Cretan wine. To punish myself for the sin of gluttony, I finished off with a large shot of raki, made from grape skins and stalks and resembling the Italian grappa, only rougher, much rougher. This atmospheric town was where Zorba the Greek was filmed.

We headed back towards Heraklio and stopped in the town of Rethymnon. Rhethymnon, which had been the Ottoman capital of Crete, was smaller than Hania but even better preserved. The old town was dominated by the massive Fortetza on a headland to the west, said to be the largest Venetian castle ever built, and on the site of the ancient acropolis. Opposite the entrance to the Forteza, the former prison was now the Archaeological Museum with Minoan artefacts and statues from the Greco-Roman period. South of the Museum, the narrow streets and alleyways of the old town were lined with Venetian period houses with wrought iron balconies, bright with floral displays. Some wooden Turkish-style houses remained with overhanging wooden balconies with oriel windows and there were still some minarets visible – retributions against Turkish rule had obviously been less drastic here. The Neratzes Mosque remained intact but was now a music college. The Rimondi Fountain in Paleologou Street was reminiscent of its look-alike in Heraklio with lions again spitting water: further east, another old Loggia was now the Museum shop. Busy Arkadiou Street had shops selling leather and textiles. The quayside of the small, picturesque Venetian harbour, full of fishing boats and pleasure craft, was lined with fish restaurants and tavernas, its entrance signalled by a 16th century lighthouse. Fishermen were mending nets among the milling tourists.

Just south of the harbour, a sandy beach was backed by a palm tree lined esplanade, giving it an exotic, almost North African, atmosphere. The open-air cafes, bars and restaurants along the esplanade were already filling up in the late afternoon when we left to return to Heraklio.

I caught a Hydrofoil Superjet across to the island of Santorini in the Cyclades group, a 127 kilometres (80 miles) journey across the Aegean Sea. Arriving by sea from the south was definitely the most dramatic way to approach the island, the inner face of the volcanic crater towering 300 metres (975 feet) above us as we berthed at the little port of Athinios. I found a taxi to take me to the main town, Thira, where I was staying. (This name was often given to the whole island and it was sometimes spelled "Fira" – the English transliteration of Greek place names was highly variable and confusing.) The taxi driver tried to negotiate a price but I tapped the meter and said "Put meter" in my best pidgin Greek. He seemed reluctant and I started to get out: he sighed like a martyr and switched it on. When we arrived at the Aressana Hotel, I discovered that they had double booked me but had arranged an alternative at the nearby Theoxenia. Swearing pro-fusely, I watched while a porter loaded my suitcase onto a trolley – the Theoxenia was located in a pedestrian only area the Receptionist said. Expecting to be shunted to a lower standard flea-pit a la Philipposis in Athens, I couldn't have been more wrong. The Theoxenia was one of the most beautifully located and fitted out hotels I have stayed in – I later discovered that it was a Member of the exclusive Small Hotels of the World club. It was on the pedestrian street called Ypapantis run-ning along the edge of the crater rim. The view out across the caldera and along its rim was spectacular.

Santorini was small, just 73 square kilometres in area, measuring 20 kilometres (12 miles) long by 7 (4 miles) at its widest. Its popula-tion of 13,600 was distributed between Thira town and a dozen or so villages. The highest point near the village of Pyrgos, just inland from the ferry port, rose to 565 metres (1855 feet). Just before 1600 BC, a huge, explosive, volcanic eruption had blown out the former central volcano, the sea flooding into the massive caldera which now gave the island its spectacular landscape and creating the tsunami which had devastated the coastline of Minoan Crete. The offshore islands in the middle of the caldera were still volcanically active. The town of Thira was perhaps the most picturesque place I had seen on all my travels. Perched on the edge of the caldera and cascading down its upper slopes, with its dazzling whitewashed buildings interspersed with the bright blue domes of church roofs and flowers everywhere, it was the sort of place that ate camera film and memory cards. The Orthodox Cathedral with its twin bell towers shared a square with the Atlantis Hotel at the south end of town. At the other end of the caldera-top promenade, Ypapantis Street, a cable car dropped down to the tiny port of Skala Firon, 270 metres (885 feet) below. The alternative was 580 stone steps, although donkeys and mules were on hand to take the strain off the leg muscles. Between the two, the street was packed with shops aimed at the tourist trade: the southern section had so many jewellers it was sometimes called Gold Street. The sheer number of tourists was overwhelming. I counted 8 large cruise ships anchored in the bay below. At times it was difficult to move on Ypapantis street: it must have been a pick-pocket's paradise.

Buses went all over the island from near the main square, Plateia Theotokopoulou. I took a trip up to the village of Oia at the north end of the island to watch the sunset. Oia was if anything even more picturesque than Thira. It had been seriously damaged in an earthquake in 1956 measuring 7.8 on the Richter scale (as had Thira) but since then sensitively restored, its white and pastel coloured houses with red pebbled walls, clinging to the caldera face. There were "skafta" (cave) houses with barrel-vaulted roofs designed to resist earthquakes and the ubiquitous blue domed churches. Numerous cafes, tavernas and restaurants were strategically located for sunset watching. Another day, I went out to the beach at Monolithos. The shallow water, red-hot black sand and sharp pebbles were not my idea of a beach idyll and the peace was shattered every now and then by low flying aircraft landing and taking off from the nearby airport. I explored the vineyards around the village of Pyrgos, where some of the wineries held tastings. Santorini produced some quite good wine in spite of the lack of surface water and dry, cinder-like, pumice soil. Wheat, tomatoes and eggplants were also grown but agriculture must have been an uphill struggle. The goats and donkeys seemed more at home in the parched landscape. I went out to Akrotiri, right at the south end of the island. In 1967 a remarkably well preserved town had been excavated from beneath layers of volcanic debris and lava, complete with frescoed murals, Knossos style, still retaining their bright colours, one showing a youth holding blue and yellow fish, another, two boxers. Akrotiri had been destroyed by the 1600 BC volcanic eruption. It had been a thriving town, a colony of the Minoans. No bodies had been found on the site, suggesting that the people had had pre-warning of the eruption. The site was closed to the public. A couple of years earlier, a section of the roof which had been constructed over the excavations had collapsed, killing one tourist and injuring several more. This seemed to me to be symptomatic of the general malaise affecting the Greeks' care of their historical heritage.

On my last night, I went for a meal in one of the restaurants clustering around the end of the stepped lane leading down to Agiou Mina, a pedestrian promenade running below Ypapantis Street and leading to the funicular. There weren't many customers, which should have made me suspicious – it was an attractive location with the upper terrace looking out across the caldera. I ordered an octopus dish as a starter followed by moussaka and a carafe of house wine. Nothing happened for a while and then a waitress appeared with a Greek salad and plonked it down in front of me. I explained that I had ordered the octopus but she shrugged and said casually that they didn't have it so she had brought a salad instead. I gave her a dirty look but I was quite fond of Greek salad so I didn't argue. It's difficult to imagine how it's possible to make a mixture of tomato, cucumber, onions, olives and feta cheese unpalatable but this restaurant had achieved it. Even the feta cheese was insipid. A waiter appeared with the wine. It bore no resemblance to anything I had tasted at the local wineries. I strongly suspected that it had been watered down. The moussaka arrived. This baked dish of layered eggplant, potato, and minced meat topped with cheese sauce was one of my favourite Greek meals. But this one was practically inedible: it was greasy, tasteless – I suspected that it had been left over from lunch time and just warmed up and not very warm either. I left half of it and thought I would push my luck and order baklava for dessert; surely it would be third time lucky. It wasn't. The layers of pastry in the syrup cake were tough and greasy and it was nauseatingly sweet. I couldn't finish it. The bill arrived. I had thought things couldn't get any worse but they did: they'd charged me for the octopus which hadn't materialised and the inedible moussaka was substantially dearer than quoted on the menu. I went ballistic and stormed downstairs to where I'd seen a manager at a till on the way in. " Look," I said, "Not only have you served me the worst fucking meal I've ever not eaten but now you've overcharged me for it. What the fuck is wrong with this place?" There was no apology, he just amended the bill – I got the impression that it wasn't the first time he'd had an irate customer breathing warmed-up moussaka fumes over him. The following morning at the Airport, I got a clue as to what the fuck was wrong with Santorini. This tiny island had 29 flights showing on the Arrivals and Departures boards. Coupled with the eight cruise ships I had seen in the harbour earlier and the constant stream of ferries from Athens and the other islands, it was being smothered by tourists arriving like a cloud of poisonous pyroclastic dust and ash from an exploding volcano.

Before leaving New Zealand, I had pre-booked the Philipposis Hotel again for my last night in Greece on my return to Athens from Santorini and so couldn't avoid it. This time they'd managed to double book my room which proved a blessing in disguise as they shunted me to their nearby sister hotel, the Herodion, which was a bit better - not an internal staircase in sight. I had been disappointed with Greece. The problems I had encountered with hotel bookings were too numerous to be just coincidence: it was clearly down to ineffi- ciency and incompetence and what was worse, a couldn't- care-less attitude towards customer care. For a country so dependent on tour- ism this was tantamount to suicide. I, for one, wouldn't go back. The dishonesty and indifferent service I had found in restaurants was part of the same malaise as were the cheating taxi drivers, although you find them in plenty of other places as well. To be fair, part of the prob- lem was the sheer number of tourists, particularly in Santorini. When visitors are coming in droves regardless how you treat them, there isn't much incentive to encourage repeat customers – just rip the punters off, there'll be another invasion of new faces off the cruise liners and ferries and through the airport gates tomorrow. I had also been disappointed with the standard of care and presentation of the archaeological sites. Greece had so much history but little effort was made to bring it alive for visitors: again the overwhelming impression I came away with was of a couldn't-care-less attitude to this heritage. Perhaps Lord Elgin had got it right after all: "I think I'll just nick those marble friezes; these Greek buggers aren't capable of looking after it." The cradle of Western civilization had become a bit of a basket case.

10

NEUSCHWANSTEIN CASTLE, BAVARIA, GERMANY JUNE 2009

IN JUNE 2009, on my annual trip back to the Shetland Islands from New Zealand, I stopped off in Munich, intending to hire a car and drive the length of the German Alpine Road, visiting Neuschwanstein Castle, one of the short-listed Wonders of the World which I had not yet seen, on the way. I had also become interested in King Ludwig II of Bavaria, known as Mad King Ludwig, who built Neuschwanstein, and planned to visit the places associated with his birth, life and death. Along the route of the Alpine Road, I was intending to take side trips into Liechtenstein, Switzerland and Austria, spending around three weeks in total.

I had been to Germany several times before, including two longish trips. The first had been a tour through the former Hanseatic League ports of Hamburg, Bremen and Lubeck in 1986. The Hanseatic League, a consortium of merchants and ship owners from a number of ports along the North Sea in the Low Countries, Germany and the Baltic, had dominated trade with the Shetland Islands from the time they became Scottish (on default by Denmark on a royal dowry agreement with Scotland) in 1469, until the early 18th century. I had been involved in the restoration of one of their trading posts on my home island of Whalsay as a tourist attraction – the Hanseatic Booth - believed to have been operated by merchants from Hamburg trading locally produced "stockfish" (dried ling and cod) for fishing gear, salt, food, drink and household goods. I had been keen to see the other end of this trade route. The second long trip, three weeks in all, had been by train taking me from Amsterdam in Holland to Cologne, down the Rhine Valley and then via Frankfurt to Wurzburg and the Romantic Road to Rothenburg ob der Tauber, probably the best preserved walled medieval city in Germany. I had continued on to Munich, Regensburg, on the Danube and via Prague in the Czech Republic, to Berlin, not long after the wall had fallen. I had completed the circuit back to Amsterdam via Hamburg. I'd been back to Hamburg since and to Berlin towards the end of my Trans-Siberian Railway trip in 2005. So I was familiar with German culture and reasonably fluent in the language, having put myself through a number of self-tuition packages over the years.

The important thing to remember about the German Alpine Road is that it doesn't exist. That way, when you're confronted with a junction where both roads appear from the map to lead to your destination, you won't sit there frozen with angst about which one is the 'real' Alpenstrasse. You'll toss a euro and drive on. The doubts set in before I left New Zealand after consulting the internet and a mound of guide books. The few maps I found showing the route differed. Some pundits even suggested taking short-cuts across Austria. Things didn't improve when I arrived in Munich to pick up my hire car. I went into a book shop and asked in my best German for a map of "Die Deutsche Alpenstrasse". The assistant looked at me as if I'd asked her for a map of Mars. She did however sell me a very detailed map of the Alps which had the name of the fabled route annotated in red against sections of road here and there but conspicuously absent elsewhere. However, some basic facts were clear. The road started in Lindau on the Bodensee (Lake Constance) and finished at the Konigsee, near Berchtesgaden, a distance of about 500 kilometres (312 miles). The road numbers at each end weren't in dispute. Leaving Lindau, you turned off the Munich autobahn onto the B308. At the other end, the B305 led all the way from Bernau on the Chiemsee to Berchtesgaden. It was just the middle that was a black hole.

In Munich, I stayed in the Cortiina Hotel, an excellent boutique style establishment in Ledererstrasse, right in the historic centre and within crawling distance of the Hofbrauhaus beer emporium. At the far end of the street was the Haxnbauer Restaurant, fronting Sparkassenstrasse, with the best pork knuckles in Munich. Munich was not a city for teetotallers or vegetarians. The site had first been settled by Benedictine monks who gave it its name – "munchen" meant "monks" in medieval German. It had come under the control of the Wittelsbach family ("Mad" King Ludwig's dynasty) in 1240. They later became the royal line of Bavaria. Now it was a bustling city of well over a million people with the BMW car plant and home to the Siemens electronics empire as well as a host of new technology firms. At the heart of the historic centre (the Altstadt) was Marienplatz, just a short stroll from my hotel. In the centre of the square a golden statue of the Virgin Mary, balanced on a crescent moon, stood atop a tall column and dated from 1638 – the Mariensaule (Mary's Column). Bavaria was a strongly Catholic state. Marienplatz was dominated by the neo-gothic Neues Rathaus (New Town Hall) built between 1867 and 1909. The 85 metres (276 feet) tall steeple housed a glockenspiel (carillon) with 43 bells and 32 brightly coloured copper figures which entertained the crowds three times a day. The show re-enacted two historical events: the top half portrayed a jousting tournament with knights celebrating a wedding; and the lower half the "schafflertanz – coopers (barrel makers) dancing to mark the end of an epidemic of the Black Death. The building was decorated with gargoyles, statues and sculptures, a dragon crawling up the roof turrets. On the east side of the square, the oldest part of the Altes Rathaus (Old Town Hall), the tower, had been part of the city's fortifications, built between 1180 and 1200. The Rathaus itself had originally been built in 1310 but replaced in 1464. The present building was an 1861-64 rebuild in neo-gothic style: the tower had had to be reconstructed after World War II on the basis of plans dating from 1493. Just across from the Altes Rathaus, Peterskirche was the oldest church in Munich, dating from 1180 AD. It had been built on the site of the monks' settlement that the city derived its name from. Its 92 metres (299 feet) tall tower and spire housed eight clocks and seven bells and there was a spectacular view over the city from its viewing gallery. Just beyond, and almost as old, the Heiliggeistkirche (Church of the Holy Ghost) dated back to the 14th century but had been refurbished in baroque style in 1724. These churches formed the impressive setting for the Victualienmarkt (food market) with stalls laden with fruit, vegetables, mushrooms, wurst (sausages), cheese, hams, olives, jams and pricey truffles. There were sections with meat and fish. It was a lively scene and very much part of city life, not laid on for the benefit of tourists.

I headed back west along pedestrianised Kaufinger Strasse past the Neues Rathaus to have a look at the Frauenkirche, a Munich landmark with its 99 metres (320 feet) high onion-domed twin towers. Built between 1468 and 1488 in the Renaissance period it was the largest Gothic building in southern Germany. Town Planning laws restricted any new building from obscuring views of it. I continued west along Neuhauser Strasse, a continuation of Kaufinger, a busy shopping street which extended to the Karlstor Gate, retained when the old city walls were demolished in 1791 to allow the city to expand. This was effectively the edge of the Altstadt on the west side. I backtracked and went into Michaelskirche, built by the Jesuits in 1597. This was where Ludwig II, the "Mad" King of Bavaria, was buried. I walked down the stone stairs to the dank, dark crypt where his tomb stood, surrounded by fellow members of the Wittelsbach dynasty spread out around the low walls. The dim lighting produced a sombre but peaceful atmosphere. His portrait hung on the wall behind and a replica crown stood on top of the tomb. There were artificial flowers and candles. I lingered a while, going over in my mind what I knew about his life and rehearsing the places associated with it that I hoped to visit. A little further along, I stopped outside the Hunting and Fishing Museum, which was housed in a white painted, disused Augustinian Church, to interfere with a bronze statue of a wild boar.

Legend held that rubbing it brought good luck: I noticed that the area around its testicles was the shiniest.

I walked north up Theatinerstrasse on the west side of the Neues Rathaus The street was named for the magnificent, lemon-yellow, baroque Theatinerkirche, one of Munich's finest buildings. Work had begun on it in 1663 but it hadn't been completed until 1765. The domed twin clock and bell towers rose to 70 metres (230 feet) in front of the central superstructure and dome. Across the road was the Residenz, home to the Wittelsbach family until the revolution in 1918 which drove them from power. It was an imposing building, built around a series of courtyards, dating back to 1385 but rebuilt in the baroque and rococo styles in the 17th and 18th centuries. At the next junction, the Odeonsplatz, was where Hitler's abortive coup in November 1923, known as the "Beer House Putsche" had been nipped in the bud. He had led a group of 600 of his brown-shirted SA troopers to the Burgerbraukeller (Citizen's Beer House) where the Bavarian State Commissioner, Gustav von Kahr, was delivering a speech to an audience of 2,000 people. Hitler's intention was to persuade them to start a revolution against the unpopular left-wing national "Weimar Republic" government which had emerged after the First World War and the departure of the Kaiser. Bavaria was in political turmoil at the time. In 1918 a revolution had ousted the Wittelsbach dynasty and set up the Bavarian Free State. The following year a far-left group had attempted to set up a Bavarian Soviet Republic along the lines of the Bolsheviks in Russia but that had been quelled. Since September 1923, there had been a State of Emergency in Bavaria and the State Prime Minister had appointed Kahr to administer the State with dictatorial powers. Kahr himself had aspirations about seizing power at national level as a dictator. Hitler and his fledgling Nazi Party at that time were just part of a wider movement known as the "Kampfbund" seeking to remedy the wrongs they felt had been done to Germany at the Treaty of Weimar which had ended the First World War and also to forestall a takeover of the country by the communists. At the Burgerbraukeller, the Brownshirts surrounded the building and set up a machine gun in the auditorium. After meeting with Kahr and other senior officials present and addressing the meeting, Hitler won support for his revolution attempt and the group set out to take over the city. However, at Odeonsplatz, they were met by a force of police and army loyal to the existing order which opened fire on them, killing 16 Nazis and the rest fled. Hitler was arrested a couple of days later and sentenced to five years in jail. However, he only served 8 months, during which time he wrote "Mein Kampf" and the rest is history. During the shoot-out at the Odeonsplatz, Hermann Goring was wounded in the groin. A couple of centimetres to the side and he could have featured with Rommel, Himmler and Goebbels in the famous World War II song "Hitler has only got one ball."

North of the Residenz, the formal, manicured Hofgarten had the Temple of Diana in its centre with a statue of her on the domed roof. Just beyond, the Englisher Garten was landscaped in the style pioneered by landscape gardeners such as Capability Brown in England with oak and maple trees, paths and water features. It had been laid out in 1789 as a "garden for the people", the rulers perhaps mindful of what was going on next door in France where the French Revolution was getting up a head of steam. Surfers could ride an artificial wave on the Eisbach stream. I followed the stream northwards through a meadow dotted with nude sunbathers. Germans will get their kit off at the drop of a hat: everything else would quickly follow. I had a beer and some lunch at the Chinesescher Turm (Chinese Tower), a wooden five-tier pagoda style "folly" with a beer garden and an oompah brass band clad in lederhosen, knee-socks and green hats with a feather. The waitresses wore the traditional dirndl skirts and could carry more "mass" (litre glasses) of lowenbrau (lion brew beer) in one hand than I could have lifted with both. I wouldn't have fancied a clip round the ear from one of them. I walked back down Residentzstrasse to Maximilianstrasse, called after Mad King Ludwig's father, King Maximilian II who had ruled from 1848 to 1864. He obviously suffered from a touch of egomania and perhaps paranoia himself: a large statue of him looking pompous, 13 metres (42 feet) tall, stood in the centre of the street which ran grandiosely down to Maximilian's Bridge across the wide Isar River (a tributary of the Danube) from where the imposing façade of the Maximilianeum, the Bavarian State Parliament, faced back along the avenue. Had he slipped slightly further over the edge he could have become known as "Mad Max". His street was the most opulent in the city, lined with designer emporiums – Prada, Armani, Bulgari, Hermes – the luxurious Kempinski Hotel, the Opera House, theatres, museums, galleries and very up-market cafes.

That evening, I went for dinner at the Hundskugel Restaurant, an atmospheric little place in an attractive old three-storey building in Hotterstrasse, which claimed to be the oldest restaurant in Munich, founded in 1440. The roast suckling pig was excellent. Bavaria was hard on the arteries: apart from the ubiquitous calorie laden pork-knuckle cholesterol bombs, local specialities included baked udder and fried cows' heads. To wash down the pig, I went along to the Hofbrauhaus beer cellar in Am Platzl, just up from my hotel. It was an attractive, white, three-storey building with a stepped gable above, arched doorways and long colourful banners strung along the front-age from beneath the eaves. There was an outdoor beer garden with chestnut trees and a fountain. It had started of as part of the Royal Brewery founded in 1589 and been opened as an inn in 1830 by no less a personage than King Ludwig I himself. (I can't imagine Queen Elizabeth II performing the opening ceremony for the equivalent of the Rover's Return in Coronation Street.) The Neo-Renaissance exterior of the building was the result of an 1896 refurbishment. Inside, the cavernous ground floor could hold 1,000 drinkers seated communally at long tables. It was a very convivial way to drink if you were on your own. I got chatting with a very entertaining Swedish couple at my table who were in Munich for a Conference (they were both married to other people I discovered but you know what Swedes are like.) I sneaked a peek at the Festsaal, a ceremonial hall seating 1300, on the first floor. There were also smaller side rooms called Trinkstuben where you could have a more private piss up. This was large scale, industrial drinking but a lot of fun.

The following morning, I caught a tram outside the Hauptbahnhof (Central Station) to visit the Schloss (Castle or Palace) Nymphenburg where Mad King Ludwig was born in 1845. I sat in the rear of the tram opposite two late-middle-aged women, one of them a hard faced blonde. A brightly coloured wasp-like winged insect was fluttering around in the back window, settling on me for a moment and then flitting over to the window sill. I stretched my hand out towards it and it climbed onto the back of my hand. I saw the blonde watching me through slit-like eyes. "Why don't you kill it?" she said in German. "Ich bin Hindu" (I'm a Hindu) I replied. "Vieleicht ist es meine Grossmutter" (Perhaps it's my grandmother.) She gave me a very dirty look. I got up to get off at the Schloss and wished them a cheery "Tschus" (Goodbye). The blonde sidled along the seat, delivered a vicious forehand smash to the innocent insect and looked at me triumphantly. I was planning a trip up to Dachau to see the Concentration Camp. It occurred to me that the woman would have made an excellent warder there. Schloss Nymphenburg was a splendid Italian style palace with an ornamental lake in front, populated by swans and ducks and with fountains playing. The five-storey central building had been built in 1675 for the Wittelsbach Elector's wife (the rulers of Bavaria later came to be known as Kings rather than Electors): the perfectly symmetrical three-storey flanking pavilions attached to the main building by galleries had been added in 1702. Stables and an orangerie had been included after 1715. The whole impressive façade stretched for 600 metres (1,968 feet). A French style garden out back flanked a canal. Upstairs, the two-storey rococo style Steinerner Saal had been the dining hall, with elaborate stucco sculpturing and fresco paintings. The Gobelinzimmer was full of colourful tapestries, the Chinese Laquer Room decorated in the fashionable Chinese style of the day. In the south wing was the Schonheitengalerie (The Gallery of Beauties), a portrait gallery of beautiful women from all walks of life and parts of the world – King Ludwig I's personal porn collection. Also in the south wing was a stunning porcelain collection and the Marstallmuseum, a collection of coaches and riding equipment including Mad King Ludwig's rococo style sleigh with oil lamps for night riding. The reclusive monarch used to rampage through the snow at night on it when there was no one around to see him. By all accounts, Ludwig did not have a happy childhood in the Palace. His father, King Maximilian II,

in typically Victorian paternal style, largely ignored him and his education was beaten into him. He developed an early interest in opera,
particularly Richard Wagener's work, which was to become an obsession in later years. In 1864, his father died and he became king at the
age of 18.

I took the S Bahn up to Dachau to visit the former concentration
camp, now preserved as a memorial. The entrance was marked by the
notorious, cynical Nazi slogan "Arbeit Macht Frei" (Work Makes You
Free). Inside, the barracks where the prisoners were housed and the
gas chamber were still there. An intricate wrought iron sculpture symbolised the fate of the former inmates. A forlorn looking statue of
a Jewish victim stood in a little clump of trees. Apart from the Jews,
a range of other groups considered to be social misfits by the Nazi
regime were consigned to the concentration camp system, including
homosexuals, gypsies, Jehovah's Witnesses and the mentally retarded.
The camp was so close to the town that it was difficult to believe that
the citizens didn't know what was going on there, as they later claimed.

I picked up my hire car and headed down the autobahn towards
Lindau on the Bodensee (Lake Constance) to start my traverse of the
German Alpine Road. The old part of Lindau was built on an island in
the Bodensee, accessed from the mainland by a causeway. It had been
founded as a fishing settlement in Roman times and later occupied by
nuns. I stayed in the excellent Reutemann Hotel down by the harbour,
looking across the lake through the narrow harbour entrance between a
lighthouse and a stone lion, at the mountains of Switzerland and Austria.
Lindau had some fascinating old buildings. Just along from the hotel on
the harbour front, the tall Mangturm had been built around 1200 AD
as a lighthouse and watchtower. Its overhanging, yellow upper storey
was surmounted by a spire decorated in yellow and green glazed tiles
in a chevron pattern. I walked up to the 15th century, step-gabled Old
Town Hall ("Rathaus" in German, which, although being apt, I don't
think was intended to be a slur on local government politicians.) Its
façade was painted with colourful murals called "luftlmalerei" (open-air
paintings, known in French as "trompe de l'oeil") which I was to see on
buildings all along the Alpine Road – medieval rural scenes with people

dancing, playing music, eating and sometimes religious themes like the crucifixion. The picturesque main street, Maximilianstrasse, was lined with boutique shops, restaurants and cafes, in houses dating from the 15th to the 19th centuries, mostly gable-on to the street and many with oriel windows. There was a fascinating local museum in the baroque Haus zum Cavazzen with a steep, mansard roof and its façade painted with mythological figures, sphinxes and bunches of fruit. A bustling market was under way out in front, stalls laden with fruit, vegetables, flowers, cheeses, sausages. Two picturesque churches stood in the adjacent square: Stephanskirche dating back to the 12th century; and the Munsterkirche, originally founded by Benedictine monks around 800 AD but re-modelled in baroque style. Over in Oberer Schrannenplatz, I visited Peterskirche, white-washed and with a five-storey tower, believed to be the oldest church in the whole Bodensee region but now serving as a war memorial with a life-size sculpture of a soldier in uniform stretched out on the lid of a coffin, complete with the trademark German coal-scuttle helmet. The interior was decorated with frescoes dating from the 13th to the 16th centuries. Beside it stood the tall Diebsturm (Thieves' Tower), a watchtower built from 1370-80. The following day, I took a cruise on the lake, stopping briefly at the jetty in Wasserburg alongside the beautiful Georgkirche, its white-washed walls and mauve onion-domed tower offset by an adjacent yellow-painted building with a bright red tiled roof. We passed close to the shores of Switzerland and Austria, including the Austrian town of Bregenz, capital of the Vorarlberg province. Lindau was the sort of place you didn't want to leave, especially on a road that might not exist.

But first, I had a detour to complete - south into the little mountainous principality of Liechtenstein. Only 25km (16 miles) long by 6km (4 miles) wide, with a population of 34,000, Liechtenstein was a fully fledged member of the United Nations. It was called after the Austrian family which bought it (Schellenberg County in 1699 and Vaduz in 1712) from impoverished German nobles. It gained full independence in 1866. The head of state was Prince Hans Adam II, although the day to day running of the country was in the hands of his son Crown Prince Alois. They lived in the medieval looking

Schloss Vaduz, perched on the mountainside above the little capital, Vaduz. The Principality was famous for two things – false teeth (it was the world's leading exporter) and funny-money - tax evasion. The latter had made worldwide headlines in 2008 when a disgruntled former employee of the state's largest bank sold pirated DVD's with the names of prominent tax evaders to the American, German and British tax authorities. All hell broke loose and international efforts began to try to break down the wall of secrecy built round Liechtenstein's financial industry. With 75,000 companies registered there, more than twice the population, financial services were its life blood. The Royal family, which owned the largest bank, was estimated to be worth US$4.9 billion, much more than the British monarchy. When the scandal broke, Prince Alois was quoted as saying "We just don't behave like a nanny and ask people continuously 'Have you paid your taxes?'"

I stayed in the 600 years old Gasthof Lowen (Lion Guest-house) with its antique furniture and a vineyard out behind from which they made their own wine, served in the excellent restaurant. Further up the hill was the royal family's vineyard with the Hofkellerei wine cellar and restaurant and lanes lined with picturesque houses in the Mitteldorf area, including the striking Rotes Haus (Red House) with its half-timbered tower. In the tourist office I got a souvenir stamp in my passport (there were no border formalities) and bought some of the Principality's colourful stamps, a major source of revenue before e-mail made in-roads into the postal service.

My detour continued along the Rhine Valley south from Vaduz into Switzerland, with spectacular views of lakes, emerald green alpine meadows with brown and white cattle grazing and snow-capped mountains as I headed towards Zurich. It was dangerously beautiful. A hire car gave freedom of movement but it was difficult to drive on a Swiss autobahn and enjoy the scenery at the same time. I began to wonder if the raised middle finger was the Swiss national greeting as I hogged the so-called slow lane. I had to buy an expensive windscreen disk at a petrol station, a sort of road tax, before I could drive on Swiss roads. The cost was the same if you were going to stay all year as it was for a couple of days. They're mean bastards the Swiss when it comes to money. Zurich was an attractive city, situated where the River Limmat flowed north towards the Rhine out of the 40 kilometres (25 miles) long glacial lake called the Zurichsee. There had been a Celtic settlement on the Lindenhof hill on the west bank of the river, now the heart of the Altstadt (Old Town), superseded by a Roman fort, destroyed by barbarians. In the 9th century, a palace had been built on the hill with a trading settlement below it and the city had grown from there. Now it was the financial capital of Switzerland and its richest city and it showed. I was booked into the Seegarten Hotel on the east bank of the lake, near the opulent, neo-baroque style Opera House with a colonnaded portico and winged statues on the roof. In the evening I went for dinner in the historic Niederdorf area on the east bank of the river, a network of narrow, cobbled streets and alleyways with antique shops, art galleries, restaurants and cafes The north end of the pedestrianised main street, Niederdorfstrasse, was distinctly seedy, not what you would expect of Zurich at all. I passed a strip club and then in a beer bar a scuffle broke out between a barman, who was clearly drunk, and an elderly customer, equally drunk, who had been taking the piss out of him. Bottles fell over and spilled their contents; a glass smashed on the floor. Who said the Swiss were staid and boring?

The following morning, I walked along the lakeside promenade, Utoquai, and crossed the Quaibrucke over the Limmat to the Old Town. Bahnhofstrasse, the main street, ran northwards towards the railway station, following the line of the moat which had run along the old city walls. It was lined with up-market shops and restaurants and the headquarters of major banks. All the Swiss specialities were here for the taking if you could afford them – watches, clocks, jewellery, chocolate, leather goods, glassware and ceramics. I passed the exclusive Jelmoli Department Store. Back towards the river I walked up the historic Lindenhof and south to the mauve-painted St Peter's Kirche, famous for having the largest clock face in Europe on its tower – measuring 8.7 metres (28 feet) in diameter. Further south, the Fraumunster (Women's Church) featured stain glass windows by Marc Chagall with biblical themes, each window with a different bright predominant colour – green, blue, yellow, orange and red and navy blue. The origins of the church went back to 853 AD. I walked back across the river over the Munsterbrucke. The Rathouse, just at the other side, had been partly built on piles set into the river bed in 1694-98. The Limmatquai along the river was lined with half-timbered former guild houses, many with oriel windows, converted to shops, restaurants and cafes, including the attractive Haus zur Ruden. The east bank skyline was dominated by the aptly named Grossmunster church with its massive twin towers. It was believed to be on the site of a church founded by Charlemagne in the late 8th or early 9th century. The construction of the present Romanesque-Gothic structure had been begun around 1100 AD. This was where the Protestant reformer Ulrich Zwingli had preached the powerful sermons which spread the Reformation throughout Switzerland and Germany. In the afternoon, I took a cruise down the Zurichsee.

The following morning I got hopelessly lost trying to find my way out of Zurich towards Germany via Winterthur and St. Gallen. Eventually, I had to stop at a petrol station and ask where I was. Fortunately, I wasn't far from the main road and a helpful member of staff marked the route to get there on my map with a heavy red marker. Back in Germany, I found the B308 junction which marked the start of the Alpenstrasse, not far past Lindau and turned east. Just past the Lindenburg turn-off, I hit my first obstacle – a barber's pole look-alike stretched across the road with a sandwich board telling me the road was closed. An arrow off to the left indicated a diversion. I was having to get off the Alpenstrasse already when I had barely got onto it. But there are advantages in getting off the beaten track. This was deep rural Bavaria, green fields sloping up to wooded hills, verdant meadows filled with yellow flowers, like a medieval landscape, an impression reinforced when I rounded a corner to see a lederhosen clad yokel mowing hay with a scythe. My father used to do that back in the Shetland Islands but that was in the 1950s. I eventually got back onto the B308 - and the present - at Oberstaufen. There was a decision to be made just past Hindelang where the road forked and the B308 appeared to end. From the map, both would get me to my destination, Fussen. The right hand fork crossed into Austria to the town of Reutte, the left ran north along the German side of the border. The map in the Eyewitness guidebook favoured the right fork and my map had the minor road from Reutte towards Oberammergau annotated as the Alpenstrasse but the most convincing map I'd found on the internet followed the left fork. Most of the guidebooks I'd seen described the Alpenstrasse as running north from Fussen, coinciding with the southern stretch of the "Romantic Road". I decided to bear left and make enquiries in Fussen about where to go from there.

I arrived in Fussen, a beautifully preserved historic town at the southern end of the "Romantic Road" with a medieval castle and a 9th century Benedictine monastery, now the museum. I was booked into the Sonne Hotel right in the centre, another gem in a historic building. The standard of accommodation I had been finding on the trip showed up how far behind the rest of Europe Britain was in the hospitality industry: it made me embarrassed to be British. Fussen had been a Roman settlement on the swift-flowing River Lech. Down by the river, the façade and tower of the Heilig-Geist-Spitalkirche were decorated with luftmalerie and there was more on the arcaded façade of the castle which now housed an art gallery. However, the main attraction in Fussen was Neuschwanstein, Mad King Ludwig's fairy-tale castle in nearby Hohenschwangau, made famous by Walt Disney as the abode of Sleeping Beauty. I drove over to Hohenschwangau early the following morning. Before taking the bus out to Neuschwanstein, I walked over to the Schloss Hohenschwangau, the castle which Ludwig's father, Maximillian II, had bought in 1832 and restored in medieval style and where Ludwig spent holidays in his youth. It had been built in the 14th century but virtually destroyed in the Napoleonic Wars. It was square and bulky with cylindrical towers at the corners and painted yellow. Immediately after Ludwig became king, Bavaria became embroiled in the wars between Austria and Prussia and then Prussia against France. When Prussia forced through the unification of Germany in 1866 under a Prussian Emperor, Ludwig was left with a royal title but little political power, a figurehead. He withdrew into a fantasy world of castle building and opera, sponsoring Wagner whose operas he was obsessed by.

Neuschwanstein was the first of his castles, work on it beginning in 1869. He saw it as a monument to medieval culture and kingship, the concept of a God-given monarchy with absolute royal power which he admired and envied in his current figurehead role. I took the bus up to the Marienbrucke, a cast-iron bridge over the rushing waters of the Pollat River at the bottom of the gorge below. From the bridge, this was the Walt Disney view of Neuschwanstein, the fairy tale, wedding-cake-white, limestone-clad castle with its soaring spired towers perched on a rock outcrop, towering above the gorge of the Pollat River, surrounded by dense, dark green forest and with the cobalt blue of the Alpsee beyond. It ticked all the boxes in the cliché "magical scene". I walked down to it along the path through the forest along the river. Close up, the towering battlements conjured up visions of medieval pageantry, exactly as intended by Ludwig. The plans had been drawn up by a theatre designer rather than an architect, based on the medieval castle at Wartburg, and it showed. Inside, the main rooms were decorated with murals of scenes from the Germanic and Nordic sagas on which Wagner had based his operas such as "Lohengrin" and "Tanhauser". The Singer's Hall on the fourth floor with its magnificent wooden beam ceiling was dominated by massive chandeliers. In the Throne Hall, there was a large mural of St George killing the dragon. Ludwig's bedroom had a Tristan and Isolde theme and the huge bed had carved Gothic spires. Fourteen carvers had worked for more than four years on the bed canopy and the oak panelling. There was a little chapel with stained-glass in an alcove. The living room had murals with over 100 swans, the symbol of the royal family and after which Schwangau was named. There was a small, artificial grotto, based on the Venus grotto in "Tanhauser", with turquoise blue and pink fake-rock walls, lit by electric candles standing on a carved table with tree-like legs and matching chair. Only 14 of the castle's 200 rooms were completed by the time of Ludwig's death and he only stayed in it for about 170 days.

My inquiries at the tourist office in Fussen confirmed that I should take the Romantic Road north as the Alpenstrasse, in spite of what my map said. They recommended a visit to the Wieskirche, near Steingaden, a UNESCO listed World Heritage Site, considered to be the finest example of a Rococo church in the world, dating from 1754. I'm not remotely religious but the beauty of the interior decoration, pastel coloured angels reflecting the light streaming in through the tall windows, and the overwhelming feeling of peace created, moved even a cynic like me. But I was on the road to Garmisch-Partinkirchen, not Damascus, and the St. Paul moment passed.

I stopped in Oberammergau, the luftlmalerei capital of Bavaria, famed for its 6 hour passion play, which stemmed from a 1633 outbreak of the plague, the play being first put on to celebrate the end of it. Practically every building in the town centre was decorated with luftmalarei murals, the Schuhaus Hans Wolf with its biblical scenes and the Hotel Alte Post with its depiction of the crucifixion between the third floor windows. Just beyond Oberammergau was the over-the-top baroque Benedictine monastery of Kloster Ettal with its huge green copper clad dome and larger-than-life statues of the apostles on the façade, built round a wide courtyard. Inside, the basilica boasted exuberant rococo interior decoration, including a colourful fresco in the dome and elaborate stucco mouldings. The herbal liqueur called Ettaler Klosterlikor that the monks made wasn't bad either.

I back-tracked up a minor road shown as the Alpenstrasse on my map, to visit Linderhof Palace, another of King Ludwig's extravagances and the only one which was completed in his lifetime in 1878 and in which he actually lived. Designed in the French Baroque style, Linderhof reflected Ludwig's obsession with the 'Sun King' Louis XIV of France. It wasn't large by Ludwig's standards, just two-storeys high with a low roof line and finished in a restrained cream colour. However, it had an ornate, colonnaded, baroque style portico, with statues in alcoves at first floor level. And the approach was magnificent. A large, rectangular pond stretched out in front of it with a circular island fountain in the middle on which a golden figure surrounded by golden cherubs sprawled. The pond was surrounded by large stone urns with handles in which shrubs were growing. Curved flights of steps led up to a terrace surrounded by stone balustrades. Bare rock faces showed through the trees on the steep mountain behind. The garden behind the palace featured another fountain in a circular pond, a golden cupid with his bow marooned in the middle of it. The manicured flower garden was enclosed by tall box hedges with a large sculpture of Venus and Adonis in the middle and a couple of statues standing watching them in recesses in the hedge. The interior was opulent with gold, lapis lazuli and malachite ornamentation, velvet and silk wall hangings, crystal chandeliers, magnificent paintings and porcelain pieces. The sun symbol, representing the absolute power of kings, appeared here and there. The huge bedroom was highly decorative, with an enormous glass candelabra holding 108 candles. In the dining room, the table was designed to sink through the floor to the kitchen below like a "dumb-waiter" where it would be set and the food sent up without the servants having to intrude on the reclusive Ludwig's privacy. Reportedly, the table was always set for four and it was rumoured that Ludwig would carry on conversations with imaginary guests like Louis XIV, Madame Pompadour and Marie Antoinette while he ate. Valuable Meissen pottery was on display. In the Hall of Mirrors there was a carpet of ostrich plumes, an ivory candelabra and gilded bronze ornaments. Other rooms were hung with tapestries. The never-used audience chamber held bunches of ostrich feathers, an oriental symbol of royal power. I walked through the beautifully landscaped park, past the Moroccan House and the Moorish Kiosk. The artificial Venus grotto with fake stalagmites and stalactites, a waterfall and lake in it, still housed the seashell like golden gondola with a cherub as a figurehead on the prow that Ludwig called his swan-boat and used to float around in, to the strains of Wagner's operas.

There can't be many places in the world where you can climb a mountain in a train. In Garmisch-Partenkirchen I caught the cogwheel train that chugged along to the Eibsee, then laboured up above the snowline to 2600m on the Zugspitz, Germany's highest mountain. The final climb to the 2,962 metres (9,718 feet) summit was by cable car. The summit was still covered with snow, a tiny chapel nestling among it. It was cloudy but on a clear day the view out across the Austrian and Swiss Alps must have been spectacular. Back in Garmisch, I had a delicious dinner of roast wild boar in the Zum Wildschutz Restaurant.

Another detour off the Alpine Road took me down to Innsbruck in Austria via Mittenwald, an idyllic little Alpine town just on the German side of the border, famous for its violin making. The setting of Innsbruck was magnificent, the Alps seeming to press in on it, squeezing it into the valley of the River Inn, the peaks of the Nordkette Alps still snow-capped in June. The growth of the city dated back to 1180 when a bridge was built across the River Inn from a small market settlement on the north bank, enabling expansion onto the south bank and connecting the north-south trade route through Mittenwald south into Italy via the Brenner Pass. The River Inn provided an east-west route as well as leading north to the Danube, giving Innsbruck a strategic location for trade. The new bridge was called Ynsprugg (old German for Inn Bridge) hence the name of the city. In 1420 it became the seat of the Hapsburg Dukes of the Tyrol and reached the pinnacle of its power under Emperor Maximilian I between 1490 and 1519. I stayed at the Romantik Hotel Schwartzer Adler (Black Eagle) in Universitatstrasse, close to the centre of the Altstadt (Old Town). This boutique hotel specialised in honeymooners, their white limo allegedly featuring in Madonna's "Material Girl" video. The bathrooms were awash with Swarovski crystal and Gianni Versace had slept there – probably not with Madonna in view of his sexual orientation. The roof-top restaurant had a magnificent view of the Altstadt and the Alps.

In the morning, I walked west along Universitatstrasse towards the Hofburg which closed off the end of the street, its green copper cupolas dominating the view. It had been built as a castle in 1453, expanded by Emperor Maximilian I in the 16th century and given a full baroque make-over by Empress Maria Theresia in 1755. Inside, in the former state apartments, the rococo Riesensaal (Giant's Hall) was decorated with colourful frescoes and paintings of the Empresses sixteen children, including Marie Antoinette who lost her head in France after her off-the-cuff comment "let them eat cake" didn't go down well with the revolting and starving French peasants who were demanding bread prior to the French Revolution. The nearby Hofkirche had been built by Emperor Ferdinand I between 1553 and 1563 as a mausoleum for his grandfather Maximilian I. It had been remodelled in baroque style with an octagonal tower surmounted by a green onion dome. Unfortunately, Maximilian hadn't come along to the party – he was buried elsewhere – so his tomb stood empty, the sarcophagus surrounded by larger than life cast-iron statues of members of his family including his daughter-in-law Joanna the Mad. No wonder she was mad if he hadn't bothered to turn up to his own funeral. Charles the Bold was there as well. I could imagine him whispering to Joanna "If you're mad enough, I'm bold enough." Just north of the Hofburg, the Cathedral, the Dom St Jacob,   stood on the Domplatz, twin-towered and decorated in over-the-top 18th century baroque style. It had been badly war damaged and rebuilt in the 1950s. An equestrian statue of St. Jacob was mounted on top. The heart of the Altstadt was Herzog Friedrich Strasse, lined with fine baroque buildings. The piece de resistance was the Goldene Dachl, a Gothic oriel window above a balcony in the former residence of the Tyrolean rulers, its steeply sloping roof supported by four pillars and clad with 2,657 gilded copper tiles (I didn't count them) which glistered gold in the sun. It had been constructed by Emperor Maximilian I in 1520 so that he could watch what was going on in the street below, including jousting tournaments. Just across the street was the breathtaking frontage of the Helbinghaus, a town house which had been decorated in 1725 with some of the most beautiful rococo stucco moulding I had seen, painted in a pale mauve pastel colour. Just down from the Goldene Dachl, the clock tower and green dome of the Stadtturm rose to 56 metres (184 feet) above the red-painted Old Town Hall. I climbed the 148 steps (I did count them) to the viewing platform for a magnificent view across the city and mountains. It had been built in the 14th century but acquired its present Renaissance look in 1560. I continued walking south into what became Maria-Theresian Strasse, where a tall column, surmounted by a statue of the Virgin Mary, erected in 1703 and called the Annasaule (St. Anne's Column), stood outside the new Rathaus. Beyond it, the Triumphpforte, a triumphal arch erected in 1765, straddled the street.

I retraced my steps and then walked west to see the bridge over the swift-flowing River Inn which had given the city its name and its raison d'etre.

My next planned overnight stop was near Prien on the Chiemsee. This section of the Alpenstrasse presented a plethora of alternative routes. My map had the B307 from Wallgau annotated as the Alpenstrasse. The map in the Eyewitness travel guide also favoured the B307. But the most convincing looking map I had found on the internet showed the route going north from Wallgau past the Walchensee to Bad Tolz. Back in Germany in Wallgau, I went into the attractive Panoramahotel Karwendelhof for a coffee and advice about the route to take from there to the Chiemsee. The blonde girl who brought my coffee said she would ask her husband about where the Alpenstrasse went from there. He appeared and introduced himself as Wolfgang. We started chatting in German but after the first few exchanges, he switched to English. His wife, Jelena, burst out laughing. "I didn't realize you were British" she said. "I thought you just had a funny German accent." I suppose that was a compliment. It turned out that Jelena was Polish and that they had both lived in America for a number of years and still had a hotel property over there. They had only recently moved back to Germany. Wolfgang, being a native, had not been fooled by my masquerading as a German. There were no other customers and they were extremely friendly so we ended up having a long chat. Wolfgang told me that the Alpenstrasse route from there was really just a matter of personal choice: the B307 along the Isar Valley was more Alpine, closer to the mountains, but the scenery around the Walchensee was spectacular too. To their amusement, I tossed a euro and chose the Walchensee route.

The drive along the Walchensee lake was indeed spectacular, the cobalt-blue lake framed by forested mountains, the little red-roofed town of Walchensee nestling down by the edge of the lake. By the time I got to Bad Tolz, I was running out of time, so I continued along the B472 past Miesbach to join the Munich-Salzburg autobahn and on to the Prien turn-off at Bernau. In doing so, I think I missed a section of the "real" Alpenstrasse. With more time, I could have headed south from Bad Tolz, joined the B307 and followed it to Bayrischzell from where a minor road ran east to Oberaudorf. From there, you had the choice of dog-legging back to the Munich-Salzburg autobahn on the Inntal autobahn or cutting across a corner of Austria direct to Bernau.

Chiemsee was Bavaria's largest lake and a popular holiday resort. I stayed in the Hotel Zum Fischer am See a few kilometres south of the little harbour at Stock, where the ferries left for the two islands in the lake which were the main attraction. The Zum Fischer was a comfortable, homely, relaxing country-style hotel down by the lake shore, one of the most pleasant places I have ever stayed. The staff were friendly, the restaurant excellent with traditional Bavarian dishes and the bar lively. The clientele appeared to be entirely German. I strolled down a path to the little harbour with reed beds further along the shore inhabited by waterfowl. The snow-capped Chiemgau Alps filled the skyline on the southern shore of the lake across the shimmering blue water. The following morning I drove up to Stock with hotels, restaurants and cafes clustered around the ferry piers. Little green railway carriages hauled by a steam engine ran up and down to the town of Prien just a few kilometres inland. I caught a ferry to visit the islands in the lake, the open upper deck with slatted bench seats providing a vista of the lake, dotted with white sails, the mountain tops glistening white to the south. The larger island was the site of another of King Ludwig's palaces, the Schloss Herrenchiemsee. The Linderhof Palace had sought to pay homage to Louis XIV in a relatively modest way: the Herrenchiemsee set out to rival his Palace of Versailles in both size and magnificence. This was the one that had Ludwig's bankers hitting the panic button and threatening to foreclose on him when his money dried up in 1885. He had paid for the castles from his own funds and borrowing and had gone deeply into debt. In 1886 he applied to his cabinet for credit and when this was refused applied to the parliament for money to continue the projects. His Ministers, presumably fearful that his personal debts could eventually fall on the State Treasury, decided that enough was enough and started the process of deposing him. From the time Ludwig bought the island in 1873 until his death in 1886, he spent more than the present day equivalent of $125 million US dollars on the project, more than on Neuschwanstein and Linderhof combined. Work had started on the palace in 1878 but by the time of Ludwig's death only twenty of the planned seventy rooms had been finished: the north wing was just a shell and it was demolished in1907. Ludwig only spent 9 days in it.

From the landing stage it was a half hour's walk up to the palace, the last stretch through an avenue of trees. When it came in sight, the three-storey neo-baroque frontage was as long as a football field. The extensive garden out in front was split into four quarters: first, two manicured lawns with neat flower beds, ringed with bright red flowers; then two large ponds or artificial lakes with spouting fountains, lined with sculptures – bare breasted maidens, cherubs, Neptune – and a large conical sculpture in the centre of each, one surmounted by a winged warrior on a horse. I took a thirty-five minute guided tour of the interior. We ascended the State Staircase, an elaborate double flight affair with a frescoed gallery and glass roof. We passed through the Royal Bodyguards' Room and two Antechambers to the State Bedchamber, where Ludwig had intended to hold morning and evening audiences a la Louis XIV. The decoration of these rooms was mind-blowing – colourful frescos on walls and ceilings, paintings, wall hangings, elaborate stucco mouldings, sculptures, priceless ornaments and porcelain. The piece de resistance was the Great Hall of Mirrors, 98 metres (320 feet) long, 10 metres (33 feet) longer than the original at Versailles, and with the Halls of War and Peace at either end, taking up the whole frontage of the palace. Seventeen mirrors reflected the light from 1,848 candles in 44 candelabra and 33 chandeliers. The ceiling was painted with tableaux from Louis XIV's life. We saw Ludwig's private bedroom, all over-the-top gilded stucco and extravagant carvings. The Blue Salon and Writing Room were opulently decorated; the dining room had another disappearing table masquerading as a dumb-waiter and a huge chandelier of Meissen porcelain. We descended by the north staircase which was just bare brickwork, never having been completed. Downstairs was the bathroom with a huge bath which could be heated: the palace had gone one up on Versailles by being centrally heated. The walls were covered in colourful murals of bathing scenes and there was an elaborately decorated Robing Chamber adjacent.

I caught the next ferry to the other island, the Fraueninsel, named for the Benedictine nunnery founded in 766 A.D. The current baroque style Abbey and Convent dominated the end of the island as we came in to the landing jetty – four storeys high and five or six times as long, it was a massive building with small dormer style windows in the steeply sloping slate roof. The garden beside it was a riot of colour with flowers, rose bushes, shrubs and tall trees. Round the back, the tall clock tower with an onion-shaped dome could be seen from all over the island. There was a beautiful peaceful graveyard outside St. Michael's Chapel with ornate headstones and flowers growing on the graves. It was just a short stroll around the island on the lake-front path, a pretty, tranquil place, with picturesque traditional houses, bars, cafes and restaurants. The inhabitants, apart from the nuns, were mostly fishermen, artists and craftspeople. I saw a young woman in short shorts painting at an easel, watched intently by a little bare-footed blonde girl. Yachts were moored in little stone-faced docks. I stopped for an Inselbrau at Fritzi's Biergarten. I wished I had planned to stay longer in Chiemsee.

From Chiemsee, I followed the B305 through Reit-im-Winkl to Berchtesgaden, dominated by the Watzman, Germany's second highest mountain. I stayed in the Hotel Bavaria with a magnificent view of the Watzman and the Ammer River, running through the town below, from the bedroom window. I had a meal in the Gasthof Bier Adam up on the Marktplatz, the façade decorated with luftmalarei depicting rural scenes including two men sawing up a log. Along at the end of the street a band was playing and the pavement tables set out by the bars and cafes were crowded with drinkers.

The following morning, I took a cruise down the Konigsee, confined between steep, forested, mountain sides like a fjord, to see the church of St. Bartoloma, nestled at the lakeside, beneath the Watzman, with its red, onion-shaped domes. Why is it, when you've come half way around the world to photograph an iconic building, some Muppet buries it behind scaffolding? Do they do it deliberately? Who told them I was coming? I consoled myself with a Lowenbrau beer and a fish sandwich in the adjacent timber built Fischerei St. Bartoloma.

The following day, I drove down to Obersalzberg to visit Hitler's Eagle's Nest. The weather was atrocious, heavy rain and low cloud, so I went into the Dokumentation Obersalzberg Centre at the foot of the 1,834 metres (5,960 feet) Kehlstein Mountain, on which the Eagle's Nest perched, to wait for it to clear. The museum had been opened in 1999 to tell the story of the area and the Nazis. The exhibition covered the growth of the Nazi Party and the rise of Hitler to power, and catalogued the atrocities committed by the regime as they consolidated their control over Germany and waged war on the rest of the world, with graphic detail of the concentration camp system and the Holocaust. No punches were pulled: it was a sobering experience, illustrated with photos, documents, posters, films and sound recordings. I rented an audio guide as the labelling was only in German. There was a section on the local history of the Nazis in the Oberslazberg area. In the 1920s Hitler had had a holiday home in the area which he later bought and enlarged into his impressive Berghof residence. In 1933, when he became Chancellor of Germany, he developed the Obersalzberg area as the southern headquarters of the ruling Nazi Party. Land was bought up or confiscated, a 2 metres high barbed wire fence erected around a substantial area with guardhouses on the road accesses to keep the public out. Several Nazi top brass, including Goring and Martin Bormann moved there, an SS barracks was built and a bunker system drilled into the mountainside. The Eagle's Nest was built as a 50th birthday present for Hitler. Towards the end of the war, the Allies bombed the area flat and later the Germans themselves blew up what was left. Miraculously, the Eagle's Nest survived intact. In one of the ironies of history, there was a theory that Hitler had Jewish blood. His father was illegitimate and it was rumoured that he was the son of a Jew that his mother worked for as a domestic servant. There were also persistent rumours that he was homosexual. All that and only one ball. If he was guilty on either of these counts, according to his own policies, he should have sent himself to the gas chamber and saved the German people and the rest of humanity a lot of grief.

The weather cleared a bit, and I took the bus up the spectacular road to the Eagle's Nest. After getting off, we passed through a tunnel to a huge, brass-lined lift which took us rapidly up the final 124m (403 feet). I went outside onto the terrace, where I'd seen technicolour footage of Hitler and Eva Braun cavorting with the Nazi top brass. The development of the Alpine Road network as a tourist trail had started in 1933, the year Hitler came to power. As I enjoyed a bratwurst and a beer in the restaurant, I wondered if Adolf hadn't taken his eye off the ball on the question of the Alpenstrasse. With his track-record, you would have expected firm lines on maps, alternative routes dynamited out of existence, Austria invaded where convenient, him to provide a solution without shilly-shallying with options. A final solution. His Alpine lair was a fitting place to end my German Alpine Road trip.

But I had one more detour left; continuing on to Salzburg in Austria, home of Mozart and The Sound of Music's von Trapp family. Appropriately, I stayed in the Mozart Hotel in Franz-Josef Strasse in the "New Town" which was actually quite old. Salzburg was bisected by the Salzach River, flowing north-west to the Danube. It was hemmed in by mountains: the Kaputzinerberg dominated the south end of the New Town on the north bank; the Old Town, on the other side of the river, nestled beneath the Monchsberg. It was a stunning setting with snow capped peaks visible in the distance even in early summer. The city was named for the salt deposits mined nearby since 1,000 BC. There had also been valuable copper mines and other minerals in the immediate area. A Roman city on the site had been destroyed by Celtic barbarians and like Munich, the modern city had been founded by monks who built St. Peter's Church and Monastery around 700 AD. Forty percent of the city's buildings had been destroyed in World War II but it had been meticulously restored and declared a UNESCO World Heritage Site in 1997.

The Mozart Hotel was plush, like a decorative chocolate box or high class brothel with its predominantly red furnishings, the Reception area filled with antiques. I was even given a complimentary

Mozart's Kugeln (Motzart's Balls) – chocolate, not fossilised. I walked downhill to the Schloss Mirabel, a palace built in baroque style in 1727 for the Archbishop. The attached gardens, the Mirabelgarten, were magnificent, with sculptures, fountains, manicured lawns, flower beds and shrubs, rose gardens and leafy trees. The axis had been orientated to direct the eye to the Festung Hohensalzburg, the massive hilltop fortress on the skyline on the other side of the river. The steps near the Pegasus fountain and the gnomes in the Zwerglgarten (Gnomes Garden) was where the von Trapp children had practised their "Do-re-mes" in "The Sound of Music". Yodel-ee-hee-hee, I thought. I walked along to the Makartplatz, the first stop on the Mozart trail – he was everywhere in the city – the house to which he had moved with his parents when he was 17. Called the Tanzmeisterhaus, it was a substantial two-storey, yellow-painted building with a blue-slate roof and tiny dormer windows. It had been destroyed in World War II but restored as an exact replica. It now housed a museum to the great piano-plonker. I crossed the Salzach River over the Staatsbrucke (State Bridge) into the Old Town. The clock tower and spire of the Altes Rathaus (Old Town Hall) framed the end of a narrow alleyway. I walked along the main shopping street, the Getreidegasse, lined with expensive boutique shops in baroque style buildings. No.9 was Mozart's birthplace where he had been born in 1756 and had lived until he was 17. He'd been a precocious little sod, composing his first music at age five and performing for the Empress Maria Theresia a year later. At the age of two, he reputedly identified a pig's squeal as G sharp: in a later era he would probably have correctly recognised Julie Andrews' high notes in "The Sound of Music" as identical to the sound made by a rat caught by the gonads in a spring-loaded trap. In later years, he became a bit of a piss-head, famed for his heavy drinking sessions. He had died in Vienna at the early age of 35 and been buried there, so there was no grave to round off the Mozart trail in Salzburg. However, there was as a statue of him in the centre of the nearby Mozartplatz.

The adjacent Residenz Platz was dominated by the Residenz, the opulent former home of the Prince-Archbishops of Salzburg, who had been the religious and secular rulers of the whole Province since the

Middle Ages until absorbed into the Austro-Hungarian Empire. It was now mainly government offices. A spectacular marble fountain, the Residenzbrunnen, stood out in front, ringed by four horses spouting water and surmounted by a Triton holding a conch shell. The magnificent Cathedral (Dom) with its bulbous copper dome and twin spires was a Baroque masterpiece. It had first been built in 774 AD but rebuilt in Baroque style and consecrated in 1628. Its façade featured large sculptured figures of saints. The cavernous interior had allegedly been designed to hold 10,000 worshippers but it would have been a tight squeeze, a paedophile priest's paradise, offering endless opportunities to grope small boys. In the Kapitelplatz behind the Dom, there were horse-drawn carriages for hire and a huge chess-board marked out on the flagstones, with outsize pieces. Street performers prowled around and pavement artists were in session. The Stiftskirche St. Peter was where the city had its origins when Benedictine monks built the church and monastery around 700 AD. The present buildings dated from the 12th and 13th centuries but had been re-modelled in Baroque style, like most of the Old Town, in the 17th and 18th centuries. The Friedhof (Cemetery) out behind was a beautiful, tranquil place with intricate stonework in the tombstones and filigree crosses. There were sculpted cherubs, one cradling a skull. The flowers and shrubs were a riot of colour and leafy trees provided shade. I took the funicular from Festungsgasse up to the Festung Hohensalzburg, high above the city. The fortress had been built in 1077 during the "holy war" between the Holy Roman Emperor and the Papacy. The present structure mainly dated from a re-build between 1495 and 1519 with some later 16th century additions. It had been a military barracks in the 19th century but was now just a tourist attraction. There were some old cannon in the fortress area at the north end of the site. A gateway led through to the residential area where the Schulhaus and Kuchelturm (Schoolhouse and Kitchentower) stood, whitewashed, with a conical tower and blue-slate roofs. There was a tall, old salt warehouse in the Small Courtyard. The Goldene Stube (Golden Room) had a gold studded ceiling imitating a starry night-sky and a weird, gothic-styled stove with gold coloured tiles. The Reckturm (Corner Tower) had been a torture chamber, complete with racks, wheels and assorted bodily suspension systems – a sado-masochist's paradise. According to the promotional leaflet, people had been tortured here as recently as 1893. Salzburg had a long history of torturing people, right up to the soundtrack of the "Sound of Music" – "The hills are alive with the sound of screaming." In the evening, I had fish soup and a rack of lamb in the Zum Eulenspiegel Restaurant just off the Getriedegasse, opposite Motzart's birthplace.

I drove back to Munich. I had one more pilgrimage to make – to the spot where Mad King Ludwig had died. The following morning, I took the S Bahn railway down to Starnberg on Lake Starnberg. I'd managed to pick a public holiday for my trip and everything was closed in the little town including the Tourist Office and no buses were running – it was like a ghost town. I finally met a woman walking down by the lake shore and asked her how I could get to Berg, further down the lake, where Ludwig had drowned. She told me that the ferry was running and pointed to the jetty where I could catch it. Ludwig's body and that of his psychiatrist, Dr. von Gudden, was found floating in knee deep water just days after he had been declared insane and deposed from the Bavarian throne. From the ferry terminal at Berg, I walked out through the estate still occupied by the descendants of the Wittelsbach family to the place where the bodies were found. The attractive little Votivkappele chapel, built in his honour, stood overlooking the lake, and in the shallow water below it, a large white cross marked the spot where the bodies were found. The official verdict was that Ludwig had committed suicide. Quite why his psychiatrist had joined him in some bizarre suicide pact was never explained. At the time, fishermen reported hearing shots. Ludwig had been deposed because he was squandering vast sums of his own and borrowed money on his castle building projects and his government was concerned that he could be dragging the kingdom towards financial ruin. He was diagnosed by Dr. von Gudden as suffering from paranoia which today would be classified as schizophrenia. Recent medical evidence suggests that he was suffering from a form of meningitis and was far from insane. He was homosexual and reclusive but despite his oddity, he was popular with his subjects. After his death rumours circulated that he had been assassinated by members of his government to ensure that there was no possibility of him being restored to the throne. In 2007, new evidence emerged in the form of a sworn affidavit from a Munich banker claiming that when he was a child, a Countess, who looked after some of the Wittelsbach family's assets, showed him and his mother a coat which she claimed Ludwig had been wearing the day that he died, with two bullet holes in the back. The coat was later lost in a fire in 1973 in which the Countess and her husband died. The banker's claims were backed up by a Bavarian art historian who published a photograph of a portrait of Ludwig painted hours after his death showing blood oozing from the corner of his mouth. Calls for the body to be exhumed for a post mortem were refused by the surviving members of the Wittelsbach family.

Flying out of Munich, I reflected that if Ludwig were miraculously to be resurrected from his grave in Michaelskirche, he would be pleased to see that his fairy-tale castle at Neuschwanstein was now so much appreciated – a candidate for the New Seven Wonders of the World no less. It certainly hadn't been appreciated during his lifetime by his political enemies and its construction may indeed have led to his murder.

11

KIYOMIZUDERA, KYOTO, JAPAN SEPTEMBER 2009

THE NEXT ON my list of new Wonders of the World runners-up meant a trip to Japan. I had never heard of the Kiyomizudera Temple in Kyoto until I saw the New 7 Wonders web-site. I decided to return to New Zealand from my 2009 trip to Shetland via Tokyo. I booked a tour of Honshu Island which included Kyoto.

I didn't know much about Japan before the trip and so I was by no means burdened with preconceived ideas about it other than those stemming from World War II and watching Japanese tour groups in action outside their country, perhaps not the best preconceptions to carry with me. I had also broken my golden rule about trying to absorb some basic language beforehand so I was not as well prepared for the trip as I usually am. I knew that the Land of the Rising Sun was also the Land of the Rising Yen: that in spite of a stagnating economy since the early 1990s and years of deflation, especially in the property market, it was still the most expensive country on the Planet for foreigners. I also knew that, like New Zealand, it was on the Pacific "Ring of Fire", prone to devastating earthquakes and volcanic eruptions. I had read that the Great Kanto earthquake of 1923, 7.9 on the Richter scale, had caused 100,000 casualties in Tokyo and destroyed 45% of its buildings; and that Mt. Fuji had last erupted in 1707, covering Tokyo in 10 centimetres (4 inches) of volcanic ash. But since it was mostly such a black box to me, I was looking forward to a peek up the Japanese kimono

The trip didn't start well. While I was in Shetland, I had an e-mail from my travel agent in New Zealand telling me the bad news that the tour I had booked with Travel Indochina had been cancelled due to lack of numbers. However, the good news was that she had found an alternative with JTB Travel which started just a day later and went to all the places covered by Travel Indochina except Himeji-jo Castle and Hiroshima. I was disappointed to miss seeing the place where the first atomic bomb in the world had been dropped but otherwise the problem was solved and I would have an extra day in Tokyo, hopefully at the expense of my travel insurance company.

My initial impression of Tokyo on the drive in from Narita Airport was not favourable. The buildings seemed bland, monotonous and designed purely for function rather than any aesthetic appeal, as if all the architects had worked from the same set of standard designs. In retrospect, I realize that this was hardly surprising. Tokyo was completely destroyed by the Americans in World War II by saturation bombing and the subsequent fire-storms among the predominantly wooden buildings. The civilian death toll of 80-100,000 was higher than in Hiroshima and Nagasaki, destroyed by the atom bombs dropped on them. The city therefore had to be rebuilt from scratch and quickly, so a degree of uniformity could hardly have been avoided. The sheer scale of the city was overpowering, the built-up area extending as far as the eye could see in every direction. With a population of over 35 million, metropolitan Tokyo was by a long way the largest conurbation in the world.

I stayed in the Shiba Park Hotel in the Rappongi area, not far from the Ginza District and close to Tokyo Tower. I had a day to spare before the tour began so I decided to see if I could master the city's rail and metro system and visit some of the places that the tour wasn't scheduled to include. Like many things in Japan, the Tokyo rail system was something of a black box. There were few concessions to non-Japanese speakers and without the help of some English speaking locals – and there didn't seem to be many of them – I don't think I would ever have got out of the first station. In particular, I couldn't figure out the fare between stations so that I would know which ticket button to press. I subsequently discovered that the best idea was to select the cheapest fare and then use the machines at the other end which would tell you how much you had under-paid. Once I got the hang of the system, it proved to be an excellent, cheap and quick way to get around the city. However, in 1995 it had proved to be a not too safe means of transport. Members of a death cult called Aum Shinrikyo had placed bags of deadly liquid sarin gas on the floor of carriages on five subway lines. Twelve passengers had died and hundreds been injured. As I travelled around, I realized why it wasn't felt necessary for the system to be user-friendly to non-Japanese – there were hardly any of us using it. For the most part, mine was the only non-Japanese face in the carriage. Tokyo was the most un-cosmopolitan place I had ever been. It was as if the clash in 1853 had never taken place, when Japan was opened up to the West, for the first time in over 200 years, at the gun-points of the American navy. The first Europeans to visit Japan had been three Portuguese merchants shipwrecked there in 1542. They were soon followed by the Jesuits: St. Francis Xavier, whose tomb I'd seen in the Basilica of Bom Jesus in Old Goa in India, established a Catholic mission at Kagoshima in 1549 and Christianity started to spread. The port of Nagasaki was developed in 1571 to serve Portuguese traders. However, the Japanese authorities became concerned at the threat these outside influences posed for Japanese culture. In 1597 Shogun Hideyoshi had six Spanish priests and 20 Japanese Christian converts crucified. In 1637 a Christian insurrection against the government broke out, which was put down and the Portuguese expelled the following year. Christianity was banned and savagely suppressed. A small artificial island had been built in Nagasaki harbour for the Portuguese traders. After 1638 the Dutch were allowed to trade there on the basis that no missionary work was carried out, but only 14 traders were allowed and only very limited contact with the natives – some officials, traders and prostitutes. Apart from that and a Chinese trading post in

Nagasaki, all other contacts with the outside world were banned until the Americans took things into their own hands. In 1853, Commodore Perry sailed into Tokyo harbour with four heavily armed "black ships" to force the Japanese government to open up the country to diplomatic and trade relations. This was followed up by a treaty of friendship and trade between the two countries in 1858 and similar agreements with other western nations followed soon afterwards. But even now, in the 21st century, restrictions on immigration and foreign workers ensured that Japanese racial purity was preserved. Even some of the red light establishments wouldn't allow gaijins (foreigners) over their doorsteps in case they contaminated the local whores. Although outwardly very polite to foreigners, I suspected that Japan was the most racialist society in the world. That would explain their callous behaviour in World War II when they maltreated their enemies and prisoners as if they were another species or from another Planet.

I went to visit the Yasukuni Shrine, built in 1869, where the ashes of the war dead since the Meiji Restoration in 1868 (when the Shogun system ended and the Emperor resumed a political role) were enshrined, including World War II war criminals, among them war-time militarist Prime Minister, Tojo Hideki. The complex was very Japanese with an imposing red "torii" gate entrance, eight storeys high, cherry trees, a pond garden and a tea house. Unlike the Dokumetation Salzburg museum in Berchtesgaden, Germany, where the horrors of the Nazi regime were spelled out warts and all, the little war museum at Yasukuni made no concessions to contrition on the part of the Japanese. A Zero fighter plane and a locomotive from the Burma Railway stood proudly in the main hall. The whole complex was teeming with visitors. There was obviously no sense of national shame about World War II – quite the contrary. A recent visit to the shrine by the Japanese Prime Minister had brought virulent protests from the Chinese and Korean governments, countries which had suffered atrocities at the hands of the Japanese during the war including the "rape of Nanking", where 150-300,000 civilians had been massacred and the use of Korean women as sex slaves by the army. After the opening up of Japan to the West, "westernization" proceeded very rapidly with the construction of railways, industrialization and particularly a build-up of modern military capability. By 1895 they were able to defeat China in the brief Sino-Japanese War and in 1904-06, Russia, in the Russo-Japanese War, including the annihilation of the Russian naval fleet sent round from the Black Sea. They annexed Korea in 1910 and then in 1931, occupied Manchuria, setting up the last Chinese Emperor, Pu-yi (who had been deposed in China) as a puppet ruler. Following international protests, Japan left the League of Nations, becoming virtually an international pariah. After widespread social unrest in the 1920s and 30s, the Military were effectively in control of the country again, an echo back to pre-1868 days when the warrior Shoguns had ruled the roost with the emperors as figureheads. In 1937 they invaded China and then in 1941, desperate at sanctions by the USA restricting their supply of oil and other key resources, bombed Pearl Harbour and invaded Singapore, Hong Kong and other European outposts in the Far East, bringing them into conflict with the Allies lined up against Nazi Germany. At the end of the war, following the atomic bombs dropped on Hiroshima and Nagasaki, the leaders were hanged as war criminals. However, the Emperor was spared in spite of obvious guilt but the new constitution drawn up post-war made it clear that he would now be a constitutional monarch without the old connotations of divinity. (According to Japanese mythology, the emperors were descended from the Sun Goddess, Amaterasu.) The country was demilitarised. American aid poured in and by the 1960s the Japanese economy had outpaced the European countries and was second only to the USA.

Starting the tour, we climbed the Tokyo Tower for an overview of the conurbation - a bright red Eiffel Tower clone built in 1958, when it had been the tallest structure in the city at 333 metres (1,093 feet). It confirmed my initial impression of the overpowering size of the sprawling Metropolitan Area. Our guide pointed out where Mount Fuji would be visible if it wasn't for the cloud cover. We went on to see the Imperial Palace: it wasn't open to the public but we viewed the towers protruding above the surrounding walls and the wide encircling moat bordered by colourful planting. From the picturesque Niju-bashi

Bridge across the moat we could see the upwardly curved roof-lines of the Fushimi-yagura lookout turrets of the original Edo Castle, work on which had begun in 1590 and which had become the largest castle in the world at the time. I had read that, following the Emperor's radio announcement that Japan had surrendered in World War II, numerous soldiers had disembowelled themselves outside the palace, rather than admit defeat or surrender to the Allies. The current Emperor, Akihito, who succeeded his father, Hirohito, in 1989, was still held in God-like reverence by the people in spite of the constitutional change, although he no longer wielded much in the way of political power. We continued on to the Senso-ji Temple, also known as the Asakusa Kannon after the Buddhist Goddess of Mercy, Tokyo's most sacred and oldest temple, dating back to 628 AD. This was the area, Shitomachi, where Tokyo had its origins as the village of Edo on the banks of the Sumida River. Shogun Tokugawa Ieyasu had made it his military capital in 1603, reclaiming marshy land along the river for expansion and building the massive citadel of Edo Castle where the royal palace now stood. Edo grew to be the largest city in the world in the early 1700s with over a million people: London didn't reach that size until well into the 1800s. The name Tokyo (Eastern Capital) wasn't applied to the city until 1868 when it became the national capital after the rule by Shoguns ended and the Emperor moved from Kyoto to a new palace in the Castle grounds. We passed into Senso-ji Temple through the huge, red, wooden Kaminarimon (Thunder) Gate between twin guardian statues of Fujin, the God of Wind and Raijin, the God of Thunder. Feeling protected by the appropriate Gods, I glanced round and risked releasing a fart I'd been suppressing since I got off the bus. The Gods had obviously looked kindly on me; no one appeared to have heard it. A large, red, paper lantern hung above the entrance, inscribed with the Chinese ideogram for "thunder". Japanese script was a strange mixture of Chinese ideograms and two home-grown syllable-based systems, each using 46 characters. One system appeared to be mainly used for transcribing foreign words (an amazing number of which had been absorbed into the language) almost like using italics in western writing. The guide told us that you needed to know at least

2,000 of the Chinese ideograms to be able to read a newspaper. I was glad that I hadn't attempted to learn any Japanese for the trip. I had already discovered that even counting was a nightmare: while there were "general numbers" used when counting on your fingers, different suffixes had to be added to those depending on what you were counting, for example, three bottles, three stamps and three people all had different words for the "three" part of the expression. On the plus side, I had discovered that there was no tonal system to master like in Chinese and Thai. Indeed, Japanese wasn't related to Chinese at all: it belonged to the Altaic family of languages, most closely related to Mongolian and Turkish. There had been people in Japan for thousands of years, including the Ainu who still survived in small numbers in the northern island of Hokkaido and may have shared Caucasian blood with ancient Europeans but the present Japanese stock were mainly derived from a series of immigrations of Mongoloid peoples from the Korean Peninsula in the two centuries before Christ and then again around 250 AD. The early migrations brought the skills of growing paddy rice and smelting and forging iron into tools and weapons. The later migrants were warrior horsemen, wearing iron armour and with superior iron weapons who became the aristocracy and from whom the line of emperors descended. Buddhism had been introduced from Korea in 552 AD and from then Chinese influences on the culture grew, including on the architecture and the adoption of the Chinese ideographic script. Beyond the Thunder Gate, the Nakamise-dori (street) was an arcade of craft shops selling kimonos, fans, dolls, hair combs, and Buddhist artefacts. In Japan, commerce and religion appeared to mix happily. A giant, bronze, incense burner stood in front of the main hall. Worshippers were burning sticks of incense and wafting the fumes over their clothes. The cavernous main hall housed a golden statue of Kannon and a magnificent golden and lacquer altar. There were votive paintings on the walls and a dragon motif painted on the ceiling surrounded by angels and lotus flowers. A five storey pagoda stood at the edge of the compound. Elsewhere in the grounds, the bronze Nade Jizo bodhisattva statue was believed to "relieve ailments if you rub the part of its body that troubles you". I'd seen a Japanese man furtively watching three mini-skirted Japanese girls posing provocatively for photos of each other on a low wall. I now saw him approaching old Nade, walking as if he had a painful erection. Glancing around to see if he was being observed, he reached out and gave the statue a quick wank. The expression on his face was too inscrutable to tell whether or not he had obtained any relief from his affliction.

The afternoon was free, so I took a train on the Yamanote line around through Shibuya to Harajuku and on to Shinjuku. The Harajuku area was the place to go to see young Japanese trying to be anything except Japanese – punk rockers, Elvis, every bizarre fashion imaginable with dyed hair colours ranging from blonde through blues to pink. I spent the evening in Shinjuku, the main night-life centre of the city, including the Kabuki-cho "pleasure quarter", with glaring neon flashing everywhere among the towering skyscrapers. It was impossible to tell a brothel from a bakery as all the signs were in Japanese and I couldn't read them. I found it all a bit overpowering and I had never felt so alien anywhere else in the world. It was as if I had found myself in a scene from the 1982 film "Blade Runner" with me as an alien android "Replicant". I decided to catch a train back to the hotel before Harrison Ford loomed out of the neon to "retire" me. I think I would have been overcome with emotion and nostalgia if I had come across a Macdonald's.

The following morning, we took a local train down to Kamakura, Japan's military capital from the 12th to the 14th century when the first Shogun (military leader), Minamoto Yoritomo had made it his headquarters. This began the system of government by a Samurai warrior class, remotely located from the emperors living in the national capital of Kyoto and performing a ceremonial, figurehead role. Kamakura's importance at that time was reflected in its 19 Shinto shrines and 65 Buddhist temples. From Hase Station we walked to the Hase-dera Temple and up to the bronze statue of the Great Buddha (Daibatsu). Cast in 1252, the 13.5m (44 feet) tall statue had survived tidal waves, earthquakes, fires and typhoons. In the afternoon we walked up the tree lined Komachi-dori shopping street to the Hachiman- gu Shrine, dedicated to the God of War and approached past two island studded lotus ponds.

Our next tour took us north by bus on a two hour drive to Nikko to visit the Tosho-gu Shrine, where one of Japan's most famous Shoguns, Tokugawa Ieyasu, was buried. It was he who developed Edo (Tokyo) as his military capital and founded a dynasty of Shoguns more powerful than the emperors. In 1333, the then Shogun had abandoned Kamakura and moved his headquarters to the Imperial capital, Kyoto. There, relations with the royal family deteriorated further and the emperors were pushed even more into the background. After a Shogun was assassinated in 1441, the Shogunate began to lose control of the country and in 1467 the century long Age of Warring States saw regional warlords called "daimyo" fighting over territory. Eventually three of these warlords in succession started the process of re-unifying the country, the last of them, Tokugawa Ieyesu, finally succeeding after winning the battle of Sekigahara in 1600 where 100,000 samurai clashed in armies representing alliances of warlords from eastern and western Japan. He went on to found the Toshugawa Shogunate in Edo which lasted until 1868. After his death he was enshrined as a god. Nearing the shrine, we passed the ornate, red-lacquered, wooden Shinkyo Bridge, spanning the Diaya River. We approached the shrine along an avenue of Japanese cedars and entered it through a granite torii (gate). Just to the left was a five-storey pagoda, each storey representing an element – earth, water, fire, wind and heaven, in ascending order. We climbed some steps to the Omete-mon Gate, guarded on either side by the two Nio gods of Buddhist theology, fierce looking creatures with staring, bulging eyes, one with its mouth open, the other with it closed, representing life and death, the beginning (or the first letter of the Sanskrit alphabet) and the end (or the last letter of the Sanskrit alphabet). The open mouth was supposed to fend off evil, the closed one to keep in good spirits. Further into the complex we passed the plain wooden sacred stable, decorated with a carving of the three wise monkeys. The Three Sacred Storehouses were built in the traditional style of Japanese rural architecture with carvings of elephants around the eaves of one. A Sacred Fountain, covered by a massive ornately carved Chinese style roof, was intended for ritual bathing before entering the inner sanctum of the shrine. We climbed more steps to a terrace with twin bell and drum towers. Off to the side, the Honji-do building had a painting of a "crying dragon" on the ceiling. The guide demonstrated how the echo appeared to make it roar by clapping two sticks together near its mouth, an effect that didn't seem to happen anywhere else in the room. The next level was reached through the massive Yomeimon Gate, lavishly decorated with gold leaf and intricate carvings of mythical beasts, dancing girls and flowers. Two seated figures on either side of the entrance were statues of former imperial ministers. A further flight of steps took us up through the smaller Karamon Gate into the forecourt of the building housing the Haiden (Sanctuary) and the Honden (Inner Sanctuary) decorated with paintings including the "kirin", a mythical beast, half giraffe, half dragon and on the ceiling, over 100 dragons were depicted . A covered walkway supported by red-lacquered pillars ran around the edge of the upper terrace. An exquisite carving of a sleeping cat (the Nemuri-neko) at fascia board level at the entrance way to Ieyasu's tomb, was supposed to signify tranquillity and that all evil spirits had been expelled. A path with over 200 stone steps led up through lofty cedar trees and past an honour guard of seated stone samurai statues to the tomb on top of the hill. The return trip to Tokyo took us through the forested Nikko National Park, past the placid Lake Chuzen-ji and the Kegon Falls, which dropped 96m (315 feet) to the Diaya River. Having seen the Iguacu Falls in Brazil, I found these ones distinctly underwhelming.

The following morning we took a bus down to Mount Fuji, at 3,776m (12,390 feet), Japan's highest peak, dormant since 1707. It was in cloud as we approached and remained so when we climbed up to the highest road access point at 2,300m (7,475 feet), the mist-shrouded 5th Station, where there were some shops, restaurants and open air food stalls selling "yakatori" (grilled meat on skewers). We finally saw it in all its snow-capped glory on the drive round to the Mount Kamagatake Aerial Ropeway but by the time we got there only the summit peeked above the cloud layer. So my only photograph of Japan's most iconic physical feature was a hazy trapezoidal shape barely visible through the clouds. We ended the day with a cruise down Lake Ashi on a Pirates of the Caribbean style galleon, about as typically Japanese as the blonde-haired punk rockers at Harajuku. We docked at Hakone and spent the night in the Kowaki-en Hotel.

In the morning, we boarded the shinkansen (bullet train) at Odawara station for Nagoya. This sleek train was impressive; you could feel the g-force as it accelerated out of the station. We were met off the train by our guide for the next section of the tour. She was elderly, how elderly difficult to tell, most Orientals weather well. Her English was excellent but very old-fashioned, as if she'd practised it on a diet of novels by Charles Dickens and Sir Walter Scott. Her favourite word was "really" pronounced in a very rotund way, perhaps to demonstrate that she had no ploblems with plonouncing the letter "r" and she could roll her Rs with the best of us. She would say things like: "Really, this is the biggest Buddha in all of Japan." She turned out to be extremely friendly and helpful, solicitous in a fussy, motherly way and obsessed with the health and safety of the group: "careful here" at a foot wide water channel; "mind the step" for a six inch doorstep; "careful with the traffic" when there wasn't a Toyota in sight. The only time she appeared aggressive was when her mobile phone rang. She would snatch it out of her pocket and snarl "Moshi-moshi?" (Hello) into it. I recognised a kindred spirit: to me, mobile phones were the most anti-social, privacy-invading invention that mankind had ever inflicted on itself. I'd had to have one when I was working as a Town Planning Consultant but when I packed that in, I threw it in the waste bin and had resisted all the blandishments of persistent telecom marketeers ever since. The tour guide had introduced herself to us but I hadn't caught her name. I came to think of her as Mrs. Moshi Moshi. In Nagoya, we visited the Toyota Museum and Nagoya Castle. The castle was surrounded by a high dry stone wall. Corner towers rose above the walls, upwardly curved roofs, clad in green tiles, projected out at each storey level, giving the impression that the whole structure was in the process of floating upwards. It looked much flimsier and insubstantial than the typical solid European castle and the architecture showed distinct Chinese influences. The white walls were broken by a symmetrical window pattern. The castle had been built on the orders of the Shogun,Tokugawa Ieyasu and completed in 1612. Much of it had been burned down in World War II air raids. Restoration of most of it had been completed in 1959. Just inside the sturdy main gate was a 600 year old Japanese Nutmeg tree. At the corner of the central part of the fortifications, the South west Tower had overhanging sections at second floor level where trap doors could dump rocks or other missiles on attackers. We passed through the Omote-ninomon Gate into the central compound containing the "donjon", the main keep. The Homaru Palace had also once occupied the centre of this area, where visiting Shoguns had stayed but it had been destroyed in the wartime bombing and not yet restored. There were two golden dolphins, 3 metres (10 feet) long, one at each end of the main ridge of the donjon. They were replicas of the originals which had been destroyed in the bombing raids. Inside the Donjon, a small museum housed treasures which had belonged to the Tokugawa clan and documented their family history. There was also armour and weaponry and beautiful paintings of a bamboo grove, a leopard and a tiger on sliding door panels which had been salvaged from the bombed out Homaru Palace. At the Fumei-mon Gate in the north wall, 30 centimetres long spearheads protruded from the beam below the eaves to foil efforts to scale the wall. Just outside the gate, the guide pointed out inscriptions on stones in the wall identifying which feudal lord had been responsible for placing them – the castle had been built using "free" labour required to be provided by the aristocracy. The eastern end of the complex was occupied by the Ninomaru Garden complete with a tea house where the traditional Japanese tea ceremony was carried out. I went to the toilet, half expecting Mrs. Moshi Moshi to come with me in case I splashed my boots. I could picture her standing there beside the urinal saying: "Really, that must be the biggest one in all of Japan" while thinking "really, I have seen bigger things in a tadpole pond." We took a local train to Toba, on the Ise Peninsula, where we stayed at the Toba Hotel International, once patronised by Queen Elizabeth and Prince Phillip, whose mug shots were proudly on display. I was surprised that Prince Phillip's one hadn't been removed after his foot in mouth gaffe on a subsequent visit to China where he'd remarked to a British student, over there to study Chinese: "Don't stay here too long or you'll go all slitty-eyed." The Ise Peninsula was home to the famous Ama female pearl divers. We visited their huts at Osatu and sampled some of the seafood that they now dived for instead of pearls. One of the women was seventy-seven years old and still diving. While we were enjoying a traditional seafood snack in their primitive hut, a cell phone suddenly went off and one of the women dragged it out from the folds of her traditional costume to answer it, looking embarrassed. It rather spoiled the impression of rustic timelessness they were trying to create. We later saw young divers demonstrating their diving techniques in a display laid on for tourists in the little harbour at the Mikimoto Pearl Island in Toba. The Japanese had perfected the technique of growing cultured pearls here by inserting pieces of grit into live oysters around which pearls would grow artificially. This had killed the pearl-diving business not just here but elsewhere in the world such as the Persian Gulf, where it had previously been a major industry in places like Dubai.

At the Ise-jingu Shrine, ("really, the holiest Shinto shrine in all of Japan" according to Mrs. Moshi Moshi) I was reprimanded in Japanese by a local woman for photographing a white-robed Shinto priest blessing a woman in a low-walled compound beside the main shrine. I gathered that it was taboo to photograph the priests, although perhaps she was just having a bad day. I was a bit puzzled about Japanese religion. Shinto was the traditional faith but it seemed to be mixed with Buddhism in most of the temples. Shinto was basically a form of animism or shamanism, all natural objects such as trees and rocks as well as animals were believed to have spirits which need to be appeased. It seemed to be blended into everyday life in a fairly low-key way rather than the subject of public, communal worship or ritual. In the inevitable little commercial centre associated with the shrine, Okage Yoko-cho, a number of traditional wooden buildings had been assembled in order to conserve them. While we were wandering through them, we came across a street drumming performance, the group hammering hell out of an array of large drums with heavy drum sticks, before a large, appreciative audience. We also had a look around a Kibuki Theatre, another of these exclusively Japanese preoccupations which remain largely a mystery to outsiders. Back in Nagoya, we said goodbye to Mrs. Moshi Moshi. Really, it was like losing a mother.

Arriving in Kyoto by train, we visited the Kinkaku-ji temple (the Golden Pavilion), all three storeys covered in gold leaf and topped by a bronze phoenix. Sited at the edge of a lake in the midst of a maple forest, it had started life as the retirement villa of a Shogun but had been converted to a Zen Buddhist temple on his death in 1408 AD. A deranged priest had burned it down in 1950 but it had been painstakingly re-built by 1955 and last re-gilded in 1987. Each of its three storeys was in a different architectural style: the ground floor in the palace style; the second level in the style of a samurai house; and the top floor in Zen-temple style. Kyoto had been the capital of Japan until 1868, when Tokyo took its place, although Tokyo (then known as Edo) had become the centre of government in 1600 AD when the shogun Tokugawa Ieyasu made his headquarters there. Kyoto was spared the saturation bombing that Tokyo was subjected to during World War II and so its historic buildings had survived. At Ryoan-ji, the Temple of the Peaceful Dragon, we were invited to contemplate the Zen meditation garden laid out in 1479 AD. An oblong area of pale, raked, gravel enclosed by a low wall had fifteen rocks placed apparently at random on the surface, each fringed with green moss. The guide said that the longer we looked at it the more we would see. He suggested that we should try thinking about the sound of one hand crapping. I muttered: "Really, this is the most ridiculous idea in the whole of Japan" until I realized that he'd said "clapping". His diction wasn't as good as Mrs. Moshi Moshi. I saw very little but I found myself having some very profound thoughts:-

When Yoko Ono sings, it is time for seppuku (ritual disembowelment);

How many sushi portions can you make from a whale killed for scientific research purposes?

Salary man with hole in pocket feels cocky all day.

I was raised from my Zen reverie by the guide summoning us on to see Niko Castle which had been built in 1603 as the Kyoto residence of the Shogun Tokogawa Ieyasu. It was surrounded by a dry stone wall and moat but didn't have the tiered towers and fortifications we had seen at its Nagoya counterpart. I later learned that an Inner Palace with a five storey donjon (tower) had been built in 1626 but had burned down in 1750 and not been replaced. The main interest was the interiors of the Ninomaru Palace, a complex of five single storey rooms, arranged in a staggered pattern as if laying down dominoes and interconnected by covered wooden walkways. The walls and sliding panels were covered in exquisite paintings: Chinese style landscapes; tigers, leopards and panthers crouching in bamboo groves; wild geese and herons in a winter landscape; swallows; peacocks; and pine and cherry trees. In one room, mannequins representing feudal lords were kneeling before the Shogun, who was seated on a dais, to illustrate how audiences were held. Those Shoguns were powerful men. The wooden floors were designed as "nightingale" floors – to chirp like a bird when trodden on – intended to provide an early warning system for intruders. It probably also served as a deterrent to any errant courtier sneaking round to get his leg over one of the Shogun's concubines.

We continued on to see the old royal palace, occupied by the emperors until after 1868 when the Court moved to Tokyo. The original had been built in 794 AD but the complex had been destroyed by fires numerous times and rebuilt, the present building dating from 1855. The Palace itself was off limits without a special visitor pass but from what I could see of it through some open gateways, didn't look particularly interesting – all lurid red lacquer pillars and walls like a brothel. The garden, however, was beautiful with plenty of trees and ponds. The guide told us that there were spectacular displays of cherry and plum tree blossoms in spring.

In the afternoon we went by bus to Nara, founded in 710 AD and capital of Japan for 74 years. It developed as a centre of Buddhism and was Japan's terminus of the Silk Road trade route. We passed through Nara Park, accosted by tame deer, demanding to be fed, and arrived at the Todai-ji Temple, the largest wooden building in the world. The temple was completed in 752 AD to house the 16m (53 feet) high Great Buddha, who sat flanked by two golden bodhisattva (enlightened beings), the grotesque heavenly guardians Koumokuten and Tamonten watching his back. Todai-ji was a striking building with golden horns on its roof line and curved lintels. Across Nara Park and through a wood was the Kasuga Grand Shrine, a Shinto shrine whose approaches were lined with 3,000 stone and bronze lanterns donated by the public. A striking dead tree soared above the shrine.

We had the following day free to explore Kyoto so I made my way towards Kiyomizudera. The approach to the temple was through a preservation district along the Sannenzaka and Ninenzaka (Stone Paved Roads), lined with shops in old wooden buildings. I entered the temple through the Nio-Mou Gate (Gate of the Diva Kings) flanked by two ferocious looking guardians, four metres tall. The temple was built in 778 AD on the site of a sacred spring (the name meant Clear Water Temple) on the side of Mount Otawa (Sound of Feathers Mountain) part of the Higashiyama Mountains which hemmed Kyoto in to the west. It was dedicated to Kannon Bosatsu, the Buddhist Goddess of Mercy, an eleven-faced, thousand-armed and thousand-eyed image of whom was housed in the Hondo (Main Hall). Outside the hall, a large platform over-looked Kyoto, jutting out 10 metres over the edge of the cliff falling 12 metres to the wooded valley below. A little Shinto shrine devoted to "love and good matches" stood in the grounds. On the stairway up to it, a statue of a god was flanked by a large stone rabbit standing on its hind legs. I presumed that rabbits had the same reputation in Japanese culture as they did in the West. It looked as if it should have had an erection to complete the effect. Perhaps I had already seen too many temples in Japan and become blasé but Kiyomizudera did not strike me as particularly wonderful.

In the afternoon I took a taxi up to the Ginkaku-ji temple (the Silver Pavilion). It was similar in style to the Golden Pavilion only in this case it never got its coating of silver as war intervened and the wealthy Shogun sponsor died before it was completed. It was set in a beautiful garden of ponds and pine trees. From there I took the Philosopher's Walk back into town. To fortify myself for the walk on a hot afternoon, I managed eventually to liberate a soft drink (I had no idea what it was as the labelling was all in Japanese) from one of the ubiquitous vending machines standing at the entrance to the walk-way. These machines were all over Japan like a rash, often in the most unexpected places. You half expected to open a toilet door and find one standing next to the urinal. Whatever the soft drink I'd selected was, I would have preferred the contents of a urinal any day. The Philosopher's Walk was a peaceful path along the Shishigatani Canal, lined with cherry and maple trees. It had been named for a Kyoto University Philosophy Professor who had used it for his daily exercise. There were restaurants, cafes, craft shops and boutiques along the way and several temples accessed from it. After completing the walk, I wandered through the Gion entertainment district with tea houses, small inns and geisha houses. In the late afternoon it was deserted. In the evening I went into a bar in Pontocho Alley, a street of pubs and restaurants flanking the Kamo River. As I was taking a seat at the bar, the barman came scurrying round in a panic muttering "shoes, shoes" and escorted me back to the door to take my shoes off. He was clearly uncomfortable about my presence although the tiny bar was empty, probably worried that a gaijin (foreigner) would deter his local customers. I had a quick Sapporo beer and left. Japanese racialism was getting on my nerves. My mood was improved when I found a genuine French restaurant called Le Bouchon where I had a confit of duck as good as you'd find anywhere in France. I was becoming a bit tired of Japanese food by this time which I found as bland as the scenery and architecture.

We caught the shinkansen train again to Nagoya and transferred to a limited-express train for Takayama, an ancient city in the Japanese Alps. The Japanese Alps did not measure up to my expectations, none of the soaring snow-capped peaks of the European or indeed the New Zealand Alps, just rolling mountains forested to the summits, nothing in the way of spectacular mountain scenery. I was disappointed gener-ally with the Japanese landscape. I saw nowhere that remains imprinted on my memory and I even have difficulty envisaging Japanese rural scenes. The countryside was as bland as the urban areas.

In Takayama we visited the Yatai Kalkan Hall where traditional colourfully decorated festival floats were displayed. Festivals known as

Matsuri were held twice a year to coincide with the planting season and harvest time. They involved Lion Dances to drive away wild animals and evil spirits. We later passed the ornate Lion Dance Ceremony Exhibition Hall. Takayama's remote location away from Japan's frenetic east coast had enabled older buildings to survive. We walked along Sannomachi Street, lined with old wooden buildings, several sake (rice wine) breweries and shops identified by the large cedar balls hanging from the eves outside. We went into one to see what was on offer. The proprietor poured us little shots of the three grades: nikyu (2nd grade); ikkyu (1st grade); and tokkyu (special). I was tempted to ask if the third rate, bootleg, practically undrinkable, rot-gut stuff was called fukyu but resisted the temptation. A bridge across the Miyagawa River nearby had two grotesque sculptures on the rails looking along the river. Two small markets had some fruit and vegetable stalls but there was none of the exotic bustle of street markets in China or elsewhere in South -East Asia: it was more like something you'd see in Tunbridge Wells on a Saturday morning. We stayed in the Hida Hotel, a nondescript concrete pile down by the railway station. I had a look at a menu in the Shabu-Tei Bar in the hotel which featured "Fish guts preserved with salt and Japanese ginger" and "Bowels of a cod preserved with salt". This reminded me of an article about an incident in Japan that I'd seen in a newspaper before I left for my tour headed "Blowfish Testicles Poison Seven". Apart from anything else, that blowfish must have been amazingly well-hung to be able to feed seven people. I wasn't tempted to have a snack with my Kirin beer. I walked along to the traditional Suzuya Restaurant, just off Kokubunji Street, advertised as specialising in "mountain vegetable and Hida beef". According to the English translation in their brochure, I had "Sansai Teishoku" (wild plants table d'hote with much mountain and fluvial products) "Houbamiso" (pastoral miso soup) "Susuginabe" and "Misotakinabe" (selected vegetables and meat served in the hot pot.) I wasn't impressed. It was lacking in flavour like most of the Japanese food I'd sampled. You needed to add the savagely hot, green "wasabi" (made from a root related to the horseradish and mustard family) or soy sauce to put some bite into it. It seemed to me that there was more emphasis on what the food looked like than what it tasted like – high marks for artistic presentation; "nul points" for tastiness. I'd had the hot pot style of meal before on the tour for lunch. It was a bit of a magical mystery tour unveiling the individual dishes which were piled on top of each other, one forming the lid to the one below. I'd visited the sushi restaurant in the Shiba Park Hotel in Tokyo where I'd stayed. I was quite fond of sushi, the little circles of vinegared rice wrapped in skins of kelp (seaweed) and topped with raw tuna, salmon, avocado or a variety of other toppings but it needed wasabi and soy sauce to impart some flavour and I never felt as if I'd had a full meal afterwards. I quite liked the pure raw fish "sashimi" but it was nowhere near as good as the Polynesian "poisson cru" (raw fish) which was flavoured with lime juice, onions, hot red chillies and coconut milk. I didn't think the various noodle dishes were on par with their Chinese counterparts: the thin, brownish, soba noodles were made from buckwheat, served with wasabi, spring onions, "mirin" (a sweet sake dip) and shaved flakes of dried bonito; the thick, off-white, udon noodles and the vermicelli-thin somen were made from wheat. The tastiest of the lot were of Chinese origin, ramen noodles, served with soy broth, bamboo, spring onions and roast pork. "Tempura" - fish, shellfish or vegetables, dipped in batter and deep fried was also tasty but again was a Chinese import. I never developed a taste for the ubiquitous "tofu" (bean curd) or "miso" soup.

We set out by bus for Kanazawa on the Sea of Japan to the west. On the way we visited the village of Ogimachi in the Shirakawa-go district. Nestled in a narrow, green valley, this village of thatched Gasso-zukuri houses was a UNESCO World Heritage Site and was the most picturesque landscape that I saw in Japan. The steep-roofed houses – the name meant "praying hands' – were designed to shed the heavy snow which blanketed the area from December to March. Traditionally, silk worms were raised in the upper floors. Small rice paddies surrounded the houses and I passed a field of red chilli peppers climbing bamboo stakes.

In Kanazawa we visited the Kenroku-en Garden, one of the most famous formal gardens in Japan. The Japanese were obsessed with formal gardens which seemed to resonate with their love of order and uniformity. Every bush and tree was immaculately trimmed, every rock looking as if someone had polished it. The nearby Kanazawa Castle was another one off the Japanese Castle production line. It bore a striking resemblance to the one we'd seen in Nagoya, as if the architect had stolen the plans. By this time, I had come to realize that all Japanese castles looked alike – if you'd seen one, you'd seen them all. They seemed to reflect the Japanese love affair with imitation and conformity. The tour I had originally booked had included a visit to Himeji-jo castle, reputed to be the best of them all and UNESCO listed as a World Heritage Site. I was relieved now that we weren't going there. One more castle off the Nippon production line and I think I would have puked. We walked through the Higashi Pleasure District, once the liveliest red-light area outside Tokyo and Kyoto but now a quiet area of craft galleries and restaurants with old fashioned street lamps and wooden lattice windows, all a bit twee and sterile. We visited the former Shima Geisha House, furnished and decorated as it was in the 19th century but lacking any of the Mango-comic sub-genre "hentai" (pervert) style illustrations of the former goings-on there which would have made it interesting.

Back in Kyoto, I had one more night there. By this time I had had my fill of Japanese food and took a taxi to the French restaurant that I had found on my earlier stay. The following morning I was picked up for a car transfer to Osaka Itami Airport for a flight to Tokyo to connect with my New Zealand flight. I wasn't over-impressed with Japan. It was the most impenetrable society that I had found anywhere in the world, the language barrier re-enforced by the absence of any effort to reduce it for foreigners. Many aspects of the culture remained obscure to me from the Shinto religion to Kibuki theatre; and some of their obsessions unfathomable – Mango comics, Sumo wrestling and eating poisonous fish. I didn't think that the Kiyomizudera temple warranted its short-listing among the New 21 Wonders of the World either. Japan just didn't do "Wonders". Blandness, imitation and uniformity were more its style.

Like the rest of humanity, I was horrified to watch TV pictures of the tsunami which hit north-east Honshu on March 11, 2011 following a massive earthquake, force 9 on the Richter scale, centred just offshore. There was nothing much anybody could do about a force of nature on that scale. But it puzzled me that a nuclear reactor had been built in the firing line without adequate safeguards built into it. You would have thought that a country twice bitten by atomic disasters wouldn't have relied on a "thild time rucky" philosophy. They had effectively nuked themselves in the foot. My mind went back to Mrs. Moshi Moshi and her obsession with health and safety and I imagined her shaking her head and muttering: "Really, this is the biggest cock-up in all of Japan."

12

HAGHIA SOPHIA, ISTANBUL, TURKEY MAY 2010

AND THEN THERE were two. By May 2010, the only New Wonders of the World on the short-list I still had to see were the Haghia Sophia Cathedral in Istanbul, Turkey and Timbuktu. On my way back to Shetland from New Zealand, I stopped off in Istanbul. I was getting lazy in my old age: I hadn't bothered to learn any Turkish. They had gone over to using Latin script rather than Arabic in the 1920s after deposing the Sultan and Mustafa Kemal Ataturk had set about modernising the country, so at least I could read the signs even if I didn't know what they meant. I had figured that with the number of Turks who had worked in Germany, I would get by with German and English, coupled with a Turkish phrase book. I had bothered to learn how to pronounce Turkish words – "c" and "i" in particular held idiosyncratic pitfalls for the unwary.

I had booked into the Orient Express Hotel, down near Sirkeci Station (pronounced "Sirkejy"), the terminus of the train made famous by Agatha Christie in her novel "Murder on the Orient Express". This small boutique style hotel turned out to be one of the best I had ever stayed in. The rooftop Imbat Restaurant and Bar and its outdoor terrace looked out over the Bosphorus and up to Topkapi Palace on the hill above (the "i" had no dot above it and was pronounced "uh"; "i" with a dot sounded like a "y"). The tram line serving the central city ran right past the door. The main tourist attractions, Topkapi Palace, the Haghia Sophia, the Blue Mosque, the Grand Bazaar, the Spice Market and the Galata Bridge were all within easy walking distance. The weather was still surprisingly cool for May, which made walking a pleasure.

Istanbul was one of the great cities of the world. Its location on the border of Europe and Asia gave it a unique, exotic character, the Sea of Marmara and the Bosphorus dividing the two continents. To the north of the city, the Bosphorus led to the Black Sea, Russia's front door. To the south, the narrow channel of the Dardenelles led to the Aegean Sea and the Mediterranean. The European part of the city was separated by the drowned valley of a little river known as the Golden Horn, crossed by the Galata Bridge; the older part, where I was staying, lying to the east. As Constantinople, Istanbul had been the capital of the Eastern Roman (Byzantine) Empire from 395 AD when the Roman Empire was split until 1453 when it fell to the Ottoman Turks. It had originally been founded by Emperor Constantine in 330 AD. There was so much history packed within its ancient walls that it was difficult to know where to start.

I started with the Haghia Sophia (Holy Wisdom) built as a church but now a museum, the prime objective of my trip. The original church on the site had been built in the 4th century AD shortly after Christianity was made the official religion of the Roman Empire. It was destroyed in an earthquake so the existing building, which was inaugurated by Emperor Justinian, dated from 537 AD. It was the largest cathedral in the world for nearly a thousand years until Seville Cathedral in Spain was completed in 1520. Seen from the outside the building was impressive, although the various buttresses added later to strengthen it against earthquakes reduced the visual impact. But once inside the sheer scale of the construction was awesome, the dome soaring 56m (184 feet) above the vast space of the main hall (the nave) belying the rather squat external appearance. Light poured in from the stained glass windows high in the walls. The interior was decorated with brightly coloured Byzantine mosaics, including one at the end of the south gallery depicting Christ flanked by Emperor Constantine IX and his wife, Empress Zoe. In 1054 AD, the Great Schism had split the church into two branches, the Eastern Orthodox and Western Catholic. One of the bones of contention had been whether leavened or unleavened bread should be used in the Eucharist sacrament to represent the body of Christ. The mind boggles. The Orthodox Church later split into Greek and Russian Orthodox branches, perhaps over whether ouzo or vodka should be used in the Eucharist to represent the blood of Christ. After Constantinople was captured by the Turks, the Haghia Sophia was converted to a mosque and the four minarets added. Arabic calligraphy on roundels, the Mihrab (a niche showing the direction of Mecca) and the Minbar (a pulpit for the Moslem preachers) also remained from this period. In 1934 it had become a museum.

Next door to the Haghia Sophia, across the Sultanahmet Square, a beautifully landscaped garden with a fountain playing, stood the Blue Mosque, commissioned by Sultan Ahmed I and built between 1609 and 1616 AD. Externally it was even more beautiful than the Haghia Sophia, with its six soaring minarets. The inside was decorated with dazzling blue Iznik tiles, from which it got its name. Intricate designs with arabesques (flowing, intermingling lines of decoration representing foliage) were painted onto the interior of the domes. The Moslem religion had first come to Turkey in 637 AD with invasions into the south-east of the country by Arabs from the Arabian Peninsula, spreading the new religion at the point of the scimitar (sword). It gradually spread towards Constantinople as the Byzantine government lost territory to Moslem converts. Mustafa Kemal Ataturk had secularized the country in the 1920s, a civil code replacing the former religious laws. Iconic oriental symbols like the red flower-pot-like "Fez" hat and the turban had been banned in a campaign of "westernization". However, the Moslem religion had made a come-back and the religious AK Party were now in power and while by no means fundamentalist, were one of the stumbling blocks in Turkey's path to European Union membership.

The following day, I walked up to the Topkapi Palace, home of the Sultans until 1853, when the Dolmabahce (pronounced "Dolmabahjay") Palace on the Bosphorus was built. It has been a museum since 1924. Rather than a single building, Topkapi was conceived as a series of pavilions set in four large courtyards, to reflect the tented encampments of the originally nomadic Ottoman Turks. The entrance was through the imposing Gate of Salutations, flanked by twin towers. I took a guided tour through the harem, a labyrinth of rooms where the Sultans' wives and concubines had lived in a hotbed of palace intrigue, plotting to jockey their sons into line for succession to the throne. In the third courtyard I visited the throne room, an exhibition of ornate imperial costumes and the treasury, where an array of precious objects were on display including the emerald studded dagger which Peter Ustinov stole in the 1964 film 'Topkapi' and the 86 carat Spoonmaker's diamond. The marble library of Sultan Ahmet III was perhaps the most striking building in the whole complex. In the fourth courtyard, a balcony between the Circumcision and Baghdad Pavilions looked out over the Golden Horn. The excellent Konyali Restaurant occupied the other side of the courtyard. The Turks were nomadic horsemen and soldiers from Central Asia who had been recruited as mercenaries by the Arab Caliph in Baghdad. In the early 11th century, one of their tribes, the Seljuks, had set up a state in Persia (Iran). In 1071 they expanded into Turkey after defeating a Byzantine army. Another Turkish group, the Turcomans, fought as mercenaries for the Byzantines. After the initial fighting was over, they remained and settled in parts of Anatolia to found mini-states under Seljuk suzerainty. It was from one of these groups that the Ottomans came. A Turcoman warlord rescued a Seljuk Commander from an invading Mongol army detachment and was rewarded with a fiefdom in Western Anatolia. This was the base from which the Ottoman Turks spread to establish their empire, initially under a leader called Osman. They took advantage of the weakness of the Seljuk Empire and the chaos in Anatolia, following an invasion by the Mongols in the 1220s. The remains of the Byzantine Empire was also weak after sackings by successive Crusader armies and the struggle against the Seljuks. The Ottomans hadn't originally been Moslem but following conversion to the Sunni sect, they became fanatical proselytisers. They defeated much larger Byzantine armies twice and took control of most of Anatolia from the Seljuks. In 1337 they crossed the Dardanelles to Europe and conquered Thrace. In the second half of the 14th century, Sultan Murat I expanded the empire further into Europe, getting as far as Kosovo before he was murdered during a battle. Murat's son, Beyazit, conquered the Serbs and in 1396, in what is now Bulgaria, heavily defeated an army of 100,000 raised in Western Europe in the last Crusade. Sultan Murat II overran Greece in 1422 and in 1448, at the second Battle of Kosovo, beat a combined army of Hungarians and Wallachians (now part of Romania) under the Hungarian King Hunyadi and Vlad the Impaler (who was the original Dracula) and gained control of these territories. In 1479 they finally subdued Albania. They also expanded their empire into the Levant, Mesopotamia, Persia, the Arabian Peninsula and North Africa, becoming the most powerful military and political force in the world at the time. The magnificence of Topkapi Palace reflected that status.

Across the street from the Blue Mosque, the Hippodrome had been a stadium holding 100,000 people where chariot races were held. It was now a pleasant park lined with obelisks and columns including the Egyptian Obelisk, dating from 1500 BC and brought here from Luxor by Emperor Constantine; and the Serpentine Column, dating from 479 BC and brought here from Delphi in Greece. I walked up Yenicelirer Caddesi   (Street; pronounced "Jaddesy") to the Grand Bazaar. It was a warren of streets and arcades covered by painted vaults and lined with reputedly 3,600 shops selling everything imaginable – I saw carpets from all over Central Asia, brass coffee pots, Ali Baba style slippers and Fez hats (no longer illegal but strictly for tourists). There were little cafes with customers smoking nargile (hookah) pipes where the aromatic tobacco smoke was filtered and cooled through water. I bought a little blue and white good-luck charm pendant with the evil eye symbol on it from a charmless one-eyed hag who was giving me the evil eye as I perused her souvenir stall. I got the distinct impression that if I didn't buy something from her, no good would come of it for me. I carried on past the University to the Suleymaniye Mosque, built between 1550 and 1557 for Sultan Sulyeman the Magnificent by the great architect Sinan, its towering minarets visible from all over the city. The Ottoman Empire had reached its peak under Suleyman, who ruled from 1520-66. He doubled the size of the Empire and his navy dominated the Mediterranean. On his watch, architecture reached its peak under Sinan. Suleyman was a patron of the arts, which flourished: painters produced miniatures of court life and military campaigns to rival those produced later under the Moguls in India; calligraphy became a high art form; beautiful glazed tiles and textiles, including carpets, were produced; woodwork and metalwork, including gold smithing, was of a very high standard; and literature and poetry blossomed. But there was also a barbaric side to the regime. The practice of fratricide, started by Beyazit, who had his younger brother Yakub strangled to prevent him becoming a rival for the throne, continued for 200 years. In 1595 Mehmet III had 19 siblings strangled when he became Emperor. The military might of the Ottomans depended heavily on the Janissary system: sons from Christian families within the empire were taken away at an early age, brought up as Moslems and trained as soldiers. Brainwashed into complete loyalty to the Sultans they were a bloodthirsty bunch to whom atrocities in battle were second nature. After Suleyman, the Empire began a steady decline. Their siege of Vienna in 1683 failed and that was as far as they penetrated into Europe. In 1571 a combined navy from Spain, the Papal States, Genoa and Venice heavily defeated their navy at the Battle of Lepanto and ended their domination of the Mediterranean. Events in the wider world also hastened their decline. The voyages of Columbus to the Americas in 1492 and Vasco da Gama to India in 1497 eventually broke the Ottoman monopoly on the trading routes to China via the Silk Road and India through Red Sea ports. Gold and silver flooding into Spain and Portugal from the Americas debased the Ottoman currency. They also contributed to their own decline on the intellectual front. From the 8th to the 11th centuries, Moslem scholars had dominated the fields of mathematics, medicine, astronomy, literature and the arts

generally. The later growth of fundamentalist Islamic beliefs and practices inhibited further intellectual growth: for example, Islamic clergy
banned the use of printing presses until 1727, nearly 200 years after
they had been introduced into Europe. The opposite was happening in Europe where religious dogma and repression had strangled
intellectual development throughout the Dark Ages. The movement
west of scholars fleeing from the doomed Constantinople brought the
intellectual legacy of ancient Greece and Rome back, initially to Italy,
and fuelled the Renaissance from the late 14th century.

I headed down towards the Golden Horn below. This area of the
city was badly run-down with crumbling streets and houses in a poor
state of repair. The historic areas of Istanbul had been added to the
UNESCO list of World Heritage Sites in 1985. It looked as if progress
with restoration was slow, at least in this area. Back down near Galata
Bridge, the square in front of the New Mosque was busy with stall-
holders selling "simit" bread rings and corn on the cob. I bought a
"balik emek" (fish sandwich) for 4 Turkish Lira (about 1.50 pounds
sterling) from a gaudily painted boat moored at the quay. Underneath
the bridge was a little fish market and the bridge was lined with men
armed with fishing rods but not catching much as far as I could see.
The nearby Spice Bazaar was on a more manageable scale than the
Grand Bazaar but still displayed a vast array of goods as well as the
oriental spices which lent it its name.

The scene on the Beyoglu side of the bridge was dominated by the
round 60m (196 feet) high Galata Tower, with its conical top, dating
from the 6th century, when it was used to monitor shipping. I took the
Tunel funicular up to Tunel Square where I caught the quaint old fashioned tram along Istiklal Caddesi to Taksim Square. I was looking for
the bus company offices just near the square to book my onward passage down the Adriatic coast. Nobody in the office spoke English but
I managed to book the first leg down to Kusadasi. I couldn't, however,
manage to get hold of a route map so I had effectively booked a magical mystery tour as there appeared to be a variety of possible routes.
In the evening, I ate in a meyhane (restaurant) in Nevizade Sokak,
a street lined with restaurants and heaving with people. A tempting

selection of mezes (starters) was brought round on a trolley and I eventually chose vine leaves stuffed with rice, herbs and pine nuts followed by a shish kebab with grilled peppers. Mezes were a distinctive feature of Turkish cuisine, often comprising "dolmalar" (stuffed things) – aubergines, peppers, tomatoes and grape leaves filled with rice, pine nuts, currants, herbs and spices: they also included fish and shellfish dishes, courgette frittata and I even came across more substantial starters like lambs liver and onions. Main courses tended to be dominated by grilled and spit roasted meats like the ubiquitous doner and sis (shish) kebabs although there were also excellent meat stews served in ceramic pots. Among the fish dishes, swordfish, skewered with peppers and tomatoes was delicious. Borek, filo pastries filled with meat or cheese were a meal in themselves. I steered clear of some of the more idiosyncratic concoctions such as "koc (fortunately pronounced "koch") yumurtasi" (lamb's testicles); raw lamb's brains; and spit roasted lamb offal wrapped in gut. The "baklava" dessert, which I had previously come across in Greece, layers of filo pastry with honey and pistachio nuts, was delicious but you needed to have an ambulance standing by to race you to the cardiac unit. Turkish tea ("cay", pronounced "chay") and coffee were very strong, the coffee consisting of fifty-fifty liquid and grounds. I really liked the "elma cay", apple tea. The Lonely Planet guide book described it as "wholly chemical" and claimed that "locals wouldn't be seen dead drinking the stuff." But don't believe everything you read in Lonely Planet: it was delicious and very refreshing on a hot day.

The next day I took a cruise up the Bosphorus, past Dolmabahce Palace where the Sultans lived after 1853, then under the Bosphorus bridge linking Europe to Asia. Just before Fatih Bridge, the majestic Rumeli Hisari (Fortress of Europe), stood on the shore, surrounded by trees and flowers. It was built by Sultan Mehmet the Conqueror opposite the Anadolu Hisari (Fortress of Asia) on the other side of the channel, to seal off Constantinople before his final assault on the city in 1453. Mehmet had become Emperor in 1451 and set about finally capturing Constantinople. By this time, all that was left of the once powerful Byzantine Empire which had stretched from North

Africa through the Levant to Italy and included southern Spain for a time, was the city of Constantinople itself; and the city's population had dwindled to 40,000, just a fraction of the 600,000 during Emperor Justinian's time in the 6th century and nearly a million at its peak. Mehmet installed heavy ordinance in the castles which effectively sealed off the approach to the city along the Bosphorus. A new fleet of ships completed the blockade. Finally, he had even heavier cannon built by a renegade Hungarian called Urban for use on the massive city walls. They were effective and the city was stormed, the last Byzantine Emperor dying in the fighting. Three days of raping and pillaging ensued. The last bastion of Christianity in the Balkans and South-East Europe had fallen. The aftermath of the Moslem Turkish occupation of the area was to continue into modern times, still producing ethnic cleansing in the former Yugoslavia into the 1990s. We stopped for lunch at Anadolu Kavagi on the Asian side where there was a good view out to the Black Sea from the ruined castle on the hill above the town.

I had booked a tour down to Gallipoli and Troy. We drove down the European side of the Sea of Marmara to the little museum at Kabatepe dealing with the history of the ill-fated Gallipoli campaign of World War I where the Allies tried to take Turkey out of the war, open up a supply line to Russia and attack the German/Austrian forces from the rear, through Bulgaria. We saw Anzac Beach where the Australian and New Zealand forces landed. Looking up at the steep receded old cliff line above the beach, rising to the towering peak known as the Sphinx, it was easy to envisage the carnage that took place as men tried to scramble up under heavy fire from the defenders. Up at the battlefields extending up to the Nek and Chunuk Bair, traces of the trenches still remained - the opposing sides amazingly close to each other. The casualty rates had been horrific: by the time of the withdrawal of the allied forces in January, 1916, they had lost 220,000 men, dead and wounded, a 59% casualty rate and the Turks 251,000, a 60% rate. The various graveyards were immaculately cared for including the New Zealand Cemetery and the Australian one at Lone Pine. The memorial at the New Zealand Cemetery included a statue of the Turkish commander Mustafa Kemal Ataturk. He went on to become president of Turkey after the war - when the Sultan was deposed - and to modernise the backward state. The text of a moving tribute by Ataturk was also on display on a plaque, reflecting the mutual respect between the opposing forces:-

Those heroes that shed their blood and lost their lives... you are now lying in the soil of a friendly country. Therefore rest in peace. There is no difference between the Johnnies and the Mehmets to us where they lie side by side here in this country of ours...You, the mothers, who sent their sons from far away countries, wipe away your tears; your sons are now lying in our bosom and are in peace. After having lost their lives on this land they have become our sons as well.
Ataturk, 1934.

Attending Gallipoli on ANZAC Day (April 25th, the anniversary of the combined Australian and New Zealand landings on Anzac beach in 1915) had now become something of a pilgrimage for young New Zealanders and Australians. We crossed the Dardanelles for an overnight stay in Canakkale where there was a replica of the little mine layer 'Nusrat' which went out the night before the British and French fleets tried to storm the Dardanelles at the start of the Gallipoli campaign and laid the mines which played havoc with the attack..

There wasn't much of Troy left to see, just a maze of stone foundations, in places overgrown with red poppies. Outside the site was a large replica of the famous wooden horse, a party of school children climbing into it. The site had originally been excavated by the German archaeologist Heinrich Schliemann in 1873 and various levels have been identified dating from 4000 BC to around 300 AD, including remains from around the 13th century BC when the siege during the Trojan Wars chronicled in Homer's Iliad took place. Greece and Turkey had a long history of enmity, extending into modern times. Back in Canakkale, at the Anzac House Hostel (the base for our tour company, the "Hassle Free Travel Agency") after we'd watched an excellent documentary film on the Gallipoli campaign, I got chatting to the tour guide. Over complimentary cups of "elma cay" (apple tea) he told me that Turkey maintained a standing army, navy and air force of 900,000, mainly to counteract the perceived threat from Greece, with Cyprus, divided between a Greek and a Turkish sector, a potential flash point. The ownership of some of the Aegean islands was also still in dispute. Helen's honour may have been avenged at Troy but over 3,000 years later, the Trojan War still wasn't really over.

My magical mystery bus tour to Kusadasi took me across the Bosphorus Bridge to the Asian side and on to Gebze where we caught a ferry for a 30 minute trip across an arm of the Sea of Marmara to Yalova and then through Bursa to Izmir. I was very impressed with the standard of bus services in Turkey. An attendant in white shirt and black bow tie served free tea, coffee, biscuits and cakes after each major stop and the bus was immaculately clean and comfortable. Izmir had been the scene of horrific events in September 1922 with thousands of Greeks slaughtered and burned alive in fires which swept the city. The Greeks had been settling on the Aegean coast of Turkey, which they called Ionia, for millennia, the foundation of some of their cities going back to around 1,000 BC. They had survived occupation by the Persians until Alexander the Great liberated them. While the Byzantine Empire started life as the eastern wing of the Roman Empire, the language and culture had soon become Greek. After the fall of Constantinople, Greek communities had remained in various parts of Turkey under the Ottoman Empire and had been allowed to retain their Orthodox Christian religion. However, in the aftermath of World War I things had gone pear shaped. In the 1920 Treaty of Sevres, Turkey had been dismembered, leaving it as a rump state centred on Ankara. The British military occupied Istanbul; the Bosphorus and Dardanelles were "internationalised"; France got a part of south-east Turkey adjacent to their mandated territories of Syria and the Lebanon; Italy took the Dodecanese Islands and the coastal area from Bodrum to Antalya; the Kurds and Armenians were given independent states in eastern Anatolia; and the Greeks were given territories on the eastern Black Sea coast, eastern Thrace and the port of Smyrna (now Izmir) and its hinterland. In May 1919 a Greek expeditionary army had landed at Izmir to consolidate their territory there but became greedy and started to move further east into Anatolia. This fuelled the Turkish War of Independence. In April 1920, Ataturk set up a National Assembly in Ankara, independent of the Sultan who was based in Istanbul under British control and readied the army to resist the Greek advance. In August 1921, the Greek advance was halted before they could capture Ankara. In the resulting stalemate the French and Italians withdrew from their Turkish territories. Then in August 1922 the Turks counter-attacked, decisively defeated the Greek army and pushed it back to Izmir, where it was evacuated in disarray. The triumphant Turkish army set fire to the Greek and Armenian sectors of Izmir and ran amok among the civilian population of these areas. The survivors were eventually evacuated mainly by British and American ships which had stood idly by in the early stages of the massacre. Following an armistice in October 1922, the 1923 Treaty of Lausanne established Turkey's present borders and provided for the transfer of populations between Greece and Turkey, internationally sanctioned ethnic cleansing. A million and a quarter Greek Orthodox Christians moved from Turkey to Greece and 450,000 Moslems of Turkish descent living in Greece moved in the opposite direction. Diplomatic relations between the two countries had never recovered from that.

We continued on to Kusadasi (pronounced KuSHAdasuh) where I was booked into the Club Caravansarei, an old 17th century inn formerly serving the camel train routes from Central Asia. It was surrounded by a high stone wall with battlements, neon lit now in the evening. The courtyard, where tables were set out from the restaurant, was used to display carpets for sale which added to the atmosphere. My room was up a wide flight of stone stairs from the courtyard and furnished with Ottoman antiques, the floor covered in Turkish carpets and kilims. I had dinner in the hotel restaurant which was excellent and then an early night: it had been a long day on the road and although I hadn't actually been on a camel, I had been travelling with the Kamil Koc (pronounced "coach") bus company so I felt at home in a caravanserai. In the morning, I had a look around Kusadasi. It was situated on a wide gulf, the mouth of which was partly closed off by the Greek island of Samos. The town was clearly geared to tourism but it was still quiet in May, although there was a large cruise ship moored down in the harbour. The bazaar area, just west of the hotel, was aimed at the tourist market with carpets, leather goods, hookah pipes, cheap jewellery and souvenirs. The old part of town, Kaleici, just behind the post office, was more interesting with narrow lanes lined with shops and some inviting looking restaurants, cafes and bars. There was a busy yacht marina down at the harbour with some fishing boats as well as pleasure craft. I walked west along the waterfront and out the long causeway to Pigeon Island where there was a 14th century Genoese fortress, now used for handicraft exhibitions. In the evening, I had a crawl through Barlar Sokak (Bar Street) which wouldn't have looked out of place in Dublin with the number of Irish bars, but it was remarkably quiet this early in the tourist season. I tried to liven myself up with a few "raki", the fiery local grape-based spirit with an aniseed flavour like the French Pernod, which turned cloudy white when you added water and ice. This area had a reputation for hedonistic night life in the tourist season but that night you could have brought your Irish great-granny.

The following morning I took a guided tour of Ephesus, about 20 kilometres (12 miles) north-east of Kusadasi. Allegedly originally founded by Greeks from Athens around 1,000 BC, it was reputed to be one of the best preserved Roman cities anywhere in the world, second only to Pompeii. Now 5 kilometres (3 miles) inland, following silting of the River Menderes (Meander) which had flowed into its harbour, Ephesus was once the chief port of the Adriatic: Emperor Augustus had made it his capital of Asia Minor, the residence of the Governor of the Province. At its peak it had had a population of a quarter of a million. St..Paul had arrived there in 51 AD, penned his Epistle to the Ephesians and been run out of town by acolytes of the Roman goddess Diana (equivalent to the Greek goddess Artemis) – Pagans 1 Christians 0. We entered by the Magnesian Gate through the Hellenistic period city wall, little of which now remained. A colonnaded street lined with Ionic and Corinthian columns led from the Baths of Varius, past the remains of the Odeon Theatre with its marble seats and the large square of the Upper Agora, which had been the administrative centre, to the Temple of Domitian. Hercules' Gate, with depictions of the hero of Troy carved into the posts, led into the paved Curetes Street which had been the Champs Elysees of its day, lined with shops. Four well-preserved Corinthian columns supported an arch with the bust of a goddess in its centre in the Temple of Hadrian. The stony face of Medusa with her fearsome dreadlocks appeared on a rear wall. A headless marble statue of Scholastica stood outside the baths called after her. Sculptures of gods and goddesses included one of Nike, now the goddess of footwear. Murals in the form of mosaics and frescoes in the houses opposite the Temple of Hadrian showed everyday scenes. By this time, I was coming to realize that my guide was a waste of time. She was young, fat and bone idle, carrying an umbrella to protect her from the sun even though it wasn't particularly sunny. She took every opportunity to sit down in the shade after she'd delivered her rote-learned spiel on the various buildings while I was exploring a bit more and taking photographs. My attempts to elicit further information not in the script had proved fruitless. She clearly belonged to the school of philosophers who shaped their lives around the principle of "always put off till tomorrow what you couldn't be bothered to do yesterday either". The piece de resistance of Ephesus was the remarkably well preserved two storey Library of Celsus, with elegant columns at ground and first floor level and statues of the four Virtues in niches in the façade. Just across from it was a brothel. Presumably the good citizens of Ephesus could spend a leisurely afternoon leafing through the pornography section in the library and then nip across the road for a bit of light relief. Afterwards they could adjourn to the nearby communal men's latrines where, seated on companionable side by side long drops, they could discuss the virtues of the ladies in the brothel. Marble Street led past the Lower Agora, once the food and textile market, to the well preserved theatre, carved into the flank of Mount Pion. It had been designed to seat an audience of 25,000. Opposite the theatre, Harbour Street ran down to the former harbour and rather poignantly now ended in a field, a tall column marking the former water's edge. On the way to the exit through the Lower Gate, we passed the Gymnasium of Vedius - which had included a swimming pool - and the stadium. We drove up a long winding road to a hill above Ephesus to visit the Meryemana (House of Mary) now a Pope-endorsed shrine to the Virgin Mary. St. John the Evangelist was alleged to have brought her here in 37AD, where she had lived until her death in 48 AD. Now, the Virgin Mary and Mary Magdalene had been seen after Jesus' death in more places than Elvis after his. But his Holiness the Pope had swallowed this one whole and who was I to suspect that it might be bogus? After all the location had been hit on in a dream by a German nun who had never been near the place and in fact had never left her convent, so how much more proof did you need? However, the chapel was at the end of a very pleasant walk from the car park along a wooded path beside a mountain stream so even if it was all bollocks it was a very picturesque spot. Needless to say, the tour guide didn't come with me, just pointed the way and retreated into the shade of the Café Turca to fill her ample face with something fattening.

I had booked in for the night in the Rebetika Hotel in the little town of Selcuk (pronounced "Seljuk"), just a few kilometres (couple of miles) from Ephesus. It looked out on all that remained of one of the original Seven Wonders of the World, the Temple of Artemis – a single column with a stork's nest on top of it. Some other broken columns lay scattered around and there was a drawing of the original temple on a display board. It was an object lesson on the transience of man-made wonders. An early version of the temple had been burned down by some loser who wanted his name to be remembered by posterity, like what's his name who shot John Lennon. When Alexander the Great got there in 334 BC work was already under way on the magnificent replacement. But neglect following Emperor Theodosius' edict making Christianity the state religion and his fatwa against pagan worship, coupled with earthquakes, had taken its toll over the years. Stone from it may even have been used in the 6th century Byzantine citadel on the adjacent Ayasoluk Hill. I walked back towards the hotel, past the oval-shaped roofs of a disused medieval "hamam" (bath house). Just round the corner from the hotel, the Isa Bey Camii (Mosque) had been built in 1375. Just up the road, the Basilica of St. John had been built in the 6th century by Emperor Justinian, allegedly on the site of the Apostle's grave. It had been carefully restored. I walked up the steep hill to the citadel, with its well-preserved towers, through its massive Byzantine gateway. The square in the town centre had gardens, pools and fountains with outdoor tables from the surrounding cafes and restaurants spilling out into it. The remains of an ancient Roman aqueduct ran along the edge of the bordering street with storks' nests on top of it. It was a very pleasant spot for a beer. Ephesus Museum, down by Selcuk's bus station, housed artefacts not just from Ephesus but also from the site of the the Temple of Artemis. The prize exhibit was a headless marble statue of Priapus, the Greek God of Fertility, which had been rescued from the brothel in Ephesus. He was balancing a tray of fruit on his enormous willy. There were also two marble statues of the multi-breasted Artemis, holding what appeared to be eggs – again presumably a fertility symbol. A bronze statue depicted Eros interfering with a dolphin. A room was devoted to a display illustrating the lives of gladiators – their weapons, training and gruesome injuries. In the evening I had dinner at an outdoor table across the road from the Amazon Restaurant, looking right out at the lone column of the Temple of Artemis with its guardian stork. That night in the Rebetika Hotel, I spent my most uncomfortable night ever. I had read a diatribe in the Trip Advisor web-site on the internet by a former customer, about the hardness of the mattresses and laughed it off. But it was true: it was like lying on a concrete floor and sleep was well-nigh impossible. In retrospect, the Akay Hotel, just across the road, looked as if it would have been a better choice.

Another lesson on the transience of man-made "wonders" awaited me down the coast in Bodrum when I went to see what remained of the Tomb of Mausolus, another of the original Seven Wonders of the World. Mausolus had been the "satrap" (ruler) of the Kingdom of Caria under Persian suzerainty and had died in 353 BC. Work had started on his mausoleum two years earlier and had continued under the direction of his wife who was also his sister. Built of white marble, it had stood 41 metres (134 feet) high, consisting of a colonnaded structure with 36 columns standing on a podium, with a stepped pyramidal roof surmounted by a horse-drawn chariot carrying Mausolus and his wife. Again there was nothing to see but rubble. A poster on the wall of the entrance kiosk showed all seven of the original wonders, none now remaining, other than in ruins, except the Pyramids. In a little museum on the site was a model of the tomb, which must have been a magnificent sight in its day. Apparently it was reasonably well preserved in spite of earthquake damage until 1552 when the Knights of St. John, successors of the Crusaders, came across from Rhodes and demolished it to build the Castle of St. Peter down by the harbour. I later visited the Castle which now housed the Museum of Underwater Archaeology with fascinating exhibits from shipwrecks in the Mediterranean. The castle dominated the waterfront and divided the harbour in two, the enclosed West Harbour on one side and open Kumbahce Bay to the east. Work had started on the massive structure in 1406 and it hadn't been completed until 1522 – the towering battlemented walls and five towers, one for each of the main nationalities represented by the Knights, explained why it had taken so long. The year after it was completed it was abandoned without a fight as Suleyman the Magnificent had defeated the Knights in nearby Rhodes and they withdrew to Malta. The entrance was via a stone ramp, a marble Crusader coat of arms on the wall on the landing. There was an ancient mulberry tree in the main courtyard and a display of amphorae, the large ceramic jars which had been used to store and transport olive oil, wine and grain – they had all been salvaged from shipwrecks. A peacock was wandering around. In the former chapel, there was a model of a Roman ship and a full-size reconstruction of its stern which you could clamber over. I climbed up to the next level. In the Glass Shipwreck Hall, the original timbers of a 1025 AD Byzantine ship were supported in a steel frame. The glass which it had been carrying was on display. The English Tower was fitted out as a refectory with a long central table, stags' horns, suits of armour and standards (flags) hanging on the walls. The Uluburun Wreck dated from the Bronze Age, the 14th century BC. There was a life-size replica of the ship and artefacts found in it were on display – gold jewellery, bronze daggers and ivory boxes. Below the Gatineau Tower, the dungeon had been a torture chamber. A sign above the door said: "Where God does not exist". The display inside featured mannequins having despicable things done to them to a soundtrack of groans and screams. I'm sure nasty old Jehovah was there after all, lapping it all up.

I stayed in the Su Otel, up on the hillside above the West Harbour, accessed through a maze of narrow lanes. Its whitewashed walls, with bright blue trim, was typical of the architectural style of the town. Bougainvillea and other flowering plants hung over trellises, providing a riot of colour in the courtyard around the central swimming pool. There was an excellent restaurant and friendly bar. It was another candidate for the best hotel I had ever stayed in. With the exception of the rock-hard bed in Seljuk, I was becoming impressed with the standard of accommodation in Turkey. In the evening, I strolled out along the waterfront. Bodrum was an up-market tourist centre, as the standard of the yachts in the West Harbour showed. It was an important centre for the "blue voyage" industry, cruises along the Aegean coast in motorised sailing craft called "gullet". On the seaward side of Dr. Alim Bey Caddesi, fronting Kumbahce Bay, some attractive restaurants stretched out over the beach, with stunning views across to the castle. At the far end was the massive Halikarnas disco club.

I moved on to Marmaris, another popular seaside resort, a down-market sister of Bodrum. I was booked into the Royal Maris Hotel on the esplanade, Ataturk Caddesi, which ran along the back of the beach in to the town centre. It had a rooftop terrace with a swimming pool and a section of private beach out in front. Marmaris lay on a near perfect natural harbour, ringed by pine-clad hills. I walked eastwards along the waterfront towards the centre and came to a crowd of people surrounding a temporary stage where a concert of folk music and dancing was under way in front of a large grim-looking statue of Mustafa Kemal Ataturk, who didn't look to be enjoying it. The seaward side of Kordon Caddesi was lined with "blue cruise gullets" for hire. The castle out on the headland had been re-built by Suleyman the Magnificent after 1522 and now housed a small nautical museum. The Old Quarter around it had been a Greek enclave, ethnically cleansed in 1924 and fallen into decay. But it had now been restored to become the most attractive part of the town with open-air restaurants, bars and cafes. Further on, the Netsel Marina was crammed with yachts. Inland, the bazaar (carsi) was full of tourist bric a brac. Haci Mustafa Sokagi was another "Bar Street" but like its counterpart in Kusadasi, very quiet – the tourist season didn't get under way until June.

From Marmaris, I took a choppy catamaran crossing over to the Greek island of Rhodes, the site of another of the original Seven Wonders – the 30 metres (100 feet) tall bronze statue of the sun god Helios, known as the Colossus of Rhodes. He was usually depicted standing straddling the old Mandraki Harbour entrance, now flanked by statues of two deer. However, up in the Palace of the Grand Masters, now a museum, I saw among the displays that he was believed to have stood on the hill above the town where the remains of a number of ancient temples were located and from where he would have been visible for miles out to sea. He lasted less than 100 years, being toppled by an earthquake in 227 BC. The town of Rhodes at the north tip of the island dated back to 400 BC. The old part of town was one of the best preserved examples of a medieval walled city, the walls extending for 4 kilometres (2 miles). Inside, the narrow, cobbled Street of the Knights was lined with the Inns where the Knights of St. John lived from 1309 AD after their Crusader forebears had been driven out of Jerusalem and then Cyprus. They were finally expelled by the Turkish Sultan Suleyman the Magnificent in 1522, moving to Malta. From their former headquarters, the Palace of the Grand Masters, I took a walk along the top of the old walls. The trip back to Marmaris was on a small ferry carrying perhaps a dozen passengers, two and a half hours in choppy seas with the spindrift flying, the sun shining and the mountains of Turkey looming up clear ahead against a blue sky through the spray off the bow. It was a magical trip.

I flew inland to Cappadocia on the Anatolian Plateau via Istanbul from Dalaman Airport, just south of Marmaris. We landed in Kayseri, the main town in the province, which in a previous incarnation as Caesarea, had been the Roman capital of the area. It was now a big, bustling industrial centre with a population of over a million. I was picked up from the airport by a driver from the tour company which

I had booked to show me the delights of Cappadocia over the next three days. Heading west towards my hotel, an hour's drive away in Uchisar, the 3,916 metres (12,848 feet) snow-capped peak of the volcano Mount Erciyes dominated the horizon to the south. This was one of the three volcanoes which had created the landscape I had come to see. The sight of snow drew my attention to the fact that it was cold after the Mediterranean coast. The Anatolian Plateau lay at over 1,000 metres (3,250 feet) above sea level. The name "Cappadocia" meant "Land of Beautiful Horses" in the old Persian language. The Romans had sourced brood mares from the area and the open, rolling, grassy plains did resemble the American "Wild West" in Wyoming. A bit further on was a reminder of the past, a restored caravanserai, one of the overnight stops for camel caravans travelling the silk route from China to its terminus in Constantinople. The driver pointed out Uchisar up ahead as we approached. It was like something straight out of Lord of the Rings, a towering honey coloured volcanic outcrop, riddled with holes like a gorgonzola cheese - the doors and windows of cave houses - and on the very top, a fairy-tale castle. At the foot of the road leading up the steep base of the outcrop, an enterprising local was offering camel rides. I was booked into the Museum Hotel, perched half-way up the pinnacle. A porter showed me to my room via a terrace with a small pool in front of the bar and restaurant. The view out across the Anatolian Plateau brought home how the world had changed. Strabo, the Greek geographer, who lived around the time of Christ, wrote that a monkey could travel across Anatolia from the Mediterranean to the Black Sea without ever having to get down from the trees. Now, it was bare, khaki coloured grassland, just a few straggly belts of trees along the water courses. The porter led me down a flight of stone steps and opened a door into the rock face. My room was a cave. I'd been called many things during my long career as a Town Planner but now I had become a troglodyte and crawled under a rock as I'd occasionally been invited to do by irate customers. But it was amazingly cosy and comfortable. There was a small window at one end with a low bench covered in colourful cushions below it, facing the TV. The bed was at a lower level, the floor covered in Turkish carpets and kilims (flat-woven rugs).

The walls were just smooth, natural volcanic tuff. I discovered later that the temperature in these caves stayed around 18C all year round which must have saved a fortune on heating and air-conditioning.

My tour guide arrived in the morning and introduced himself as Mustafa. He was in his mid twenties and fluent in English. He later told me that he had graduated from University, specializing in tourism related subjects. There was just me, him and the driver from the previous day in a land cruiser so this was going to be a personal tour. We drove down to Goreme, tourist central on the Cappadocia trail. Goreme was a picturesque little town with plenty of cafes, restaurants and small hotels – many with cave rooms like the Museum Hotel. About 2 kilometres from Goreme on the road to Urgup, we called into the Goreme Open-Air Museum. The landscape in Cappadocia was the weirdest I had seen anywhere in the world. Apparently it had been formed by three volcanoes erupting different types of material, sometimes blasting out deep layers of soft volcanic ash called tuff, at others, lava flows producing harder layers of basalt rock. The soft tuff had eroded over time through the action of water, wind and in winter, frost, into pinnacles, cones and peaks. Where layers of basalt lay above it, great pillars of tuff had been preserved with basalt boulders perched on them, like giant toadstools; harder layers of tuff above softer material produced spear-like pillars. The scenery in the Open-Air Museum was particularly spectacular, almost surreal – you could easily imagine that you were seeing troops of elves and gnomes emerging from the caves. Over the centuries, the local people had carved houses out of the soft tuff rock. In the early days of Christianity, when converts were being persecuted by the Romans, who ruled the area at the time, monasteries and churches were also carved out, where they could worship in secret - even more had been excavated after the invasion by Persians and Moslem Arabs after the 7th century. Mustafa said that there were hundreds of them. We went into St. Basil's Chapel, the colourful Byzantine style frescoed paintings of bible scenes still visible on the walls: St. Basil himself was there; a Maltese cross; St. George and St. Theodore slaying the dragon, a symbol of paganism according to Mustafa, who, in spite of being a Moslem (a non-practising one he told me), was well versed in all the Christian mumbo-jumbo. Apparently, St. George had been a Roman soldier, born in the Levant (modern Israel and Lebanon) with a Cappadocian father (he was now the patron saint of Cappadocia). He had been martyred by the Roman Emperor Diocletian in 303 AD for refusing to renounce his Christian faith. The English had stolen him and adopted him as their own during the Crusades. In the apse, Mary was holding the baby Jesus. We visited the Apple Church, overlooking a valley of poplar trees and with more frescoes and the Chapel of St. Barbara, which Mustafa said had been excavated during the "iconoclastic period" when the Old Testament horror at "graven images" had been re-activated by the clerics and the representation of people made more impressionistic. The Snake Church was a bit of a misnomer: the snake was really a dragon, being dispatched by St. George again in a fresco – it did look more like a snake, as if he'd let the wind out of a blow-up dragon with his sword. This Church was dedicated to St. Onuphrius. The legend, according to Mustafa, was that the Saint had started life as a virtuous young girl who in order not to lose her virginity to a suitor prayed to become a man. God had granted her wish and she grew a beard, going to live in the Egyptian desert for the rest of her life as a hermit, wearing a loin cloth of leaves and eating only dates. There was a picture of him/her holding a palm leaf over his/her genitals. I said to Mustapha "Anybody who would go on a date with a geriatric, bearded, smelly old hermaphrodite deserved to be eaten" but I think it went over his head. I had to pay extra to go into the Dark Church, but in spite of my scepticism about religion, it was worth it: the frescoes here were the best of the lot, including one of the betrayal of Christ by Judas.

We went on to see the villages of Zelve and Cavusin. This area had been badly damaged in an earthquake in 1950 which had led to the evacuation of Zelve's cave houses, many of which had originally been monastic retreats, spread through three valleys. The Fish and Grape Churches had been named after prominent frescoes in them. The old part of Cavusin had been abandoned after a rock fall in the 1960s, leaving a ghost-town like a honey-combed abandoned ant hill. We drove north to Avanos for lunch. This was a larger, more modern town on the Kizilirmak (Red) River, from which the red clay was extracted for the pots for which it was famous. We saw them on display as we drove in, brightly painted in turquoise and earthy brown and yellow colours. Over our sis kebabs, Mustafa said that we would be visiting a pottery after lunch and asked me if I would be interested in trying my hand at throwing a pot. I'd had a few glasses of the local red wine by this time and was becoming facetious so I said: "Oh, I don't think so. They looked quite nice and smashing any of them would be mindless vandalism." I think he just took this as a "No", wondering what sort of idiot he'd landed this time. He was more or less a chain smoker and I had come to think of him as Mustafa Fag. He also appeared to have a weak bladder judging by the number of trips he'd made to the toilets all morning. It occurred to me that he might be a split personality, also masquerading as Mustafa Pee. After the visit to the pottery, we drove down to Pasabagi, a valley half-way along the turn-off road to Zelve. This was the best area for the basalt capped pillars. You could describe them as fairy chimneys, toadstools or mushrooms if you liked but after a bellyful of red wine at lunch time there was only one image that came into my sick mind. There was no point in beating about the bush or being politically correct. What they most closely resembled were giant penises, rampant erections, great throbbing cocks with bulging basalt knobs, a forest of willies – a nun's nightmare. We continued on to the Devrent Valley where the rock had been eroded into all sorts of weird shapes. It was also known as the "Valley of Imagination" and you were supposed to let your mind run riot in interpreting the shapes: Mustafa pointed out a camel, a seal, a dolphin, kissing birds, Napoleon's hat and the Virgin Mary: I saw more big willies and a nun. We drove around Urgup, a less touristy version of Goreme, but with a lot of small boutique hotels, again using caves, and restaurants and cafes. There were vineyards nearby and it was known for its wines. On the drive back towards the hotel, we saw some sheep, goats and donkeys and occasional patches of cultivation but agriculture seemed to be on a very small scale. We stopped at a café on the road up to Uchisar, perched on the edge of the valley which ran down to Goreme, with spectacular views across the bizarre scenery.

The following morning, Mustafa was waiting for me at Reception, fag in mouth as usual. We drove off to visit the village of Ortahisar. Ortahisar was like a miniature Uchisar, its 40 metres (130 feet) high pinnacle riddled with cave houses and topped with a Byzantine castle, a slim minaret rising beside it from a mosque and small, flat-roofed houses covering the slope below. We had a look in Crazy Ali's antique shop and then visited the Culture Folk Museum on the main square, where interpretive panels and displays featuring mannequins in traditional dress illustrated local life, including making bread and kilims. The town of Mustafapasha had been a largely Greek settlement, subject to the ethnic cleansing of 1924 when the Orthodox Christians had been expelled to Greece. The impressive mansions of the richest merchants remained and the huge Orthodox Church of Saints Constantine and Helena in the town centre was an echo from a former era, its state of disrepair a reminder of how things had changed. We had lunch in the atmospheric Old Greek House Restaurant where the "kofte" (meatballs) were excellent and the red wine even better. Mustafa went to the toilet and was away so long that I thought he must have morphed from a split personality into a full-blown schizophrenic –adding Mustafa Shit to his multiple personalities. In the afternoon we visited the village of Guzeloz with its Byzantine period rock tombs and then continued south to the Soganli Valley where the steep valley side was riddled with dovecotes cut into the rock face, the entrances picked out in white rings to attract the birds, as Mustafa explained, after I'd asked if it was pigeon shit. Pigeons had been kept so that their droppings could be used as manure. The advent of chemical fertilisers had ended the pigeon fancying. South of here, we could see the Ala Daglari mountain range with the volcanic peak of Mount Demirkazik rising to 3,756 metres (12,207 feet) the second of the trio of volcanoes which had produced this unique landscape. Back in Avanos, we visited a carpet emporium where, plied with cups of "cay", I eventually bought a magic carpet (the price went down like magic when I made to leave). I had actually been meaning to buy one for the old family home back in the Shetland Islands which I had inherited when my mother and brother had died. In the evening, I went for dinner in Le

Mouton Rouge (The Red Sheep), a French style bistro just uphill from my hotel in Uchisar, where the coq au vin was first class. (The restaurant in the Museum Hotel was also excellent.) Uchisar was extremely picturesque as I strolled round it, passing an impressive statue of a black horse but the steep slopes were hell on the leg muscles.

I had booked a hot-air balloon flight for the following morning. The weather had been unseasonably cold and windy since I'd arrived and the balloons hadn't been flying but when I got up at 5.00 am it seemed promising and sure enough the driver from the operators Kapadokya Balloons arrived before dawn to drive me to the launch site. There were about half a dozen of us waiting to get into the basket while the balloon was filling with air and the propane gas burner was warming it. When it was straining to go, held down by heavy ropes, we climbed in and it was lift off, skimming over the poplar trees and soaring up to over a kilometre above the ground. The views of the jagged landscape below us were breathtaking, like flying over the Planet of the Apes; swooping lower, we could see people going about their early morning chores – beating carpets, loading up donkeys. We drifted over Uchisar and I had a bird's eye view of my hotel and the lanes I'd walked around the previous evening. We descended towards an open field where the support crew were ready to trap us like a butterfly, hanging onto the dropped ropes for dear life. We were treated to a champagne breakfast.

Back at the hotel, Mustafa picked me up again to visit the underground city of Derinkuyu. He said that 37 of these troglodyte metropolises had been re-opened and that there were believed to be at least another 100 in the area. It wasn't certain when they had first been excavated but there was some archaeological evidence that some of them could go back as far as the Bronze Age Hittite civilization which flourished from 1800 to 1200 BC. What was certain was that they had been dug as shelters from invaders and there had been plenty of them – Persians, Greeks, Romans, Arabs (and Persians again) Seljuk Turks, Mongols and finally Ottoman Turks - over the centuries. We ventured down into the claustrophobic maze of tunnels, passageways and chambers. As well as residential quarters there were food stores, stables, wine presses, kitchens, churches, wells and ventilation systems, every-thing to sustain a substantial number of people for long periods of time. Mustafa said it went down 60 metres (197 feet) with seven levels (Wikipedia says 85 metres (276 feet) and 11 levels, the lower ones not re-opened) and could accommodate 10,000 people (Wikipedia says 35,000 to 50,000 but the internet is a notoriously unreliable source of information.) Large wheel-shaped "millstones" were set back into recesses and could be rolled forward to block entrances against intrud-ers. The city had been connected to its counterpart at Kaymakli to the north via an 8 kilometres (5 miles) long tunnel, which presum-ably could have served as an emergency exit. We continued south for a 4 kilometres (2 miles) hike through the Ilhara Valley, along the little Melendiz River, snaking through the valley floor between steep cliffs with churches and old cave dwellings carved into the rock. The path ran through groves of shady trees and swung round picturesque piles of eroded boulders. It was very relaxing and peaceful after crawl-ing around in the bowels of the earth at Derinkuyu. We stopped at Belisirma for lunch at a restaurant beside or rather in the river (there were tables on little islands accessed by timber walkways) and I had some excellent grilled trout. I took a photograph of Mustafa with a donkey standing behind him. The resemblance was uncanny. After lunch, we drove down to Selime at the end of the valley to visit yet another rock-hewn church with impressive Byzantine frescoes. From here, the third of the volcanoes which had spewed out the raw mate-rial for the Cappadocia landscape dominated the horizon, capped with snow – the 3,268 metres (10,621 feet) high Hasan Dagi.

Turkey had been one of the most fascinating countries that I had visited. In areas that I hadn't seen were the remains of some of the oldest towns in the world such as Catalhoyuk and ancient civilisations such as the Hittites and Assyrians. Turkey had been an important part of the ancient Greek and Roman empires. It had been vital to the development of Christianity, St. Paul spending much of his time there. The fall of Constantinople to the Turks in 1453 contributed to the Renaissance in Europe and the voyages of discovery by the Portuguese and Spanish, trying to get around the monopoly by the Turks on the

Silk Road to the Far East and sea routes to India. Modern Turkey was trying to get into the European Union but on-going problems with the Kurdish minority and a pro-Islam party in government were working against that. However, most of the people I discussed these issues with seemed to be fairly secular in their views and there were few burkas to be seen in the streets. It occurred to me that the Haghia Sophia, starting off as a cathedral, becoming a mosque and now a neutral museum with exhibits from both faiths was perhaps an omen that Turkey could in time become an integral part of the European Union. But like Mustafa, it was clearly schizophrenic. It didn't know whether to point east or west or which cap to wear – the fez and turban or the baseball cap. And as regards relations with Greece, the ghost of Helen of Troy was still there, lurking in the shadows.

13

TIMBUKTU, MALI
NOVEMBER 2010

AND SO IN 2010 there were no more Wonders left except Timbuktu. It was a fitting final destination. Timbuktu had come to symbolise remoteness, the ends of the earth. During my time working for Shetland Islands Council, whenever I was setting off on holiday to some exotic location, my mother would say cynically "Where is it this time, Timbuktu?" It attracted seasoned travellers who wanted to be able to say "I've been everywhere, man!" The attraction of the town arose from its fabled wealth. With its strategic location on the edge of the Sahara Desert, gold, ivory and slaves were traded northwards and salt from the desert southwards for distribution along the River Niger. In 1336, Kankan Musa, king of the Mali Empire, had gone on a haj pilgrimage to Mecca and dished out so much gold along the way that he flooded the market and the price of gold plummeted in the Middle East and Europe. On his way back, he commissioned the Dyingerey Ber Mosque in Timbuktu which became a centre for Islamic scholarship and worship. The town's reputation for inaccessibility arose from the desire of its fervent Moslem inhabitants and the desert dwelling Tuareg tribesmen to protect this holy city from prying infidels. The first European to get there and come back alive was the Frenchman, Rene Caillie in

1828. Many others had perished in the attempt, including the Scottish explorers Mungo Park and Gordon Laing: Laing had got there but had been murdered by Moslem tribesmen shortly after he left.

The Australian firm Peregrine Adventures were offering tours through Mali and Burkina Faso, taking in Timbuktu, so I signed up. Climatically, November seemed to promise a period of slightly cooler weather between the end of the rainy season and the start of sand-storms blowing out from the Sahara Desert. My 65th birthday was also in November so it seemed appropriate for a travelling man to spend it on the road to Timbuktu. Mali wasn't the easiest of places to get to. My route took me from Auckland via Sydney to Johannesburg and then onwards to Dakar in Senegal for a connection with Air Burkina to the Malian capital, Bamako. The return from the tour end in Ouagadougou, the capital of Burkina Faso, went through Accra in Ghana back to Johannesburg. I arranged stopovers in Johannesburg and to spend some time in Senegal and Ghana.

I had been in South Africa before, a couple of years previously, when I went to visit my brother's grave in Malawi. I had spent some time in Cape Town, Durban and up in the Drakensberg Mountains en route to the mountain kingdom of Lesotho, but had only passed through Johannesburg Airport. In Johannesburg, I arranged a tour of Soweto with Jimmy's Face to Face Tours. Jimmy himself had been brought up in Soweto and so was the ideal man for the job. It wasn't nearly as grim as I had expected. I had seen far worse slums in Nairobi, Bombay and Rio de Janeiro. There was electricity, piped water and sewers and a perfectly adequate road network. There were patches of corrugated iron and cardboard shacks visible as we drove around but they appeared to be the exception. We saw Nelson Mandela's for-mer house, now a museum and nearby, Archbishop Tutu's residence. We also visited the memorial to Hector Pieterson, a student killed by security forces in the 1976 riots who became a symbol of the struggle against Apartheid. On a hillside above the township the brightly deco-rated twin Orlando Cooling Towers made an incongruous landscape feature. We went on to the Apartheid Museum, its tone set by the separate entrances for black and white visitors. The displays covered the development of the Apartheid policy and the struggle against it. A mock-up of a solitary confinement cell, strings of nooses to symbolise the political executions and a big, yellow Casspir armoured vehicle used to quell riots featured among the exhibits.

I flew on to Dakar in Senegal, arriving at 1.00 o'clock in the morning. Dakar was a notoriously dangerous place. The Lonely Planet guidebook said "Taxis wait outside the airport, behind throngs of touts, hustlers and thieves." I should have been warned. My hotel, the Savana, was supposed to have provided an airport pick-up but I saw no signs of anyone with a placard. As I was about to go and look for somewhere to make a telephone call to the hotel a well dressed young man in white shirt and tie came up to me and asked in perfect English which hotel I was heading for. When I told him, he said "Ah! The shuttle bus. Come with me." Like an idiot, I didn't ask to see any evidence that he was from the hotel. I was tired after the flight, relieved that my problem appeared to have been solved. I dropped my guard. He took me out to the parking area to a beat-up car with the driver already in it. There were a number of other taxis around, all equally decrepit, so I assumed that this was just the standard level of transport in Dakar. As we drove into town, the collar and tie man chatted away in good English. Then he said "Which flight did you come on?" Alarm bells rang. If he had been sent to collect me he would have known which flight I was on. Moments later, my suspicions were confirmed. The driver turned into a petrol service station and collar and tie said he would need some money for petrol. I acted surprised, said that I had pre-paid for the transfer and in any case hadn't found anywhere at the airport to change money. Collar and tie said that this wasn't the "normal" hotel shuttle and that I would have to pay for it. I said that we could sort that out when we got to the hotel. They drove on, conversing in their own language. Suddenly the driver turned into a dark side-street and stopped the car. Collar and tie turned round and asked me what sort of money I had. I told him just some foreign currency in small notes left over from previous trips, some US dollars and Euros. He said "Show me." One trick I had learned over the years of travelling was to distribute money around my person in case of events like this. I took out my wallet and made a show of counting the small denomination US dollars and Euros. I had New Zealand dollars and South African rand elsewhere. He looked at the small wad of notes and said "That's not enough" but took it. They conferred together again and then turned round back to the main road and continued on the way to the hotel which I recognised from the maps I'd studied before the trip. They spoke together some more and again we pulled up in a dark side street. Collar and tie turned round again. "Are you sure you haven't got any more money?" he asked. I thought I would stall for time again so I said "Oh! Yes. I might have some South African rand. I produced some from a back pocket. He muttered about the lousy exchange rate on rand but eventually took it. I had now given them about US$40, at least twice the normal fare from the airport. I held my breath. The driver counted this latest contribution to his retirement fund, exchanged a few more words with collar and tie and then to my relief drove on. We arrived at the hotel and I got out. I still don't understand why they didn't just mug me in the dark alley and drive off with my luggage. It was a lesson that no matter how seasoned a traveller you are, if you drop your guard you can be taken for a ride. It wasn't a good omen for the rest of the trip.

In the morning, my guide, Yusuf, from Africa Connection Tours turned up to take me on a city tour. We stopped at a bank in the city centre so that I could get some money from the ATM. Immediately I was surrounded by street vendors waving wooden carvings at me, becoming aggressive when I ignored them. We had a look at some of the city markets, the Marche Kermel and one specialising in herbal medicines and fetishes. Outside the Presidential Palace, I photographed a guard colourfully dressed in a red tunic and helmet and baggy blue breeches. We stopped at the ornate colonial style railway station and the Grande Mosque where I saw a woman in a burka lying flat out sleeping in the middle of the open square outside. On the way up to Les Almadies, where there were some attractive beach-front restaurants, we passed the gigantic Monument of the African Renaissance. The Soviet-style bronze statue, built by North Korean workers, was the brain-child of President Abdoulaye Wade, and depicted three figures

- a man holding a woman behind him and a child aloft, pointing out to sea. The figures in it were modelled on President Wade and his family, according to Jusuf. The monument had been inaugurated earlier that year as the highlight of the 50th anniversary of the country's independence from France. At 49m (160 feet) it was higher than the Statue of Liberty and cost US$27m (18m pounds sterling). It had come in for savage criticism locally because of the cost in one of Africa's poorest countries and because the scantily clad woman was considered to be un-Islamic. Just beyond it, the picturesque cream coloured Mosque de la Divinite stood down by the sea beneath a cliff.

The following morning Yusuf took me out to Goree Island, a twenty minute, 4km (2.5 miles) ferry ride from Dakar. The island was only 28 hectares (70 acres) in area with a permanent population of about 1000 which was swollen during the day by an army of hawkers who travelled out on the ferry. No cars were allowed on the island, which gave it a peaceful, other-worldly atmosphere. Goree had developed as a centre associated with the trans-Atlantic slave trade. It was doubtful whether many slaves were exported directly from the island as it wouldn't have been practical to accumulate and feed large numbers of slaves on such a small island. However, it was a thriving trading community dealing in commodities required by the slave trade and other African products such as ivory and gold. The Portuguese had first landed there in 1444 when it was uninhabited. They were pushed out by the Dutch in 1588 who were superseded by the French in 1677. It had been declared a UNESCO World Heritage Site in 1978.

We visited the House of Slaves and saw the dungeons where slaves were kept. The door of no return leading out to the sea seemed unlikely to be authentic as the water was far too shallow for vessels to have berthed there. Upstairs was an interesting interpretive display on the island and the slave trade. There was a statue called "homage to the slaves" just outside. We walked up to the castle at the southern tip of the island, past long-horned cattle grazing alongside some small fields of maize and vegetables. At the other end of the island was Fort d'Estrees, now the historical museum. We had lunch on the terrace of the Hostellerie du Chevalier de Boufflers, overlooking the little harbour.

Next day we went up to Lac Rose, north-east of the city. The lake got its name from the reddish tinge the water took on at certain times from the algae in the salty brew. Salt was extracted from the lake bed and we saw fleets of dugout canoes working offshore. At the lakeside, men were unloading canoes and piling up salt to be taken away by lorries. We were besieged by a group of women clamouring to be photographed with baskets of salt on their heads, for a small fee of course. Lac Rose had been the terminus of the Paris Dakar Rally, which had been abandoned five years previously due to security problems in Mauritania and Northern Mali where a branch of Al Qaeda was operating. This had hit the tourist industry in the area badly. We carried on to Cayar, a fishing village on the coast, where the canoes were just arriving with their catch, the beach crowded with people in the colourful local costume of loose flowing robes. The Senegalese national dish was thieboudieune, fish and rice, and the main ingredient was on display here in abundance.

I flew on to Bamako to join the tour group. On the way into the city, just before the bridge over the wide, braided, River Niger, the driver had to stop for a traffic jam. I saw a man's body lying in a pool of blood at the edge of the pavement, presumably the victim of a car accident. Nobody seemed to be doing much about it. Bamako was an unimpressive place, polluted with fumes from the heavy traffic, poorly surfaced roads, litter everywhere, the buildings badly maintained and nothing much to be seen in the way of monumental buildings, old or new. A lot of new, modern buildings were going up over to the west in what I later learned was to be a replacement city centre, romantically named ACI 2000. I was booked into the Grand Hotel just north of the railway station. At lunch time I walked east into Koulikoro Street and into the open-fronted Relax Restaurant, a busy place with a mixture of locals and expatriates. The "poulet yassa" (grilled chicken in an onion and lemon sauce) was good and I washed it down with a bottle of Castel lager. In the afternoon, I walked down past the National Assembly building on Place de la Republique, through the fetish market stalls with its gruesome monkey heads, assorted bones and unidentifiable dried objects (UDOs) and on into the teeming central market area, Le Grand Marche – block after block of traders of food, clothes, textiles and household goods – noisy and smelly. In the evening, I took a taxi up to the Route de Bla Bla where there were several lively pubs playing tracks by Salif Keita and other local heroes on sound systems but no sign of any live groups.

The following morning our fourteen strong tour party headed east out of Bamako in a mini-bus, accompanied by our tour guide, Mohammed, driver Temoko and bus "boy" Dembo - luggage shifter and general factotum. A three hour drive took us to the town of Segou on the banks of the River Niger with some interesting old French colonial style buildings. In the atelier of Boubacar Doumbia we were shown how "bogolon" (mud cloth) was made. The first thing we learned was that the cloth wasn't made from mud at all, just the designs on it. With that little misunderstanding out of the way we were given the opportunity to create our own artistic masterpieces to keep: I shall treasure my obscene effort for ever. Our first night was to be spent in a "homestay". As darkness fell and we still hadn't arrived there was some speculation about what lay ahead. "Ah, well. Just go with the flow" said Ali, who with her sister Kirsty, was from Hawkes Bay in New Zealand. The ages of the group ranged from late twenties to around seventy and the nationalities were as varied: four Australians; three New Zealanders; two Americans, one of whom was originally Hong Kong Chinese; two Norwegians, one of whom was Philippine by birth but had lived and worked in Norway most of her life; a Canadian; an Austrian girl who was the youngest in the group; and myself, a hybrid Shetland Kiwi. Females outnumbered males 9 to 5. I was later to discover that even the younger members were already seasoned travellers: Ken and Carol had recently been up the Sepik River in Papua New Guinea and in the jungles of Borneo; Solve, a Norwegian oil-rig platform design engineer had been on a tour through reclusive North Vietnam the previous year. Later on the trip, over a beer, he asked me how many countries I had been to. I had kept a record and told him 87, including Mali. "That's odd," he said, "that's exactly the same number as me." But he looked as if he was still in his 30s and was clearly going to beat me hands down eventually. He had a strange hobby: he collected airline sick-bags, unused ones fortunately. He said that they invariably had the airline's logo on them and it was a good way to keep a record of the airlines he'd flown with. "Young" Ian, he was just in his early 60s, had been a senior official with the Australian Federal Government department dealing with overseas aid and that had taken him and his wife Maree all over the world. "Old" Ian had been born and brought up in New Zealand but had later served in the British Merchant Navy, emigrated to South Africa and then moved on to Australia during the unrest prior to the end of the Apartheid system. He now went somewhere exotic most years. We all had the travel bug – badly.

What lay ahead was a village of mud huts. We were treated to a meal of fried chicken, guinea fowl, rice, fried bananas, groundnut sauce, tomatoes and salad greens spread out buffet style on the ground. Afterwards we were shown the facilities by torch light. The toilet was a door-less, mud-walled enclosure, open to the night sky, with a hole in the ground in the centre. Washing arrangements consisted of a large earthenware jar of cold water and a wooden ladle. Mats were arranged along the edge of the compound for sleeping, with mosquito nets suspended over them. A dance was laid on for our entertainment, the throbbing music provided by drums and large xylophones called "balakon". The men and women danced separately, the men retreating backwards, still dancing, to the edge of the encircling crowd to be replaced by a gyrating wave of women and girls, the process repeated as if at some given signal. After the long day's drive, the open-air sleeping arrangements were surprisingly comfortable.

I got up for an early morning walk through the village compound. The mud-walled, thatched huts were in a poor state of repair: the poverty was palpable. But the children were all smiles, shyly calling out "Bonjour". Women were energetically pounding millet in tall ceramic tubs, using elongated "pestles" like fat baseball bats. Some donkeys were tethered outside a hut and chickens were scrabbling around in the dust. Further on, a long-horned cow was lying down chewing the cud and a long-eared sheep was rooting around among some rubbish like a pig. After breakfast, which Mohammed had brought on the bus, we were shown round the village, which was called Niamana, by Youchauo Traore, son of the former mayor. We saw the run-down school. The mud-brick teachers' houses had collapsed in the rainy season some years ago and there was no money to repair them. It was therefore difficult to recruit teachers. "In any case," Youchauo said, "little money gets through from the government for education. It's embezzled by politicians and civil servants." I asked him if things were worse now than in Colonial times. "Oh, yes" he replied, "much worse, we had good schools then." We saw a solar-powered project provided by a private aid donor that had pumped water from a reservoir for irrigation but had broken down and there was no money or expertise available to repair it. We saw a diesel-driven machine for grinding millet which would have saved the women several hours a day of pounding. Again it was broken down. The group had a whip round and raised enough money to go a fair way towards the repair cost.

We carried on to Djenne on an island in the Bani River, a tributary of the Niger. Its mosque was the largest mud building in the world and it had a bustling market on Mondays, which was the following day. At the ferry across to the island, we were engulfed by a swarm of hawkers who piled aboard with the bus. I was confronted by one calling herself Ms. Best Price Mimi. I stalled her by promising to maybe see her "après", French for "later" – an old trick for temporarily warding off hawkers. On the way back, a couple of days later, she collared me again. That time there was no escape and I paid her a few hundred CFAs (Central African Franks, exchanged at 730 to the pound sterling) to pose for a cheesy photo with Mohammed, the tour guide. We stayed in the Hotel Djenne-Djenno, separated by a narrow arm of the Bani River from the main part of town, a causeway leading across. It was an atmospheric, low, mud walled place built round a courtyard and run by a Swedish lady – I saw her later, returning from a ride on a stylish looking horse, dressed like a Sloane Ranger competing in a show-jumping event– her, not the horse. The room was comfortable and tastefully decorated, a stylish contrast to our previous night's lodgings.

The following morning, the market around the mosque was full of sheep. Mohammed explained that an important Moslem festival, Tabaski, was coming up when every family had to kill a fat sheep, commemorating the Old Testament event when Jehovah allowed Abraham to sacrifice a sheep instead of his son, Isaac. Most people were dressed in the colourful traditional flowing robes and turbans. The mosque was off-limits to infidels but Ken and Carol had managed to bribe their way in. When they came out, Carol was shaking her head. "Ken managed to step on someone who was lying on the floor in the darkness while he was taking photos," she said. "You can't take these Australians anywhere" I remarked. The original mosque on the site had been built in 1280 AD. It had fallen into disrepair and the current building had replaced it in 1907, carefully retaining the original Sahel-style, mud-brick architectural design. Wooden poles protruded from the walls. They were part of the structure but also served to support the scaffolding used for the re-plastering of the mud walls after each rainy season. The streets around the mosque were teeming with hawkers. One approached me waving bootleg music DVDs. I pretended I couldn't hear him, cupping my hand behind my ear. He repeated his sales spiel more loudly in French. "Ah,non," I said, "Je ne veux pas de la musique. Je suis sourde." (Oh,no. I don't want any music. I'm deaf.) He laughed uproariously and went away. I had learned a new trick in the war against persistent hawkers. The street-scape was very distinctive, many of the mud-brick houses rising to three storeys – traditionally the owners would have lived in the top level, the slaves below them with the ground floor used for commercial purposes or storage. The doors, window frames and shutters were decorated in Moorish style. The streets were dusty and many of the houses in a poor state of repair but there was an air of former gentility which hadn't completely gone away. We had lunch in the open-air restaurant of Le Campement, a sort of low-cost hostel in the town centre. Paying individually for drinks afterwards was the usual shambles. Small change was as scarce as hen's teeth in West Africa. Mohammed explained that some businessmen had spotted a business opportunity hoarding coins and small denomination notes and selling them at more than their face value. I was sitting beside Mary from Canada. I had noticed that she made copious notes about everything and I asked her if she was writing a book. "No," she said, "I just don't trust my memory any more." I knew the feeling but I did my scribbling surreptitiously at night in case the other members of the group got the same idea about me and clammed up. In the afternoon, we went to visit a Fulani village on the north side of the river reached by a bridge. The Fulani tribe had their own distinctive costume, hairstyle and personal decoration. Many of the women were strikingly beautiful with Arabic features. They wore heavy gold earrings and silver coins in their braided hair. Both men and women had tribal markings around their eyes and mouths which had been inscribed into their skin as children

In the morning, we left Djenne and headed east, stopping for lunch at the Ambedjele Hotel in Sevare, run by a Spanish lady, which we were due to come back to after two nights living rough in Dogon country. We left most of our luggage there and Mohammed and the crew disappeared into town to lay in provisions for the next two days. After lunch we headed south for Dogon country. The Dogon people lived along the 250 kilometres (156 miles) long Bandiagara Escarpment, a 500m high sandstone cliff, following a fault line, which provided the major physical feature in an otherwise mostly flat Mali landscape. Their isolation had enabled them to preserve their local traditions, cosmological beliefs and animistic religion against incursions by Islamists and French colonists. We transferred to 4WD vehicles in the little town of Bandiagara. A corrugated track took us through Dogon millet and onion fields to the edge of the escarpment. Half way down, we had to stop in a narrow gorge to allow a donkey cart to come up. The two donkeys yoked between the shafts looked exhausted, I could see it in their eyes. They staggered under the load of sacks of millet piled on the cart, the drivers mercilessly whipping them with tree branches.

We spent the night in the open air on the roof of a Campement or hostel in the village of Tireli. The facilities were an improvement on the earlier "homestay", a cold shower and sit-down toilet but Spartan nevertheless. In the morning, we trekked up the base of the escarpment to the village centre for a dancing display. To the rhythm of drums, the grotesquely masked dancers, some on stilts, paraded around a tree, their pink and green raffia-like grass skirts and cloaks swaying, elaborately carved, tall, wooden fetish symbols balanced on their heads. It felt very authentic, sending a frisson through me, as if

I had been transported back in time. Afterwards I chatted in French with the village headman. He told me that they still performed the dances for themselves at funerals and harvest times so it wasn't just a tourist gimmick. The architecture of the village was very distinctive, the cylindrical granaries with conical thatched roofs a photographer's dream. Paths meandered between piles of weathered boulders among scattered trees. It was the sort of timeless African landscape which brought back fond memories of the more remote parts of East Africa I had seen in my youth.

Following the dance, we trekked about 10 km along the base of the escarpment to Ireli village, a UNESCO World Heritage Site. Along the way we passed a crocodile pond, a couple of its denizens immobile on the bank. When we arrived at the Ireli Campement, some of us were approached by a stall holder who had some wooden carvings and masks for sale. He rummaged around in a box near the display and furtively un-wrapped a bronze pornographic "art" object displaying a daddy Dogon and a mummy Dogon busy making a baby Dogon. The salesman claimed it dated from the time of the Tellem people who had lived in caves high up in the escarpment until they were displaced centuries ago by the invading Dogon. "Young" Ian, who was obviously a bit of an art connoisseur, reckoned it was from the Dogon doggy-style period. We'd had to bring our own food (and beer) with us from Sevare as there were no restaurants in the Dogon campements. Muhammed and the crew rustled up a very tasty dinner of grilled chicken and rice with groundnut sauce, salad and vegetables. Afterwards, some of us were sitting around a rough wooden table having a beer when some-one suggested that what was needed was some Tellem jokes. The germ of an idea had been brewing in my mind ever since I'd heard the name "Tellem" and now it crystallised. "Once upon a time," I began, to groans, "there was a little Tellem boy called William, who used to stand around balancing an apple on his head. Everybody called him Little William Tellem." More groans, particularly from Susanne, the Austrian girl, who worked in Switzerland. "Now for months a particu-larly nasty Dogon witchdoctor had been prowling around picking off Tellem with his bow and arrow and carrying them away to cook them and eat them. One day when he was passing, the witchdoctor saw Little William standing there, apple on head as usual and being partial to a spot of tender roast Tellem with apple sauce, the dastardly Dogon lined him up in the sights of his bow and let fly with an arrow. The arrow missed William but scored a bullseye on the apple. Now his target wasn't actually Little William Tellem at all: it was Big Bad Bill Tellem, the roughest, toughest, meanest dude on the whole escarpment, cunningly disguised as Little William Tellem. Big Bill sprang into action, grabbed the Dogon witchdoctor, stuffed the apple with the arrow still attached up his arse and told him to bugger off and never come back. The moral of the story is – an apple a day keeps the witchdoctor away."

"Young" Ian thought about that for a while. He had already proved himself to be an authority on donkey jokes (no, not that sort) (as well as Dogon pornographic art) and sure enough he rose to the occasion. "One day" he said, "a stranger was passing through Tellem country when he saw Little William Tellem standing there with an apple on his head as usual. The stranger spotted a donkey standing nearby so he asked it: "Why is that little Tellem boy standing there with an apple on his head?" Now the donkey suffered from a serious speech impediment, a painful stammer but it wanted to create a good impression on the stranger and give him a meaningful insight into the local culture so it took a deep breath and started: "Hee haw, hee haw, he hawlways does that." Nobody tried to improve on that one. "It's the way he tells 'em," I said. That night, some of us decided to sleep down below in the courtyard of the Campement as the roof was a bit congested. Around midnight, a strong wind blew up. It would rise to a near gale force crescendo, then fall away only to build up again to a new peak. There was a lot of sand around at the base of the escarpment from erosion of the sandstone rock. A sandstorm developed. During the night my blanket blew away and in the morning a sizeable sand dune had built up in my belly button.

The following day, we drove back to the Ambadjele Hotel in Sevare, where Diane, one of the Americans, made a beeline to get a beer before we'd even checked in. She was tiny, not an ounce of fat on her but she could drink beer like a Liverpool dock worker. She also read "chick-lit" novels in the bus, tearing out the pages and throwing them away as she finished a chapter to save the weight of carrying them around. In the afternoon, we drove the short distance to the major river port of Mopti, where the Bani River flowed into the Niger. The Niger here resembled a sea rather than a river as we set off on a cruise in an open-sided launch with an overhead canopy to protect us from the sun. It was hard to believe that in the dry season it shrank until the river boats plying up to Timbuktu couldn't operate. In the bustling market along the river bank we saw the blocks of salt carried down from the Sahara to Timbuktu by Tuareg camel caravans and distributed along the rivers through Mopti. The market stalls were also laden with dried fish, pottery, brightly coloured textiles, food, clothing and household goods of every kind. The smells and sounds of darkest Africa filled the air. The recently restored Great Mosque towered over the old part of town just inland from the port area.

We never made it to Timbuktu. A branch of Al Qaeda had been operating in the desert north of Timbuktu and in 2009 had kidnapped and killed a British tourist when no ransom was paid. Early in 2010 a French aid worker had suffered a similar fate. More recently, seven mine workers had been kidnapped in neighbouring Niger and were reputedly being held in Mali. Mauretania had sent army units into Mali under a cross border agreement and they had skirmished with Al Qaeda and Tuareg groups within 50 miles of Timbuktu. Western governments all issued no go warnings and Peregrine deleted the Timbuktu leg of the tour. History had repeated itself and fanatical Moslems had again sealed off Timbuktu to infidels like us. Between 1588 and 1853, at least 43 European explorers had tried to reach Timbuktu and only four had made it, three getting back alive. So we were in good company.

We could still have got to Timbuktu. A couple of planes a week flew in from Bamako and Mopti, river boats plied up the Niger while the water level was high enough and there was road access for 4WD vehicles in the dry season. But with the current security situation it was for the foolhardy only. In any case, according to the guide books, there was no longer much to see there. By all accounts it was a dusty, fly-blown backwater, a sprawl of low, shabby, flat-roofed buildings, the streets filled with sand blown in from the desert and with lousy tourist accommodation. The old mosques were still there, the Sankore and Sidi Yahiya as well as the Dsingerey Ber; the Centre for Historical Research and some private collections still held the religious, historical and scientific manuscripts from the former Moslem universities; and there were the houses where the few early European explorers who had got through had stayed – the Frenchman Rene Caillie; Heinrich Barth, who had made it in 1853; and the ill-fated Gordon Laing. But there was apparently nothing particularly "wonderful" about it any more: in fact it was a wonder that anyone bothered to go near the place.

The following year, 2011, another incident was reported on TV and in the newspapers concerning the security situation in Mali. A Frenchman who was planning to marry a local girl in neighbouring Niger had gone to a bar in the centre of Niamey, the capital, for a stag-night drink with his best man, a fellow Frenchman. They had been kidnapped from the bar in full public view by an Al Qaeda group and carried off towards the Mali border. The Niger Security Services had caught up with them at the border and in the ensuing shoot-out, both the Frenchmen had been killed. Then, in March 2012, I saw a TV report of a military coup in Mali, the leaders frustrated at the lack of resources being given them to fight a full-blown rebellion by Tuareg tribesmen in the north of the country. The ringleaders in the rebellion had been part of Colonel Gaddafi's security forces and army in Libya and on his demise, when he discovered the hard way that all his people didn't love him after all, had come back home to Mali, armed to the teeth with Libyan weapons. They had captured a town in the northern desert and were closing in on Timbuktu. It was later reported that they had taken Timbuktu as well and set up an independent Tuareg state. If it had been difficult to reach Timbuktu before, it was now looking well nigh impossible for anybody in their right mind.

We flew back to Bamako from Mopti and transferred to a flight to Ouagadougou, the capital of Burkina Faso. Like Bamako, Ougadougou didn't inspire much enthusiasm, run down buildings, poorly maintained roads, rubbish clogging any areas of open space. The perhaps appropriately named suburb of Pissy became the Cannes of Africa each year when the pan-African Fespaco film festival took place there. The face of the President, Blaise Compaore, in power since a military coup in1987, was everywhere, even on the labels of the mineral water bottles. Our hotel, the Azalai, was supposed to be one of the best in town and on the surface looked impressive with a huge swimming pool, but the air conditioning in my room wasn't working and it was infested with mosquitos and other flying insects. After a sleepless night, they showed me an alternative room, where the bathroom was dirty and which smelled of smoke and musty furnishings. Eventually, I was given a room where I reckoned I had a fighting chance of a night's sleep.

We drove down to Bobo-Diolasso in the south-west of the country. The scenery was monotonous, flat and forested. The rainfall was higher in the south of the country so the landscape was noticeably greener as we progressed. In Bobo-Diolasso we visited the chaotic market and the old mosque, which resembled a hedge-hog due to the protruding wooden poles sticking out from the walls to take scaffolding for the annual re-plastering of the mud walls. We walked through the Kibidwe District, the oldest part of the city, bordering a litter-strewn stream. A wizened old man in a white robe played a bamboo flute, gathering a small crowd on the red, dusty, street. A hair-dressing session was under way, two girls sitting on a rug beneath a tree with two others braiding their hair. An older woman sat beside them on a chair with a baby in her lap. There was a lot of giggling from them as we queued up to photograph the scene. The front wall of the Museum of Music was attractively decorated with murals, one showing a man playing the large xylophone-like balafon. Inside there was a display of traditional instruments including jungle drums used to transmit messages over long distances, different ones for different occasions like funerals or weddings or war. Bobo-Dialasso was known as the music capital of Burkina Faso. In the evening, we were entertained during dinner at our hotel, the Auberge, by a local group going through their repertoire of traditional tunes and songs.

The following morning we set off for Banfora, on the way visiting some interesting rock formations at Sindou and a chain of hills where sandstone pinnacles were overlaid with caps of rocks more resistant to erosion, resembling the landscape in Capadoccia in Turkey, but nowhere near as spectacular. We clambered up to the Karfiguela Waterfalls where some of the group took a dip. We over-nighted in the picturesque Hotel La Canne a Sucre.

Next day we headed for the little town of Gaoua in the south-east of the country. This was the home of the Lobi people. I remarked to Diane that her President, Obama, had it in for these people. "When he was running for election he said that when he got to the White House he was going to sort out these lobby people," I said. She failed to get the joke and Solve, the Norwegian, had to explain it to her. When I mentioned this to "Young" Ian he said "Americans don't do irony." We visited a Lobi home, owned by a headman with a staggering number of wives and children. Mohammed, the tour guide, told us how many but it was so unbelievable that I've forgotten. Unusually for Africa, Lobi homes stood on their own out in the fields, not in villages. For security purposes, the houses were built with high, mud brick walls and small slits for windows, like miniature fortresses. Later, we walked around an old stone-built fortress at Loropeni. It was a sizeable structure with high walls, the sides measuring about 100m (310 feet). The local guide who showed us round said that it was believed to have been associated with the slave trade, perhaps acting as a staging post on the way to the coast.

I flew down to Accra, in Ghana, from Ouagadougou. I had booked into the La Palm Royal Beach Hotel, a luxurious establishment on La Beach, on the eastern fringes of the city, with a magnificent pool and a casino. I booked a city tour. We stopped in Independence Square to photograph the imposing Independence Arch with its slogan Freedom and Justice, commodities in short supply in most of Africa, surmounted by a black star. We walked down into the massive, deserted square. The guide explained that I could not take pictures in the direction of Osu Castle, built by the Danes around 1659 and until recently the seat of government. Paranoia still reigned even though the original excuse for it had gone. A group of soldiers and plain clothes security men were sitting down by a grandstand to enforce the anti-photography rules. My guide said that they would expect some money since I had been taking photos, even though I hadn't pointed my lens anywhere near Osu Castle. I swore and handed over some cedis.

The next stop was Kwame Nkrumah Memorial Park. Nkrumah had been Ghana's first President at independence in 1957 and developed serious delusions of grandeur. The effect of the imposing memorial beside the small museum dedicated to the great man was somewhat diminished by his adjacent headless statue, vandalised when he was forced out of power after leading the country to near bankruptcy. Inside the museum there was an almost pathetic collection of his old clothes and furniture. Again hands were extended by Museum personnel for "dash" (gift/bribe) money for doing their jobs. On the way back to the hotel, I called at an ATM machine to get some money. It carried out the transaction complete with receipt but delivered no money. It had obviously learned the "dash" trick from the kleptomaniac locals. Down in Jamestown, the old part of the city, we climbed the lighthouse tower for the view. More bribes for watching the parked car and entrance to the lighthouse. The view was not rewarding, ramshackle buildings, a filthy beach, a corrugated iron and cardboard shanty town down by the harbour breakwater. The old James Fort looked neglected.

I hired a driver to take me along the coast to Elmina, where I was booked into the Coconut Grove Beach Resort. On the way we were stopped twice by policemen, in each case having to pay them a substantial bribe not to find anything wrong with the car or the driver's papers. "They're worse than usual at the moment" the driver said ruefully. "Christmas is coming." Christmas had already come for the police. The government had doubled their salaries in the hope of breaking their habit of taking bribes for doing their job. It obviously hadn't worked.

In Elmina, I visited the old slave castle of St George. It was an imposing building situated at the end of a rocky peninsula. Built by the Portuguese in 1482, it was captured by the Dutch in 1637 and finally ceded to the British in 1872. During the Dutch period, it served as the headquarters of the Dutch West Indies Company. I visited the grim dungeons where the slaves were held prior to shipment out across the Atlantic and the punishment cells. Unlike at Goree Island in Dakar, the door of no return here was the genuine article. The Portuguese built church housed a small museum. Facing the castle across the lagoon was the much smaller Fort St. Jago, a UNESCO World Heritage Site like the castle itself. It had been built by the Dutch between 1652 and 1662 to protect the castle. The view across the small town and the busy fishing harbour was superb. In a little square in the town centre stood an Anglican church with an orange trimmed tower and beyond that another little square with a statue of King Nana Kobina Gyan who had reigned from 1868 and according to the plaque fell out with the British and was exiled to Sierra Leone. On a hill above the Dutch cemetery stood an attractive Catholic church, a large dead tree in the form of a cross in front of it.

I took a taxi into the little town of Cape Coast to visit Cape Coast Castle, another of the slaving centres. The imposing whitewashed building made an impressive closure to the street scene at the seaward end of the town centre. Inaugurated by the Dutch in 1637, then expanded by the Swedes in 1652, it was captured by the British in 1664. It was the headquarters of the British colonial administration until Accra became the capital in 1877. Canons lined the battlements facing seawards and there were piles of cannon balls in the interior courtyard. The dark dungeons and punishment cells for the slaves contrasted with the airy bedroom of the Governor, with floor to ceiling windows overlooking the ocean. The museum on the first floor had displays on the history of Ghana and the slave trade. The door of no return led towards the crowded beach where fishing canoes were hauled up beyond the foaming surf, colourful flags flapping above them.

I celebrated my 65th birthday alone back at the Coconut Grove Beach Resort, the only customer in the attractive, open-sided beachfront restaurant, surrounded by swaying coconut palms, the sound of the sea lapping at the beach in the background. I wasn't surprised to be the only customer: it was a nice enough hotel (although I'd been waiting three days to get a fused light bulb replaced) but Ghana was a basket case, populated by kleptomaniacs from the guardians of the security of the disused parliament building to the police, right down to the ATMs. I reflected that I had come a long way since my childhood in the far off Shetland Islands. I had seen the best of the wonders the world had to offer. It was time to think about filing away my passport - but perhaps not just yet. I hadn't made it to Timbuktu but I was in good company there – many had died in the attempt; and it looked like it might be a while before any more tourists in their right mind got there. Anyway, I thought, bugger Timbuktu. The Dogon country is the new Timbuktu. If you haven't slept under the stars in a Dogon village during a sandstorm, you haven't been anywhere, man.

Ends

About the Author

James A. Anderson, a proud Scotsman and Shetland Islands native, earned an MA in geography, with honors, from the University of Aberdeen in 1967. After a two-year stint as an education officer with the Kenyan government, he embarked on his lifelong career as a town planner in New Zealand. He has since worked as a planner with Shropshire County Council in Shrewsbury, England, and as the director and deputy director of planning with the Shetland Islands Council. In 1997, he returned to New Zealand, where he worked as the district planner for Dunedin City Council and then a planning consultant until he retired in 2008.

Anderson has visited 104 of the 194 UN member countries, and he's not done yet. He recently completed a course on freelance travel writing and plans to pen more books about his adventures. His previous book was *To the New 7 Wonders of the World.*

8813666R00193

Printed in Great Britain
by Amazon.co.uk, Ltd.,
Marston Gate.